D1528910

A POLITICAL ECONOMY OF URUGUAY SINCE 1870

A POLITICAL ECONOMY
OF URUGUAY SINCE 1870

M. H. J. Finch

St. Martin's Press
New York

St. Martin's Press, Inc., 175 Fifth Avenue, New York, NY 10010
Printed in Hong Kong
First published in the United States of America in 1982

ISBN 0–312–62244–9

Library of Congress Cataloging in Publication Data

Finch, Martin Henry John.
  A political economy of Uruguay since 1870.

  Bibliography: p.
  Includes index.
  1. Uruguay – Economic policy.   2. Uruguay –
Economic conditions.   I. Title.
HC232.F56 1981   330.9895′06   80–21047
ISBN 0–321–62244–9

For Liz, Robert and Patrick

Contents

List of Tables

List of Figures

Preface

Writing this book has taken a very long time, during which others—principally those to whom it is dedicated—have suffered at least as much as the writer. However, this is not the moment to agonise, but to give thanks. Whatever the final outcome might suggest, this project was not a modest one. It was only made possible by generous financial assistance from the Ford Foundation (made available through the Overseas Development Institute) and the University of Liverpool, and I record my appreciation for their support.

During the period of these labours I have been helped immeasurably by many friends in Uruguay, and it would be right to acknowledge them here by name. I cannot do so, however, because the nature of academic and intellectual life in contemporary Uruguay is such that I might place individuals and institutions in peril. I must be content, therefore, with an expression of my deepest gratitude, and my admiration of their continued pursuit of free intellectual enquiry.

Happily, other debts can be acknowledged. F. E. Watson made his contribution long ago, in Suffolk. The decision to undertake research on Uruguay originated in a conversation with the late Professor David Joslin, who was an important source of inspiration and encouragement. In Uruguay I was made welcome as a visiting member of the now-closed Instituto de Economía, and in thanking two of its Directors, Enrique Iglesias and Raúl Trajtenberg, and a fellow-visitor, Alberto Fracchia, I also thank the good friends I made there whom it is now discreet not to name. In Liverpool, Professor C. T. Smith and Professor A. Beacham encouraged me to bring the work to a conclusion. Elizabeth Finch and Rosemary Thorp read the entire manuscript in an earlier draft, making numerous suggestions for its improvement. My sincere thanks go to all. No-one other than myself is in any degree responsible for the interpretations and conclusions of this work, still less for its errors and omissions.

Finally, my thanks to Heather Ainscough, Gill Brown, Jackie Fawcett and Joan Ovens, for preparing the typescript.

August 1979   HENRY FINCH

List of Abbreviations and Notes

AEBU	Asociación de Bancarios del Uruguay
AFE	Administración de Ferrocarriles del Estado
AFTE	Administración de Ferrocarriles y Tranvías del Estado
AMDET	Administración Municipal de Transportes
ANCAP	Administración Nacional de Combustibles, Alcohol y Portland
BCU	Banco Central del Uruguay
BOLSA	Bank of London and South America
BROU	Banco de la República Oriental del Uruguay
CECEA	Centro de Estudiantes de Ciencias Económicas y de Administración
CGTU	Confederación General del Trabajo del Uruguay
CIDE	Comisión de Inversiones y Desarrollo Económico
CLEH	Centro Latinoamericano de Economía Humana
CNA	Consejo Nacional de Administración
CNG	Consejo Nacional de Gobierno
CNT	Convención Nacional de Trabajadores
COPRIN	Comisión de Productividad, Precios e Ingresos
COSENA	Consejo de Seguridad Nacional
CSU	Confederación Sindical del Uruguay
CUR	Central Uruguay Railway
CUTCSA	Cooperativa Uruguaya de Transportes Colectivos, SA
DGEC	Dirección General de Estadística y Censos
DSHCR	Diario de Sesiones de la Honorable Cámara de Representantes
ECLA	United Nations Economic Commission for Latin America
EFCSA	Establecimientos Frigoríficos del Cerro SA
EEC	European Economic Community
EFTA	European Free Trade Association
FAO	United Nations Food and Agriculture Organisation
FO	London, Public Record Office, Foreign Office Archives
FORU	Federación Obrera Regional Uruguaya
FUNSA	Fábrica Uruguaya de Neumáticos SA
GRISUR	Grupo de Información y Solidaridad Uruguay

IMES	Instituto Militar de Estudios Superiores
IMF	International Monetary Fund
IMPROME	Impuesto a la Producción Mínima Exigible
IQI	Instituto de Química Industrial
LAFTA	Latin American Free Trade Association
MAF	Ministry of Agriculture and Fisheries (United Kingdom)
MGA	Ministerio de Ganadería y Agricultura
MUR	Midland Uruguay Railway
NWUR	North Western Uruguay Railway
OIT	Oficina Internacional del Trabajo (International Labour Organisation)
ONT	Oficina Nacional de Trabajo
UEE	Usinas Eléctricas del Estado
UET	United Electric Tramways of Montevideo
UGT	Unión General de Trabajadores
UNR	Uruguay Northern Railway
USU	Unión Sindical Uruguaya
UTE	Usinas Eléctricas y Teléfonos del Estado

Notes

A billion is equal to a thousand million.

Unless indicated otherwise, tons are metric tons, and $ refers to the Uruguayan peso. In 1975 the new peso, equal to a thousand pesos, was introduced.

For the pronunciation of Batlle's name, the reader is reminded that in the River Plate countries 'll' is pronounced similarly to the French 'j'.

Uruguay: Railways and population centres, 1963

1 The Ideology of *Batllismo* 1870–1970

Whoever wishes to have something by which to distinguish Uruguay from its many sister republics, the size and character of each of which are unfamiliar to many of us in Europe, may learn to remember that it is the smallest of the South American states, and that it has neither mountains, nor deserts, nor antiquities, nor aboriginal Indians. Nevertheless, it is by no means a country to be described by negatives, but has, as we shall presently see, a marked character of its own. (James Bryce, *South America: Observations and Impressions* [1912] p. 349.)

Introduction

The hundred years of Uruguayan history after 1870 represent a cycle which began and ended with military *coups*. In 1870 Uruguay was on the eve of a decade of military government which would lay the foundations of a strong centralised state and a transformed economy. A century later civilian government was again deposed by the armed forces, in the *coup* of 1973 which effectively marked the death of what may be termed *batllista* Uruguay. (The political economy of the military regime is examined in a later chapter.) The purpose of this opening essay is to analyse the conditions which made *batllismo* possible, its changing nature during this century, and the factors bringing it to an end.

The Uruguayan experience of the twentieth century until the beginning of the 1970s was unique. In a continent whose institutions have been typically authoritarian and unstable, Uruguay was celebrated for its pursuit of an unorthodox career, in which the early development of social and labour legislation, the growth of the public sector of the economy, the prominence of the middle classes, as well as adherence to (and innovation in) constitutional and liberal forms of government, were characteristic aspects. For external observers of the country, as well as for the Uruguayans themselves, the achievement was exceptional. In the 1950s, in a mood of national complacency, it was said that 'there is nowhere else like Uruguay' (*como el Uruguay no hay*). But by the end of the 1960s all that was finished. Since then approximately 10 per cent of the population has emigrated, and those who remain speak

1

with bitter irony of the Latin Americanisation of their country. The bitterness is all the greater for the severity of the political repression, and for the decay in the living standards of the mass of the people, in a country which previously took pride in living well and speaking freely.

The expression 'batllista Uruguay' requires some clarification. In essence it refers to the highly distinctive social and political achievement of President José Batlle y Ordóñez in the early years of this century. In a wider sense, batllismo was the ideology of the faction of the Colorado political party which Batlle led until his death in 1929 and which subsequently based its identity on his memory. But in its most general meaning, batllismo refers to a national style or ideology of development within which Uruguayan public life was conducted from early this century until the end of the 1960s, with a brief interruption in the 1930s. The hallmark of the national style was above all the use of techniques to redistribute income in the interests of securing a high level of social consensus, and, related to this, a marked social preference for political compromise rather than confrontation.

The unorthodox nature of the economic and social policy of the batllista mode of government and its long survival pose fundamental questions about the nation's structure and development. What features of the Latin American economic and social process in the nineteenth century were particular to Uruguay? What were the boundaries imposed on the unorthodoxy in this century, and what factors resulted in its recent termination? The hypothesis which offers a starting point to answer such questions is that from the late nineteenth century onward the state and political system in Uruguay were characterised by a substantial degree of autonomy from the dominant economic interests. Such autonomy could not of course be absolute, since the logic of the capitalist process entails that the class which owns the means of production will exercise ultimate control over the apparatus of the state.

Poulantzas has argued that the relative autonomy of the state is a structural condition of capitalism, since it is a function of the state to mediate between conflicting fractions of the dominant class.[1] Without entering the controversy which this argument has aroused, it is sufficient to point out that the postulated relative autonomy of the Uruguayan state is not seen here as necessarily deriving from a general structural condition of capitalism, but rather from the particular nature of capitalist modernisation in Uruguay in the late nineteenth century, and the implications it had for the political system. Specifically, the nature of the economic transformation permitted the survival of traditional (i.e. non class-oriented) political structures in the period of mass politics, as a consequence of which the normal function of political parties in articulating interests and fabricating alliances within the dominant class was not fully developed. The political process was therefore less, or less immediately, responsive to the requirements of the dominant class, and was even enabled to act at times contrary to the interests of it, on behalf of subordinate class interests or other class fractions. The participation of members of the economic power bloc in the political system was limited. The practice of politics as a full-time profession developed very early, and to an increasing degree the political system was manipulated in the interests of its own practitioners, such that at least one authority has spoken of the emergence in Uruguay of a 'political class'.[2]

Much of the theoretical discussion of the state has related to metropolitan capitalism, particularly in its post-competitive phase.[3] The problem of analysing the state in peripheral capitalism over an extended period of time is plainly more complex. Thus the period studied here saw the effective creation of the capitalist state in Uruguay and the modernisation of the economy eliminating pre-capitalist vestiges, a transformation whose terms were given by the dependent status of the society. The effect of this process in general in Latin America was to create a specific kind of social formation, strengthening traditional landowning oligarchies in alliance with groups linked to export sectors, and inhibiting the emergence of an industrial bourgeoisie. The dependent status of Latin America has been secured and consolidated essentially by the penetration and shaping of internal power structures by the dominant interests of the metropolitan countries. An implicit alliance may be said to exist between foreign capital, which thus secures favourable treatment, and collaborating domestic groups, whose capacity for continued social and political domination probably relies on, and is certainly strengthened by, participation in the benefits of the dependent relationship. A community of interest is thus created in which the leading fraction of the dominant class receives sufficient reward for its capacity for control to be maintained against the claims of competing fractions. During the export-led phase of development typical before 1930, dependent status was associated with liberal treatment for imports of capital and goods from the metropolitan countries. This inhibited the development both of a domestic market, through the internal pattern of income distribution and the remission abroad of factor incomes and interest on foreign debt, and of domestic industry to serve such a market, through the lack of protection.

In defining further the historical pattern of dependent development, a basic distinction is to be drawn between societies in which domestic groups were able to retain control of the productive system—that is, where land owned by nationals was used on an extensive basis in production for export—and societies based on enclave export development.[4] In the former case, which includes Uruguay, foreign capital played an important but generally subsidiary role in the development of the export sector, most frequently in the provision of infrastructure and processing capacity. But the existence of a domestic (landowning) bourgeoisie at the centre of the growth sector resulted in an important process of capital accumulation. Domination by this class of modernising landowners was exercised through alliances embracing traditional landowners, and commercial and financial interests in which foreign capital was prominent. The dynamism of the export economy and the diffusion, even though partial and limited, of its benefits to the rest of society, stimulated the diversification of the economy and gave rise to urban and rural groups producing mainly for the domestic market, whose interests diverged from and competed with those of the export sector. It is this plurality of conflicting interests within the dominant class which it is the function of political parties to articulate and resolve in the context of liberal democratic forms of government, without jeopardising the dominant position of the power bloc.

The emergence of the *batllista* ideology is therefore to be seen as a remarkable response to singular political and social conditions. The relative autonomy of the state which permitted it may be regarded in a general Poulantzian sense as a structural necessity given by the early emergence of an urban bourgeois class, but is interpreted in this chapter more narrowly as the result of internal conflict within the landowning class during the period of capitalist transformation of the livestock sector in the late nineteenth century. The inadequate political representation of the landowners thus gave rise to the development of a petty bourgeois ideology which incorporated mechanisms to consolidate the control of an 'autonomous' political system over the state apparatus. These mechanisms proved remarkably enduring—though eventually in a corrupted form—and sustained *batllista* Uruguay virtually intact until the end of the 1960s, long after the urban interests promoted by the ideology had begun to disintegrate.

Modernisation, 1870–1900

Although many of the contemporary characteristics of Uruguay are the result of political developments in the early years of this century, the process of modernisation, both political and economic, was effectively the product of the last three decades of the nineteenth century.[5] The first dynamic impulse in the economy came with the growth of sheep production during the 1860s; but though wool exports expanded, perhaps the principal significance of the decade was to demonstrate the limitations imposed by the economic and social structures characteristic of the livestock sector. During the 1870s two institutional developments began the progressive, if only partial, removal of those limitations. In 1871 the Asociación Rural was founded, and immediately became propagandist for improved practice in livestock production and acknowledged representative of the modernising *estancieros*; and in 1876

Colonel Lorenzo Latorre displaced the weak administration of President Varela, and imposed central authority over factional interests in the country for the first time in Uruguayan history.

A major achievement of the Asociación Rural was to secure the widespread adoption of wire fencing in the late nineteenth century. Until its introduction in the 1870s, the territory of Uruguay consisted almost entirely of open pasture. Though world demand for animal products was in any case limited, the frequent outbreaks of civil war and the accompanying loss of livestock discouraged investment in fixed assets or improved livestock. Property rights depended on the physical capacity of landowners to defend them, both collectively, by rallying to regional *caudillos* and the standard of the Blancos or Colorados, and individually, in defence of ill-defined tracts of land and against the raids of cattle-thieves. The claim to property was legitimised by possessing it, while the only group which could normally secure recompense for losses during civil conflicts were immigrant landowners, mainly British. A labour supply in the rural sector was thus required not only for the purpose of production, but also to secure the rights of individuals to the product of the land; and therefore a substantial rural population participated, if only marginally, in the income derived from the land. The relationship between landowner and worker in this semi-feudal context was one of mutual dependence for protection. In the absence of central authority, the *estancia* was to a considerable extent a self-governing political and social system.

Before the modernisation period, the roles of landowner and *caudillo* tended to coincide, since the one normally presupposed the other. Nonetheless, the roles were not identical; and by the 1860s there were already degrees of emphasis apparent between two groups, whose interests steadily diverged to become incompatible by the end of the nineteenth century. In the more fertile lands of the south and west (the Littoral), the concentration of immigrant landowners produced a progressive capitalist group which was pre-eminent in the growth of wool production in the 1860s, and in the foundation of the Asociación Rural in the following decade. In the centre and north of the country, however, land continued to be held to a far greater extent as the basis for social and political control of the region. The state apparatus and central government in Montevideo was comparatively weak. The urban political group (the *principistas*), mainly of the Colorado party, was in disarray when it was displaced from power by the military in 1876. The reduction of its wealth during civil wars, and its limited direct participation in either the livestock or commercial sectors, reduced its status to that of a professional, intellectual, and above all political, elite group. Its ideology was imported from Europe, combining anti-state liberalism from England with the aristocratic life-style of its forefathers, the *patriciado*, and was unrelated to the needs of the rural and urban economic elites. The urban bourgeoisie, like its rural counterpart with which to some extent it overlapped, was dominated by immigrants engaged mainly in commercial and financial activities. The failure of the political system, preoccupied still by the rivalry of urban intellectual *doctores* and rural *caudillos*, to express the interests of the dominant sectors of the economic system, induced them to bypass the institutional structure and take control of the apparatus of the state.

Militarismo faithfully reflected the interests of both urban and rural fractions of the dominant class. Reduced public expenditure and the withdrawal of inconvertible paper currency won the confidence of the financial and commercial sectors. The financial rectitude and internal stability promoted by the military administration of Latorre was warmly welcomed also in London. Its major achievement, however, was to provide the institutional framework needed for the rapid development of the export sector. Increased livestock production to meet growing demand in European markets meant adaptation and improvement of existing animal stocks. The introduction of valuable pedigree animals and selective breeding required wire fencing, which was the physical expression also of property rights. While these technical changes were promoted by the Asociación Rural, property rights received legal definition in the Código Rural of 1875–9, with strengthened police powers and sanctions for their enforcement. At the same time government forces, aided by the extension of the railway and the telegraph, were beginning to curtail the power of the regional *caudillos*. Though military government lasted only a decade, and though the succession of civil wars was not yet concluded, the establishment of a modern state which guaranteed property rights was a permanent achievement.

The process of modernisation in the livestock sector was accompanied, however, by two features which were to have profound social and political significance. First, though effective central authority and the consolidation of rights in property were a prerequisite of the transformation of the economy, it did not follow that modernisation would occur uniformly. The example of the progressive immigrant *estancieros* of the Littoral found slow acceptance in the remoter regions, whose *caudillos* did not willingly or wholly resign themselves to government from Montevideo. Not until the late 1880s did the Central Uruguay Railway penetrate into the northern half of the country and thus extend its centralising influence. Moreover, although the leaders of the Asociación Rural mostly remained apart from traditional political loyalties, the military hierarchy, like the civilian government it deposed, was drawn from Colorado families; while the *caudillos* of the northern region were preponderantly Blanco in their allegiance.

The second feature of the modernisation of the economy was that it was accompanied by a massive displacement of the rural labour force from participation in the livestock economy. Investment in the fencing of pastures reduced the amount of labour required directly in production and indirectly in safeguarding the stock. It also tended to eliminate the population which lived by grazing a few animals on marginal land. Thus fencing was the agent of economic and social change by which the functions and status of labour were altered, and its share in the product of the land reduced. Probably the greater part of this population migrated to the neighbouring regions of Argentina and Brazil. Others moved to Montevideo or found employment in the construction of the railways (which subsequently, with the growth of the meat export trade after 1905, expelled additional labour from traditional occupations). But the problem of rural poverty was a preoccupation of the Asociación Rural for the instability it engendered. The preoccupation was both well-directed and ineffectual, for it was from this dispossessed labour force that the armies of the Blanco *caudillo* Aparicio Saravia were recruited at the end of the century.

By then the political structure had changed substantially, for the period of military rule did not endure and the eclipse of the political elite was short-lived. The restoration in 1886 of civilian government—government by politicians—was owed in part to the increasingly corrupt administration of the military under Máximo Santos which eroded their support among the powerful groups in Montevideo. More important were changes occurring in the organisation of the traditional parties and the structure of the economy. Early in the 1880s attempts began to revitalise the Colorado and Nacional (Blanco) parties,[6] and this resurgence was based in part on the growth of middle-class or petty bourgeois interests antagonistic to those of the rural and urban elites. The traditional division within each party between the intellectual *doctores* of Montevideo, who reached their nadir in the early 1870s, and the *caudillos* of rural Uruguay, capable of mobilising instinctive adherence, began to close. The career of Julio Herrera y Obes, from *principista* in the 1870s to Colorado leader and president during 1890–4, illustrates the change: 'El elemento principal que el Presidencialismo urbano y doctoril de Herrera ha debido apropiarse es el tradicionalismo partidario . . . El doctor Herrera, el principista Herrera, el intelectual Herrera, se acaudilla, se agaucha, para poder dominar.'[7]

The revival of the political parties coincided with adverse conditions in the principal sectors of the economy linked to export and import flows, and the emergence of competing urban interests producing for the domestic market. The livestock sector, following a period of heavy investment in wire fencing, faced falling world prices for its principal products in the second half of the 1880s. In the following decade the trend would be reversed, but for the commercial sector the decline was permanent. The large volume of import trade conducted through Montevideo, and to a lesser extent through Salto, included an important transit trade attracted to Uruguayan ports by their natural advantages compared to those of Argentina and southern Brazil. Those advantages were lost, and with them the trade, with the modernisation of the ports of the two neighbouring countries and with protectionist legislation for their shipping.

The declining influence of the importing houses of Montevideo could be observed in the granting of tariff protection to domestic producers of light manufactured goods, initially in 1875 but with substantial increases in 1886 and 1888. In addition, a central issue of public policy at the end of the nineteenth century was that of the money supply. The restoration of convertibility in 1876 favoured powerful groups in the economy— importers, *saladero* owners (see p. 133), the large banks, and some of the largest *estancieros*—who made payments abroad in gold, required monetary stability for the successful conduct of business, or who benefited from high interest rates. But in the conditions of the 1880s the issue returned. Whereas the former group, the *oristas* (i.e. those who favoured a gold-backed currency), represented the conservative and wealthy interests of Montevideo, the *papelistas* (i.e. those wanting an inconvertible paper currency) included debtors and those resentful of the shortage of credit and high interest rates—small farmers and *estancieros*, and manufacturers. But they included also the political elite, whose limited participation in the dominant economic sectors deprived them of a secure economic base; whose capacity to use the apparatus of the state they controlled was limited by the necessity to borrow from the *oristas* or secure loans in London; and who found a political base in representing those interests which demanded an expanded money supply. Thus the Banco Nacional was founded (with the participation of British capital) in 1887; and though its failure in the aftermath of the Baring crisis was in part a demonstration of the strength of *orista* opposition, it is significant that the attempt could be made, and that the political elite was neither displaced nor discredited by its failure. Indeed the foundation in 1896 of the Banco de la República, a state bank which substantially liberalised the availability of credit, confirmed the tendency.

The political and economic configuration of Uruguay in the final decades of the nineteenth century does not therefore fit a simple model of political domination exercised directly or indirectly by economically dominant classes in alliance with foreign capital. Though there were representatives of the 'oligarchy' in government office, the political elite was a distinct group which sustained its position after the mid-1880s by its use of the press, by clientelism, and by the elevation of *caudillo* modes of leadership and political loyalty into a more or less viable political system. On this basis it was able to pursue policies (though not necessarily successfully) which did not wholly conform to the interests of the economically powerful. The capacity of the political system to function with such a degree of autonomy may be explained by two factors. First, the principal sectors of the economy, both urban and rural, were dominated by foreigners and immigrants who identified the traditional party groupings with the civil wars and anarchy of the pre-modernisation period. They themselves generally lacked the family connections and political antecedents required for political eminence, and they failed to perceive the potential capacity of the parties for mass political mobilisation. Second, there were substantial differences and conflicts of interest within the economic elite itself. The landowning class was divided between those influenced by the modernising efforts of the Asociación Rural, for whom land was essentially an economic asset, and the *caudillos* who regarded landownership as a political base. The former group of progressive *estancieros* was in turn divided between the wealthiest, who also had urban interests (especially in commerce and banking), and the majority who were frustrated by the inadequacy of credit. The urban economy was also divided between the massive but declining influence of those who imported, and the claims of those who produced for the domestic market. Thus the transformation of the economy and of the state apparatus was not accompanied by the displacement of inherited political structures through which control of the state by the power bloc had to be exercised. The (urban) political elite identified interests of its own, which it could pursue in alliance with fractions of the dominant class. At the same time the important role of foreign elements in the modernisation process paradoxically weakened the position of the economic elite, since it partially explains the failure of the elite to penetrate the political system.

Batllismo, 1900–1930

There has been a tendency in the writing of Uruguayan history to see the presidencies of José Batlle y Ordóñez (1903–7, 1911–15), and his continuing influence until his death in 1929, as a discontinuity or watershed in the life of the nation. Of the decisive importance of the early years of the century to the subsequent development of Uruguay there can be no doubt. The last armed conflict between Colorados and Blancos ended in 1904, and the consolidation of democratic forms of government and political parties was achieved at this time. The legislation which has misleadingly caused Uruguay to be called a 'welfare state' has its origins in this period. The value of exports doubled between 1900 and the outbreak of the First World War, following the introduction of the frozen meat trade. Manufacturing activity increased, and there were important extensions to the urban and national infrastructure. The very extent of these changes prompts the view that, without detracting at all from the significance of his work, it might be more correct to see Batlle as the creation of his times, rather than (as Vanger describes him) their creator.[8] For Batlle's achievement may be regarded as a response to two processes which were already evident at the close of the last century: the social instability of the livestock sector, and the rapid growth of the urban economy. The phenomenon of *batllismo* was a liberal, humanitarian, middle-class settlement of the political and social tensions which resulted from these processes. Though at times it may have taken a radical form, particularly in protection by the state for the economically and socially weak, the underlying design of *batllismo* was fundamentally conservative—it was to expand the functions of the state in order to secure an equilibrium of class forces, while enhancing the role of the political system.

The instability of the rural sector reached its climax in the armed uprising led by Saravia in 1904. As the work of Barrán and Nahum makes clear, the civil war waged by Saravia was in no sense a bid by landowners as a class to defeat the growth of antagonistic urban interests.[9] Rather it represented the efforts of a *caudillo* landowner, at the head of part of the Nacional party and commanding the support of the conservative landowners resistant to modernisation, to defeat the immoral, intolerable, and above all Colorado government of Batlle. The war broke the alliance between the two fractions of the landowning class. Saravia's forces were recruited among the rural poor dispossessed or displaced by modernisation; and this was ironic, since the interests most directly threatened by Saravia were precisely the progressive landowners who had invested in improved livestock and fencing, only to see them slaughtered and destroyed by the armies. For this reason they attempted to secure a peace based on a new pact between the parties. Their efforts failed, however, essentially because they lacked control of the parties; and in 1904 Batlle secured a military victory.

This last civil war was of great significance in determining relations between the essentially urban government of Batlle and the landowning class. In spite of the physical damage and losses they had sustained, and though their political isolation was fully revealed, the landowners could be well content. The financial conduct of Batlle's government, in spite of war expenditures, was impeccable. More important, the conclusive demonstration of the power of central authority was in the long run to be a far more effective guarantee of internal peace and stability than a further party agreement on territorial spheres of influence. Such agreements, the traditional form of *coparticipación* (i.e. the coparticipation of the opposition party in government) by which the parties had maintained an uneasy peace since 1872, were at an end. For the landowners, it was made clear during 1904 that the Colorados did not plan an attack on the principle of private landownership, nor an attempt to rescue public lands (the *tierras fiscales*) which landowners had absorbed. The autonomy of the political system was plainly a privilege that the politicians could not afford to abuse by policies which attacked the very basis of the rural sector, and thus a pact implicitly emerged. Nonetheless, the paradox of the landowners' political vulnerability, that an economically dominant group should fail to control the political apparatus, was recognised in 1916 when the landowning class united to form the Federación Rural as a pressure group operating within both political parties.[10]

Thus for all the dangerous ideas that were being voiced in Montevideo, the rural interests had little to fear. Batlle's agrarian policy was effectively neutral. Since a direct attack on property rights would encounter severe opposition not only from the rural sector, Batlle resorted to measures designed to produce a gradual transformation of an indefensible structure. But the measures enacted—higher land taxes, taxes on inheritance and absentee ownership, minimum wage legislation, colonisation schemes, credits to small producers—were easily evaded or had minimal impact. In the long term the failure to reform the agrarian structure was to have serious implications for the development of Uruguay. On the other hand, the rapid growth of exports, and the wisdom of political conciliation, were sound reasons for avoiding a confrontation with rural interests. And in the short term there was a conclusive consideration: that the urban economy, whose interests Batlle directly represented, had scope for expansion without bringing it into conflict with the unreformed rural structure.

If it was the strength of the inherited political tradition which made the phenomenon of *batllismo* possible, its cause was the rapid growth of Montevideo and the diversification of urban interests and social classes. By the end of the nineteenth century Montevideo already had 30 per cent of the total population, and was predominantly a city of immigrants; in the 1889 census of the city 47 per cent of its inhabitants were foreigners.[11] The great majority of the new arrivals had little or no capital; few had skills. But just as commerce and finance had earlier included a large number of immigrants within their elite ranks, so the early industrialists, benefiting from the legislation of the 1880s, included a disproportionate number of recent arrivals. With the growth of the city, small capitalists, professionals, clerks, skilled and unskilled workers, were absorbed into light manufacturing, construction, distribution, public services and government administration. Agricultural production in departments close to Montevideo expanded. The inflow of population increased during the early years of this century, coinciding with the establishment of the meat-packing industry, extension and improvement of the tramway system, and construction of the port of Montevideo. The turn of the century was thus a period of substantial economic change, led by the growth of exports and sustained by urban growth and protection for domestic manufacturers.

Batlle's economic policy did not achieve any important modification of the economic structure. In addition to the protective tariff already available, tax concessions were granted to new manufacturing enterprises. But in the absence of a progressive fiscal policy the market remained limited, and it was left to the socialist Emilio Frugoni to point out the regressive nature of protection for articles of mass consumption.[12] The growth of the public sector, a feature of *batllismo*, undoubtedly favoured rather than prejudiced national capital. The state monopoly of some insurance business was at the expense of foreign, not Uruguayan, companies. Private capital showed no interest in the electricity utility until it became potentially profitable, and it was retained in the public sector. Nationalisation of the principal banking institutions (Banco de la República and Banco Hipotecario) was undertaken to maintain financial stability and the availability of credit to small borrowers.

Batlle's hostility towards foreign capital, on the other hand, was unfeigned, but it amounted to very much less than a confrontation of imperialism. It was largely confined to the British-owned public utilities, whose inadequate and expensive services were already a matter of general comment before the end of nineteenth century. It coincided with the end of the expansive phase of British imperialism, and did not affect Uruguay's willingness to borrow in New York after the First World War. Indeed, an ally for the government, in its criticisms of the railway system, were the landowners, who had long been dissatisfied with the service for which they paid heavily.[13]

If the economic aspects of *batllismo* had modest results, the social and political achievement was substantial. Mass immigration introduced new interests to Montevideo—class-based institutions and ideologies—which cut across the patterns of allegiance to the traditional parties which showed no coherent class base. Working-class organisation strengthened after 1895, and discontent intensified during the decade of rapid growth preceding the First World War, creating alarm among the large employers. Equally threatened with the urban bourgeoisie, in the face of working-class militancy, was the traditional political structure, ill-equipped to articulate the new demands. Batlle's response was to elevate the state, and therefore the political system, into a form of benevolent neutrality which would allow it to deny the reality of class conflict, while enabling it to mediate where such conflict threatened. Legislation secured the primary objective of the working-class movement, the eight hour day, in 1915. Additional social legislation anticipated the claims of labour, and the traditional political process was thus able to draw strength at the expense both of the trade union movement and still more of class-based political parties. While political clubs served as devices for the social and political integration of the new population of Montevideo, the enactment of old age and retirement pensions, provision for rest days and workmen's compensation for industrial accidents, and minimum wage legislation, all consolidated the loyalty of wage and salary earners to the state apparatus which protected them. Such legislation was the price to be paid by the rising class of small industrialists and businessmen for political and social stability.

The ideology of *batllismo* was fundamentally middle class or petty bourgeois in character. Though no group was excluded from the *batllista* alliance, those most positively represented were small-scale producers and the mass of salaried employees in the bureaucracy and the financial sector. Egalitarianism combined with guarantees for property, belief in the value of social mobility expressed in the growth of educational facilities and equality of opportunity, and support for the 'neutral state above classes', were characteristic. *Batllista* policy was therefore to maintain an equilibrium between increasingly antagonistic social forces by concessions to each, while conserving and strengthening the independence of the political system through its capacity to mediate. To fit it for such a role, and also to secure the agreement of Batlle's opponents to the introduction of the collegiate executive (Consejo Nacional de Administración) in the constitution of 1919, substantial changes were required in the political system. Most important was the establishment of parliamentary democracy based on free elections, with the degree of political participation greatly increased. At the same time the transition of the two traditional parties into a radically changed political system, from elite politics to universal suffrage, required important internal changes within the party system. One such, which resulted from the denial of class politics at a time of increasing social differentiation, was the growth of factions within each party; and this was met by the Ley de Lemas (i.e. law governing the electoral use of party names) of 1910 which enabled the supporters of each *lema* (Colorado or Nacional) to unite for electoral purposes without penalising the tendency of each to factionalise in *sub-lemas*. A second change in the party system was the reintroduction in 1918 of *coparticipación* as a device of government. In its new formulation, the minority party (i.e. the Nationalists) received a limited participation in appointments to the central administration and public corporations. The right to give jobs in the bureaucracy, now shared by the two parties, was held exclusively by them, and resulted in a substantial growth of public employment (and hence the authority of the parties) in the 1920s. The use of patronage to secure or reward political loyalty was far from novel in Uruguay, but in subsequent decades clientelism came to assume massive proportions, and was fundamental to the survival of the parties.

Thus for all the significance that the *batllista* period has had in the subsequent development of Uruguay, it neither initiated the growth and diversification of the urban economy, nor wholly expressed the ascendancy of a new social class. Still less did it achieve a significant modification of the terms of Uruguayan dependence. The inheritance of a comparatively autonomous political system was employed to secure the political isolation of the dominant but divided economic group, the landowners, and to establish a degree of equilibrium between urban capital and the urban labour force, between domestic and foreign capital, and between British and US capital. The state became a neutral mediator in conflicts of interest, and the control of the Colorado and Nacional parties over the greatly extended apparatus of the state was confirmed.

Batllismo Deposed and Restored, 1930–1955

On four principal occasions in this century the *batllista* ideology and style of government has been challenged. In 1916, when the reaction of the conservative classes to Batlle's more radical second administration imposed a brake on the process of reform, and in 1958, when the electoral victory of the Nacional party gave rural interests greater representation in government, the autonomy of the political process was threatened but survived. Indeed, although at these junctures the power bloc was successful in obtaining policies rather more closely aligned to its interests than those pursued in each previous decade, the control of the parties over the machinery of the state was essentially unimpaired or even strengthened. The two other crises in the political system had more severe implications for *batllismo*. The early 1970s saw the total elimination of the political parties for a decade at least, while the *coup* of 1933 also dispersed—if only partially and temporarily—the political elite.

Batlle's own proposals for constitutional reform, and the 'alto de Viera' of 1916,[14] produced a split in the Colorado party which left the *batllistas* as a fraction only, though the dominant fraction, of the Colorado party. Moreover, the Colorados held only the narrowest electoral advantage over the Nationalists. The result, during the period of the first collegiate constitution (1919–33), was a politics of compromise which reflected also the relative stability in the 1920s of relations between the constituent classes of the *batllista* alliance. The basis of compromise was apparent at the beginning of the 1930s in an agreement with a fraction of the Nacional party which permitted the *batllistas* to extend state participation in directly productive activities in exchange for increased Nationalist participation in state patronage.

This 'pork-barrel pact' of 1931 was exploited by Gabriel Terra, as evidence of the corruption of government by a bi-party collegiate executive, in the campaign preceding his *coup* eighteen months later. It was also useful to him in helping to secure the neutrality and eventual co-operation of Luis Alberto de Herrera's faction of the Nationalists, which was excluded from the pact. However, the divisiveness of the political elite was a reflection fundamentally of the impact of the depression on the landowning class, and of their comparative political impotence within the *batllista* scheme. For livestock product exporters, the fall of world prices at the beginning of the 1930s came at the end of a decade in which prices had initially collapsed after the war, stabilised at 30 per cent below the war-time peak in the mid-1920s, and then resumed their deterioration. In volume terms the performance was scarcely more encouraging; the average of 1926–30 was only some 20 per cent higher than the pre-war level. This stagnant performance was in sharp contrast to the rapid growth of export values in the pre-war decade, which had coincided with the radical phase of *batllismo*. During the 1920s the Federación Rural in particular expressed the growing hostility of the landowners to the political groups and the expanded state system, to bureaucratic employment and the fiscal burden. In 1929 it played a leading role in the formation of the Comité de Vigilancia Económica, an alliance of the conservative classes in defence of capital. But only where its interests coincided with those of the political system, in their joint opposition to the operations of the meat trust which depressed cattle prices, was the rural sector at all effective. For livestock producers the creation of the Frigorífico Nacional in 1928 was to defend them against domination by foreign capital of the meat export trade; for the parties, it would extend their area of authority.

A significant aspect of the depression period in Uruguay is that, in comparison with other countries of the region, the political reaction was delayed. The economic impact reached its maximum severity in 1932, when exports fell to 58 per cent of their 1930 value. Budget deficits, balance of payments deficits and the depreciation of the peso automatically followed, but the storm was beginning to abate by the time of the *coup* in March 1933. Though the policy of the collegiate executive in its last two years in imposing trade and exchange controls was directed basically at redeeming the trade and revenue deficits, there is good evidence that these measures corresponded to traditional *batllista* objectives.[15] Import restrictions were structured to have protectionist effects; the stabilisation of the depreciated peso at a level above the market valuation penalised the export sector; the amortisation of foreign debt and remission of dividends to the UK was interrupted; the pork-barrel pact allowed the creation of a state enterprise (ANCAP) to produce refined fuels, alcohol and cement; and the reduction of the budget deficit was sought as much by an increase in revenue as by a reduction in spending.

The *coup* of 31 March 1933, though it resolved for the dominant economic group the crisis of its lack of representation in government policy, was partly generated by divisions within the political elite itself, was sustained by political devices as much as by repressive techniques, and in thus failing to destroy the political system it was in turn superseded a decade later by a revival of *batllismo*. Terra had himself been a member of the *batllista* group, was elected as such to the presidency in 1931, and conducted the political campaign preceding the *coup* on the grounds of the corruption and ineptitude of the presidential committee.[16] From the beginning of 1933 he could count on the acquiescence of Herrera, who had important connections among the landowners. The *coup* itself, with the declared objective of constitutional reform, aroused minimal popular resistance. But the strength of the two-party tradition in the country, and Terra's dependence on the support of a Nationalist group, meant that the new constitution rested on an inter-party agreement. Coparticipation continued to be the *modus vivendi* of political life. 'One can argue that the real difference between the 1918 and 1934 constitutions was that in 1918 coparticipation was between the two parties, but in the 1934 charter it was restricted to one faction in each of the parties . . . In essence, the 1931 pact had been informally constitutionalized.'[17] And since the substance of coparticipation was the admission of the party faithful to the bureaucracy, it is significant that the budget for 1937 lists 39,400 central government posts, compared with 30,100 in 1924–5 and approximately 33,000 in 1931–2.[18]

Though the mode of political operation was traditional, the orientation of policy represented a break with *batllista* ideology. The fraction of the dominant class most obviously rewarded were the landowners. The new line was made clear in the presidential message accompanying proposals to reduce the land tax: 'The initiation of a policy of rectifications and corrections in favour of the rural sector, through these laws which have a direct influence on rural life, indicates the beginning of an historic stage in the economic life of the Republic.'[19] Other direct financial benefits included the suspension of mortgage payments on rural property, bonus payments to livestock producers, and the devaluation of exchange rates applicable to exporters. The alliance with other sectors of the economic elite was constructed on the basis of opposition to further social legislation and to the incursion of the state into manufacturing industry; accordingly, there was an almost complete cessation of such legislation.[20] Nonetheless the alliance was based on interests which only partially converged. The regime of trade and exchange controls (which continued after the *coup*) limited the freedom of the commercial sector, while industrial interests were adversely affected by depreciated exchange rates though policy remained protectionist. An orientation guided exclusively by the rural interests would have been insupportable in a country whose political life had been determined for the previous thirty years by the mass of the population, concentrated in Montevideo. Thus policy after 1933 was in effect defined by economic diversification and downward pressure on wages as much as by the restoration of landowners' prosperity.

A further dimension to the breakdown of the autonomy of the political system was the role of the imperialist power and its effect on the behaviour of domestic groups. Though the reaction of the conservative classes to their lack of representation through the political elite was growing before 1930, it was clearly the crisis of the capitalist system itself which precipitated the internal crisis. Uruguay had been born and raised under British tutelage, but by 1914 the ties were evidently loosening, as British investment reached its peak and a modest and diminishing proportion of exports was directed to the UK. The irony of the 1920s was that the growth of the chilled and frozen meat trades, for which the UK was the main market, tied the landowners to an imperial system which by then had nothing else to offer, but from which withdrawal was unthinkable. Worse, Uruguay's position in the market was marginal. In 1930 all her chilled beef, 83 per cent of frozen mutton and 39 per cent of frozen beef were consigned to Britain, but Uruguay's share of South American shipments (themselves threatened by Dominion producers) was small, and diminished further during the course of the depression. The implications for both sides were clear. In the view of the Foreign Office, frustrated in dealings with the *batllistas*, 'Nothing but strong measures will bring the Uruguayans to their senses, and in Ottawa we have a strong weapon ready to hand.'[21] For the landowners, with their principal market threatened—the UK absorbed a quarter of total exports—and with negotiations on the meat quota imminent, the removal of the *batllistas* became a matter of urgency. The Foreign Office had already expressed its admiration of Terra: 'If he succeeds [in cutting the authority of the National Council of Administration] this will be all to the good from our point of view.'[22] When the time came, assistance of a more tangible form was provided from the private sector: just four days after the *coup* a million dollar loan was offered by the Atlas Electric and General Trust in exchange for the promise of more favourable treatment of its Montevideo tram company. Further relief for foreign capital came in 1936, when the Baltar Law denied the right (such as had been granted to ANCAP in 1931) of public enterprises to establish legal monopolies to which they were entitled by their laws of foundation.

One effect of the international economic crisis, in Uruguay as in other dependent nations where the process of industrial growth had already begun, was to promote further industrialisation. This result was not the consequence of the displacement of an elite group (i.e. the landowners) from its pre-eminent position in the power bloc by a previously subordinate group (i.e. the industrial bourgeoisie). On the contrary, in Uruguay as in Argentina, the withdrawal of support by the imperialist power required the landowning class to increase its direct representation in the political process, in order to secure the internal changes which the new international conjuncture required for the landowners to maintain their pre-eminence. Why then was the new regime unable to maintain control of the state apparatus, being gradually ousted from 1938 onwards until the *batllistas* were restored to government under the new constitution of 1942? Part of the answer is that the political life of the country was not completely interrupted. By later standards the repression of dissidents was mild, and there was no attempt to eradicate traditional political allegiances (though opposition party factions were not permitted to express their opposition effectively). Indeed, support for the 1933 regime was based on an inter-party pact, and this involved the traditional distribution of patronage. Thus the rural interests were unable to maintain control of the state because in fact they never sufficiently secured it. In part their failure was also due to a weakening of the ruling political alliance as a result of international political developments. Terra decked out his regime with some rather half-hearted fascist traits, but among the Herreristas there was unquestionably considerable sympathy with the Axis powers, which was sustained into the Second World War. Such feeling was not in general shared by the Colorado group in the pact, especially after Alfredo Baldomir replaced Terra in 1938, and it carried the further embarrassment that in spite of considerable German economic penetration in the 1930s Britain remained by far the most important export market.

The market was not expanding, however, and both the lack of dynamism of the export sector and its incomplete recovery during the 1930s, compared with the appreciable and accelerating rate of growth of manufacturing, were the fundamental cause of the decline of the rural interests from late in the decade. The greater profitability of industry was the result of the collapse of world commodity prices and the necessity for increased self-sufficiency. The process of import substitution was furthered by emergency measures taken from 1931 onwards and continued by the Terra regime. It was not the result of favourable political change; on the contrary, the resurgence of the urban sector itself contributed to the restoration of *batllismo*, which in turn developed policies conducive to rapid industrial growth.

The breakdown of the Terra–Herrera alliance and the revival of *batllismo* produced the new constitution of 1942 and a revival of *batllista*-inspired legislation. The conception of the state as mediator between labour and capital was greatly strengthened by the institution of wages councils in 1943. The expansion of the social security system was resumed in the 1940s, and late in the decade the state sector was expanded by the incorporation of public utilities acquired from their British owners. After the Second World War the economy experienced ten years of rapid industrial growth, financed mainly by domestic capital and utilising accumulated foreign exchange reserves and the proceeds of the Korean War export boom. Prosperity in the export sector was a condition of the new *batllismo* as it had been of the old, but in other respects the two versions differed. The appeal of Luis Batlle, the nephew of Batlle y Ordónez, and the dominant figure from 1947 until the late 1950s, owed little to the expressed social idealism of earlier times and much to a demagogic populism. Redistribution now favoured industrial capital and its mass market, the urban working class. The strength of the inherited political tradition was again seen in 1951, when constitutional reform reintroduced the collegiate executive, and with it the sharing of power and patronage between the two parties was again institutionalised.

The End of the Batllista State, 1955–1970

In the mid-1950s the Uruguayan economy entered a period of almost complete stagnation which lasted until the beginning of the 1970s. The unparalleled severity of the crisis, resulting from the long-run stagnation of exportable production in the livestock sector and the end of the rapid growth phase of import-substituting industrialisation entailed almost continuously declining *per capita* incomes for two decades. This concluding section does not examine the performance of the economy during the crisis period, which is the subject of a later chapter, but is concerned with the way in which *batllista* Uruguay was able to survive so long in extremely adverse economic conditions and the reasons for its eventual collapse at the end of the 1960s.

The capacity of the political system early this century to implement policies of social reform and the return to this tradition of social innovation in the 1940s, combined with a high degree of political stability and constitutional inventiveness, gave rise to Uruguay's textbook reputation as a socially and politically modern country, a 'laboratory of social experiment'. Had the reputation still been valid for the crisis period, then one might expect to find initiatives from within the political system aimed towards fundamental change and reform. Alternatively, the social tensions inherent in economic stagnation would be such as to endanger the stability of the institutional structure, if the political system should fail to develop policies capable of ending the stagnation. In practice it was possible for the *batllista* state to survive for an extended period without generating a positive response to the economic crisis.

The political reaction to stagnation was in fact very limited. In 1958 the Nationalist party won an electoral victory—their first—on the basis of dissatisfaction in the rural sector, especially among small producers, with the complexities and distortions of Colorado interventionist policy, notably the trade and exchange control system, multiple exchange rates, subsidies to industrial producers and to consumers. The Monetary and Exchange Reform Law of 1959, designed with the aid of the IMF, was intended to dismantle these policy instruments and redistribute income in favour of the export sector, but the objectives of the reform proved as difficult to sustain as the structuralist recommendations of the Comisión de Inversiones y Desarrollo Económico (CIDE), the planning commission, were impossible to implement in the mid-1960s. The inability of the political system to identify problems and pose alternative solutions was fully revealed in the election of 1966, which was fought on the apparently irrelevant issue of further constitutional reform. However, the significance of the constitution of 1967, which restored the one-person presidency, was revealed in 1968, when the concentration of the executive power was employed to begin the destruction of the *batllista* state.

The basis of its survival until then, and the explanation of the extended period of political inaction and institutional stability in the face of acute economic problems lay in the autonomy of the political system. Employing traditional redistributive techniques, notably the right to appoint to the bureaucracy and the public sector, and the capacity to secure privileges from the welfare state apparatus for those with political backing, the two parties achieved a massive enlargement of their clientele base. By using their privileged access to the resources of the state, the parties could mediate between the individual and an increasingly hostile economic environment. There was thus a cumulative interaction between the economic crisis (stagnation of production), which created social tension (declining real income, unemployment, inflation), which in turn enhanced the role of political mediation (public employment, preferential treatment in dealings with the bureaucracy). The worse the crisis became, the more important it was to have political connections and demonstrate political loyalty, so that a perverse result of the crisis may even have been to strengthen the short-term position of the political elite. Certainly the political consequences of the crisis helped to perpetuate economic difficulties, since the enormous expansion of public employment reduced the proportion of income available for capital expenditure, while the monopoly of the political system by the two parties stifled its capacity to develop meaningful political alternatives. In short, the redistributive devices of *batllismo*, designed to reduce social conflict under conditions of rapid export-led growth, were used in a corrupted form by the political elite to maintain the privileges and status of the political system under conditions of economic decay. What had formerly been an ideology of innovation and reform had become a doctrine promoting social stasis.

The accession of Jorge Pacheco Areco to the presidency at the end of 1967 was a decisive moment in the destruction of traditional Uruguay. The introduction in June 1968 of a prices and wages freeze to consolidate the effects of devaluation, and the semi-permanent employment of emergency security measures for the repression of trade unions and other dissident groups, represented a deliberate attempt to end the redistributive, consensus policies of previous administrations. The culmination of the process came in June 1973 when with the backing of the armed forces Juan María Bordaberry (elected president in 1971) dissolved the legislature, imprisoned political opponents, banned working-class organisations and ended free political expression. The significance of the process consists not merely in the abolition of civil liberties in a country which, more than most, had traditionally valued them: the ultimate object of the right-wing offensive was to destroy the political system itself through which the *batllista* state was organised. The separation of the parties from their patrimony was first to be seen in the composition of Pacheco's administration, strongly representative of the private sector interests in whose favour the economic strategy was constructed.[23] The main assault on the parties was conducted by the military in the wake of their successful campaign against the Tupamaros in 1972. Invited to uphold the *status quo*, the military questioned its moral and political basis, and attacked the political elite either for their involvement in corrupt dealings or because they were implicated by information secured from the Tupamaros. In spite of internal divisions within the military on the role of the military in politics, and between progressives and conservatives, the short-term cleansing policy inevitably strengthened the hand of those seeking to take power, by challenging the strength of support for political leaders who would resist a military takeover. By March 1973 a systematic denigration of the political class had begun, and the *coup* was inevitable.

Perhaps the most surprising aspect of the political crisis in Uruguay is that it was so long delayed, given the severity of the post-import substitution economic crisis. If the autonomy of the political process in the context of a stalemate between the leading contending factions of the dominant class explains the period until 1968, it then becomes necessary to identify factors which became critical at that time, making the continued lack of representation of the dominant class insupportable. Clearly, the removal of the Consejo Nacional de Gobierno under the constitution of 1967 was important primarily as an enabling measure. A more fundamental explanation is that the autonomy of the political system was tolerable to the dominant class as long as its interests were adequately safeguarded. The onset of stagnation in the 1950s threatened the position of the political elite, and the Blanco electoral victory of 1958 expressed the determination of the rural sector to increase its political representation and impose a new economic strategy. The attempt failed, however, for a variety of reasons. In the first place, the redistributive techniques of the *batllista* state were still viable, and were utilised by the Blanco party no less than by the Colorados. Secondly, the social stability which they secured was still a desirable objective, particularly for urban interests. Thirdly, although the distortions in the economy were severe, they did not prevent the profitable employment of capital: the banking sector grew spectacularly in the early crisis period, and there was speculation in foreign currency, commodities, land and urban real estate.

During the course of the 1960s these conditions ceased to be valid. The role of the parties in exercising social control through income redistribution depended on their capacity to protect adequate numbers of people from the economic effects of the crisis, and therefore on the capacity of the state to secure a sufficient share of the nation's resources to sustain this role. In fact although the share of government in total consumption increased from 10.8 per cent (1955–7) to 16.1 per cent (1964–6), the ratio of government income to GDP remained almost constant during the first decade of the crisis.[24] Thus the burden of maintaining traditional consensus policies was borne by a substantial shift in the composition of public expenditure in favour of consumption, and after 1961 by allowing current expenditure to exceed income. To have continued the traditional role of the state would have implied either an enlargement of the government's share of the national income by fiscal measures, or an acceleration of the inflationary process. Neither of these alternatives was acceptable to the dominant sectors of the economy by 1968. Inflation in 1967 exceeded 100 per cent for the first time, and the seriousness of the balance of payments position made renewed approaches to the IMF unavoidable. The stability of the capitalist class as a whole was threatened not only by the rapid rate of inflation but also by serious bank failures in 1965, as well as by the groundswell of trade union and student discontent and the early indications of Tupamaro guerrilla activity. The *batllista* state, incapable of giving expression to any strategy which would resolve the *impasse* between the urban and rural sectors and incapable also of maintaining internal security and stability, could no longer be sustained. Following the intermediate regime of Pacheco, under which the authority of the political parties and legislature were curtailed but the threat to the capitalist system increased, the stage was set for the military *coup* of 1973.

2 Population and Society

What have they done with this their heritage? What are they doing even now? They are sitting dejected in their houses, or standing in their doorways with folded arms and anxious expectant faces. For a change is coming: they are on the eve of a tempest. (W. H. Hudson, *The Purple Land* [1904 ed.] p. 12.)

I. Population

Growth and Structure

The population history of Uruguay is in several respects quite unlike that of Latin America as a whole, or of any other Latin American country except Argentina. Not the least of its peculiarities is the remarkable absence of a general population census between 1908 and 1963, which, because the assumed contemporary rates of population growth in the inter-censal period were exaggerated compared with modern historical estimates, has meant that the supposed population of the country was (in the late 1950s) up to 12 per cent greater than it is now believed to have been. Errors of estimation have been particularly grave in attempting to determine the net contribution of immigration, due to a lack of attention paid to permanent emigration to neighbouring countries. As a result there are substantial variations in available population estimates, and the data needs to be treated with caution.

However, the most striking demographic characteristic of Uruguay is the very low rate of population growth, especially during the last forty years. In the 1960s the total rate of increase of between 1.2 per cent and 1.3 per cent was lower than for any other Latin American country, and less than half the rate for the region as a whole. Even this represented a partial recovery from the rate of 1.1 per cent in the early 1940s (Table 2.1). It is clear from the table that changes in the crude birth rate explain most of the decline in the total rate of growth down to the late 1930s. Since then it has remained remarkably constant at between 21 and 22 births per thousand population. The modest increase in the natural growth rate in the post-war period was attributable to a very slight increase in age-specific fertility, and to a decline in the rate of mortality

23

TABLE 2.1. Estimated total population and demographic rates, 1895–1975 (five-year averages)

	Total population (thousands)	Births	Deaths	Natural increase	Migration	Total increase
			(Rate per thousand)			
1895–9	826.3	43.4	14.8	28.6	0.1	28.7
1900–4	934.8	38.9	13.7	25.2	0.9	26.1
1905–9	1054.5	37.6	14.0	23.6	2.2	25.8
1910–14	1189.5	36.5	13.5	23.0	1.3	24.3
1915–19	1318.8	31.9	14.1	17.8	0.2	18.0
1920–4	1448.4	30.1	12.6	17.5	2.6	20.1
1925–9	1606.5	28.6	11.9	16.7	3.9	20.6
1930–4	1758.8	25.8	11.5	14.3	1.2	15.5
1935–9	1880.6	22.3	11.1	11.2	0.6	11.8
1940–4	1991.6	21.6	10.3	11.3	—0.1	11.2
1945–9	2111.5	21.1	9.1	12.0	0.5	12.5
1950–4	2263.4	21.2	8.5	12.7	1.4	14.1
1955–9	2436.4	21.8	8.8	13.0	0.4	13.4
1960–4	2611.4	22.0	8.6	13.4	0.4	13.8
1969–71[1]	n.a.	22.1	9.6	12.5	n.a.	n.a.
1975[2]	2781.8	21.1	9.9	11.2	—5.4	5.8

Notes: 1. Three-year average. 2. 1975 only.

Sources: (1895–1964) Ana M. Rothman, 'Evolution of Fertility in Argentina and Uruguay', International Population Conference, London, 1969, vol. I, (International Union for the Scientific Study of the Population, Liége, 1971) vol. 1, p. 716. (1969–71) UN Demographic Yearbook (1975), V Censo de Población, 1975, Muestra de Anticipación.

which, however, seems now to have stabilised or even increased slightly, probably as a consequence of the changing age-structure of the population towards a higher proportion in old age-groups. The low rate of population growth is not a remarkable phenomenon simply of contemporary Uruguay: at no period in this century did the total rate of growth including immigration reach the level of 2.88 per cent recorded for Latin America as a whole in the 1960s.[1]

In view of the importance of immigration as an element in the social formation of Uruguay, its low level relative to natural population growth indicated in Table 2.1 is notable. Estimates of the net contribution of immigration based on contemporary migration data have been subject to drastic downward modification. For example, the migration rate for 1910–14 of 1.3 per thousand in Table 2.1, based on the estimates made by Cataldi, is a considerable reduction even on the figure of 2.4 per thousand estimated by Pereira and Trajtenberg, and of a different order of magnitude to the rate of 16.2 per thousand for 1911–15 indicated by Narancio and Capurro Calamet.[2] The effect of the reassessment is to show that Uruguay could not compete with Argentina as an ultimate destination for immigrants: in the decade 1905–14 the ratio of new immigrants to total population for Uruguay was only one-tenth of that for Argentina.[3] For many migrants Montevideo was simply a staging-post on the way to Buenos Aires or to Rio Grande do Sul. While a similar revision for pre-1895 migration statistics has not been made, it is most unlikely that it would relegate immigration to such a marginal position as a determinant of population growth. Contemporary estimates by Vaillant and census data on the number of foreign-born inhabitants testify to the importance of immigration during the second half of the nineteenth century. The inadequate supply of land available for colonisation, and the expulsion of labour from the *estancias* during the period of rural modernisation, meant that Montevideo retained a disproportionately large number of the new arrivals. The census of the capital in 1889 found that 100,739 inhabitants (46.8 per cent of the total) were foreign-born.[4] Of that number, 47.0 per cent were of Italian origin, and 32.0 per cent from Spain. An estimate for 1860 had found a slightly higher proportion of foreign-born in the capital,[5] and in the 1908 census the ratio was still 30.4 per cent. For the country as a whole in 1908 the proportion was much less, at 17.4 per cent, with the share of Italian and Spanish arrivals accounting for two-thirds, and Brazilians and Argentines, who were disproportionately numerous in rural areas, a further 25.0 per cent. During the 1920s immigration substantially increased in importance as a source of population growth, with central and eastern Europe supplanting the Mediterranean region as the principal source.

It is likely that throughout this century Uruguay has itself been a source of migrants for Argentina and Brazil, as well as a destination for migrants from (mainly) Europe. In this respect Uruguay's relationship to her neighbours has been somewhat analogous to that of Canada with the United States. The rate of emigration in recent years is not known exactly, but it is likely that with the onset of economic stagnation increasing numbers would seek employment outside Uruguay. Rather surprisingly, Table 2.1 indicates that the rate of net immigration in the first decade of crisis remained stable and quite high at 0.4 per thousand. However, during the following decade the suspicion grew that emigration was proceeding rapidly. In 1973, a private but authoritative estimate[6] suggested that in the previous five-year period the net loss by emigration totalled 240,000. The estimate was effectively supported by the census of 1975, which found a total population of 2,788,400, such that the actual increase in the twelve-year inter-censal period was a mere 193,000, compared with a predicted increase of about 416,000 (on an assumed natural growth rate declining from 12.5 per thousand to 12.0 per thousand during the period).[7] The actual rate of increase therefore averaged approximately 6 per thousand, and the rate of net emigration was probably of a similar magnitude. Argentina received more than half of this mass exodus, but there were also significant flows to the United States, Australia, Spain, Brazil, and Canada.[8] The full extent of this disaster, which appears to have accelerated in the late 1960s, is perhaps better stated as a loss by emigration of the order of 10 per cent of the actual 1975 population.

TABLE 2.2. Population age-structure, 1908, 1963, and 1975 (per cent)

Age-group	1908	1963	1975
0–14	40.9	28.3	27.0
15–59	55.2	60.1	58.7
60 +	3.9	11.6	14.3

Sources: (1908 and 1963) census of population; (1975) *V Censo de Población, 1975, Muestra de Anticipación.*

The low rate of population increase has been accompanied by a changing age-structure of the population (Table 2.2). The main explanation of this change resides in the decline in the crude birth rate, supplemented by a decline in the mortality rate. Between 1908 and 1963 there was a very marked reduction in the proportion of the population aged under 15, and an increase in those aged 60 or over. The ratio of those of economically 'active' age to 'inactive' in fact increased during the period. Evidence on the inter-censal period, however, indicates that the ratio is now declining. Though their estimates are not directly comparable with the census data, Pereira and Trajtenberg found that most of the relative deline in the 0–14 age-group had occurred by 1939, when its proportion of total population was 30.1 per cent. However, the over 60 group had by then increased only to 5.8 per cent of the total, and the proportion of 'active' population in fact remained over 64 per cent during the 1940s. Thereafter it has declined quite sharply, due every largely to a marked increase in the proportion of the population over 60.[9] This phenomenon appears to be attributable in part to the high level of net immigration of young adults in the 1920s. Between 1963 and 1975 the reverse process operated on the age-structure, namely the high rate of emigration. A large proportion of emigrants were young adults, so that the 'ageing' process in the population structure was greatly accelerated.

In comparison with the rest of Latin America, the demographic age-structure resulting from the very low rate of population growth is exceptional, and more closely resembles that of European populations. Data for 1970 indicates that Uruguay has the smallest proportion under fourteen of any Latin American population, and the highest proportion over sixty-five.[10] Only Argentina has a population whose age-structure is even remotely comparable.

The peculiarity of Uruguay's population history and structure is mainly attributable to the fall in the crude birth rate. The decline in the mortality rate had a less pronounced effect, while migration was significant less for its total contribution to the population than for its abrupt changes and the effect of these on particular age-groups. In explanation of the falling birth rate, it is important to emphasise that this was almost entirely the result of falling age-specific fertility rates. Indeed, the slight revival in the birth rate after the late 1940s is also associated with slightly increased fertility.[11] An estimate of the number of women of child-bearing age (15–49) as a proportion of the total population shows remarkably little variation during 1909–59, at between 24.8 per cent and 26.4 per cent.[12] The reasons for declining fertility in Uruguay can only be suggested. The phenomenon has been associated in other societies with urbanisation, the reduction of illiteracy to low levels, the growth of employment opportunities for women, and rising standards of living: all of these processes have operated in Uruguay and may be taken as partial 'explanations' of the adoption of the practice of family-size limitation. The unusually large proportionate size of the middle class, aspiring to social and economic improvement, is also doubtless relevant.

The question arises whether the poor economic performance of Uruguay since the 1950s can be associated in any way with its peculiar demographic characteristics. Generally it is believed that rapid population growth impedes the process of economic growth, 'swamping increases in output, and thereby preventing the establishment of a sustained growth of per capita output'.[13] A survey of the literature on the effects of population growth on economic development cautiously accepted the conventional wisdom, but also argued that 'whatever the influence of population on economic growth, it is relatively small in comparison with other influences'; not surprisingly, perhaps, the possibility that slow population growth might slow the process of development was not discussed.[14]

In the case of Uruguay it is difficult to find positive evidence for any direct effect. It has been suggested that the low rate of population growth is a symptom of pessimism about the future of the country, which is communicated to or shared by those deciding whether or not to invest in new productive capacity.[15] The argument hardly seems plausible, especially since the period of rapid economic growth based on the domestic market coincided with fertility rates which were lower even than those of the crisis period itself. Nor does it seem likely that the pattern of demand created by a society which had reduced its average family size was inappropriate to the industrial structure of the early 1950s: on the contrary, the emergence of industries producing consumer durables required a large middle class market whose expenditure patterns were not dominated by demand for non-durables. Of course it may be true that the small absolute size of the population has inhibited the growth of such industries, but this constraint will not be removed for many decades by any imaginable rate of growth of the population.

It is perhaps clearer that the changing age-structure of the population has had adverse implications for the growth of the economy, though here too the effects have probably been mixed. The ratio of 'active' to 'inactive' population is much higher than for the region as a whole, but is declining as the proportion of population over 60 increases. Thus the burden on the active population of supporting its dependents appears to be increasing, but on the other hand the proportion of young (0–14 age-group) population is declining: and if, as seems likely, social expenditure per head of the dependent population is greater for the young (education, health and child welfare) than it is for the old, then it is not clear that the actual burden has increased. A further potential adverse effect of an ageing population is that the age of the labour force and the relatively small number of new entrants to it may reduce its flexibility and inhibit the reallocation of resources and the absorption of new skills.

Although these demographic characteristics may have long-term implications for the Uruguayan economy, it is impossible to believe that they were significant factors in the economy's recent performance. They have in any case been overshadowed by the scale of population loss by emigration from the late 1960s onwards. The explanation for this movement must be based on the deterioration of the economy, resulting in the erosion of living standards and high unemployment. Nonetheless it did not take on major proportions until the crisis was already a decade old, and is therefore evidently associated with the end of *batllista* redistributive policies from 1968 and the attack on the traditional political system (which administered and depended on these policies). The loss to the country has not simply been concentrated on the young adult age-group, but has been especially severe on the intellectual and cultural elites, whose members have been compelled by the repression of political and human rights to leave the country.[16]

Urbanisation

A further characteristic of the Uruguayan population is its extreme degree of urbanisation. According to the 1963 census, 46.3 per cent of the total population—more than 1.2 million persons—lived in the almost entirely urban department of Montevideo.[17] Only two other cities, Paysandú and Salto, had more than 50,000 inhabitants. The urban population, defined as those living in centres of more than 20,000 inhabitants, amounted to 61.3 per cent of the total population, and this proportion rose to 71.7 per cent if the definition of 'urban population' is extended to include those living in centres of more than 5000. On the more restricted definition, an estimate for 1970 found that the proportion had risen to 70.5 per cent, the highest concentration of population in urban areas of any Latin American country.[18] These figures are particularly remarkable in view of the importance of rural production to the national economy, and of the modest level of population density— 15 per square kilometre, approximately the average for Latin America as a whole—in a territory almost all of which is economically utilised.

The spatial distribution of the population in this way poses two immediate questions: firstly, why the level of urbanisation should be so high, and secondly, why the process of urbanisation should have continued, at least until very recently.[19] As to the first, it is important to recognise that the large size of Montevideo relative to the rest of the country is not new. Since Independence it is likely that the capital has always accounted for at least one-quarter of total population,[20] and in the censuses of 1889 and 1908 the proportion had increased to about 30 per cent. The original military function of Montevideo to defend the Banda Oriental declined in significance in the nineteenth century, but the growth of the city was then sustained by the immense natural advantages which the port enjoyed in trade between the River Plate basin and the rest of the world. While the rural economy continued to be based on primitive livestock production requiring a very limited settled population, Montevideo grew on the basis of its commerce and as the formal administrative capital of the republic. The arrival of European immigrants in the late nineteenth century confirmed the predominance of Montevideo. The limited supply of land suitable for arable production, the absence of unclaimed land available for extensive colonisation and settlement schemes, and the reduction of the labour requirement in livestock production with the adoption of wire fencing, all encouraged the majority of immigrants either to move on to Argentina or to remain in Montevideo. It is true that the growth in agricultural production which began in the late nineteenth century was largely attributable to the participation of immigrants, who formed a majority of the farmers producing for the urban market, but such immigrants were not typical of the main stream.[21]

Between the censuses of 1908 and 1963 Montevideo increased its share of the population from 29.7 per cent to 46.3 per cent. While the average annual rate of population growth in the inter-censal period for the country as a whole was 1.67 per cent, of the nineteen departments only Montevideo (2.50 per cent) and neighbouring Canelones (1.96 per cent) had more rapid rates. The increasing concentration of population in Montevideo is not explained by a higher rate of natural increase. On the contrary, while there is very little regional variation around the national average death rate, the crude birth rate is markedly higher in the interior than in Montevideo, both in 1908 and 1963, and the difference between them increases still further when allowance is made for under-registration.[22] International migration could explain some of the differential growth, but on the extreme assumption that all immigrants since 1908 have remained in Montevideo, only 15 per cent of the differential population growth rates is explained.

The overwhelming cause of the rapid growth of Montevideo has in fact been internal migration. Knowledge of its extent and characteristics is very limited, and mainly based on the 1963 census and survey data relating to 1959.[23] According to the census, 29.7 per cent of the Montevideo population was born in the interior, and only 56.8 per cent in the capital itself. The number of internal migrants was equal to or exceeded the number of Montevideo-born in all age-groups from 40–44 upwards. The major sources of migrants to Montevideo are the urban areas of the interior—three-quarters of migrants in the census were urban-born (though the definition of urban is not known and is probably juridical rather than by size of population nucleus). According to the 1959 survey the distribution of urban/rural-born migrants by departments of origin is uneven, and is apparently linked with their economic structure. Campiglia found that the rate of migration was greatest from those departments in which livestock production, especially cattle raising, made the greatest contribution to the GDP of the department, and concluded: 'The *latifundio* is at the root of migration to Montevideo.'[24] The way to the capital for those born in rural areas generally includes a period of residence in an urban area in the interior.

The failure of the livestock sector to employ the natural increase in labour supply—the displacement of the human population by cattle, in Martínez Lamas's phrase[25]—forms a continuous theme in the last hundred years of the social history of Uruguay. Census data on the decade in which internal migrants still living in 1963 arrived in Montevideo suggests that the flow has been continuous, but does not indicate how the rate may have varied. However, the 1959 Montevideo survey yielded evidence that the rate of migration between generations has accelerated. Of 500 male heads of families born in Uruguay, only 20 per cent had had grandfathers and fathers born in Montevideo. Four per cent had grandfathers born in the interior, 16.5 per cent had fathers born in the interior, and 59.5 per cent had themselves migrated to Montevideo.[26] The role of the capital city in the *batllista* scheme, with its superior employment opportunities and a concentration of health, education and welfare facilities, was to absorb the social tensions generated by primitive and unproductive land utilisation policies favoured by the land-owning class.

This escape-valve is functional to conserve agrarian structures without too much fundamental change. While it is necessary that agrarian activity should partly finance urban development, it is as if this price is accepted as the unavoidable cost of maintaining traditional or semi-traditional agrarian structures, though the beneficiaries of the latter do all they can to reduce it.[27]

Indeed, it was argued in the previous chapter that further increases in this price were perceived as intolerable by the 1960s. As a result, Montevideo was no longer able to absorb the rural exodus, and increased emigration has been the inevitable consequence.

II. Social Structure

Rural

The most frequent generalisations made about the social structure of Uruguay concern the large size and significance of the middle class. Estimates of its size have been made in order to suggest its importance, to which in turn certain national social values, especially preference for security, conservatism, reliance on institutions and the importance of family, have been ascribed.[28] In a more general way, the extent of the middle sectors has been taken as an indication of an advanced degree of modernity, implying stability, consensus, and an absence of social conflict. No one is likely to underestimate the important role which 'the middle class' has played in the development of Uruguay, but quite apart from the general difficulties of definition and identification of a social class, it should be borne in mind that 'the middle sectors' often appear to comprise not so much a social class as a collection of occupational groups unified mainly by their failure to fit in the capitalist/landowner or proletarian/peasant categories.[29] Indeed, the relatively high degree of coherence within both 'upper' and 'lower' classes, in terms of location in the productive process, income level, political stance and cultural habits, suggests that the 'middle sectors' may be defined as a residual rather than a class by itself.[30] A further difficulty with the 'middle class–modernisation' hypothesis (in Uruguay) is the implication it carries that the rise of the middle class is owed to a process of economic diversification in which authority previously held by an oligarchy came to be vested in institutions and diffused through the large middle sector contingent on which the running of a modern state depends. It is suggested in Chapter 1 that such an implication in the case of Uruguay is misplaced; but of course it is true that the social and economic conditions which have given rise to a large population which is neither bourgeois nor working class have been of basic significance to the development of Uruguay.

This population is characteristically urban; the rural social structure, with its extremes of wealth and poverty, is not marked by a substantial middle sector, though its importance has increased in the course of this century. The rural upper class is more easily identifiable than its urban counterpart since its power derives from ownership of the land. The social formation of modern rural Uruguay effectively dates from the period of capitalist modernisation initiated under the military government of Latorre, and the concentration of landownership is its principal characteristic. The census of 1908 provides the first systematic (though incomplete) information: it indicates that there were 1391 farms greater than 2500 hectares—3.2 per cent of the total—occupying 41.6 per cent of farm land. From this small group were drawn the leaders both of the traditional *latifundistas* of the north and centre of the country, ruling their territories as *caudillos* and resistant to the progressive practices and production techniques of the other component of the rural elite, the modernising landowners of the Littoral and south. The alliance between the two systems of domination—the former paternalistic, semi-feudal and informal, the latter operating through the creation of a settled wage-labour force and regulated by institutions—broke down for the last time with the revolt of Aparicio Saravia in 1904, and was resolved in favour of the latter by the decisive intervention of urban interests. Technological progress and capital formation in livestock production required a substantial change in the status of rural labour. The immediate effects of the change were to reduce the level of employment, through the labour-saving effect of fencing, mechanical shearing, and the more general use of other equipment, and to depress rural wage rates. But the release of labour from the livestock sector, especially from the cattle regions, produced a stratification of the rural poor, to include not only the fixed labour force but also a sector of *minifundistas* producing at subsistence level on the remaining areas of *tierras fiscales* not absorbed by the landowners, and a marginalised population living in extreme poverty in crude communities designated (as early as the 1880s) *pueblos de ratas*. A large part of this displaced rural population also migrated to Argentina and Brazil, and to Montevideo.[31]

The rural middle class may be analysed as those groups in occupations which are necessary to and dependent on the activities of the dominant class, and also aspirant members of the dominant class occupying a subordinate position within the rural economy itself. In the first category are those exercising managerial, technical, professional and administrative functions in the rural sector. Their number has tended to increase during this century, but the primitive nature of the livestock sector, in particular the poor quality of management and slow rate of technical change, deprives this category of great importance.[32] The second category, consisting of rural producers of intermediate size, is far larger. Its defining characteristics include inadequate farm size (i. e. smaller than the producer aspires to) and dependence on credit, while a large proportion are tenant farmers. In the late nineteenth century the rural middle class was particularly associated with sheep production, with farm units too small for cattle production or the cost of improving cattle herds excessive.[33]

The rural social structure was further diversified from the late nineteenth century onwards by the growth of arable production. In the 1870s the area cultivated was not more than 200,000 hectares, and the sector had changed little since the colonial period. By the 1900s the cultivated area exceeded 450,000 hectares, and although production continued to be technically backward the sector was clearly responsive to the growing demand, and the increasing preference due to Italian immigration for cereal products, of the Montevideo population. Nevertheless, agriculture remained a subordinate part of the rural system. It is true that the livestock interests, through the Asociación Rural, relaxed their early hostility to a potential competitor for land, seeing in the arable sector a safety valve for the absorption of their surplus labour displaced by wire fencing. But the meagre supply of land and its poor quality, the impossibility of securing credit when even the larger landowners were starved of capital, and the unsuitability of the *gaucho* labour force to arable production, defeated the plan. The growth of agriculture was in fact largely the work of immigrants, but even so they were a minority of immigrants who decided to settle in rural Uruguay rather than in Montevideo. Nor did they bring with them knowledge of improved farm practice from Europe: mostly urban in origin, few had experience of agriculture before they arrived. Hence although the ideology of the rural elite by the end of the nineteenth century had broadened to include advocacy of arable production, and of immigration to introduce the skills and aptitudes which Uruguayans themselves neither possessed nor particularly valued, the principal consequence was a limited increase in the area cultivated, an impoverished sector of small-scale producers, and a concentration of immigrants in the capital. There was no dilution of the hard core of livestock-raising *estancieros* in the rural elite. Indeed, although the number of arable farm units may have increased somewhat, while the crop area per unit evidently did so (Table 3.4), arable producers have not been able to exert any effective power.[34]

The social formation of rural Uruguay which took shape in the final decades of the nineteenth century still retains the essential stratification which became apparent at that time. The lower class is composed of wage-labourers, *minifundistas*, and the population concentrated in the *pueblos de ratas* or *rancherios*.[35] Wage-labour offers relatively stable employment, and produces a higher per capita income than that of the other two strata. However, a high proportion of labour is employed in livestock production such that labour is dispersed over wide areas and for that reason is less able to defend itself. The problem of wage rates below the legal minimum level is still found. Employers discriminate in favour of unmarried men or those unencumbered by obligations to their families, so that normal social responsibilities are evaded by employers and the work force. The massive sex imbalance in this stratum of the rural population is reflected in a preponderance of women in the rural population concentrations. The inhabitants of the *pueblos*, the lowest rural stratum, have neither continuous employment nor access to land, form a large reservoir of surplus labour, and live in conditions of extreme poverty. Occupying an intermediate position are those with access to land but on a scale too small to produce a minimum acceptable income. Living standards are directly related to the size of the landholding, but the per capita incomes of *minifundistas* are much below those of wage labourers. In practice there is a considerable overlap between the two strata, and the age-structure of the two sectors suggests some tendency for labourers leaving employment to acquire *minifundios*. In general, however, though mobility is probably greatest between these two groups, the *minifundio* sector appears to be somewhat stable with a high degree of continuity in the ownership of plots. Taken together, these three principal strata of the rural poor account for approximately two-thirds of the rural population.

In defining the rural upper and middle classes (excluding professional groups), the fundamental distinction between them exists in the concentration and control of the land by the former, with the consequent ability to determine the structure of the rural economy and to influence policy affecting it. In this respect the important change occurring in the twentieth century has been the increase in the number of farm units up to the mid-1950s—to rather more than double the 1908 figure—followed by a slight contraction. In Chapter 3 it is noted that the increase has occurred largely by the subdivision of medium and small units, and this process is clearly evident in Table 3.3. Although the number of farm units in excess of 2,500 hectares has fallen slightly between 1908 and the 1960s, there has been a remarkable degree of constancy in the number exceeding 1000 hectares: indeed, in recent censuses it has been increasing, and with it the proportion of the land held in large units. The number of medium-sized units has also remained relatively constant since 1913, but declining from the mid-1950s, though this category has seen a tendency to increasing farm size in the last two decades. It is believed that the number of large farm units overstates the number of large landowners because of single ownership of a number of units.[36] But even without allowance for that there is no evidence in

Table 3.3 that in this century the control of the land by a small number of owners has been reduced. Solari has observed that the continuity of landownership within single families appears to be less than in Argentina, but the pattern of mobility is not vertical but horizontal, reflecting the close association of landowners with the urban economy.[37] There is thus a relatively free movement of capital between the rural and urban sectors, while the leadership of the rural upper class is exercised through its institutions, the Asociación Rural and Federación Rural.

Urban

It is impossible, in analysing the urban social structure, to ignore the predominant position which most observers believe is occupied by the middle class. An early modern estimate by Grompone (1949) found for Uruguay as a whole 68 per cent of the population in the middle class.[38] Subsequent estimates have tended to reduce the proportion (though two raised it above 70 per cent), the lowest estimating the middle class at 31 per cent.[39] More recently, Solari estimated on the basis of survey data for Montevideo a proportion between 47 and 66 per cent, but probably about 51 per cent.[40] All these estimates agree that the middle class is proportionately most important in the Montevideo population. The reasons for the variation are partly matters of definition, and partly the lack of census material, which made techniques in which the middle class was estimated as a residual particularly hazardous. In any case, the important conclusion is that the middle class component in Uruguay is large, and probably larger than in any other Latin American social formation.

To trace the origins of the expanded middle class, and the determinants of the social structure in general, it is necessary to return to the last quarter of the nineteenth century. The factors which emerge as of primary significance in this period are the insertion of Uruguay in a global economic system substantially directed from London, and the mass inflow of new population from Europe. By about 1870, though the economic structure was as yet little changed, the penetration of the economic elite by foreigners was already very substantial. Political domination by the traditional ruling group of families known as the *patriciado* had been undermined in the course of the nineteenth century by the loss of their interests in land, commerce, and the *saladeros*, to Europeans who had the overwhelming advantage of immunity from losses during civil wars. The political heirs to the *patriciado*, lacking a substantial economic basis for the exercise of power, were removed from government in 1876 by a military regime which proceeded to lay the institutional base for the capitalist transformation of the rural sector.

This transformation was not achieved rapidly, since as we have seen in Chapter 1, it provoked the opposition of *caudillo* landowners who were reluctant to cede their authority to Montevideo.

The urban ruling class, though still with some direct interests in the land, was fundamentally concerned with commerce and finance. Its close links with London, and the influential position of the London and River Plate Bank alongside the Banco Comercial in the Uruguayan money market, underwrote a local hegemony based on its monopoly of credit. But the conflict aroused by the conservative financial policies of the dominant class, particularly its opposition to the Banco Nacional which was founded in 1887 to cheapen credit, is important evidence of the diversifying social structure of the country. For by the 1880s the sprinkling of immigrants of earlier decades, who from modest beginnings had risen to occupy commanding positions within the economic elite, had been joined by a flood of new arrivals from southern Europe. Their arrival contributed to the rapid growth of the capital, created a 'mass' domestic market for the first time, and also introduced the enterprise to exploit it. The new manufacturing even secured a degree of protection in tariff legislation, and a small number of enterprises had by 1900 reached the size of factories. But there was no incipient 'bourgeois revolution'. Some individual immigrants achieved wealth through manufacturing, but the economic structure at the turn of the century was still firmly based on trade and livestock production.

The census of Montevideo taken in 1889 reveals the importance of immigrants in the city, and is also suggestive of the way they were absorbed into the labour force.[41] Of the total population of 215,061, 46.8 per cent were foreign-born. However, the age and sex composition of the immigrant population gave it an even higher proportion of the active population, at 68.6 per cent: almost two-thirds of the foreign-born were economically active, compared with one-quarter of Uruguayan nationals.[42] Data on the distribution of employment by occupational groups suggests the broad conclusion that immigrants introduced enterprise, skills and labour, while nationals contributed capital and occupied the 'dependent middle class' stratum. The scale of business undertakings was typically very small indeed. Of a work force of 95,000, 34,000 were described as self-employed, of whom immigrants comprised 70 per cent. Among the 3,864 *rentiers*, however, the immigrant proportion fell to 40 per cent. Male working-class occupations were heavily comprised of immigrants: 83 per cent of labourers, 88 per cent of bricklayers, 85 per cent of metal workers, 87 per cent of shoemakers, 93 per cent of seamen, 80 per cent of waiters, and 81 per cent of carpenters, were all foreign-born. A total of 30,658 men were employed in these trades or occupations, representing 41 per cent of total male employment, of whom 85 per cent were born outside the country. In a wide range of other trades, of which millers, bakers and tailors may be taken as representative, the relative number of immigrants was overwhelming. Within the male labour force (79 per cent of the total employed), the only large occupational groups with a disproportionate representation of nationals were the army (85 per cent), employees (presumably of the government) (68 per cent), and clerks (45 per cent). The professions also had a preponderance of nationals, especially as lawyers, journalists, surveyors, cashiers, etc. In the female labour force the ratio between nationals and immigrants was much less marked because of the large number of the former employed as dressmakers.

If it is true, as Germán Rama argues, that the immigrants were easily assimilated into the social system because it was relatively flexible and lacking major obstacles to social mobility,[43] it is clear nonetheless from the preceding data that they were absorbed into the labour force at fairly well-defined socio-economic levels. It is not therefore surprising that the ideology of Uruguayan trade unionism should have close European connections, nor that industrial enterprise even in the 1920s should still be regarded as the monopoly of immigrants. But the social environment in the late nineteenth and early twentieth centuries was, in many respects, conducive to individual advancement. The immigrant community as a whole was not a small minority group systematically excluded from possibilities of social improvement, and the urban economy was growing rapidly in the 1880s and again after 1900. The threshold of entry into small commerce or workshop manufacturing was low. Moreover, the foundations of general educational opportunity had been laid by Varela in the 1870s, and the university played an important role in preparing the sons of immigrants for higher level occupational positions. Although immigrants came to Uruguay typically as tradesmen or labourers, their sons found no rigid barriers to their entry into the professions or public employment. The permeability of the dependent middle-class stratum was evidently a major factor in the rapid integration of immigrants.

By the turn of the century the size of the middle-class sector appears already very large. The national census of 1908 indicates that only 28 per cent of those whose occupations were known were employed in the primary sector, compared with 40 per cent in the secondary, and 31 per cent in the tertiary sectors.[44] Such an occupational structure appears remarkably modern, particularly in the high proportion in the service sector. Twenty per cent of the total were employed in commercial or professional activities or by the state, though the divisions between these groupings were left unclear in the census, and certainly included a number of working-class occupations. The concentration of commerce and banking, government, and cultural activities in Montevideo meant that the proportion in these occupational groups increased from 20 per cent nationally to 32 per cent in the city. Such crude figures can only give

a very general picture of the extent to which middle-class employment
was growing, but it was evidently an important phenomenon. Germán
Rama has estimated using 1908 data an upper and middle sector
component of 28.8 per cent, three-quarters of which was based on
secondary or tertiary sector employment.[45]

In the opening chapter the ideology of *batllismo* has been represented
as essentially a doctrine of equilibrium between social classes, rooted in
the aspirations and interests of the urban middle class. The political
development of Uruguay in the *batllista* period, in particular the
conversion of the traditional parties into instruments capable of
articulating political interests in the transition to mass electoral politics
which was completed with the constitution of 1919, would scarcely have
been possible without the foundation of a strong middle-class element.
The political conditions permitting the ascendancy of the middle class
were fundamentally the loss of control of the political process by the
economic elite, and the latter's internal divisions in the rural sector, and
in the urban sector with the decline of Montevideo's entrepôt trade. The
economic conditions promoting middle-class growth were the expansion of exports, the high level of per capita incomes,[46] and the growth of
small-scale activities supplying domestic demand. But the possibilities of
social advance in the pre-Batlle period were constrained by Uruguay's
very small size, and by the terms on which Uruguay was integrated into
the world economy. Even with the level of protection which it was
politically feasible to secure, an urban consuming market of about
300,000 persons in 1900 did not offer limitless opportunities to the sons
of the petty-bourgeois manufacturers and tradesmen. The rural market
scarcely existed, since the labour surplus in the livestock sector resulted
in extreme income inequalities only slightly modified by the more equal
size of landholdings in agriculture and sheep raising. Hence it was to the
'dependent middle class' stratum, to administrative and managerial
posts and professional activities which carried prestige and from which
their fathers had tended to be excluded, that the sons of immigrants
looked for economic and social advancement.

For the class of small producers the implications of Uruguay's
dependent status were ambiguous. On the one hand their attempts to
secure a wider share of the domestic market were opposed by the high
commercial interests involved in overseas trade, and the concentration
of land in the hands of the rural elite inhibited the extension of the
market to rural Uruguay. On the other hand the growth of the market
itself was entirely linked to expanded European demand for the output
of the rural sector. *Batllismo*, in furthering the interests of this middle-
class sector, largely confined itself to tax concessions to new import-
substituting enterprises requesting them, and an attempt to raise the
minimum level of rural wages. The dependent middle sector was less well
served by Uruguay's position in the British imperial system, with almost

the entire public utility sector, many of the banking and commercial houses, and soon the *frigorífico* industry, owned by foreign capital. Though a small number of professional men, especially lawyers, were retained by these companies as advisers, the general practice was to recruit staff and even skilled workers from the country of origin rather than locally. Thus the route to social improvement for an important segment of the middle class was blocked. The growth of state participation in the economy in the *batllista* period served a variety of purposes: it met the absence of a large-scale urban-industrial bourgeoisie, capable of capital formation on the scale required by, for example, the electricity supply industry; it lowered the price and increased the availability of services both to consumers and to the petty bourgeoisie; and not least it increased the supply of prestigious administrative posts beyond the considerable level already available in central government.

> The most original and characteristic achievements of the triumphal middle classes under *batllismo*, which go a long way to determine the Uruguayan society of the future, were: the extension of education to a degree unprecedented at that time in any country, and the growth of state activities in commerce, industry, and the social services.[47]

The dependent middle class grew with the size of the state apparatus to which it had access via the traditional political parties. The latter also served to integrate the urban working class. *Batllista* ideology encouraged workers to see themselves not as members of a social class whose interests were necessarily antagonistic to those of employers, but as potential members of the middle class. This, and the tangible benefits of Colorado government, were undoubtedly factors which deprived the working-class political movement of mass support.

Changes in the urban social structure in the post-Batlle period have been consequences of the changing structure of the economy, and of its overall performance. In numerical terms there is no doubt that the increased proportion of the middle classes has been the principal development. To some extent this reflects the growth of tertiary sector activities which is normally associated with increased demand for services at higher per capita income levels and higher productivity in the primary and secondary sectors. But the process in Uruguay has a more specific explanation. Since 1950 the level of employment in the rural sector has declined in absolute numbers, and although the growth of industry until the late 1950s was able to absorb some part of the increasing labour supply, the stagnation of industry has swollen the numbers in the tertiary sector. Most of the increase is accounted for by employment by the state, and in particular in public administration. Employment in manufacturing has shifted away from the preponderance of small-scale enterprise. Although 95 per cent of establishments in 1968 employed fewer than 10 persons, their share of the industrial labour force was only 41 per cent.[48] Large-scale operations employing more than 100 accounted for 36 per cent, some 62,000 workers, but this nucleus of an industrial proletariat, while altering the nature of trade unionism, did not lead to a desertion of the traditional multi-class parties.

The social harmony achieved before 1930 depended to a considerable extent on social mobility, on the prospect of individual advancement to a higher socio-economic level. Opportunities for advancement could be manipulated by the state, but their creation depended fundamentally on the process of economic growth. The cessation of growth therefore carried implications for the behaviour of social groups, since the possibilities of social advancement have deteriorated over time, particularly for the lower strata.[49] The reaction of a predominantly dependent middle-class population to economic decline probably would be defensive, seeking to conserve the levels it had attained, and resisting potential encroachments on its position from below. A generalisation on these lines perhaps helps to explain the overwhelming loyalty of the electorate to the traditional political parties throughout this century. The clientelist system offered security of status and an income which was regular, if modest. In addition, the parties were a guarantee of conservatism. Their inability to analyse the causes of the economic decline and to construct coherent policies which would reverse it, and their capacity to ignore diagnoses which implied reform of existing structures, were positive virtues to all but a small minority.

III. Social Welfare

Origins

The legislative achievement of the *batllista* Colorados in the field of social welfare was one of the most remarkable aspects of Uruguayan development in the first three decades of this century. This was particularly true of labour legislation and of social security, in which Uruguay was a pioneer in Latin America and by the 1950s had a system affording more complete coverage than any other country in the region. It was this legislation which gave rise to Uruguay's reputation as a 'welfare state', and is in many ways the most significant aspect of Batlle's social policy. But it should also be seen in the larger context of what was a programme of extraordinary breadth and radicalism. Educational reform, especially the provision of secondary education in rural areas, the expansion of the university and night classes for adults, has been noted already. In addition, there were reforms inspired by Batlle's secular, humanitarian philosophy which limited the influence of the church, liberalised the divorce laws, defended the rights of women and illegitimate children, abolished capital punishment, and banned entertainments which involved cruelty to animals. Such reforms, many of them implemented before the First World War, were not only advanced among Latin American countries, but also frequently preceded their adoption by other societies with much longer histories of liberal humanitarianism. Any account of *batllista* social policy which fails to acknowledge the contribution made by the reforming spirit and social conscience of Batlle y Ordóñez and his collaborators is patently incomplete. Nonetheless it is argued later in this chapter that some part of the inspiration for labour legislation can be found in the attempt to integrate the urban working class into the ranks of the Colorado party; and the case can also be made that the advanced and very generous social security legislation was the product neither of misguided altruism, nor of 'misplaced modernity',[50] but owed its characteristics to social and economic conditions prevailing at the time of its introduction.

The labour legislation instituted by the *batllistas* was in no sense extreme. The most important single item was the restriction of the working day to eight hours (1915), a measure complemented in 1920 by the legal requirement of a day of rest following six working days. There was an attempt in 1918 to regulate night work which proved very difficult to enforce. From 1914 employers were obliged to take measures to protect workers exposed to danger in their occupations, and from 1920 were required to indemnify those who suffered accidents at work. Various proposals to institute minimum wage levels were made, but by 1930 only a limited number of occupational groups were covered, principally government employees and rural workers. In 1943 a revival of government interest in this area resulted in the formation of wages councils (Consejos de Salarios): but in recent times the responsibility for the protection of labour ceased to be the prerogative of the state, and became instead the primary function of mass membership trade unions. Indeed, the pre-1930 measures affecting private employers in their relations with labour appear—to the extent that they could be enforced—basically to have accelerated trends that were in process already. The eight-hour day had been a principal objective of organised labour for at least a decade before its introduction. Hanson observed that 'at the turn of the century the standard working day was twelve hours';[51] but by 1908, when the commission of the House of Representatives reported on Batlle's proposal for a general eight-hour day, a number of occupational groups were said to have secured it already.[52] This proposal was defeated. In 1911 a similar measure was proposed, and was eventually accepted largely because over a third of wage-earners had already secured the eight-hour day and in most other occupations the length of the working day was shortening. It is interesting to compare the success of the *batllistas* in securing this measure, for which labour was expressing a clear demand, with their failure in the minimum wages issue over a decade later. By then *batllista* radicalism was much more muted, the conservative classes better organised, and labour apparently uninterested in general legislation of this kind.

The characteristic expression of social policy in the early twentieth century, and one which was to have far-reaching consequences, was in social security provision. Retirement pensions had been paid almost since Independence to the military and public employees. In 1896 a fund had been established for schoolteachers with qualification set at the age of 55 (45 for women) with 25 years' service.[53] In 1904 the fund for public employees was reorganised, with eligibility at age 60 with 30 years' service. The principle of retirement pensions was extended to the private sector in 1919; employees of the (mostly foreign-owned) public utility sector qualified with 30 years' service at the age of 50. During the 1920s there was considerable pressure for the creation of schemes for other occupational groups and some were absorbed into existing schemes. In 1925 bank employees became eligible on the basis of 60 plus 30. This was followed by a scheme in 1928 to cover employees of almost all joint-stock companies in industry and commerce. Meanwhile a proposal by Batlle in 1914 to institute an old-age pensions system had been approved in 1919, with the age qualification set at sixty. A law of 1926 introduced pensions to women employed for at least 10 years in industrial and commercial occupations who left employment to have children.

During the 1930s, the financial difficulties of the social security funds and the hostile attitude of the regime which came to power in 1933 halted any important extension to the system. During the 1940s, however, the least organised groups were incorporated: domestic servants in 1942, and rural workers in 1943. Other important forms of welfare expenditure originated at this time. Family allowances were introduced in 1943 for workers in industry and commerce, and were extended in the 1950s to other groups. In the mid-1940s unemployment compensation became available to workers in industries processing exportable products and was extended in 1958 to workers in industry and commerce. During the 1960s there was some expansion in the availability of welfare benefits to groups not previously covered, but the only innovation of significance was the gradual introduction of health insurance schemes.

From this abbreviated account of the introduction of labour and social security legislation it is possible to make two general observations. First, the welfare system as it had developed before 1930 appears remarkably advanced and extensive in comparison with practice in the rest of Latin America, but it nonetheless contained certain characteristics or biases. The most obvious of these was that it benefited almost exclusively the urban population. Rural labour was excluded from the provisions of the 1915 eight-hour law, and was the last major occupational group to be covered by a retirement pensions scheme. It was also the last group to become eligible for family allowances, and by 1970 was still not covered by unemployment insurance. True, rural workers were the first to be the subject of minimum wage legislation, though it is not clear what inspired a measure on behalf of a group which was incapable of expressing a collective demand for any improvement in its condition. In any case, the law was widely disregarded following its introduction in 1924, and is still not fully implemented.

The second characteristic of social policy is rather less well-defined, but is essentially that the welfare measures were of such a nature as to have less impact on the quality of labour than on the quantity of labour time available to the economy. It is not easy to draw a clear distinction between these two effects, since many social policies to some extent produce both simultaneously—for example, secondary education reduces the present supply of labour but increases its future quality. Nonetheless it can be argued that in the pre-1930 period there was a greater emphasis on provision for old age and retirement—in particular, *early* retirement—than on, for example, the supply of housing for the working class, medical facilities, medical insurance, or subsidised food supply. This is not to deny the important work in the field of public health performed by the Consejo Nacional de Higiene (created in 1895) and the Consejo de la Asistencia Pública Nacional (reorganised in 1910) which administered the hospital service. Indeed, three new hospitals were opened during 1907–11, and another in 1913, but private philanthropy was the major source of finance for these foundations, and there were still reports of serious hospital overcrowding before the First World War and in the 1920s.[54] The crude rate of mortality at the turn of the century does not appear in fact to have been high (Table 2.1), but it is significant that it does not begin to decline until the 1920s; and in that decade a substantial inflow of young adults contributed to the fall.

The early appearance of social welfare legislation, and its bias towards a reduction in the aggregate supply of labour, are not easily explained in a systematic way. Attempts to relate welfare expenditure to particular levels of development or social characteristics have not been markedly successful. 'Societies as diverse as Germany, the United States of America, Tsarist and later Soviet Russia, Australia and Uruguay were embarking on social legislation, which contained many similar elements to the Liberal reforms, at roughly the same time.'[55] Rostow suggested that welfare was a function of economic maturity, but such an explanation is not helpful to the case of Uruguay. Rimlinger in 1966 formulated the hypothesis that 'the development of modern health and welfare programs is at least in part a response to the rising productivity and increasing scarcity of labour in the course of economic development', but was forced to the conclusion that 'in no country did labour productivity or manpower considerations play a visibly decisive role . . . '.[56] Indeed, it will be argued that in Uruguay there was no evidence of a scarcity of labour. Bjork, in discussion of Rimlinger, proposed that 'social policies designed to give a measure of income security to the individual would be forthcoming as the need for them increased'—by urbanisation, income growth and an ageing population structure—but was equally pessimistic about the availability of supporting evidence.[57]

Urbanisation can in a sense be regarded as the 'cause' of Uruguay's distinctive social policies, but that is not by itself very helpful. The important point is that at the beginning of the twentieth century the urban population, especially the economically active part, was predominantly immigrant, and therefore lacked traditional bonds of loyalty to the existing political parties. The aspiration of the working-class majority of this population for higher living standards and greater economic security tended to be directed towards the working-class movement, which threatened the mass urban support on which the Colorado party of Batlle y Ordóñez was based. Labour and social security legislation had Bismarckian objectives in seeking to integrate the new population into the traditional institutional structure, while at the same time strengthening the role of the state as guardian of the under privileged masses and neutral mediator between classes. The reasons for the extensive programme of social legislation must therefore be sought broadly in the requirements of the political system itself.

The particular nature of the legislation requires a different kind of explanation. Many of the important labour and social enactments tended to restrict the availability of labour. Between 1900 and 1915 the length of the average working day declined from about twelve hours to eight, a remarkably rapid change. The decline was to some extent a gradual one, as employers conceded the demands of their work force, but nonetheless the immediate effect of the eight-hour legislation in 1915 was to create approximately 2 000 new jobs in Montevideo.[58] It is likely too that the effect of the retirement pension schemes was to shorten the period in which individuals were economically active. Quite clearly the schemes permitted retirement at remarkably early ages, far earlier than is the practice in high-income welfare states. A possible explanation for this apparent bias in the legislation is that apart from the increased unemployment of the First World War period, and paradoxically for an economy with a high ratio of natural resources to labour, Montevideo may have had a long-run excess supply of labour in the period preceding the expansion of industry in the 1930s. An alternative formulation of this hypothesis is the possibility that the inability of Montevideo to retain more than a small fraction of the immigrants who landed there—in itself evidence that jobs may not have been in ready supply—required social welfare policies of sufficient 'generosity' to increase the city's relative attraction.

Unfortunately, evidence on the level of unemployment is indirect and limited. Some contemporary observers indeed believed that the problem did not exist. In 1910 it was said that 'as in general in all new countries it is easy to find work in Montevideo'.[59] This belief was based partly on the ratio of natural resources to population, an argument somewhat discredited by the expulsion of labour from the resource-using sector of the economy; and partly on data recording the demand for and supply of labour in 1909 in the newly formed employment bureau of the Oficina Nacional de Trabajo (ONT). It is impossible to know how representative the data is of the employment situation that year, but in 1914 it was improved by the inclusion of similar data from the private employment offices. In 1909 (and 1910) demand for labour did indeed exceed supply, but thereafter until the data expires in 1933 there were more people seeking work than there were jobs available in every year except 1922–4 and 1930.[60] It should be stressed that the data for the 1920s and 1930s looks susupiciously even and is not to be relied on, but it tends to confirm rather than contradict the 'unemployment hypothesis'.

A second observer to doubt the existence of long-term unemployment was the deputy Eduardo Perotti, who in 1926 proposed (with the collaboration of the ONT) compulsory unemployment insurance for workers in industry and commerce. Of the 90,000 workers who would be covered, 81,000 had permanent work, and '9000 workers are threatened by more or less probable, more or less extensive, more or less prolonged unemployment'. But this was presented as a seasonal and cyclical problem. 'As a new country, whose productive capacity grows with every passing year, Uruguay does not display the endemic unemployment of the old world countries resulting from the constant excess of labour which finds no employment in the market.'[61] The timing of this initiative, and its justification, are both rather curious. It is true that the seasonal nature of operations in the *frigorífico* industry was a major cause of temporary unemployment, but there had been no major downturn in the general level of activity since the recession of 1920–1. The denial of endemic unemployment appears to be something of a rhetorical flourish, perhaps designed to disarm conservative opposition to the proposal. An appraisal of the state of the labour market at this time should also bear in mind the fate of the 103 employees of the defunct Tranvía del Norte of whom only two or three were known to have found work in the private sector.[62]

It is difficult to assess whether the growth of new employment opportunities was sufficiently rapid to absorb new entrants into the labour force. Between 1908 and 1929 the total population grew at the rate of 2.1 per cent, and the total labour force at 2.5 per cent; in Montevideo the population increase was 3.5 per cent annually (to 1930), and with the concentration of immigrants in Montevideo the growth of the labour force was probably at least 4 per cent.[63] Assuming a constant average level of productivity in the urban labour force, a level of employment in 1930 equivalent to that of 1908 would have required a rate of growth of output equal to that of the labour force, i.e. a minimum of 4 per cent. This is substantially greater than the rate of growth of exports between the eve of the First World War and the depression (Table 5.2), but more or less in line with the increase in the value of imports (Table 6.1). Most of the increase in foreign trade occurred before 1920, the succeeding decade being relatively stagnant, and there is a clear evidence of an increased level of domestic activity—the establishment of the *frigorífico* industry, public utility construction, new manufacturing industry—as well as an increase in net immigration, in the decade preceding the First World War. By the 1920s there were three *frigoríficos* active in Montevideo, domestic house-building was at a higher level,[64] and street paving and road construction were important, and in effect new, sources of employment. Manufacturing industry continued to grow, and the bureaucracy was already very substantial. It is not clear, however, that these new developments explain why tens of thousands of immigrants should have landed and remained in Montevideo in the 1920s, whereas before the First World War the net contribution of immigration was very much less.

A significant comment on the low level of net immigration was made by Frugoni in 1913:

> Our country ought to be a country of immigration for strong and healthy men from all parts of the world, attracted not by fraudulent promises and cheap transport paid for by those who live and work here, but by the reality of excellent living and working conditions. Instead, it is a country of emigration, since many thousands of Uruguayans have gone to establish themselves in other countries, fleeing from a discouraging economic situation.[65]

The ratio of net to gross immigration is uncertain, but the rate of net inflow of population estimated in Table 2.1 for 1900–14 is only one-tenth of the rate—presumbly of gross immigration—quoted by Oddone.[66] Clearly, a large proportion of the immigrants who landed in Montevideo subsequently moved on to Buenos Aires, in addition to the Uruguayans of the interior who moved to Argentina or Brazil. The reasons why so many immigrants chose to move across the River Plate to Argentina in the early twentieth century surely relate to superior economic conditions to be found there—in particular, higher wages, more abundant employment opportunities, and more land available for settlement.

If it is necessary to abandon the surplus labour hypothesis for lack of hard evidence, it remains the case that employers in Montevideo seem never to have complained of difficulties in recruiting labour. But the most probable explanation of the lack of a pressing unemployment problem is that the superior attractions of Buenos Aires drew off the surplus labour. The role of social policy may therefore have been not simply to integrate the settled immigrant population, but also to induce a greater proportion of River Plate immigrants to remain in Montevideo by offering improved working conditions. Legislation which reduced the hours worked per day, and gave retirement pension rights after comparatively short periods of service, increased the demand for labour and at the same time promoted social mobility by offering the prospect of accelerated personal advancement.[67] The effect must have been to increase the relative attraction to immigrants of permanent settlement in Montevideo.[68]

Operation

The administration and operation of the social security system have been the target of criticism almost from its inception. The 'generosity' of the system in terms of the eligibility for benefit, and the inefficiency of its administration, have permitted it to be abused at various times both by its direct beneficiaries and by the political system which controlled its functioning. The origin of many of the defects in the system is to be found in the unplanned, piecemeal manner in which it was constructed, giving rise to inconsistencies, duplications, and a lack of overall control. The pension funds were also created at a time when few models existed elsewhere whose experience could be drawn on, and when demographic conditions were unstable. By the 1960s the system had been corrupted to a point where its original functions were scarcely recognisable, but one of the root causes of its corruption—the economic crisis since the mid-1950s—has also been attributed to social welfare itself, especially by external observers.[69]

The age at which eligibility for retirement benefit is reached, generally for men at between 50 and 60 years, may reasonably be described as premature in relation to practice in other societies and to the capacity of the economy to service this burden. The latter has worsened over time, with an ageing population; in 1929 an estimated 5 per cent of the total population was 60 or over, compared with over 14 per cent in 1975.[70] However, for a variety of reasons the average age at which eligibility for pension benefit is reached is likely to be lower than the prescribed age. One way for this to occur is through the substitutability of years of service for years of age: thus a public employee may reach the required coefficient of 90 at (for example) age 55 with 35 years' service, instead of sixty plus 30. Pensions for physical incapacity are related to the period of service, with a minimum of 10 years, where the disability is not incurred at work; but unrelated where the disability is suffered at work. Perhaps the most contentious form of entitlement has arisen in the case of dismissal where no blame attaches to the employee. Though the funds varied somewhat on this point, the principle was accepted by all that a discharged employee should be entitled to a lifetime pension after a minimum of 10 years employment, the size of the pension related to the length of employment and not conditional on his remaining unemployed. The pension paid to women withdrawing from the labour force after ten years of employment to have children is similarly an unconditional, lifetime annuity.

Pensions resulting from dismissal have proved to be far more numerous than could have been envisaged when provision for this benefit was made. Hanson suggests that the number was inflated by deliberately provoked dismissals by those wishing to take with them a pension from their old employment when moving to a new post.[71] In the public utilities fund, for example, dismissal was the cause of over 45 per cent of pensions throughout the 1930s, a level reached before the impact of the depression was felt and exceeding those awarded on normal retirement;[72] five years after the institution of the industry and commerce fund dismissal was the cause of 28 per cent of pensions. The size of these pensions was each relatively small, of course, though the average duration of payment was longer than for retirement. In subsequent years this high proportion was reduced, but in 1963 the Caja de Jubilaciones de Industria y Comercio—the largest of the funds—was paying only 56 per cent of its pensions to those who had qualified by age and service, compared with 14 per cent for invalidity, 12 per cent dismissal, and 12 per cent maternity.[73] Of the dismissal pensions, over 70 per cent of those for which information could be found were held by persons under 50 at the time of first payment; and of total pensions paid by Industria y Comercio in 1963, 55 per cent were to persons who had become eligible under the age of 56. Ironically, in an attempt to raise the average age of retirement, bonus payments (*beneficio de retiro*) were introduced in the 1950s for those who retired with at least 30 years' service.

The old-age pension, the first of the large-scale pension funds, is unlike the other schemes in that it is non-contributory. But remarkably, the pension originated in a proposal by Batlle himself in 1914 which in two respects was less liberal than the measure accepted by the legislature in 1919: firstly, Batlle proposed that the fund should be basically financed by contributions from those in employment whereas in fact taxes were imposed on consumption and land with no contributions from employees; secondly, the age qualification was reduced from 65 to 60 (though physical incapacity gives the right to benefit at any age).[74]

The pension was designed to protect against poverty, and was granted only in the absence of other means of support: any immigrants attracted by this kind of relief were not those which Uruguay most needed.

The retirement pension funds have been financed mainly and increasingly by contributions from employers and employees. These contributions have themselves increased substantially in recent years, but there has been no attempt to standardise the contributions between the different funds. The teachers' fund demanded employee contributions of 3 per cent of salaries in 1904, but this was raised to 5 per cent in 1909. Public utility contributions were 4 per cent (employee) and 8 per cent (employer) in 1919, while the bank pensions scheme had rates of 5 per cent and 12 per cent respectively. Table 2.3 summarises the evolution of contributions in the Caja de Jubilaciones de Industria y Comercio, and compares the rates in 1962 with those of the other principal Cajas. The notable features are the cut in the level of employers' contributions made by the Terra regime in 1935, the enormous increase in rates which occurred in the 1950s and early 1960s, and the wide variation which still existed between the three principal funds at the end of the period. The contribution made by the state has ordinarily occurred through assigning the product of specific taxes, but in recent years both this and interest receipts on the funds' reserves have declined in relative

TABLE 2.3. Rates of pension contributions, Caja de Jubilaciones de Industria y Comercio, 1919–62 (per cent of salary)

	Employer	Employee	
1919–34	8	4	(public utilities)
1928–34	9	5	(*sociedades anónimas*)
1934–5	9	5	
1935–47	6	5	
1947–50	7	5	
1950–1	9	7–10	
1951–2	10	7–10	
1952–7	11	8–11	
1957	12	8–13	
1957–60	12	8–14	
1960–1	13	9–15	
1962	18	10–16	
1962	20	13–16	(Caja Civiles y Escolares)
1962	11–18	7–14	(Caja Rurales y Domésticos)

Note: The financing of the *beneficio de retiro* imposes an additional 1 per cent on both employer and employee.

Sources: Kneit, *Previsión Social*, p. 205; Hanson, *Utopia*, p. 169; OIT, *Seguridad Social*, p.51.

importance; contributions by members which were 78 per cent of income to the three funds in 1957 had increased to 90 per cent in 1965.[75]

The critical state to which the social security system had been reduced by the 1950s was not altogether unprecedented. Many of the pension funds had found themselves in financial difficulty within a few years of their foundation. The number receiving old-age pensions grew rapidly from 2100 in 1919 to 15,600 in 1921 and 22,000 in 1923,[76] and the reserves built up in the first two years quickly evaporated, principally because of 'laxity in the granting of pensions, practical difficulties in the collection of certain taxes, expensive administration and the unusually low age qualification.'[77] Little could be done about any of these except to reduce tax evasion and increase the value of the assigned taxes in 1925. The public employees' fund created in 1904 also built reserves in its early years but saw them soon dissipated.[78] By 1925, when new resources rather than economies were voted, the fund was in deficit. The Caja Escolar (teachers) also received an increase in the level of state subvention on several occasions.

It is likely that further crises would have attended the operations of the various funds; in fact the effects of the depression produced a generalised crisis throughout the social security system. Demand for pensions grew: 28,100 old-age pensions in 1928 became 35,900 in 1931. Income, however, declined with the increase in unemployment and the reduced yield of taxes. Administrative costs in 1932 were 8 per cent of revenue in the joint-stock companies' fund, 9 per cent in that of the public utilities, and pensions were paid in arrears. By the early 1930s all the major funds were in deficit. Even Acevedo Alvarez, Finance Minister under the Consejo Nacional de Administración which was deposed by the *coup* of 1933, observed subsequently that the position of the pension funds was 'one of the most important problems left unresolved by the former regime'.[79] Predictably, the Terra government sought economies in administration, stricter rules on eligibility, and in some cases a reduced level of benefit, rather than an increase in revenue. Indeed, as we have seen, public utility and joint-stock company employers had their contributions cut in 1935. The severest impact of the economies was apparently felt in the old-age pensions sector, where the number of recipients fell from 35,900 in 1931 to 26,000 in 1939. It is hard to believe that so great a decline could be achieved simply by weeding out the ineligible, nor was it that the extension of retirement pension schemes had reduced demand for the non-contributory benefit. Life for the indigent was not made easier after 1933. On the other hand there is clear evidence that the pension funds had been politicised and abused during the 1920s, if not on the scale that was to occur in the 1950s; and some of the new principles adopted in 1934—'that it is socially desirable for a man under fifty years of age to seek a wage and not a pension. . . . that remunerated activity was incompatible with receipt of a pension'[80]—were not necessarily harsh. Nor was their adoption to be permanent.

By the late 1950s the social security system was irretrievably corrupted. The extension of its benefits to a larger proportion of the population aggravated and widened the implications of its crisis, and its politicisation ensured that its fortunes were bound up with those of the political elite which was replaced at the end of the 1960s. There is little exaggeration in saying that the function of the system had ceased to be the economic protection of the needy, and became instead a device for maintaining political control. These were functions which could coexist while the resources of the system were adequate, but certainly by 1960 had become irreconcilable.

The measure of the crisis is to be found less in the size of deficits incurred by the major funds, than in the availability and size of benefits. In the mid-1960s it was said that the level of pensions and family allowances was 'absolutely inadequate',[81] but there was further deterioration later in the decade.[82] More remarkable were the delays which elapsed between application and approval of the pension, and delays in making the actual payments. The former were particularly serious. In 1963 the International Labour Organisation (ILO) study found that the Caja Industria y Comercio had 83,000 pension applications which were being processed, compared with approximately 190,000 being paid. Of pensions granted in the previous year, only 30 per cent had waited less than a year; 27 per cent had waited at least five years for their applications to be approved.[83] The delays were the result partly of administrative inefficiency and dilatory methods appropriate to a bureaucracy, partly of an attempt to reduce pension claims to the level of the fund's income. They also served to emphasise the importance of political backing for an application, which, by securing *pronto despacho* (i.e. rapid clearance), was invariably required for approval within twelve months of application.[84] 'In the Caja interminable queues of people form, many of them very old, scarcely able to walk, who hope to be able to talk to a member of the Directorio, or to some official, in the hope that someone will push their applications more rapidly.'[85] One consequence of this has been that while waiting for approval, applicants would attempt to find another job, which would either qualify them in due course for another pension, or, if pension contributions were evaded, might be at below the minimum wage. The practice of multiple occupations, especially among the professions, clerical staff, and public employees, is long-established. The result is that especially within the middle class a significant (but unknown) proportion has more than one job, or more than one pension, or a combination of the two.[86]

The administration of social security has also been defective in the collection of revenue. While the value of the reserves (and hence of interest on them) has been eroded by inflation and the lack of a current surplus, employer/employee contributions have increased as a proportion of total revenue. Although since 1950 employee contributions have been related to some extent to the level of income, the lack of a substantial state contribution to the funds has implied a fundamentally regressive system in the distribution of the burden. This is reflected in the very high rates of contribution (Table 2.3), which has in turn led to an increase in the rate of evasion. Between 1955 and 1961, when contribution rates increased some 30 per cent, CIDE estimated an increase in the rate of evasion of 20 per cent.[87] Kneit estimated that 65 per cent of potential resources were lost by evasion. Though the public sector itself is the largest debtor, within the private sector the non-payment by some firms of their contributions, and the low likelihood of their having to make restitution of arrears—'the system does not know who its debtors are'[88]—relieves those firms of some 30 per cent of direct labour costs, and has an obviously distorting effect on competition between firms.[89]

Defective administration is therefore one of the major problems of the social security system. Its cost is high—in 1962 it was approximately 6.5 per cent of total payments[90]—largely because of the expansion of its bureaucracy, but the major faults have been the arbitrary, political nature of direction, and the lack of systematic data collection which is required for effective control. Statistical materials are not elaborated regularly, but drawn up on an *ad hoc* basis, as and when required. The politicisation of the funds was possible mainly through the nomination by the two traditional parties of the directorates, whose principal qualifications were party affiliation, and whose principal functions were to interview pension applicants seeking *pronto despacho*, and to select new employees. In both cases the criteria employed were mainly political recommendation.

The National Plan of 1965 followed the report of the ILO in most of its recommendations. In general the Plan proposed better administration, and better definition of priorities. Immediate measures proposed to relieve the problems of the pension funds were: retirement age of not less than 60 for men and women, irrespective of occupation (the ILO proposed a minimum 65 for men); abolition of dismissal and maternity pensions; severe restrictions on the pension rights of surviving dependents; suppression of *beneficio de retiro*; and less liberality in pension awards to those still working or receiving pensions from other funds.[91] In practice, the major change by 1970 had been the creation under the 1967 constitution of the Banco de Previsión Social, which has since then administered the three major funds (Industria y Comercio, Civiles y Escolares, and Rurales y Domésticos). None of the Plan's reform proposals were implemented. The Plan for 1973–7 also envisaged a reorganisation of the social security system, but this has yet to be achieved. However, employers' contributions were greatly reduced in 1979, while pension benefits in real terms fell by approximately 30 per cent between 1972 and 1977, a fall broadly in line with that of real wages.

It is impossible to defend the inefficiencies and inequities of the social security system, but the temptation to identify it as a basic cause of Uruguay's problems should be resisted. Social security was far more a victim of the general economic crisis which began in the 1950s than it was responsible for the crisis. The increased cost of employing labour due to the scale of contributions—and the sharp increase in contributions was a feature of the crisis period itself—may have had some effect in depressing employment and raising production costs, especially in small-scale enterprise, though there is no satisfactory information on the way in which delinquency in making contributions has been distributed.[92] But compared with the effects of economic stagnation on the level of employment, and the effects of the low level of competition within the highly protected industrial structure on costs, the burden of social security payments was probably only marginal. Stagnation and inflation, however, had devastating effects on the pension funds by attacking the real value of their reserves held in the form of government securities, by the financial inability of the government to meet its commitments to the funds, and by increased demand for pension benefits. The cost of the whole system became immense, estimated at 14 per cent of GNP in the early 1960s, and it is not difficult to make the case that these resources were misallocated. But although data is not available for the pre-crisis period, the burden on the economy must then have been considerably less. Moreover, by the 1960s the real function of the system had ceased to be protection against need, and had become the arbitrary distribution of inadequate protection as a device to limit social tensions in the interests primarily of the political groups. Political patronage and control had certainly been elements of the system in its formative period before 1930. In the crisis period they became dominant elements as demand for economic protection increased mainly because of adverse economic conditions, but also in part because the ageing population structure increased the proportion of the population entitled to claim pension benefits.

IV. The Working Class Movement

Although the formative years of the trade union movement in Uruguay were the two decades preceding the First World War, the earliest recorded attempt to form a workers' association occurred in 1865, and the union of printing workers was established in 1870. Other occupational groups doubtless also formed unions at this time, perhaps as much as friendly societies as for economic protection or for political purposes. There were a number of strikes during the 1880s,[93] but on present knowledge it is impossible to assess their significance in heightening class consciousness, or to know how directly they were related to the formation of trade unions. Even in the 1870s, however, the dominant ideology of the movement, anarchism inspired by the doctrines of Proudhon and Bakunin, was evident in the Uruguayan section of the First International, the Federación Regional de la República Oriental del Uruguay.[94] By 1895 the list of occupations for which unions existed had lengthened considerably. Most, like the printers, were probably skilled trades, and included carpenters, stone masons, shoemakers, hair-cutters, bricklayers, etc. Most, also, only had members in Montevideo, where the urban population was of course concentrated. Early exceptions to one or both of these generalisations were found in unions of stone and marble quarrymen, and the port construction workers at Paysandú,[95] but they were few.

In the mid-1890s the level of union activity increased, reflecting the recovery of the economy from the crisis of 1890. 'The year 1896 saw the beginning of a stronger organisation of the proletariat, in its increased tempo, in the number of unions created, in the number of workers who joined, and in the occupations they held.'[96] The movement was checked by repressive government policy at the time of the first rising of Aparicio Saravia (1897) but resumed its expansion at the beginning of this century. By 1905 a total of thirty-eight associations existed, almost all based on crafts or occupations. In that year two new institutions reflected the growth of the movement: a union of workers of different crafts in the port of Montevideo, and the first modern federation of unions, the Federación Obrera Regional Uruguaya (FORU).

Until the early 1920s FORU represented and characterised the trade union movement, which clearly continued to grow though evidence as to its size is conflicting. Errandonea and Costabile enumerated 105 unions in 1922, of which 64 had national membership or were based on the capital.[97] Total membership of FORU unions has been estimated at 7000 in 1912,[98] but another estimate has the same total for all unions in 1927.[99] On other aspects of unionism at this time the picture is clearer. For example, though the ratio of union members to working-class population was low in relation to subsequent periods, membership tended to be much more active and militant. Recruitment was selective, and required an ideological commitment from members in a high degree. Union activists were the vanguard of the movement, and in spite of their limited numbers the size of some strikes and manifestations of solidarity support the view that 'by 1911 FORU controlled the 90,000 industrial workers'.[100] In 1913 an estimated 50,000 workers withdrew their labour in solidarity with the tramway workers then in dispute.[101]

Indeed, although the tactics and immediate objectives of the movement were expressed in the industrial context, and participation in the conventional political process was avoided, FORU was by ideology a political rather than economic institution. The movement drew much of its membership, and most of its leaders, from the tide of immigrants which reached a peak in the early years of this century. Predominantly from Italy and Spain, they brought with them the anarcho-syndicalist doctrines which characterised the early working-class movements in those countries. The radical nature of union activity in Uruguay was intensified, to the disgust of the conservative classes, by Batlle's policy of unrestricted admission of those deemed to be dangerous extremists who had been expelled from Buenos Aires.

The tactics of FORU were essentially the promotion of strikes, made more effective by the boycott of enterprises showing their lack of sympathy to the movement, and sometimes by the destruction or sabotage of equipment. The level of strike activity fluctuated considerably in the early years: one of the few periods for which a breakdown is available, 1908–12, is summarised in Table 2.4. The very limited classification which it is possible to make as to the causes of strikes suggests that although the eight-hour day was probably the primary aspiration of the movement at this time, the length of the working day was responsible for fewer disputes than demands for higher wages or for the reinstatement of dismissed workers. It is also noticeable from Table 2.4 that the great majority of strikes in this five-year period were unsuccessful, but that the rate of failure was slightly greater during the presidency of Claudio Williman than in the first two years of Batlle's second administration. The contrast between the railwaymen's dispute in 1908, the only strike of importance that year, which ended in the dissolution of the Unión Ferrocarrilera, and the successful tramway workers' strike in 1911, is highly indicative of the changed political climate.

TABLE 2.4. Strike activity, 1908–12

	1908	1909	1910	1911	1912
Total strikes	13	9	13	41	24
Total won by labour	3	0	9	16	6
Working days lost (thousands)	145	4	23	323	58
Cause of strike					
wages	3	2	7	17	5
hours	2	2	1	13	2
reinstatement of workers	4	5	1	5	7
other	4	–	4	6	10

Source: DGEC, *Anuario Estadístico* 1911–12, pp. 717–18.

Until the introduction of divisions into the working-class movement following the Russian Revolution and the formation of the Third

International, trade unionism in Uruguay was almost synonymous with anarcho-syndicalism. Although the immediate objectives of the movement did not differ substantially from those of later, mass trade unionism, the ultimate aim was revolution and the liberation of the proletariat. The unions acted not merely to defend their own class interests, but also as a means to attack the private ownership of the means of production, and the system of state authority. Direct industrial action was the only means available, since participation in the political process and the conquest of power was repudiated, and the admission of non-proletarian elements into the movement was resisted. The emancipation of the working class could be achieved only by the working class itself. The route lay not through legislation, but through self-education, the dissemination of ideas—the published output of left-wing groups was prodigious—and confrontation with capital.

Though trade unions guided by anarcho-syndicalist doctrines were the most characteristic expression of the working-class movement in the early years of the century, FORU's abstention from party politics enabled other philosophies to claim representation of the working class, and this was to have long-term implications for the left in Uruguayan politics. A striking feature of Uruguayan political experience has been the failure of left-wing parties to make any substantial inroad into the electoral base of the traditional parties.[102] The reasons for this failure must be sought in the first instance in the period of transition from elite politics to mass representation, and particularly the history of the Socialist party in its relations with the labour movement on the one hand and with the *batllista* Colorados on the other.

The origins of the Socialist party are to be found in the growth of leftist activity and the foundation of the Centro Obrero Socialista in the later 1890s, a period which also saw a revival of trade unionism. Socialists, if less actively than anarchists, found in the Centro Internacional de Estudios Sociales (an extremely active centre of revolutionary ideologies established in 1898) a base from which to launch their ideas. The formation of the Socialist party itself, however, was bound up with the political activity of Emilio Frugoni, who remained until the end of the 1950s its outstanding figure. Frugoni had fought with the government forces as a supporter of Batlle against Saravia in 1904. The experience persuaded him not merely of the evil consequences of the *caudillo* landowners and the *latifundia* system, but also that they could only be effectively combated by the working class through its own political party. Frugoni thus moved away from Batlle's Colorado party, at this time still relatively conservative, and also confronted the anarcho-syndicalists who repudiated ideological as well as traditional parties. At the end of 1904 Frugoni and others founded a socialist club, the Centro Carlos Marx, from which an attempt was made to forestall the institution of the anarchist-led FORU. The attempt failed, and the socialists were thus deprived of the support of a major part of the labour movement.

The first attempt to mobilise the left as an electoral force, and indeed the formation of the Socialist party itself, came with the elections of 1910. The decision of the Nacional party to abstain from the elections meant that the seats in the legislature which would otherwise have gone to the opposition party would go unfilled. A Partido Obrero was proposed from outside the formal ranks of the Colorados but which called for working-class support for the progressive programme of Batlle. The proposal was crushed by the response of the anarcho-syndicalists: 'The workers will not vote. They will not go to the ballot-box to leave behind their slight independence of the present, their longed-for liberty of the future. . . . We shall not fight any particular person or government, we shall always be against The Government, whatever its political colour.'[103] Nonetheless, immediately before the elections Frugoni offered himself as a socialist candidate, and was duly elected. His manifesto from the Centro Carlos Marx identified the Socialist party as a party of class, but it was impossible to escape the influence of Batlle (who had in any case effectively sponsored Frugoni's candidature[104]): '[Batlle] is, in present circumstances and given the fact of the authority of bourgeois institutions and in the context of bourgeois governments, the only candidate who can be considered a guarantee of a government which will respect the rights and demands of the working class.'[105] That was doubtless a realistic appraisal of the situation. But the hesitancy with which it was clearly made expressed the dilemma of the socialists in seeking to establish a political party of the left: they were denied the votes of the labour movement, whose aspirations were in any case far more effectively catered for by Batlle and the Colorado party.

In analysing the nature of Batlle's attitude towards the working-class movement, there is no reason to doubt that he regarded labour's demands as legitimate. The editorials of *El Dia* from the mid-1890s onwards bear witness to his concern. But he also recognised that while those demands were channelled through a revolutionary trade union movement, or through an ideological party which threatened to deprive the Colorados of their urban base, the position of the traditional parties and the viability of the established political system as a whole was in doubt. Accordingly, his policy towards labour was to guarantee the right to strike peacefully, such that a strike ceased to be in itself an act of political opposition or confrontation. At the same time labour and social laws—for example, the eight-hour day—converted the aspirations of the working-class movement into legislative achievement, not through the direct action of anarcho-syndicalism but through the bourgeois political process. At the limit Batlle adopted the style of a populist leader to sustain this policy. Indeed the great irony of one of the mass demonstrations organised by FORU in 1911, in which tens of thousands participated, was that it culminated in an address by Batlle as president of the republic pledging the benevolent neutrality of the state in the lawful pursuit of their cause.

The reaction of anarchists and socialists alike was to emphasise that Batlle was an exceptional figure within the bourgeois system; that the Colorado party might well be oriented very differently after his departure from office; and that the reforms he enacted would only endure and be effective if they were guarded by an organised and militant working class. That this was a substantially correct appreciation of the situation was shown by the policies of Feliciano Viera following his accession to the presidency in 1915. Nonetheless the Colorados were winning the allegiance of the urban working class and in doing so they pre-empted the reformism of the socialists and restricted the influence of anarcho-syndicalism such that the unions—or at least their growing membership—became more concerned with conditions of employment than with social revolution.

These consequences were not immediately apparent, nor of course was *batllismo* the only influence which produced them. Another factor was that the early strength and ideological character of trade unionism was the result less of industrial growth, which was limited, than of the concentration of immigrants in the urban population. Not all immigrants saw themselves as the vanguard of the proletarian movement. The ambition to attain a higher economic and social stratum was a powerful force, fully recognised in Batlle's liberal educational policy. Moreover, for those with aspirations to public employment membership of the Colorado party was an obvious, even necessary, route to self-advancement. 'From the artisans and workers of the turn of the century came a good part of the middle class in the following years. The sons of foreign revolutionaries attended secondary schools . . . became employees of the state enterprises or entered the University.'[106] Thus as immigrants were assimilated into the population they too joined the political clubs of the traditional parties, accepting progress and reform in place of class-oriented ideology.

Ideological changes within the labour movement were also accelerated by international developments. In the Socialist party there had been disagreement between Frugoni's supporters and a larger fraction of internationalists over his proposal to declare support for the Allies in the First World War. But the impact of the Russian Revolution was of immense significance. Within the trade union movement the general effect was to strengthen the position of orthodox Marxists in opposition to the anarchists, and a concrete expression of this was the formation in 1918 of a powerful federation of port and shipping unions, the Federación Obrera Marítima. The post-war depression produced a sharp increase in unemployment and an unprecedented degree of strike activity. In the two years 1919–20 almost $1\frac{1}{4}$ million working days were lost through strikes as labour fought to maintain real wages in the face of rapidly rising prices,[107] and this too forced a redefinition of the ideology of the movement. In 1923 the Unión Sindical Uruguaya was formed which grouped together the communist and anarcho-syndicalist unions, while a group of purely anarchist persuasion remained in FORU.

The repercussions of 1917 were also to divide the Socialist party. Frugoni led a faction whose policies were not always distinguishable from those of the *batllista* Colorados, and whose political philosophy of social democracy and reform derived from the doctrines of Eduard Bernstein. After 1917 the revolutionary faction was strengthened, and in 1921 the decision to accept the twenty-one conditions of membership of the Third International produced the decisive split: the Socialist party was reformed as the Communist party, and Frugoni departed to form a new Socialist party.[108]

The divisions within the labour movement at the beginning of the 1920s proved very difficult to eliminate. The unification of trade unions within a single central organisation was one preoccupation of trade union leadership, and on rare but brief occasions—for example, the reaction produced by government repression of the newspaper strike in 1934—solidarity overcame the ideological differences which divided the movement. But repeated attempts to forge a unified organisation failed. The inter-war years were particularly bleak. In 1928 USU and FORU together could claim only 6,200 members, less than 10 per cent of potential trade union membership.[109] During the 1920s a struggle for the control of USU developed which resulted in 1929 in the separation from USU of the Marxist-oriented unions and the formation of a third central, the Confederación General del Trabajo del Uruguay. The CGTU advanced the movement to the extent that it grouped together industry-based rather than craft-based unions, but the movement was further divided, and in no position to mobilise popular opposition to the right-wing policies of Gabriel Terra after 1933.

If the mid-1930s represented the nadir of trade unionism, from 1940 the movement entered an entirely new phase. The reasons for this reflected the changing pattern of economic development, and its political requirements, rather than spontaneous change within the movement itself. The revival of manufacturing growth in the late 1930s and the establishment of a limited number of large-scale industrial plants contributed both to a reassertion of trade unionism and was also a factor in the restoration of the *batllista* Colorados. In 1941 the report of a commission of the House of Representatives which had investigated the industrial and living conditions of the working class exposed conditions of poverty and insecurity which, if not wholly attributable to the policies of the 1933 regime, nonetheless indicated the urgent need for improvement. Its general conclusion also implied the need for a return to the traditional function of state mediation: 'There is an evident imbalance between capital and labour. The latter has no protection against wage cuts, dismissals, or the lack of adequate factory working conditions.'[110] The report led directly to the introduction of the regime of wages councils in 1943, an event of the first significance since the tripartite structure of the councils implied state mediation between labour and capital, rather than on behalf of labour.

Giving institutional status to the bargaining function of trade unions was to have far-reaching effects on the nature of the movement. Already there was evidence of growth in the formation of new unions, perhaps symbolised by the creation of a new railwaymen's union in 1942, thirty-four years after the destruction by the CUR of its predecessor. The depth of ideological divisions within the leadership was also reduced by the German attack on Russia, which united the left in opposition to fascism. Now the status of the unions was enhanced by the introduction of the wages councils, and recruitment of members increased, but in turn the character of trade unionism was slowly transformed. While the leadership continued to define the objectives of the movement in broadly political terms, and unity for that reason remained as elusive as before, both the tendency towards large unions with relatively passive memberships, and the need to carry out regular wage bargaining effectively, converted the character of the movement from one of political opposition to the defence of its members' economic interests. Strike action was employed less to attack the system than as a negotiating tactic in support of a claim for improved wages or conditions. Trade unionism of this pattern also corresponded to the interests of private sector employers in moulding a disciplined labour force whose cooperation could be secured through negotiation with its union representatives; and in extending the size of the domestic market, through higher real wages, for the output of import-substituting industries on which economic growth in the 1940s and 1950s was based.

Not surprisingly, the re-envigoration of the movement in the early 1940s was accompanied by a further attempt at unity, with the inauguration of a new central, the Unión General de Trabajadores, in 1942. The UGT was effectively the successor to the CGTU which had dissolved itself in the late 1930s, but was to prove no more successful. Almost immediately the UGT was in dispute with the *frigorífico* workers who refused to load a British ship and were therefore regarded as hindering the Allies' war effort. The UGT also lost support through its attitudes to Peronism, and to the United States. Increasingly the UGT was seen to be controlled by the Communist party.[111] The schisms within the movement—already evident in the number of important unions (meat, rubber and metal industries, for example) which because of a lack of internal ideological definition remained 'autonomous', i.e. not affiliated to the UGT—were accentuated at the beginning of the 1950s by the heightening of cold war tensions. In 1951, the UGT called a general strike in opposition to US proposals on hemispheric security, the concrete result of which was the disaffiliation from the UGT of a number of member unions, and the formation of a rival central, the Confederación Sindical del Uruguay (CSU), which rapidly assumed an anti-communist ideology.

In spite of its institutionalised status, the union movement still attracted the suspicion of government. Opposition to government proposals current in 1947, and revived in the early 1950s, to limit union power by banning public sector strikes and imposing compulsory arbitration, was one of the few issues on which the movement could present a relatively unified front. However, the onset of economic stagnation, and particularly the IMF-inspired economic policies of the Nacional government at the end of the 1950s, was to prove another and more effective stimulus to unification. With the student movement playing a leading role, the institution of a single central body emerged as the overriding objective after 1955, in spite of opposition from both the UGT and CSU, and a unified organisation was finally achieved in 1964 with the establishment of the Convención Nacional de Trabajadores (CNT).

While it is undoubtedly true, as Rodríguez argues, that a fundamental cause of the failure of earlier centrals was the diversity of ideological orientations within the leadership and its failure to concern itself adequately with the demands of the membership,[112] the achievement of a united union movement was necessarily combined with a growing acceptance of economism by union leaders. This trend was forced on the one hand by the growth of mass-membership unions, among which white-collar unions (for example, the union of bank employees, Asociación de Bancarios del Uruguay [AEBU]) had a significant place, and on the other by structural unemployment and the erosion of real wages. Both factors have tended to concentrate the attention of the CNT on the economic protection of the members of affiliated unions, rather than on opposition to government. In this the generally conservative and cooperative posture of the Communist party was also evidently influential. The declaration of principles of the CNT made in 1966 expressed the opposition of the movement to imperialism, and outlined a programme of structural reforms, including the eradication of *latifundismo*, the promotion of industrial growth, and the nationalisation of foreign trade and the banking system.[113] The confrontation of organised labour by the regime of Pacheco Areco from mid-1968 probably increased the level of class consciousness with the membership, a process which culminated in a fifteen-day general strike in June–July 1973 in protest at the dissolution of the legislature. The strike ended with the prohibition of the CNT and the banning of free trade unions, but even in mid-1973 there were deep divisions within the leadership, and between it and the rank and file, on the nature and extent of its political demands as opposed to its demands for wage increases. During the ten years of its existence the CNT did not develop as a unified and coherent political force. In general the union membership was more preoccupied by the defence of its sources of employment than by the search for solutions to the economic crisis or even by the erosion of its political and civil liberties.

One factor suggesting such a conclusion was the persistent failure of left-wing parties or coalitions to secure mass electoral support. In 1966 the combined vote of the Socialist and Communist parties was 81,000, 6.5 per cent of the votes cast. Particularly in the Socialist party, which abandoned its social democrat orientation in favour of Marxism in the early 1960s, coinciding with the displacement of Emilio Frugoni from the leadership by Vivián Trías, the left has enjoyed more consistent support among intellectuals and the disillusioned middle class than it has among the working class. In the elections of 1971 the Socialist and Communist parties combined under a single *lema* for the first time, and with the Christian Democrats and dissident members of the traditional parties formed the Frente Amplio (FA). This coalition was officially credited with 304, 000 votes, 18.3 per cent of the total, which represented an unprecedented mobilisation of the left. Nonetheless, the FA was better received in its campaigning in the middle-class suburb of Pocitos than in the working-class Cerro. A public opinion poll taken at the time of the 1971 election found that the FA drew a smaller proportion of its support in Montevideo from manual workers and the unemployed than did either the Blancos or Colorados, and a larger proportion than both traditional parties from the upper middle-class and white-collar workers.[114] Thus the urban working class, though in the previous thirty years it was drawn into trade union membership, continued to resist the appeal of the ideological left. Its traditional loyalty to the Colorado or Nacional *lema*, established during the first decades of the century, appeared to have been very little weakened by the economic crisis. Indeed, to the extent that the traditional parties until the late 1960s could still offer the prospect of economic protection and social integration, their position was probably strengthened.

3 Agrarian Structure and Performance

The economic and social history of the country is yet to be written. When it is done, one will see the fundamental and decisive influence in everything progressive of the pastures, the *estancia*, and the *estanciero*. These are the three points of the triangular base on which the national pyramid majestically rises up. (Carlos Reyles, in *La Federación Rural: Su Origen y Desarrollo* [1916] pp. 129–30.)

Because of Uruguay's almost complete reliance on the agricultural sector for its supply of exports and raw materials for export industries the growth performance of the sector has great importance as a determinant of the long-run performance of the economy as a whole. It is still more significant because the argument made in Chapter 1, that a characteristic of the social system throughout this century has been the autonomy of the political system relative to the dominant class, might be taken to explain the way in which the rural sector has developed. Bluntly, responsibility for the weak performance of agriculture might be laid at the door of the *batllistas* and their political heirs. In this chapter the structure and growth record of the sector are examined in some detail leaving to Chapter 4 analysis of possible explanations of the sector's problems and performance.

Land

The soil is Uruguay's most important natural resource, but its fertility is limited. Unlike the pampas region of Argentina, the soils of Uruguay are not suited for the growing of alfalfa.[1] It is estimated that approximately one-third of utilisable agricultural land is capable of being cultivated; with drainage the proportion could be increased, but for the most part light soils and the topography of the country rule out cultivation.[2] The territory of Uruguay consists therefore of natural grazing land, most of which has no alternative use, though the natural grasses are of course capable of improvement. A remarkably high proportion of the area of the country, almost 90 per cent, is agriculturally productive,compared with 52 per cent for Argentina and 24 per cent for Latin America as a whole.[3] Almost all the territory of Uruguay was brought into agricultural production in early times, so that a supply of new land has played no part in its economic development, and there has been no parallel in Uruguay to the role of the frontier in Argentine or US history. The pattern of land utilisation in recent years is shown in Table 3.1. The most important feature of it is without doubt the very high proportion of productive land remaining as natural pasture, at 82.5 per cent in each of the last two censuses. The proportion of this pasture which has been improved (especially fertilised) increased during the 1960s, but remains small (2.9 per cent in 1970). The second important characteristic of land use has been the slow but generally sustained increase in the area of cultivated land to 1940, its rapid growth in the 1950s, and decline in the 1960s (Table 3.2). Cereal crops continue to occupy the major part of the cultivated area, but their share has been diminishing as a result of the more rapid growth of industrial crops (linseed and sunflower seed). But in spite of this growing area devoted to crops, the cultivated area did not exceed 10 per cent of the total land available even in the later 1950s, when pasture could still claim over 87 per cent of the productive land area of Uruguay.

The regional pattern of land use shows considerable variation in different parts of the country. A classification into six zones is available, using data for 1956.[4] Zone 1, the smallest, surrounding the city of Montevideo, is largely given over to horticulture, fruit and vineyards and is characterised by very small farm units. Zone 2, extending north and east in the department of Canelones, is an important maize-producing region in association with pig and poultry rearing and some horticulture. The third zone, covering much of San José, Colonia, and the south of Florida, is the important dairy farming region of the country. Zone 4 is the Littoral region from Colonia to Salto, including much of Soriano, Río Negro, and Paysandú departments. The region is mainly devoted to wheat and other cereals, and was defined in 1956 (when wheat acreage reached its maximum extension) as having more than 20 per cent of the area under cereals. Zone 5 is a marginal band lying to the east of Zones 2, 3 and 4 and running from the far north-west to the River Plate. It is an intermediate region, primarily devoted to livestock raising but with important cultivated areas: sugar cane in the north-west, and cereals (between 5 per cent and 20 per cent of the area) in the central region. Isolated from the rest of the zone in eastern Uruguay around the Laguna Merim, is a region which combines cattle raising and rice cultivation. The final zone, and by far the largest, consists almost exclusively of pasture for sheep and cattle, extending from the Brazilian border in the north to the Atlantic coast. The classification of land use in this way necessarily ignores the variety of minor agricultural activities in each region, but it does emphasise two

TABLE 3.1. Utilisation of productive land, 1908–70
(thousand hectares)

	1908	1946	1951	1956	1961	1966	1970
Pasture							
Natural grass		12500[2]	13967	13689	13847	13383	13274
Artificial pasture[1]		271	473	458	610	804	769
Fallow		n.a.	229	270	398	295	293
Total pasture	15278		14669	14417	14855	14482	14336
Cultivated land							
Arable		944	1224	1439	1126	1059	1035
Horticultural		49	60	46	61	61	62
Fruit and vines		51	56	55	57	52	48
Total cultivated land	830	1044	1340	1540	1244	1172	1145
Woodland	n.a.[3]	407	486	554	592	568	614
Unspecified	1068						
Total productive land	17177		16495	16511	16691	16222	16095
		(per cent)					
Total pasture	89.0		88.9	87.3	89.0	89.3	89.1
Total cultivated land	4.8		8.1	9.3	7.5	7.2	7.1
Woodland	n.a.[3]		3.0	3.4	3.5	3.5	3.8
Unspecified	6.2						
	100.0		100.0	100.0	100.0	100.0	100.0

Notes:
1. Includes area under forage crops.
2. Estimated.
3. 434,000 hectares of woodland recorded at the census were presumably included in the unspecified land use category of the census.

Sources: *Censo Agropecuario*; MGA, *Recopilación de la Estadística Agropecuaria del Uruguay* (Montevideo, 1950).

factors determining the location of the main activities. The restriction of the most fertile land to the Littoral region and the area immediately north and east of Montevideo has concentrated the cultivated acreage in this part: as was pointed out earlier, the soil types covering the greater part of the country rule out cultivation. The second factor is the extreme

TABLE 3.2. Arable and horticultural land: principal crop areas, 1900–74
(five year averages, thousand hectares)

	Wheat	Maize	Linseed	Sunflower seed	Other[2]	Total[2]
1900–3[1]	290.8	167.0	12.5		2.4	472.7
1905–9	265.1	186.7	22.2		7.2	481.2
1911–14[1]	320.0	243.9	51.2		31.5	646.6
1915–19	350.2	263.3	21.8		52.4	687.7
1920–4	316.5	208.4	33.4		73.2	631.5
1925–9	407.2	190.1	70.7		79.9	747.9
1930–4	426.6	211.2	149.6		103.0	890.4
1935–9	484.2	221.7	149.9	3.6	144.3	1003.7
1940–4	406.2	215.4	146.4	56.4	165.5	989.9
1945–9	419.9	181.8	205.1	88.9	148.0	1043.7
1950–4	571.6	297.6	167.0	184.1	187.9	1408.2
1955–9	744.0	317.7	125.7	204.2	227.5	1619.1
1960–4	400.8	242.9	131.7	144.5	210.5	1130.4
1965–9	404.0	195.4	75.9	124.5	n.a.	n.a.
1970–4	322.0	188.3	65.5	98.3	n.a.	n.a.

Notes:
1. Four-year average.
2. Figures before 1920 exclude certain minor vegetable crops.

Source: DGEC, Anuario Estadístico; BCU, Boletín Estadístico Mensual.

concentration in Montevideo of urban demand for food. With the exception of some citrus production around Salto, horticulture and fruit-growing are virtually confined to the Montevideo region. The dairy industry is similarly concentrated in a well-defined region, and specialisation within it between supply of fresh milk and processed products is determined by proximity to the market.

The regional distribution of land use has a particular significance for Uruguay in the analysis of land distribution by farm size. The notorious characteristic of the Latin American rural sector, the division of the land into latifundia and minifundia, is clearly apparent in Uruguay. Basic data on land distribution by farm size is available from the agricultural censuses, and there is some information in addition for 1913. This material is presented in summary form in Table 3.3. It is evident, firstly, that the total number of farm units increased markedly and continuously to a maximum in 1956 which was more than double the figure for 1908, but fell in each of the three subsequent censuses. Secondly, the increase in the number of farms was not experienced uniformly by each of the three farm size categories adopted here. The number of large farms (i.e. at least 1000 hectares) in fact declined somewhat down to the

TABLE 3.3. Distribution of land by farm size categories, 1908–70[2]

	1908	1913	1937	1951	1956	1961	1966	1970
Number of farms								
Large	3781	3551	3485	3602	3605	3809	3866	3961
Medium	15375	18995	17467	18530	18549	18085	17174	16963
Small	24433	35984	52462	63126	66976	65034	58153	56239
Unspecified	285							
Total	43874	58530	73414	85258	89130	86928	79193	77163
Per cent distribution of farms								
Large	8.7	6.1	4.7	4.2	4.0	4.4	4.9	5.1
Medium	35.2	32.4	23.8	21.8	20.9	20.8	21.7	22.0
Small	56.1	61.5	71.5	74.0	75.1	74.8	73.4	72.9
Per cent distribution of land								
Large	64.2[1]	55.5	n.a.	56.5	55.8	56.9	58.4	58.4
Medium	30.8[1]	35.7	n.a.	34.3	34.7	34.3	33.7	34.0
Small	5.0[1]	8.8	n.a.	9.2	9.5	8.8	7.9	7.6

Notes:

1. The 1908 census did not indicate total land area by farm size. Estimates given here were made on the basis of the mean land area for each of the fourteen farm-size classes.
2. Large farms are defined as 1000 hectares and above; medium, 100 to 999 hectares; small, 1 to 99 hectares. The definitions are arbitrary, since the boundaries should vary according to the zone of the country, fertility of the soil, and nature of production; in particular, small farms might be restricted to 49 hectares, but the data for 1913 and 1937 do not break down at this size.

Sources: 1913: Martín C. Martínez, *La Renta Territorial* (Montevideo, El Siglo Ilustrado, 1918); 1937: MGA, *Recopilación*; other years: *Censo Agropecuario*.

1950s, but during the 1960s has increased and in 1970 exceeded the 1908 figure. The number of medium-sized farms (100–999 hectares) grew somewhat until the 1950s and then declined, a pattern followed in more exaggerated form by the small (below 100 hectares) farm category. Indeed it is the behaviour of this last group which explains almost all the variation in the number of farms, while the number of large units has moved inversely to the general trend.

Table 3.3 also demonstrates a high level of inequality in the distribution of land, the data for 1970 indicating that 5 per cent of farms occupy 58 per cent of the land, while at the other end of the scale 73 per cent of farms have rather less than 8 per cent. The census material on which the table is based distinguishes twelve farm size classes (rather than the three shown here), which makes it possible to calculate Gini coefficients with some accuracy, in order to assess whether the distribution of land in Uruguay has become more or less unequal over time. The statistical evidence in fact shows a tendency to increasing inequality between 1913 and 1951, with coefficients of 0.73 and 0.83 respectively.[5] Between 1951 and 1970, however, (including the intervening censuses) the coefficient shows no significant variation. Nonetheless, after 1956 there was a substantial increase in the number of large farms and a decline in the number of small and medium units. Defining *latifundia* as farms in excess of 2500 hectares, it is notable that their number had declined from 1391 in 1908 to 1162 in 1956, but in all three subsequent censuses the number has been slightly higher. Indeed while the average size of large farms (over 1000 hectares) has fallen from 2746 hectares in 1913 to 2594 in 1956 and 2437 in 1970, the proportionate fall in the average small farm size was very much greater between 1913 and 1956, and slightly greater between 1956 and 1970. Over the period to 1956, then, the greater inequality of land distribution was the net result of a strong tendency for medium and small farms to subdivide, and a conflicting but much weaker tendency for the average size of large farms to diminish.[6]

The reason for the growth in the total number of farm units until 1956, and the decline in subsequent censuses, has not received much attention in the literature on the development of the rural sector. The most reasonable hypothesis would link the number of farms with the expansion of arable farming, which also reached a maximum in 1956. Indeed, Solari compared the censuses of 1908 and 1951 and reached the conclusion that the process of subdivision of the land had occurred basically in arable production rather than the livestock sector. His evidence for this was a primitive classification in the censuses of farm units as livestock, agricultural (arable) or mixed; only 20 per cent of the total increase in the number of farms occurred in the livestock sector.[7] Between 1951 and 1970 the relationship between crop acreage and number of farms is undoubtedly very close, though the census data does not permit a positive conclusion. But for the period before 1951 there is additional annual data on arable farms covering 1912–13 to 1948–9, which is summarised in Table 3.4. This material confirms that the average crop acreage per arable farm was small, reaching a maximum of 33 hectares. The surprising conclusion to be drawn however, is that this average crop area was growing during the period, not diminishing. The total number of arable farms increased only very slightly, and was actually declining during the 1940s. Moreover, while small farms were a declining proportion of the total, the number of large farms showed a pronounced growth in the 1930s and 1940s. This evidence directly contradicts Solari's conclusion. It seems likely that the census classification of farms as livestock or arable units is too broad to be useful, and that the process of subdivision occurred in small farms which combined both activities.

TABLE 3.4. Arable farms and areas sown to crops, 1912–48
(five-year averages)

	Arable farms (000)	Crop area (000 hectares)	Average crop area per farm (hectares)	Farms sowing less than 100 hectares (000)	Farms sowing more than 1000 hectares
1912–15[1]	32.2	723.1	22.5	31.3	7
1916–20	34.4	654.8	19.0	33.8	5
1921–5	35.0	664.5	19.0	34.3	4
1926–30	36.4	825.0	22.7	35.3	4
1931–5	38.6	931.0	24.1	37.1	10
1936–40	38.7	1040.3	26.9	36.8	23
1941–5	36.3	934.9	25.8	34.3	32
1946–8[2]	33.8	1114.8	32.9	31.2	45

Notes: 1. Four-year average. 2. Three-year average.

Source: 1912–23, Ministerio de Industrias, *Anuario de Estadística Agrícola*; 1924–48, MGA, *Recopilación*.

As an index of land concentration, data on farm size somewhat underestimates the problem because of the practice of multiple landholdings. An estimate made at the beginning of the 1960s found a total of 86,900 landowners (including owners of less than one hectare).[8] The most recent census then available for comparison, 1956, had indicated a total of 89,130 farm units; however the 1961 census subsequently gave the total number of farm units as 86,928, almost identical to the number of landowners. Nonetheless there was a wide discrepancy in the case of farms over 5000 hectares: whereas the 1961 census found only 331 such farms occupying 2.6 million hectares, the CLEH-CINAM report estimated that 530 landowners held more than 5000 hectares, and that they owned a total of 4.8 million hectares. Indeed the report suggested that in terms of the distribution of economic decisions and of profits within the rural sector, the degree of concentration was still greater: 670 enterprises accounted for 5.8 million hectares (36 per cent of productive land).[9] Another estimate was that 3000 enterprises controlled almost two-thirds of the land.[10]

Concentration of farm operations, as opposed to ownership, leads to the question of land tenure. A variety of forms are found in Uruguay of which the most important are ownership and tenancy. A small amount of land is held under other forms including sharecropping and squatting. An intermediate category of great significance is that of tenancies taken by landowners. There has tended to be a presumption in the literature on agricultural development that owner-operation will in general be the most satisfactory form of land tenure, and this view is echoed in

Uruguay.[11] The objections to tenancy are principally that the tenant frequently receives inadequate protection of his interests. His ability and willingness to invest in the farm are further reduced by insecurity or brevity of tenure, and harmful agricultural practices may be employed in order to secure short-term gain.

According to census figures the proportion of owner-farmed land has been increasing in the post-war period, rising to 42 per cent in 1956, 50 per cent in 1966 and 53 per cent in 1970. The increase came at the expense of tenant land, which fell in the same years from 31 per cent to 22 and 18 per cent. Owner tenancies remained constant at 21–22 per cent. The proportion of farm units operated by their owners has also increased from almost one-half in 1956 to 55 per cent (1966) and 59 per cent (1970). The proportion of farms with tenants was very similar in all three years to the proportion of land they occupied, and this declined to 19 per cent in 1970. The proportion of farms tenanted by owners of other farms stayed constant at about 8 per cent—a much lower proportion than of the land area they cover. The explanation of this is that these units are livestock farms of substantial size and are rented by land-owners either of adjacent farms in order to create more economic units, or (more probably) who wish to expand the scale of their operations. As a proportion of the farms in different farm size classes, owner-operated farms were most important in the cases of very small and very large farms. In the medium farm size class (100 to 1000 hectares), ownership accounts for less than 40 per cent. Tenancies show the reverse distribution, accounting for the proportionately greater number of farms in this intermediate range. The patterns of land tenure within the main categories of land use in the 1970 census showed few surprising variations. However, a feature of the arable sector, which is particularly significant in horticulture and fruit-growing, is the importance of sharecropping arrangements. In one form or another they account for over 12 per cent of arable land, compared with 1 per cent of pasture.

The defects of tenancy in Uruguay have been acknowledged in legislation seeking to protect the tenant in three principal respects: the length of the tenure agreement, the rent, and the obligations of the landlord to improve the property. The efficacy of such legislation is difficult to judge; but in view of a criticism of the law of 1954 relating to land tenancy regulation, that rental contracts are normally verbal rather than written,[12] it is unlikely that legislation solved the problem. The origins of legal protection for tenants are to be found in the adverse conditions affecting the rural sector after the First World War. The rapid growth of both livestock and arable production after 1904 was accompanied by sharply rising land values; but the post-war slump did not cause land rents to decline until 1922–3 and the inter-war period as a whole was marked by an increasing ratio of rents to land prices (Table 4.3). The most serious effects of this were felt by arable farmers, a large proportion of whom were tenant farmers.[13] The contraction of arable acreage (see Table 3.2), depopulation of rural areas, and the poverty of the arable farmers who remained, were themes of the debate which resulted in the law of 1922.[14] This, the first protective measure for tenants, attempted to relate rents to the (relatively low) land values fixed for taxation purposes. In 1927 a minimum term of four years for arable farm tenancies was established, and in 1942 landlords were obliged to ensure that certain facilities were present on land they rented out. The regulations governing land tenancy through the 1960s were established in 1954: in addition to a consolidation of the kinds of protection previously granted, the 1954 law was also concerned with the manner in which the land was exploited, particularly practices leading to soil erosion, and it attempted to control the renting of large tracts of land. In thus acknowledging the wider significance of legislation on land tenure, the law pursued one of the points of the national agricultural plan of 1947,[15] and was integrated to some extent with the National Colonisation Institute created in 1948. The recommendations of the World Bank mission in 1951, however, made no mention of the desirability of land tenure changes.[16]

The agricultural colony is a form of tenure which has been a feature of agricultural development in other countries, but in Uruguay it has had almost no significance in spite of persistent if belated government policy in its favour. Before 1913 there was no effective policy and only isolated attempts at colonisation: the success of Colonia Valdense and Colonia Suiza, established at the end of the 1850s, was quite exceptional. Uruguay's failure to attract overseas migrants to settle and cultivate the land was a source of preoccupation, and in 1913 legislation enabled the state to purchase land for sale on generous credit terms to colonisers.[17] A succession of laws modified and liberalised the regime, but by 1948 only 232,000 hectares had been colonised in the 35-year period. Lack of resources and a weak institutional structure were factors hampering the scheme, but the underlying failure was the absence of state land suitable for agricultural colonisation. By 1948 the objective of colonisation policy had long since changed from attracting overseas migrants to retaining existing farmers on the land, and it was the urgent need to protect those threatened with eviction which led to the creation of the National Colonisation Institute in 1948. With the power to expropriate land (with compensation), the new organisation temporarily increased the rate of colonisation. By 1956 154,000 hectares had been acquired, but in the following ten years only a further 17,000 hectares were added.[18] The inadequate resources of the Institute available for land purchase were further reduced by its excessively large administrative structure. Thus the land acquired by the Institute was quite inadequate to its needs. In 1957 there were seven or eight applicants for each parcel of land, and by 1961 12,500 applications were registered with the

Institute.[19] Pressure to accommodate so many resulted in the allocation of uneconomically small plots: 97 per cent of successful applicants by 1954 received land sufficient to meet only their subsistence needs.[20] If that assessment seems too pessimistic, since the average allocation was 139 hectares by 1954, the general criticism of excessively small units was also made by the MGA-CIDE report, and during 1960–5 the average fell to 48 hectares.[21]

The policy of state purchase of land for redistribution has thus entirely failed to reduce the land problem in Uruguay. From the structuralist perspective, that problem has two main institutional aspects, both of which should in principle be susceptible to reform. The first concerns the size of land-holdings, notably the excessive degree of fragmentation in the arable farm sector, and the continued existence of *latifundia* in the livestock sector. The second aspect of the land problem is the defective structure of land tenure relationships. Summarising these aspects on the basis of data for 1961, it was found that only 14,200 farms (16.5 per cent of the total), comprising 3 million hectares (18 per cent), were free from problems of size and tenure, after making allowance for soil types, transport facilities, and proximity to markets.[22]

Labour and Capital

The most general conclusion to be reached about the size of the rural population is that it is remarkably small in a country whose economic structure depends on the rural sector. Moreover, as a proportion of total population it has apparently declined throughout this century, and has certainly declined in absolute numbers since the 1950s.[23] In 1963 an estimated 445,000 persons lived on farms or in population centres of less than 1,000 inhabitants, about 17 per cent of total population; and an approximately equal number were economically dependent on agricultural activities.[24] Estimates of the rural labour force are made difficult by the seasonal nature of rural employment and the relative ease of entry to and exit from the labour force in agricultural occupations. The recent agricultural censuses have exaggerated the size of the rural labour force, probably through the inclusion of occasional participants, but the declining trend they indicate is confirmed by estimates of the Banco de la República.[25] The two population censuses recorded a decline in primary sector employment from 182,000 in 1963 to 171,000 in 1975. The proportion of the total labour force engaged in agriculture is thus very low, and in recent years has been declining. From about 27 per cent of those employed in 1955, the proportion in agriculture in the 1963 census was 18 per cent.[26]

Whereas large urban centres and a process of rapid urbanisation characterise all Latin American countries, the proportionate size of

Montevideo, the ratio of agricultural employment comparable with that in some advanced industrial countries, and the importance of agriculture to the Uruguayan economy, make this a case apart. The phenomenon is neither new, nor recently recognised. It was a central theme of a highly significant book published in 1930,[27] and had attracted the attention of the government before 1914. The explanation of so deep-rooted a structural characteristic is inevitably complex. But the inability of agriculture to absorb a greater proportion of the labour supply provokes questions which are fundamental to the nature of Uruguay's development. The employment histories of the two principal sectors of agriculture, arable and livestock production, are examined separately since the forces shaping them in this century have been distinct.

The evolution of employment in crop production is more accessible than that in livestock, since for the period 1913–46 there exists annual data on the total number of persons engaged in arable production. Summarising the data as five-year averages, employment ranged from a low of 93,700 in the depressed period 1920–4, to a peak of 104,000 in the two periods comprising 1935–44.[28] For the years after 1946, coinciding with the beginning of the price support policy for wheat, greatly increased arable acreage, and substantial imports of farm machinery—a period therefore of great interest—the annual data is neither complete nor comparable, and is sharply at variance with census data.[29]

The period 1920–40 is suitable for analysis, since the data is believed to be homogeneous and the exceptional conditions of the world wars are partly avoided. The boundary years in fact correspond to the low point in cultivated acreage after the exceptional expansion of the First World War, and the highest acreage before the Second World War. During these twenty-one years the rate of growth of employment in crop production was only 0.7 per cent per annum, compared with an annual growth rate of 3.1 per cent for crop acreage. The number of hectares of crop land per person employed in the sector grew at the rate of 2.5 per cent per annum; in round figures, the area of crop land per crop worker grew from 6.5 hectares in 1920 to 10 hectares in 1940.

This evidence, incomplete though it is, throws light on an early but authoritative view that the failure of arable farming to employ larger numbers was due to the slow growth of arable farming itself.[30] Martinez Lamas was persuaded to this conclusion by selective single-year comparisons between the boom years in arable production (1913–18) and the slump in the early 1920s, though even he was obliged to notice the more rapid growth of cultivated land by 1928. In fact, in the comparisons Martínez Lamas drew with the neighbouring Argentine province of Entre Ríos, it was the relatively poor performance of Uruguay that most concerned him. Uruguay never enjoyed a period of rapid agricultural settlement and wheat export boom that was a such a feature of Argentine development before the First World War. In producing dubious evidence to show that there had been no growth of cultivation, therefore, he was attempting to make the different point that Uruguay had been left behind by Argentina.

The agricultural crisis of the early 1920s, and the public concern it aroused, did however produce important evidence on obstacles to a faster rate of growth of cultivation. An extensive survey in 1922 of the problems of arable farming concluded that the fundamental obstacle was competition for the land from livestock producers.[31] In part, it was argued, the devotion of so great a proportion of the land to livestock was rational: price trends had favoured livestock production, further investment was needed on crop-disease control and research on higher-yielding crop strains, and in any case only about 20 per cent of the land was suitable for cultivation. But an additional reason was also found:

> Employment in livestock production appeals more to the *criollo* in general, equally to the man who directs the work as to the employee or labourer who performs the manual labour. The plough and the hoe are tools which the *criollo* worker of pure blood finds it distasteful to use, as well as it being difficult or disagreeable for his employer to direct his managerial and entrepreneurial abilities towards arable farming.[32]

There was therefore believed to be an 'irrational' element in the failure of landowners to plough the land. Further evidence of it is to be found in the nature of land rental contracts at this time. In 1920 it was observed that 'Landowners prefer to rent for pasture rather than for cultivation, because of their distaste for arable farming on their lands . . .'.[33] Terra also proposed a law to nullify land contracts which prohibited agriculture on up to 20 per cent of the land area, pointing out that almost all landowners insisted on a contractual undertaking that the land was not to be ploughed.[34] Reluctance to cultivate was implied later in a law of 1933 to make cultivation obligatory, but in practice it was not applied.[35]

The slow growth of employment in the arable sector in the inter-war years thus had two components: the slow growth of the sector itself, and the rapidly declining labour input per unit of land cultivated. The first of these factors may have owed something to a non-economic preference for the more traditional activity of livestock raising, but the importance of such a preference is difficult to evaluate. However, crop producers were not restricted to the domestic market, since before 1940 Uruguay was a net exporter of wheat, maize and linseed. It seems likely therefore that the principal constraint on the growth of crop acreage was the relatively greater profitability of livestock production. Some support for this hypothesis is suggested by an examination of price trends for wheat and beef cattle, which shows a slight deterioration in the relative price of wheat during 1920–40.[36] However, in the absence of data on costs it is impossible to speak more positively on the degree to which the slow growth of crop acreage represented a rational distribution of the land resource between competing uses. But experience with the wheat price support policy after 1946 strongly suggests that farmers have been sensitive to relative price changes. The increase in the price of wheat from $8.76 per 100 kilos in 1946 to $18.92 in 1948 was only partially successful in increasing the wheat acreage. It was not until the 1952 sowing, when world commodity prices (including those of beef and wool) were falling sharply and the wheat support price had settled back to $17.50, that the major increase in wheat acreage took place.

The second factor in the slow growth of arable employment, the declining ratio of labour to cultivated land, is not explained by declining yields per hectare, nor by the substitution of crops requiring a reduced labour input per hectare. The probable explanation is to be found partly in the introduction of agricultural machinery, and partly in the growing concentration of crop land on larger farms. The mechanisation of crop farming is not easy to document because of conflict in the data sources, but it is clear that there was a substantial increase in the use of machinery. The number of threshing machines and combine harvesters per thousand hectares under cereal crops rose from 1.06 in 1920–4 to 2.08 in 1930–4 and 2.66 in 1940–4.[37] Combines accounted for a growing proportion of this coefficient, so that the labour substituting effect of mechanisation was perhaps even greater than these figures suggest. The massive import of machinery during the late 1940s, on the other hand, appears not to have been a factor in displacing labour, being utilised primarily to secure a rapid extension of the scale of cereal production,[38] though at the same time it reduced the input of labour per hectare of cultivated land.

The increasing average size of arable farms in the inter-war years has been noted already, in Table 3.4. Such a process of concentration may simply have been the predictable accompaniment of mechanisation. But it is worth emphasising, in view of the more intensive use of labour encountered on small farms, that the proportion of arable farms of less than 100 hectares fell continuously from 1920 until the data gives out in 1948: and that although the absolute number of small farms was some 20 per cent greater in the early 1930s than at the beginning of the First World War, by the late 1940s this increase had disappeared. In terms of labour employment per hectare, therefore, there was no growth in the number of small farms to compensate for the introduction of large units.

Whereas the availability of annual data on arable employment for much of the period permits some tentative analysis, for employment in livestock production there is an almost complete lack of utilisable estimates. By the 1960s the livestock sector (excluding dairying) employed about 45 per cent of the total agricultural labour force,[39] which may be compared with the proportion indicated in the data on occupational structure in the 1908 census. This found 103,300 persons— 28 per cent of the labour force—in agricultural occupations, of whom only 40 per cent were employed in livestock production. If these figures are reliable, it seems remarkable that no more than 41,600 persons were engaged in the traditional form of rural employment. In fact, if more information existed on employment trends in this sector, it would almost certainly show the major changes to have occurred in the final quarter of the nineteenth century. During this period, the practice of wire fencing previously unenclosed pasture spread rapidly, especially in the decade 1872–82. The impact of this process on the landless rural population was severe; its social implications were discussed in Chapter 1. The extent to which the labour force was reduced by the process can only be conjectural. It has been estimated that 40,000 persons previously dependent on the livestock sector were excluded from it by the early 1880s,[40] so that perhaps 10–15,000 persons lost employment.

Because the definition of the rural labour force is subject to considerable difficulties and has certainly not been kept consistent in the Uruguayan data, it would be very unwise to attempt a comparison of labour employment in livestock production in 1908 with the modern period. Probably the best generalisation is that employment has increased very slowly, and that the policy of maximising the return on labour adopted by modernising *estancieros* in the late nineteenth century has persisted to the present. Recent data on employment per thousand hectares in the livestock sector indicates a remarkably low level, ranging from 3.9 persons (farms between 200 and 1000 hectares) to 2.3 persons (farms over 5000 hectares).[41] The low intensity of employment in this sector is further shown by data from the 1950s on the average number of man-hours per year per hectare in different sectors, ranging from 13 in livestock production to 60 in dairying, 135 in agriculture, 338 in fruit-growing and 555 in vineyards.[42]

Of the trends in rural labour use which emerge from this brief examination, the best documented is the absolute decline in rural population since the early 1950s, which is undoubtedly associated with the stagnation of the livestock sector and the ending of the wheat policy. However, it would be quite wrong to suppose that the failure of the rural sector to absorb the natural increase in the labour force was simply a post-war phenomenon. The expulsion of labour from the livestock economy in the nineteenth century and the continued primitive use of natural pasture on the one hand, and the slow growth of arable farming combined with a high level of mechanisation on the other, have made rural – urban migration a persistent feature of Uruguayan social history. It has been the slow growth of output, produced by a proportionately very small and almost constant labour force, together with natural advantages in livestock production, which accounts for a level of labour productivity only 20 per cent below the average for the economy as a whole.[43] It has clearly not resulted from any process of dynamic growth.

The nature of capital formation in the rural sector throws some additional light on the evolution of agricultural employment, though here too the evidence is very uneven. In the decade 1955–64, the rate of investment in the sector, though not high and subject to very large annual fluctuations, was nonetheless rather higher as a proportion of gross product than for the economy as a whole. However, partly because of the high rate of investment in agricultural machinery which accompanied the wheat policy of the late 1940s and early 1950s, the rate of depreciation in 1955–64 was very substantial, accounting for 90 per cent of gross investment. As a result the depreciated capital stock increased by only 4 per cent in the ten-year period, and in 1970 net investment was still only 16 per cent of gross. In that year, three-quarters of the depreciated capital stock in the rural sector as a whole was in livestock production. Within the livestock sector, livestock accounted for 61 per cent of assets. The capital structure in arable production on the other hand, was dominated by machinery and equipment, which accounted for one-half, a further 25 per cent consisted of residential building. In the rural sector as a whole livestock and housing together composed 60 per cent of the capital stock.[44]

The characteristics of the capital stock strongly suggest a failure either to incorporate more advanced agricultural technology or to suit the availability of the other factors of production, with a fixed supply of land and relative abundance of labour. Increases in the stock of capital have generally taken the form of capital widening rather than deepening, and the tendency to maximise the return per unit of labour rather than of land has persisted. Most investment has taken the form of basic capital—housing, farm buildings, fences, livestock, machinery—which is necessary for agricultural production; but partly through the insufficiency of the level of investment, and partly through the diversion of resources into machinery economising on labour, there has been inadequate investment in the intensification of land use. Though the area planted to artificial pasture increased somewhat in the 1960s, such investment is an insignificant part of the total. Land use in livestock production remains extensive, irrespective of the size of the farm or the tenure form under which it is operated.[45]

There is very little systematic information on the historical evolution of the capital stock. In the livestock sector, it is likely that the proportionately greatest level of investment occurred in the period before 1930,[46] as a result of three factors. Firstly, the spread of 'modern' farm practice, involving substantial expenditure on wire fencing, was in its final phase; secondly, the start of the frozen meat trade in 1905 required the replacement of traditional *criollo* cattle by improved stock, and the introduction of new sheep breeds in place of the primarily wool-bearing Merino; and thirdly, the relative profitability of agricultural exports was much reduced after the depression. But data on investment before the 1950s is uneven, limited, and confined to physical series rather than value. Table 3.5 summarises available information on the formation of pedigree herds and flocks, and on imports of wire and posts for fencing. The growth in numbers of pedigree breeding livestock is clearly marked. The ratio of imported breeding stock to pedigree animals bred in Uruguay cannot be ascertained exactly, but seems to have declined rapidly: censuses of breeding farms showed the proportion to have dropped, in the case of beef cattle, from 10.0 per cent in 1920 to 2.1 per cent in 1928 and to 0.5 per cent in 1936; and in the case of sheep from 13.8 per cent in 1920 to 9.7 per cent in 1928, and to 4.7 per cent in 1936.[47] Imports of pedigree stock showed considerable fluctuations, with peaks in 1905–7, 1912–14, and 1917–20. Imports of pure-bred sheep achieved smaller peaks in the late 1920s and mid-1930s, but those of cattle remained at a low level after 1920.

TABLE 3.5. Agricultural investment: numbers of pedigree animals registered and index of imports of fencing equipment, 1901–40
(five-year averages)

	Beef Cattle[1]	Sheep[1]	Wire[2]	Posts for fencing[2]
			volume, 1901–5 = 100	
1901–5	471	134	100	100
1906–10	1388	1672	119	103
1911–15	1961	2076	n.a.	n.a.
1916–20	3353	1406	68	104
1921–5	5164	1580	90	80
1926–30	7809	2946	98	83
1931–5	10980	2268	48	25
1936–40			66	41

Notes:
1. Numbers of animals entered in the genealogical register of the Asociación Rural de Uruguay. Imported livestock previously registered in country of origin not included Source: Criadores del Uruguay, Cincuentenario de la Fundación de los Registro Genealógicos de la Asociación Rural del Uruguay (Montevideo, 1937) p. 428.
2. Source: DGEC, Anuario Estadístico.

Although census descriptions are not very revealing, as late as 1951 33 per cent of the cattle and 49 per cent of the sheep were of no identifiable breed. The traditional criollo animals however had disappeared by the 1920s, so it is certainly not the case that these animals were unimproved.[48] On the contrary, there is a general belief that investment in improved livestock for breeding is a satisfactory feature of agricultural practice in Uruguay.[49]

Investment in land improvements, however, has been seriously deficient. Undoubtedly the need to fence establishments absorbed large quantities of capital in the early years of the century, and the movement received a brief impetus in the period of high prices following the introduction of the *frigoríficos* in the decade before the First World War. But a law of 1913 which attempted to regularise a standard seven-strand fence for all boundaries by 1923, to reduce the spread of animal diseases, was so little observed that the ten-year period had to be extended. As late as 1928 only 30 per cent of fences were thought to have been sufficiently improved to comply with the legal requirement.[50]

Still less progress has been made in the direction of other desirable land improvements. Even in 1970 artificial pasture and fodder crops were only 4.7 per cent of agricultural land with improved natural pasture a further 2.8 per cent, and during the 1970s disinvestment in pasture improvement has occurred. In addition, the lack of adequate provision for winter feed imposes excessive seasonal fluctuations on the number of animals prepared for slaughter.[51] It is the failure to increase the feeding capacity of the pastures which is the fundamental explanation of the long-term stagnation of the livestock industry. The problem has been compounded by inadequate investment in water supply, trees for shelter, animal dips for disease control, etc. These deficiencies have been more clearly exposed in the recent crisis period, but their origins are to be found in the land-extensive nature of modernisation in the agricultural economy at the end of the last century. There has been a remarkable continuity in the criticisms made of the investment policies of the landowners.[52] The most striking expression of this is the following passage from the semi-official and generally eulogistic *El Libro del Centenario*, which could have been written at any time in the last fifty years, and applied as much in the 1970s as it did in 1925.

On a good number of *estancias* there is reliance for animal feed on the surprising fertility of the soil. The extensive pattern of production of the livestock industry, through the area of land given over to it, has not induced many *hacendados* to increase the production of the pastures to the level required by the degree of breeding and improvement of the animal stocks. They have preferred to devote to each animal a larger area of pasture on their farms, rather than solve the problem by improving the natural pastures, obtaining through a suitable crop rotation the yield required by the greater feed consumption of the superior animal types. The division of *estancias* into pastures more in keeping with the system of selection and cross-breeding employed in animal husbandry should have been accompanied by a plan of agricultural development giving the same amount of pasture permanently available through the constant renewal of natural pasture by rotations of oats, maize, wheat, linseed and artificial pasture, thus producing sufficient even in times of shortage. Nor has progress in livestock breeding been matched by measures to maximise the natural feeding capacity of the remarkably fertile land, harvesting fodder in times of plenty, even that with little nutritional value, in order to avoid costly losses at times of shortage. Many livestock owners are still unconvinced that the quality of the livestock does not depend exclusively on that of its parents, but that three-quarters of it comes from the quality of its feed and the reduction of its consumption of energy. Hence it is achieved through the provision of permanent, conveniently-located water supplies, and adequate shelter to reduce the effects of excessive heat, strong wind and sharp changes of temperature. This lack of adequate feed, especially between July and September, results in an inadequate supply of animals for industrial use and internal consumption.[53]

A further aspect of the process of capital accumulation in the rural sector concerns the relationship of investment in productive capital to the acquisition by individual producers of the basic resource, land. To a producer buying additional land, the purchase price represents to him a capital expenditure which will yield a future income (i.e. a notional rent), but which may also be regarded as a diversion of resources away from investment in new productive capital. A preference for increasing the scale of operations rather than improving the productive potential of the land has been a typical response of Uruguayan producers, and is implicit in the extensive land use pattern which characterises the rural sector and

TABLE 3.6. Proportionate distribution of agricultural capital, 1930 and 1962

	Livestock production		Arable production
	1930	1962	1962
Land	75.2	68.9	66.8
Livestock	16.4	20.5	4.4
Machinery		2.2	15.8
Housing		2.6	6.0
Fencing	8.4	2.5	2.2
Other buildings		1.8	2.9
Pasture and woodland		1.5	1.9
	100.0	100.0	100.0

Note: The derivation of 1930 data is unknown. For 1962 a survey of 146 livestock establishments and 88 arable farms was conducted.

Source: 1930, MGA, El Uruguay como País Agropecuario, 1932–36, (Montevideo, 1937) p. 33. 1962, CLEH–CINAM, Uruguay Rural, pp. 130–1.

the failure to incorporate capital deepening investments. While some possible reasons for such a preference are discussed in Chapter 4, it is interesting to notice the estimates of the value of land and productive capital summarised in Table 3.6, which show a very high ratio of land to reproducible capital in the rural sector.

Growth and Stagnation

The most significant characteristics of agricultural production in Uruguay have been its slow growth throughout this century, and its almost complete stagnation in the last twenty-five years. This characteristic has not been shared by all sectors of agriculture. In general the least satisfactory performance has been in those sectors producing for export markets. Arable production has at times grown rapidly, and dairy production has shown persistent increases. However, the overall failure of agriculture to achieve sustained increases in supply has been particularly harmful for the economy. The problem has been magnified by competition by domestic consumers for the limited supply of exportable production. The performance of agriculture is therefore an area of central concern for the Uruguayan economy. The following chapter examines some possible explanations of the stagnation; this section establishes its dimensions in the crisis period up to the beginning of the 1970s.

Because of deficiencies in the data it is not possible to construct a series for total agricultural production for the whole of this century. However, there is reliable information for the period since 1935 for the sector as a whole, with the exclusion only of the comparatively small groups of permanent pasture, fruit, market garden produce and dried vegetables. Measured at constant (1961) factor cost, agricultural production, with these exclusions, grew at only 1.1 per cent per annum between 1935–9 and 1965–9. There was thus a decline in the level of per capita production over this thirty-year period. However, the decline was not continuous. Between the pre-war period and 1950–4 the annual growth of output averaged almost 2 per cent. Thereafter the stagnation of agricultural production was almost complete. Of the two principal sub-categories in the agricultural sector, livestock production was characterised by relatively small variations around the thirty-year growth trend. Arable production was subject to much wider variations, notably a period of rapid growth between 1947 and 1954 and a subsequent decline. The contribution of arable production to total agricultural production varied between 20 and 35 per cent, most frequently in the range 25–29 per cent.[54]

Within the livestock sector there were significant shifts in the composition of production after 1935. Cattle production remained stationary over the period as a whole, and its contribution to livestock production at 1961 prices fell from 50 per cent (1935–9) to 37 per cent during the 1950s and early 1960s, rising to 40 per cent in the second half of the decade. Sheep production for meat grew during the 1940s but registered a decline over the period as a whole. The only export group to grow in relative importance in this period was wool, but at the very modest annual rate of 1.4 per cent as a result of zero growth in the 1960s. Dairy production was the only part of the livestock sector to escape the general stagnation, increasing its share of the total product from 9 per cent (1935–9) to 20 per cent (1965–9) and trebling the real value of its production.[55]

The most widely used and convenient indicators of livestock production in the century are the reports of the agricultural censuses on animal stocks (Table 3.7). They reveal the extremely slow growth of animal numbers in this century. If the 1908 figure is discounted,[56] then the evolution of livestock numbers is composed of two sub-periods. The first, a phase of modest growth, was interrupted by the effect of exceptionally severe climatic conditions in the early 1940s; it was succeeded in the 1950s and 1960s by a relatively high but stationary animal population.

Table 3.8 summarises the performance of the beef-producing sector during this century. Before 1930, two of the principal factors bearing on the volume of cattle slaughtered were the decline of the *saladero* industry (as a result of the shrinking market for *tasajo* and the rising price for freezing-quality cattle), and the growth and fluctuations of the *frigorífico* industry. The latter processed an annual total of 100,000 cattle for the first time in 1913, and reached a peak in 1919 of 663,500. This level

TABLE 3.7. Stocks of sheep and cattle, census years, 1900–70
(millions)

	1900	1908	1916	1924	1930	1937	1943
Cattle	6.8	8.2	7.8	8.4	7.1	8.3	6.3
Sheep	18.6	26.3	11.5	14.4	20.5	17.9	20.3
Cattle units[1]	10.5	13.5	10.1	11.3	11.2	11.9	10.4

	1946	1951	1956	1961	1966	1970
Cattle	6.8	8.2	7.4	8.8	8.2	8.6
Sheep	19.6	23.4	23.3	21.7	23.1	19.9
Cattle units[1]	10.7	12.9	12.1	13.1	12.8	12.6

Note:
1. Calculated on the basis of 5 sheep per cattle unit.

Sources: Solari *et al.*, *Cifras*, p. 161; MGA, *Censo Agropecuario*.

TABLE 3.8. Beef production: slaughter and yield, 1900–77
(five-year averages)

	A Cattle slaughtered			B Live weight per head (kilos)		C Meat production (thousand metric tons)
	A1 (000)	A2 (000)	A3 (1935–9 = 100)	B1	B2	
1900–4	996		86.5			
1905–9	962		83.5	471		
1910–14	871		75.6	464		
1915–19	957		83.1	469		
1920–4	1027		89.1	487		
1925–9	1284		111.5	470		
1930–4	1161		100.8	482		
1935–9	1152		100.0	496		
		1342	100.0		495	266[1]
1940–4		1361	101.4		468	
1945–9		1088	81.1		499	241.3[2]
1950–4		1390	103.6		461	305.8
1955–9		1110	82.7		463	236.0[3]
1960–4		1312	97.8		464	294.0
1965–9		1405	104.7		n.a.	298.6
1970–4		1432	106.7		460	301.8
1975–7[4]		1835	136.7		447	

Notes:
A National slaughter. Does not include allowance for export of fat cattle, or deduction for imports of fat cattle.
A1 'Controlled slaughter' only.
A2 Includes 'uncontrolled slaughter' in small slaughter houses outside Montevideo, and slaughter on farms.
B Steers (*novillos*) only.
B1 and *B2* as *A1* and *A2*. *B1* Steers for domestic consumption only.
C Indigenous animals. Includes allowance for exports, deduction for imports.
1. 1938 only.
2. 1947–9.
3. 1955 and 1959.
4. Three-year average.

Sources: DGEC, *Anuario Estadístico*: BROU, *Producción Agropecuaria*; Universidad de La República, *Estadísticas Básicas*, table 21; BCU, *Indicadores*; Celia Barbato de Silva, *Comercialización y Faena de Ganado Vacuno en Uruguay* (Montevideo, Centro de Investigaciones Económicas, 1977).

TABLE 3.9. Cattle slaughter: rate of slaughter to cattle stock, 1900—74
(census years 1900—56, five-year averages 1960—74, per cent)

	1900	1908	1916	1924	1930[1]	1937	1943[2]	1946	1951	1956
A	13.6	13.2	10.8	14.3	23.1	14.8	23.0	13.3		
B						16.3	24.2	16.5	18.2	15.3

	1960—4	1965—9	1970—4
B	16.1	18.4	15.9

Notes:
A. National controlled slaughter plus net exports of live cattle.
B. Total national slaughter plus net exports of live cattle.
1. In 1930 the price of cattle for slaughter was at its highest since 1920. Slaughter of calves was exceptionally high at 400,000 head.
2. Severe climatic conditions in 1942 induced a high rate of slaughter to reduce natural mortality.

Sources: As Tables 3.7 and 3.8.

was not achieved again until 1926, but the expansion in the late 1920s was of such proportions that 1.1 million cattle were killed by the *frigoríficos* in 1930. Recorded domestic consumption was of minor significance as a determinant of slaughter. In the rapid growth phase of the *frigorífico* industry, which coincided with the very high export prices of the First World War, mutton was substituted for beef in consumption. Subsequently, and especially after 1930, domestic consumption absorbed an increasing share of beef production which showed no sustained expansion at all during this period. Two major intervals of decline occurred in the mid-1940s, the delayed result of high mortality and slaughter after the floods and drought of 1942, and in the mid-1950s, through loss of good-quality pastures to cereal production.

The stagnation of beef production has not been confined to the numbers of cattle slaughtered. Table 3.9 expresses the number killed as a proportion of cattle stocks, from which two significant points emerge: the rate of slaughter is extremely low, and it has shown no tendency to increase. The prolonged period needed for cattle to reach maturity for slaughter is a result of deficient nutritional practice, and condemns the beef-producing sector to a very low rate of productivity per hectare. Increasing yield per animal slaughtered has provided only very minor compensation for the lack of improvement. The average live weight of steers has shown no increase at all in this century (Table 3.8). With the progressive substitution of Hereford herds for the *criollo* animal in the early years of this century the quality and quantity of meat per head certainly increased, but the full effects of this improvement had probably been felt by 1930,[57] and there has been no further increase at least since 1950.

The evolution of wool and mutton production is summarised in Table 3.10. Wool production clearly increased substantially between 1900 and the First World War, but the outstanding feature was the rapid growth of production in the 1940s and early 1950s and the complete stagnation subsequently. Trends in the production of mutton are far less easy to distinguish, due to the volume of uncontrolled slaughter for

TABLE 3.10. Sheep production: slaughter, yield and wool production 1900–74 (five-year averages)

	A Sheep slaughtered			B Av. live-weight per head	C Meat production	D Wool production	
	A1 000	A2 000	1935–9 = 100	(kilos per head)	(000 metric tons)	mill. kilos	1935–9 = 100
1900–4						36.3	68.0
1905–9	289		23.0			40.5	75.7
1910–14	595		47.4			52.0	97.2
1915–19	366		29.2			40.2	75.1
1920–4	710		56.6			40.8	76.3
1925–9	1632		130.0			56.1	104.9
1930–4	1635		130.3			52.1	97.5
1935–9	1255		100.0			53.5	100.0
		3022	100.0	36.2	64.0[1]		
1940–4		4051	134.1	39.6		59.9	112.1
1945–9		4091	135.4	40.6	74.3[2]	72.6	135.8
1950–4		3317	109.8	43.0	60.8	85.5	160.0
1955–9		3302	109.3	37.6	63.0[3]	86.1	161.1
1960–4		2718	89.9	39.6	50.2	83.5	156.1
1965–9	902				56.2	81.8	152.9
1970–4	758					64.8	121.1

Notes:
A National slaughter. No allowance for export of fat sheep or deduction for import of fat sheep.
A1 'Controlled slaughter'.
A2 Includes 'uncontrolled slaughter' in small slaughter houses outside Montevideo, and slaughter on farms.
B Ewes.
C Indigenous animals. Includes allowance for net exports of sheep for slaughter.
D Greasy wool.
1. 1938 only.   2. 1947–9.   3. 1955 and 1959.

Sources: DGEC, Anuario Estadístico; BROU, Producción Agropecuaria; Cámara Mercantil de Productos del País, Memoria Anual; FAO, Production Yearbook.

consumption, particularly in the interior. The growth in the number of sheep slaughtered from the early 1920s resulted from the introduction of the *frigoríficos* and the trade in frozen mutton and lamb which they made possible. It was for this reason that the dual purpose Lincoln and Romney Marsh breeds began to displace the Merino in the early years of this century. Since the Second World War wool production has been the dominant aspect of the sheep-raising sector, and the wool yield per head of the total flock has been raised substantially above inter-war levels but has shown no tendency to sustained increase (Table 3.11). The higher yields have been achieved in part by the introduction of new breeds, particularly Corriedale and Ideal, and in part also by the changing composition of the total flock in favour of wool bearers. Thus the proportion of lambs in the total slaughter declined from an annual average of 31.1 per cent (947,000 head) during 1935–9 to 6.3 per cent (172,000 head) in 1960–4. This decline, resulting from the relative profitability of wool in world markets, accounts entirely for the pronounced reduction in the slaughter of sheep since the 1950s.

TABLE 3.11. Wool production: yield per head of total sheep stock, census years
1900–70
(kilos)

1900	1908[1]	1916	1924	1930	1937	1943	1946	1951	1956	1961	1966	1970
1.97	1.89	3.13	3.07	3.04	2.95	3.31	4.03	3.63	3.69	3.83	3.33	3.48

Note:
1. Low yield due to presumed exaggeration of sheep numbers in 1908 census.

Sources: as Tables 3.7 and 3.10.

For the value of crop production there is complete information only for the period since 1946. Cereals have consistently been the most important group, but also show the largest variation as a result of government policy in the late 1940s and early 1950s, when high guaranteed prices induced a massive increase in production until the middle of the decade, at which time the policy was reversed. The growth period of oilseed crops came in the 1930s and 1940s, since when production has stagnated. Production of fruit and wine-grapes has been stationary or declining since 1946, and the only sustained growth areas in crop production since 1935 have been sugar crops, and to a lesser extent root crops and vegetables. Excluding the temporary expansion of cereals in the mid-1950s, the growth of new crops has still served to give arable production a slightly faster rate of growth than livestock production. Even so the process of diversification has been limited, with

cereals and oilseed crops accounting for 51 per cent of crop production
by value in 1960–4 compared with 57 per cent in 1946–9.[58] Indeed, four
crops (wheat, maize, linseed and sunflower seed) have dominated the
arable sector throughout this century (Table 3.2). However, although
there were substantial acreages devoted to wheat and maize by the
beginning of the century, the growth of oilseed production has occurred
since the 1930s, stimulated by favourable prices as part of the import
substitution process. Other cereals—oats, barley and rice—have increased in importance, and similarly vegetables and sugar-beet. Nonetheless the acreage devoted to the four main crops was 88.4 per cent of
the total crop acreage in 1920–4, and was still 86.7 per cent during
the wheat policy years of the early 1950s, declining to 82.5 per cent in
1965–9.

The summary of principal crop yields presented in Table 3.12
indicates that only in the case of wheat has there been a sustained
improvement in crop yield per hectare sown. The relative success of
wheat must be explained in part by the efforts of the research institute La
Estanzuela to produce higher-yielding strains of wheat,[59] and a higher
proportion of wheat acreage has been planted with improved seed and

TABLE 3.12 Arable production: indices of principal crop yields per hectare,
1900–74
(five-year averages, 1935–9 = 100)

	Wheat	Maize	Oats	Linseed	Sunflower seed
1900–3[1]	72.9	114.4	151.4	114.2	
1905–9	97.3	102.1	174.8	117.1	
1911–14[1]	75.6	104.2	137.8	78.3	
1915–19	78.5	113.9	119.1	77.1	
1920–4	94.8	111.1	122.0	108.7	
1925–9	103.4	102.7	136.2	114.4	
1930–4	88.3	110.1	103.9	99.2	
1935–9	100.0	100.0	100.0	100.0	100.0
1940–4	98.1	92.9	87.4	82.9	102.8
1945–9	94.8	85.7	99.8	85.6	86.6
1950–4	122.6	101.4	124.0	97.7	112.6
1955–9	115.4	98.6	119.3	89.8	93.3
1960–4	109.5	98.7	150.8	91.0	109.5
1965–9	133.7	89.7	151.2	98.7	111.3
1970–4	140.1	155.6	164.3	93.9	124.5

Notes: 1. Figures for 1904 and 1910 not available.

Source: DGEC, *Anuario Estadístico*; BCU, *Boletín Estadístico Mensual*.

receives applications of fertilisers and other agricultural chemicals than has been the case with maize, linseed or sunflower.[60] For all these crops, however, yields are conspicuously low, with inadequate expenditure on research for the development of improved strains, fertilisers and insecticides. Even more striking is the failure to achieve a general application of the knowledge which has been secured. Brannon found that national average yields for the major crops were between 25 per cent (wheat) and 60 per cent (linseed) of those of the best farmers. However, the relative lack of emphasis on cash inputs and low level of production technology did not extend to the mechanisation of arable production, which was found to be generally adequate.[61]

The problem which is common in varying degrees to all sectors of agriculture in Uruguay is not merely one of stagnating production, but also of production at extremely low levels of efficiency when compared with results achieved in other countries and regions. The relatively low yields per hectare of Uruguay's main crops are evident in Table 3.13. In

TABLE 3.13. Arable production: crop yields in selected countries and regions, 1965–9
(annual averages, hundred kilos per hectare)

	Wheat	Maize	Linseed	Sunflower Seed
Uruguay	10.0	5.6	5.9	5.1
Argentina	12.2	20.3	6.7	8.1
Brazil	8.5	13.4		
Chile	16.6			
All South America	11.9	14.6	6.6	7.9
Canada	16.1	51.0	7.3	
US	18.6	48.6	7.3	
USSR	12.1	24.8	3.1	9.6
Europe	24.4	28.9		14.7
World	12.4	24.1	4.7	11.9

Source: FAO, Production Yearbook.

the livestock sector, though meat and wool yields per animal slaughtered or sheared are not significantly lower than those of other producers, yields per head of total herd/flock are very much lower. Production of a ton of beef requires a stock of 26 cattle, compared with 12–14 in the USA, UK, and France, and 17–19 in Argentina and Australia; production of wool and mutton per head of the total flock is very low compared with Australia and New Zealand, and mutton production is low also compared with South Africa, Argentina and the USSR.[62]

The reasons for this poor performance in the livestock sector are directly related to the composition of the herds and flocks. Both are characterised by the slow achievement of maturity which results in an extended period before insemination of 3 years and 4–5 years before slaughter (for cattle). Losses due to disease or adverse weather further reduce the rate of reproduction to about 56 per cent for cattle, compared with 72 per cent, 85 per cent and 87 per cent in Argentina, Australia and the USA respectively, and to about 60 per cent for sheep, compared with 95 per cent in New Zealand and 97 per cent in the USA.[63]

The low rates of reproduction and slaughter may in turn be attributed to the low levels of feeding, health and management. Of these the problem of animal nutrition is by far the most significant. The failure to improve more than a tiny proportion of the natural pasture of the country has not only set a limit to the extensive growth of the livestock industry, but has also restricted the industry to a low-yielding, seasonal, and irregular source of nutrition. The problem of winter feed in particular has imposed a strongly seasonal pattern on the supply of animals for slaughter (Figure 5.1). The short supply during the winter months moreover has jeopardised Uruguay's position in export markets in competition with producers who market beef throughout the year. Deficient winter feeding results not only from a shortage of land naturally fitted for winter fattening, but also from a failure to conserve the relatively plentiful fodder supply on the general pastures in spring and autumn by haymaking and ensilage. The natural grasses are not high-yielding, and their performance is further diminished by lack of rotation or weed control, and over-grazing, frequently by cattle and sheep simultaneously (to the detriment of the former). Erratic weather conditions further reduce the pasture yield. 'The slowness with which modern animal feeding practices are spreading is undoubtedly the problem most adversely affecting animal husbandry in Uruguay.'[64]

A secondary but significant limitation on livestock production is the inadequate attention paid to the control and prevention of animal diseases and parasites. Estimated losses due to poor animal health were over 500 million pesos at the beginning of the 1960s, equivalent to 33 per cent of the value of livestock production.[65] Moreover, the endemic status of foot and mouth disease has at times resulted in the exclusion of Uruguayan meat exports from some international markets.

The third factor limiting efficiency in the livestock sector is the low quality of farm management. Clearly there are limits to the ability of individual producers to overcome the national difficulties of poor pasture, disease, etc., but it has been strongly argued that Uruguay has failed to assimilate modern stock-farming techniques due to the lack of rational management systems. The bias in investment patterns away from land improvements, and towards labour saving rather than the intensification of land use; the continuous mixed grazing of pastures; and primitive breeding techniques associated with a high failure rate, are examples of widespread practices which are uneconomic from the national viewpoint if not from that of the individual producer. Arable production also suffers from a low level of technology. Though the use of fertilisers was considerably higher in the 1960s than in the previous decade, it was still very low and largely confined to horticulture and pastureland. As in the case of fertilisers, little research has been done in Uruguay on the use of pesticides in relation to particular crop strains, and in both cases the use of such inputs is discouraged by their high price.[66]

4 Taxation and Agricultural Stagnation

The further north you go, towards Artigas and the borders of Brazil, the greater become the tracts of land owned by private individuals. Properties of twenty and thirty thousand hectarios are not uncommon in those parts, and despite all the politicians' professed anxiety to limit the growth of these mammoth estates and to provide land for immigrants, the rich man's mania for adding field to field is unchecked. (J. O. P. Bland, *Men, Manners and Morals in South America* [1920] p. 252.)

One of the most enduring general interpretations of Uruguay's problems is that the economy has suffered from the effects of excessive and misguided government.[1] The analysis to support such a view has frequently been unsophisticated, even reducible to the propositions that *batllista* Uruguay was socialist, and that socialism does not work. At a more serious level is the 'misplaced modernity' interpretation, which argues that the *batllista* edifice of state intervention in economic and social affairs was built on an economic foundation which was incapable of supporting the burden. It might thus be said that the freedom of the political system to develop urban-based redistributive policies penalised the rural sector, diverting away from it resources which were required for investment in a modern and dynamic agricultural economy. The most systematic presentation of such a view was published in 1930: *Riqueza y Pobreza del Uruguay*.[2] This work tackled the central problem of Uruguayan underdevelopment, the stagnation and technical backwardness of the rural sector, and its anti-*batllista* view of the Uruguayan process threw down a challenge to those holding opposite or incompatible ideas which seems never to have been taken up. The second part of this chapter presents a critique of *Riqueza y Pobreza*. It is preceded by a general analysis of Batlle's fiscal policy and the implications of it for the landowning class. The third section examines some aspects of post-1930 fiscal policy, and the fourth evaluates a number of possible explanations for the long-run stagnation of agriculture.

Batllista Fiscal Policy

The limitations of Batlle y Ordóñez's radicalism are nowhere seen so clearly as in his fiscal policy. It may be the case that his ideas in this field were less thoroughly elaborated than in others—or, more plausibly, that the political constraints operated more tightly. The best-known and most complete statement of his ideas on taxation in fact was made only a few years before his death.[3] In it he expressed his continuing opposition to taxes on income, which penalised effort. Instead, the tax base was to be placed on the land, inheritance, imports, and the consumption of undesirable commodities. The principles underlying this tax structure were in some degree egalitarian and reformist, but even more there was evidence of pragmatism; the fact was that Batlle had done little more during his periods of office than adopt a pre-existing fiscal system, and invest in it a rationale which it had not possessed originally, and which hardly fitted even after his modifications.

The tax on land was perhaps the most celebrated aspect of the *batllista* fiscal policy, though the tax itself had been introduced before Batlle. Property, it was held, belongs to society as a whole, yet it is in the hands of a very few who have made great fortunes while paying very low wages. But it would be unjust to dispossess people of their property: 'those who possess land are not to blame for the situation, because they possess it by common consent'.[4] Redistribution must proceed by evolution rather than revolution. 'A progressive land tax, that is to say, a tax which becomes even greater as the value of land increases, reduces the attraction of owning large properties, unless they are used in such a way as to produce extraordinary profits.'[5] The tax on inheritance was equally circumspect; society did not renounce the right to tax the income derived from labour and capital, but postponed it until the death of its owner, thus preventing the accumulation of large aggregations of capital. Taxes on imports were justified mainly on the grounds of protection for domestic industry, and only in passing was it noticed that import taxes increase government revenue. To the criticism that import taxes were regressive in nature, Batlle had a prompt if perverse reply: 'I would say that it is a great error to want to reduce the price of everything, because when everything is cheaper, principally the articles of prime necessity, the labour of the worker is cheapened, because if what he produces is worth very little, what he earns cannot be much.'[6] The tax on undesirable commodities was intended to limit consumption of alcohol, though there is no reason to suppose that demand was, or was believed to be, price elastic. Noticeably absent from the list of taxes to which *batllismo* was committed in this belated statement of principles were those on exports, businesses, and on transactions. The latter, being taxes on productive activities, were presumably to be reduced or suppressed.

Since this formulation of policy was made after two decades in which *batllismo* had been the dominant political force and since no significant change in Batlle's political philosophy had occurred, it would be reasonable to look for substantial changes in the fiscal system during this period. Table 4.1 summarises the data on tax revenues for the period up to 1928. Included in total revenue are indirect taxes (mainly on imports and consumption, exports, and transactions), direct taxes (mainly on property, inheritance and businesses), and licences and fees. Other sources of government income, principally lotteries and government participation in the profits of public enterprise, are excluded. So too are 'special contributions' (mostly social security contributions), which grew rapidly in the 1920s. The available material is not easy to use, because taxes were not infrequently identified by the expenditure to which they were allocated, and so the basic classification employed in the two works cited as sources has been employed here.

Though there are some discernible trends in the changing composition of tax revenue, perhaps the most striking conclusion to be drawn from Table 4.1 is that the changes were very limited, even though the total volume of revenue was growing rapidly during most of the period. In only a single year did import and consumption taxes fail to provide at least half of tax revenue. Before the war their participation was in fact increasing, but the vulnerability of a fiscal system so heavily based on foreign trade flows was demonstrated in the war years. In the 1920s,

TABLE 4.1. Structure of taxation, fiscal years 1902/3–1928/9 (per cent, three-year averages)

	Total $000	Imports and Consumption	Exports	Property	Inheritance	Transactions	Licences and Fees	Business	Other
1902/3–4/5	17421	59.8	10.4	12.6	1.4	4.5	4.4	6.0	0.9
1905/6–7/8	22652	62.3	7.4	12.6	2.0	4.5	4.8	5.8	0.6
1908/9–10/11	26283	64.0	6.8	11.5	1.4	4.7	5.0	5.7	0.9
1911/12–13/14	31904	61.9	5.3	14.3	1.5	4.3	6.4	5.7	0.6
1914/15–16/17	27361	55.2	4.3	18.2	3.1	4.7	6.8	5.9	1.8
1917/18–19/20	33726	51.2	11.1	14.5	3.9	5.6	7.4	5.8	0.5
1920/1–2/3	38163	53.7	6.1	14.3	4.2	7.2	8.0	5.9	0.6
1923/4–5/6	50275	56.0	5.6	14.0	3.9	8.3	6.6	5.0	0.6
1926/7–8/9	63508	57.1	5.0	14.0	3.9	7.2	7.8	4.4	0.6

Sources: Pedro Dondo, *Los Ciclos en la Economía Nacional*, (Montevideo, 1942); Mario La Gamma *et al.*, 'Desarrollo de los Ingresos Públicos Nacionales', *Revista de la Facultad de Ciencias Económicas y de Administración*, Year I (1940).

however, their share once more increased. Export taxes (including those on exports of sand and stone) made a relatively modest contribution which was steadily declining until the extraordinarily high values of the later war and post-war years briefly interrupted the trend. Taxes on property showed two sharp increases coinciding with the legislation of 1910 and 1915, but thereafter their relative participation remained stable. Transactions taxes and licence revenue both grew quite steadily throughout the period, while the direct fiscal burden on business activity showed a very slight tendency to fall. On inheritances, there was a sharp increase in the second half of the period compared with the first, but no further increase in the 1920s. Indeed, during the 1920s the only set of taxes to increase their share were those on imports and consumption. From the data examined here, the only evidence of a progressive shift in the burden during the *batllista* period concerns property and inheritances, in which the increases were little more than marginal and not sustained after Batlle's second administration.

In spite of its subsequent justification on protectionist grounds, the taxation of imports, which provided an overwhelming share of the government's income, was plainly intended primarily for revenue; its protectionist effects, though not disregarded, were in most cases secondary. Until 1888, the tariff was effectively *ad valorem*, since the official prices (*aforos*) on which a percentage duty was charged, were revised annually. However, the tariff law of that year created specific duties on a range of basic imported items of consumption; in addition, the *aforos* were now consolidated in a law which it would have been laborious to change, such that they remained unaltered (and the duties therefore effectively specific) until the 1920s.[7] Imports were liable also to additional taxes which were imposed from time to time. Consumption taxes, levied on both imported items and those of national production, were introduced to help meet the crisis of 1890, and were increased in 1900. The commodities taxed were mainly alcohol and alcoholic beverages, tobacco products, sugar and matches. Imports admitted free of duty were materials and equipment required by domestic activities, including agriculture and livestock production as well as manufacturing industry.

This fiscal edifice remained largely intact throughout the *batllista* period, even though its limitations were widely recognised. In 1898 it was observed that:

It would be desirable that the price of everything constituting basic consumption should be much reduced in order that the working class and the poor should not have to restrict the satisfaction of their needs. Unless they are graduated, indirect taxes are unjust because they bear no relation to the income of the contributor. The most equitable criterion would be to reduce the burden as far as possible on articles of prime necessity . . . surcharging those going to the wealthy and which are manifestations of luxury, of well-being and of the refinement of society.[8]

The regressive nature of import taxes and, because of their weight within it, of the fiscal system as a whole, was notorious. Even Martínez Lamas acknowledged that 'the articles which produce most revenue for the state are, in fact, those of prime necessity'.[9] The point had indeed already been made by the socialist Emilio Frugoni, in almost identical terms,[10] but he received no official support for his proposal that the tax base be shifted from consumption to land ownership.

Taxes levied directly on exports were a relatively small part of total revenue. General export duties, the main tax, were fixed as specific duties in 1890 and designed to yield 5 per cent on an *ad valorem* basis. By 1917 the burden of the tax had fallen to about 1 per cent of the price of wool, and the duty on wool and hides was raised to 4 per cent *ad valorem*. This increase, and the high volume and price of exports in the late war-time and immediate post-war period, largely explains the dramatic increase in the yield of export taxes in 1917–19. But from 1920 the yield returned to its pre-war level of 5–6 per cent of total tax revenue.

The main opposition of the landowning class was reserved for the direct imposition on property, the *contribución inmobiliaria*, of which about 60 per cent was contributed by the rural sector.[11] Special significance attaches to the property tax since an imposition on land had a central place in Batlle's thinking on rural modernisation and reform, and it implied a direct confrontation with the dominant fraction of the economic power bloc. A property tax was not an innovation of the *batllista* period, but undoubtedly it was developed during the first two decades of the century, and by the depression it had marginally increased its relative importance as a source of government revenue. But the impetus behind land tax policy appears to have been much less the positive desire to induce structural changes in the way in which land was owned and worked, than to increase the tax yield. During this period the price of land increased considerably, and the prime concern of policy was to secure an increase in revenue from the land (and urban property) commensurate with its increase in market value. It was basically this argument which was used by Batlle's finance ministers to press for increases in the property tax, yet for two of the most eminent of them, Martín C. Martínez and Pedro Cosio, there was the irony that at subsequent periods both were to defend the landed interest against such impositions.

At the turn of the century the *contribución inmobiliaria* was levied at the rate of $6\frac{1}{2}$ pesos per thousand pesos of the assessed value of urban and rural property. These assessments had not kept pace with the increase in land values, losses through evasion and fraud were considerable, and the method of assessment was inefficient.[12] In 1903 a proposed increase of about 10 per cent in the yield of the tax from the rural sector, and the initiation of studies leading to new assessments, aroused resistance to which the Minister responded strongly:

> It is quite false to say that rural property is heavily burdened, and even more misleading since such property has doubled and trebled in price in some parts, and not because of improvements by the landowner, who does not always work the land . . . It is a question of a tax of a hundred thousand pesos on consolidated wealth. It is well known who will bear the burden of this tax, and the capacity of capital to resist is much greater than that of the mass of consumers. If we have to increase revenue on some future occasion, we shall have to react against this system of finding it all in increased consumption taxes, and place the burden, moderately and with appropriate reservations, on capital.[13]

The re-assessment of property values was completed only slowly, but the efficiency of the tax was increased by further division of the assessment zones, from 139 to 267 in 1911, and the assessments for these regions were based on land sales data for the previous five years. The contribution from landed property immediately increased, from $1.7 million in each of the previous six years, to $2.7 million in 1911–12. In 1915 it was at last possible to introduce the system of individual assessments of the value of landed properties, excluding improvements. In defending the increase in yield produced by the change,[14] the Minister of Finance, Pedro Cosio, quoted extensively the speech of Martínez made in 1903: to the embarrassment of Martínez, 'considered one of the most brilliant minds of his generation',[15] since his natural conservatism which had enhanced the acceptability of Batlle's first administration to the landowning class now made him a highly influential critic of the *batllistas*. The increased land tax, and Batlle's proposals for constitutional reform, were critical events which persuaded the rural sector of the need to unite for political purposes, and the Federación Rural was formed in 1916. The tax was, of course, a direct imposition on the landed capitalist class, but one of very modest proportions. The reforms to the tax during the Batlle administration produced only a small increase in the proportion of the tax burden borne directly by the landowners, and was evidently in line with the increase in land prices (Table 4.3).

Riqueza y Pobreza del Uruguay: A Critique

The fundamental argument of *Riqueza y Pobreza* is that the economic and social progress of Uruguay had been slowed to rates below its potential, and below the achievement of Latin America in general and Argentina in particular. The symptoms of the crisis were to be seen in the poverty and backwardness of the rural areas, and in the rapid development of the metropolis. Montevideo was the head which had outgrown the body sustaining it. The capital operated a suction pump, impoverishing the rural sector in order to finance its own industrial, urban and bureaucratic development. Published in the brief interval between the death of Batlle y Ordóñez and the full impact of the world depression, the book is a sober, analytical and factual denunciation of public policy in the previous quarter-century. Though overt political judgements are avoided, the target is the *batllista* system of government which was to survive, with interruptions, for a further forty years. The thesis was at once general enough for it to be 'the most serious work to be written on the national reality in the first half of the twentieth century', and immediate enough for bookshops in Montevideo displaying it to receive stones through their windows.[16]

Martínez Lamas devoted much of his book to a description of social and economic conditions in the rural areas in about 1930, which cannot be challenged. The mass of the rural population he shows to be impoverished and suffering from disease, illiteracy and malnutrition. The situation of those living in *rancheríos*, squatter settlements on marginal or waste land, was particularly desperate. Though an adequate comparison with contemporary conditions is impossible, it is important to stress that rural poverty in Uruguay remains an urgent problem. A survey early in the 1960s found that in terms of food, shelter, education, social participation and family unification, the standard of living of 60 per cent of the dispersed rural population, and of 76 per cent of the rural population living in nuclei, was seriously or very seriously deficient.[17] It is safe to assume that conditions were no better in 1930. In addition, Martínez Lamas agreed that certain features of the rural economy indicated stagnation: for example, there was no process of subdivision of the land, the cross-breeding of livestock had been interrupted, and railway freight rates were extremely high due to inadequate agricultural traffic. Most serious of all was that in spite of its very sparse population, rural Uruguay was unable to employ its own natural population increase, still less attract immigrants.[18]

Thus, in spite of favourable natural conditions, Uruguay resembled, relatively, a desert. The task of policy-makers, therefore, was to establish conditions in which Uruguay's potential could be realised. The population capacity was estimated at between nine and ten millions,[19] and could be supported when extensive land use gave way to intensive exploitation of the soil. This did not mean for Martínez Lamas an improvement in pasture yield, since livestock production is throughout his work regarded as a primitive form of production to be displaced by agriculture, an argument reminiscent of Friedrich List. Crop production, specifically wheat and maize, is identified as the ideal for the rural economy; and while he did not himself indicate the area suitable for arable use, an estimate of 40 per cent of national territory (about 7 million hectares) is quoted with evident approval.[20] This figure is approximately double that of a modern estimate, which in turn is double the maximum annual crop acreage recorded in Uruguay.[21]

That this vision half a century ago of a future Uruguay is implausible does not detract from the correctness of the overall assessment: that the failure to increase the productivity of the land, then as now, was extremely damaging. What must be challenged, however, is the analysis of the causes of rural stagnation. The basic argument[22] is that the weight of the tax burden on the rural population had starved the rural sector of the capital required for its modernisation, by reducing disposable incomes in the sector and by increasing the attraction of urban investment in real estate and government bonds. Thus the rapidly-growing urban population found employment, but at the cost of inhibiting the natural evolution of the rural economy towards arable production. The maintenance of primitive livestock production in turn perpetuated the outflow of population from the rural areas. The requirements to break this cycle were stated to be an expanded flow of agricultural immigrants, and the reduction of taxes bearing on rural producers.

The analysis supporting this thesis seems to be particularly weak in two main areas: first, in the interpretation implicitly made of *latifundismo*; and second, in the estimation of the size of the tax burden and its incidence within the rural sector. As to the first, mention has been made already of the way Martínez Lamas avoided overt political judgements in favour of 'technical' arguments, showing a reticence which he was later to relax in favour of the Federación Rural.[23] It is in fact a curiosity of the book that the *latifundio* and *latifundismo* are condemned as primitive and anti-progressive but the *latifundista* and his class interests are totally ignored. The *latifundio* and its disastrous effects on employment and land use were thus reduced to a consequence of erroneous government policy, and landowners were left in helpless impotence, unable to promote the common good by sub-dividing their lands: 'There are no cultivators because the *estancia* has dispersed part of the rural population, and the men who remain on the *estancias* are in such poverty that they are unable to buy plots of land even by making minimal part-payment of its price.'[24] There is in fact abundant evidence for a contrary view, that the landowners not only systematically displaced labour from the land during the modernisation of the livestock economy in the late nineteenth century, but also remained resolutely opposed to the encroachment of arable producers on pasture land. While landowners could obstruct the extension of agriculture through restrictive conditions in rent contracts,[25] and while livestock production was anyway more profitable, it is not surprising that the *estancia* remained the characteristic rural enterprise, and *latifundistas* the controlling interest. In spite of his passing recognition of the fact that half the land was owned by fewer than 3200 owners,[26] Martínez Lamas ignored the constraint placed on the possibility of change by this degree of concentration. Rather, it was the decapitalisation of the rural sector through the fiscal burden imposed by Montevideo which he believed was acting to retard the break-up of the *latifundio*.

Ironically, it was part of *batllista* mythology that progressive land taxes would secure the gradual elimination of the *latifundio*. In fact, it appears that Martínez Lamas greatly exaggerated the rural tax burden, which does not seem to have been heavy enough to have produced either of these contradictory results. The essence of his case is contained in a calculation of the balance of payments of rural Uruguay with Monte- video for the fiscal year 1926/7. Against a rural sector income of $113 million (of which $97 million was the value of production) were to be set marketing costs ($15 million), mortgage payments, land rents paid in Montevideo, and bank services ($22 million), consumption of non-rural commodities ($48 million), and taxes ($28 million).[27] The net saving capacity of rural Uruguay was thus reduced to zero. The calculation of these estimates was made with remarkable sophistication, reflecting the detailed knowledge that the author gained while Director General of Statistical Services in the early 1920s, and they are not easily challenged. Nonetheless, the assumptions underlying the estimates of consumption and taxation, which are clearly critical to the case, do not seem to be very well founded.

The figure for consumption is based on estimates of the average rural wage ($180 per annum), of the non-Montevideo population (1 million) and of the coefficient of economically active persons in that population (36.3 per cent). All these figures in themselves seem reasonable. In 1923 a minimum wage for rural workers had been legislated, set at $18 or $20 monthly, according to the size of the *estancia*. However, 'the opinion of the leading Uruguayan observers is that enforcement was unsuccessful'[28] and Martínez Lamas himself was in no doubt that the surplus labour supply kept rural wages at subsistence level: 'they would naturally tend to fall still lower if the worker could live on less salary than the present one',[29] so that his estimate of $15 monthly is probable. His coefficient of active population is lower than a recent estimate of 40 per cent for the economy as a whole in 1926,[30] but the effect of out- migration from the rural areas, and negligible employment opportu- nities for women in the rural sector, would have substantially reduced the coefficient outside Montevideo. A more serious objection to Martínez Lamas's calculation of the rural wage bill ($65 million) is that no allowance was made for the substantial unemployed population, whose size can hardly be guessed at but which was important enough for Martínez Lamas himself to regard it as one of the fundamental evils of the *latifundio* system.

The reason why Martínez Lamas was at pains to estimate the total value of rural wages is because of his belief that rural consumption needs were basically met from outside the rural sector ($48 million); that the wage goods bore a heavy tax burden ($17 million); and that the incidence of this burden fell on the landowners. The first point to note however, is that a substantial proportion of rural wages are paid in kind. Martínez Lamas estimated the proportion at one-third,[31] which is surely an underestimate since recent analysis suggests 50 per cent in the livestock sector and 40 per cent in agriculture.[32] Whatever the exact proportion, it is impossible to accept Martínez Lamas' view that food to that full value was acquired by employers from the urban sector (i.e. imported foodstuffs) for distribution to employees. It is, after all, a familiar point that the payment of wages in kind, especially in the rural sector, diminishes the size of the market for wage goods. A major reason to explain the widespread adoption of the practice in Uruguay by rural employers must surely be that it enabled (and still enables) them to dispose of otherwise non-marketable produce while depressing wages paid in cash to below subsistence levels.

Even imputing a cash value to such payments in kind, the rural labour force was admitted by Martínez Lamas to be living at no more than subsistence level. The expenditure patterns of such a population would necessarily be dominated by basic needs for food, clothing and shelter. It is difficult therefore to give much credence to the view that 'all the commodities and goods necessary for the life of its population, with the exception of a few food items (meat, fats, flour when not substituted for by *fariña*) are bought by the rural sector in the city'.[33] With incomes at subsistence level, the basic items of diet produced in the sector, and a rural tradition of self-sufficiency, the proportion of the consumption of the rural work force supplied from Montevideo could not have been large, and would certainly have very much less than the 100 per cent alleged by Martínez Lamas. Even more damaging to his case is that of the $17 million allegedly paid in consumption taxes, $16 million were conceded to be taxes on imports (50 per cent of the national import tax yield); whereas we have the authority of José Serrato, Minister of Finance, in 1904, to the effect that 'outside Montevideo the consumption of articles paying customs revenue is very limited'.[34] Since wages were still at subsistence level, the picture could hardly have been very different in the 1920s.

The importance of this discussion on the composition of rural work force spending can be seen when it is related to Martínez Lamas' balance of payments argument, and the structure of taxation in the rural sector. The import tax burden of $16 million alleged to fall on the rural sector would constitute 50 per cent of total import taxes, an implausibly high figure. But these taxes formed 57 per cent of the total tax revenue which he claimed was paid by the rural economy to Montevideo; and they formed almost 15 per cent of the total estimated payment to the capital from the country. Hence, the volume of import taxes paid by the rural sector is crucial to his case, and his calculations appear to be very unsound.

A further criticism of the Martínez Lamas's analysis can be made. He needed to show not only that the taxes on goods consumed by rural labour were high, but also that the incidence of these taxes on consumption fell on rural producers, rather than on the labour force. If the latter were the case, real wages would be lower than otherwise, but the profitability of capital in the rural sector would be unimpaired. His authority for believing the former to apply was probably Ricardo: 'every tax on any commodity consumed by the labourer has a tendency to lower the rate of profits'.[35] The assumptions underlying this proposition are that the level of wages is no more than that required to ensure a continuing supply of labour, and that the commodities taxed are wage goods. The effect of the taxes is then to lower real wages below the level required by labourers to support themselves, and an increase in money wages results. The first of these assumptions is valid in the Uruguayan case, but the second is extremely doubtful. A rural population whose consumption is restricted to the minimum for subsistence is unlikely to have a high import component in its consumption; and basic food items, domestically produced, were also free of internal consumption taxes. Of course it is likely that there was some consumption of dutiable imported consumer goods in rural areas, but it would have been generally restricted to those with above-subsistence incomes on whom the final incidence of the tax would therefore fall. It need hardly be added that the rural labour force was absolutely powerless to press for higher money wages, and that any Ricardian pressure on *estancieros* to increase wage rates was more likely to be met by an accelerated displacement of labour from the rural economy. 'In terms of the goods that his money would buy it is probable that the peon had suffered a decrease in wages in the century after 1820.'[36]

It is unfortunate that so much of this debate, which is crucial to the understanding of the Batlle period, and indeed of the secular stagnation of the rural sector, should depend so heavily on assumptions. On the other hand there is no doubt at all that the landowning class, during the 1920s, did feel that the burden of taxes it was required to meet was excessive. Did the burden of taxes increase? Or were the landowners belatedly exercising their influence through the Federación Rural—formed in 1916—with a voice sharpened by the experience of depression at the beginning of the 1920s? Table 4.2 summarises some aspects of taxation and export growth for the period 1900–38. The table is

TABLE 4.2. Exports and taxes 1900–38

	A Exports	B Total tax revenue[1]	C Export and land taxes[2]	D B/A	E C/A	F C/B
	(Million pesos)			*(Per cent)*		
1900	32.1	17.5	2.5	54.5	7.8	14.3
(five-year averages)						
1905–9		24.0	3.4			14.2
1910–14[3]	58.2	30.0	3.9	48.3	6.2	13.0
1915–19	106.8	32.2	5.4	30.1	5.1	16.8
1920–4	84.4	43.6	6.1	51.7	7.2	14.0
1925–9	96.3	67.9	7.8	70.5	8.1	11.5
1938	96.3	89.2	7.8	92.6	8.1	8.7

Notes:
1. 'Total revenue' includes taxes, licences and special contributions. Income from lotteries, contributions from public corporations, etc. is excluded.
2. Taxes on exports (excluding sand and stone) and *contribución inmobiliaria* falling on rural property. The proportion of C.I. on rural property for fifteen of the twenty-four years was in the range 55–63 per cent, average 59 per cent, and for the other years, for which the breakdown was unavailable, was assumed to be 60 per cent. In 1938 the proportion had fallen to 51 per cent.
3. Three-year average, 1911–12 excluded.

Sources: Exports: Table 5.2. Revenue: Dondo, *Ciclos*; La Gamma, 'Ingresos Públicos Nacionales'.

admittedly crude, especially in column C, which registers only those taxes which fell directly or obviously on the landed interests. The enumeration of taxes frequently does not make it clear what was being taxed. Martínez Lamas calculated such taxes for 1926/7 at $10.3 million, compared with a figure of $7.1 million used here. However, the series in column C was collected on a consistent basis and is sufficient to show broad trends and crude orders of magnitude. A further defect in the table is that the growing value of exports in column A overstates the rate of growth of incomes of rural producers, since there was an increase in this period in the proportion of value added by urban processing (for example, frozen and chilled meat, washed wool). Column D suggests that during the period of rapid export growth up to 1914 and the export boom during the war, the value of tax revenue was growing more slowly than exports, but that in the 1920s the value of revenue grew sharply while exports stagnated. Column E confirms that export and land taxes were tending to fall as a proportion of export revenue up to the war, but reversed this tendency unmistakeably in the 1920s. It was doubtless this reversal which gave rise to the complaints of excessive taxation from the producers of exportable goods. However, column F does not indicate that these producers were bearing a disproportionate or growing share of the burden. Omitting the war-time figure, inflated by the contraction of imports and import revenue, taxes on exports and rural property appear to have been remarkably constant as a proportion of total tax revenue, and may even have fallen slightly at the end of the period.

This evidence is no more than suggestive; but it may partially explain why *estancieros* believed they were taxed excessively, while it does nothing to advance the case that the savings potential of rural producers was exhausted by punitive taxation. Moreover, data on land prices and rents for this period is available, and lends considerable weight to the view that the protestations of rural producers had little substance in fact. Table 4.3 indicates the behaviour of land prices and rents, and changes in their ratio, for the periods 1905–10 and 1918–40. Data for 1911–17 is not available. Rents show a sustained and rapid rise to the end of the post-war boom in 1921, and then a recovery from 1923. Land prices also increased to 1921, but thereafter sagged almost continuously to 1935.

TABLE 4.3. Land rentals and land prices, 1905–39
(pesos per hectare)

	Rental	Price	Ratio		Rental	Price	Ratio
1905		21.58		1926	3.60	66.08	96.5
1906		27.01		1927	3.50	65.88	98.1
1907	1.51	32.58		1928	3.65	62.37	101.3
1908	1.77	33.45		1929	3.70	65.97	103.3
1909	1.85	37.42		1930	3.71	63.18	104.8
1910	1.98	45.99		1931	3.80	63.44	104.8
				1932	3.23	56.20	105.1
1918	2.50	51.34		1933	2.96	50.57	109.2
1919	2.77	60.77		1934	2.68	47.08	109.1
1920	3.38	72.53	87.4	1935	2.81	40.02	109.8
1921	4.29	77.48	87.3	1936	2.94	49.36	111.4
1922	3.25	70.31	89.5	1937	3.14	52.90	113.3
1923	3.12	64.62	90.6	1938	3.44	54.75	108.5
1924	3.28	63.44	90.3	1939	3.68	59.00	109.8
1925	3.46	69.47	92.8				

Note: Rentals are for new contracts. Rentals and prices are averages of the eighteen departments weighted by areas of agricultural land in each department. The ratio of rental to price is expressed as a moving five-year average (1926–9 = 100).

Sources: (1905–10) Ministerio de Hacienda, *Proyecto de Contribución Inmobiliaria*, (Montevideo, Barreiro y Ramos, 1910); (1918–34) Manuel Ruiz Diaz, *Los Barómetros Económicos del Uruguay* (Montevideo, 1936); (1932–9) BROU, *Suplemento Estadístico de la Revista Economica*.

The ratio of rents to prices shows a sustained increase from the end of the First World War up to the depression, and after a slight check the increase was resumed to 1937.

The upward trend of rents relative to land prices is a phenomenon not easily explained. The rental received by the landowner is composed of interest on capital which he has invested in the land, plus a Ricardian rent which the tenant pays for the use of the 'original and indestructible powers of the soil'. The size of the interest component will depend on the volume of capital invested in the land by the landowner and the rate at which interest is paid will depend on the state of the market for 'improved' land. In the case of Uruguay the notorious lack of land improvements—except for wire fencing—suggests that the interest component was probably a small part of land rentals paid. The Ricardian rent depends ultimately on the scarcity and differential quality of land, such that if the margin of utilised land is extended as a result of increased output prices or an increased number of producers, for example, then the rent paid on all intra-marginal land will increase. This rent is of course a cost to the individual producers, but is determined in a different manner from other production costs. If demand for farm output is price-elastic (the case of a small country producing for a world market) then the effect of higher production costs should be to lower rents. The farmer on marginal land paying zero rent finds it now impossible to produce profitably because of higher wages or taxes, and so ceases production. On intra-marginal land rents must fall to persuade tenants to remain. If, on the contrary, production costs fall or the prices of agricultural products increase, then rents will rise as the margin of land use shifts outward and there is increased demand by farmers for land.

The determinants of the price of land are complex because land is not valued exclusively as a factor of production. In many societies landownership confers political power and social status. Also, during periods of rising prices demand for land is stimulated by its capacity to maintain its real value. However, the first of these factors would be unlikely to introduce fluctuations in the price of land during periods of relative social stability, while speculative demand for land has probably been of recent origin in Uruguay. Hence, it is reasonable to propose that the price of land should be related to the level of current income which it yields: i.e. to the rental payable by the farmer to the landowner. It would be surprising if for an extended period of time an upward movement in rentals should be accompanied by downward pressure on land prices.

Yet in the case of Uruguay in the inter-war years this was precisely what happened. Only in 1922–4 and 1932–4 did the level of rents fall—both were periods of agricultural depression—while in the second half of the 1920s (the period of Martínez Lamas's analysis) there was a strong upward movement of rents suggesting an active demand for rented land.

Land prices meanwhile were falling, and the ratio of rents to prices increased almost continuously during 1920–37. The buoyancy of rents is hardly consistent with increased taxes or costs, since with elastic demand for agricultural exports the burden would have been passed on to landowners in the form of lower rents. So it is hard to find any support for the 'impoverishment of the countryside' thesis in this evidence.

How is the behaviour of the rent–land price ratio to be explained? It is likely that a variety of factors are relevant. Land prices reached very high levels at the beginning of the 1920s—attributed by Martínez Lamas to the expansion of the money supply during the period of favourable trade balances[37]—and the fall in prices in the 1920s may be seen as the restoration of 'normality' in the market. Also, export prices showed a sharp fall at the beginning of the 1920s, and further deterioration at the end of the decade, which would have added to the feeling of depression which doubtless accompanied the decline in land prices. There was some growth in the acreage devoted to arable crops in the second half of the 1920s which may have pushed up rents somewhat (the proportion of rented to owner-farmed land being rather higher in arable than in livestock production), but this would not have dispelled the sense of gloom among the powerful *latifundistas* of the Federación Rural. The growth of urban outlets for the economic surplus generated in the rural sector would also have depressed the land market.

Martínez Lamas was unquestionably correct in stressing the very low level of investment in agriculture, and in observing the growth of a bureaucratic machine in Montevideo. Especially during the 1920s taxation grew rapidly while exports had lost the dynamism of the pre-war and war-time years. But his diagnosis does not stand up to examination and there is a more plausible alternative interpretation, which is that the intensification of land use was against the interests of the *latifundistas* themselves. While the foundation of the Federación Rural and the reaction against *batllismo* in 1916 enabled the landowning class to become more vocal and more effective in defending itself, the outflow of capital from the rural sector before 1930 was voluntary. Urban property development and government bonds were attracting funds away from the modernisation of agriculture.[38] The fiscal burden of the *batllista* state was borne on a regressive basis, principally by urban consumers.

Fiscal Policy and the Rural Sector after 1930

Within a few years of the publication of *Riqueza y Pobreza del Uruguay* the impact of the world depression had produced radical changes in the Uruguayan economy and political system. In the *coup* of 1933 the *batllista* faction of the Colorados was displaced from government, and its place taken by a regime whose primary and explicit objective was to defend the interests of the landowning class, not least by reducing the fiscal burden on it. Table 4.2 might appear to indicate that this was in some measure achieved, since taxes on exports and land in 1938 were the same proportion of total export value as in 1925–9, and a significantly smaller proportion of total tax revenue. Yet by the late 1930s the expectations of the landed interest that the government of Gabriel Terra would accede to its demands had been frustrated. Pedro Cosio, who on appointment as Minister of Finance in 1933 set himself the task of promoting the recovery of the livestock and farming sectors, expressed the disillusion of the landowners at the end of the decade:

> Since the intervention in the exchange market in 1931 to stabilise the paper peso, the rural sector began to support the burden of official exchange regulation, in spite of all the measures in its favour inspired by the sector's obvious crisis. It was in fact an onerous export tax which was created and which has been maintained—and even increased—with all the disadvantages of an anti-economic tax.[39]

Clearly the calculation of taxes bearing directly on exports and the land is no longer adequate to represent the burden on the rural sector under conditions of trade and exchange control.

Fundamentally, the fiscal changes legislated by the 1933 regime were less significant than the direct effects of the depression itself. These included the deterioration of the export sector relative to the domestic sector, through the decline in world trade, which tended to shift the burden of taxes towards the latter. This was outweighed by the fact of a depreciating exchange rate which offered to policy-makers new means of distributing the fiscal burden. During the 1920s there appears to have been no attempt to use the exchange rate as an instrument of policy, even though (unlike Argentina) Uruguay did not return to the gold standard. After the post-war slump the peso did in fact appreciate continuously until 1928, by when it was only fractionally below its par value of 51.06 pence, but there is no evidence of pressure from the export sector to reverse or limit the strengthening of the currency. It was the rapid fall in the peso in 1931 which introduced the era of *dirigismo* in economic policy.

A constant characteristic of Uruguayan public finance has been the dependence for revenue principally on taxes on consumption and on foreign trade flows. Though taxes continued to be levied directly on exports and imports, from the 1930s until the Exchange and Monetary Reform Law of 1959 the principal instruments of fiscal policy in the foreign trade sector were exchange control and multiple exchange rates. The latter in particular were not only a source of revenue, but were also operated to subsidise certain expenditures and certain sectors. Exchange control was introduced in May 1931 to combat speculation, and an official rate of exchange (*cambio oficial*) was established later in the year.[40] Initially the export sector was denied the full benefit of the depreciation of the peso,[41] so that alongside the official market there flourished a black market, fed by the proceeds of contraband export sales across the Brazilian border and by the concealment by exporters of part of their legitimate foreign exchange earnings. The over-valuation of the official rate was clearly an inducement to exporters to sell to the black market, and to overcome this a number of concessionary rates were decreed. Thus in 1932 a 'special free' rate was made available to exporters of non-traditional products, but it is doubtful whether this had any effect at all on the diversification of exports, and certainly did not meet the requirements of the landowning class. However its support of the 1933 *coup* was quickly rewarded by the granting of compensated exchange (*cambio compensado*) in July that year. The compensation was at different levels for different export commodities, averaging 40 per cent above the official rate, and was intended to approximate the uncontrolled market rate. The official rate continued to be used to meet public and private external debt obligations and remittances. During 1934, the exchange market consisting of black market, official and compensated rates was revised in two principal respects. First, the scope of the black market was restricted by the official recognition of a free market supervised by the Banco de la República. Second, compensated exchange was replaced by 'free controlled' (*cambio libre dirigido*), which permitted the sale of varying proportions of export earnings in the free market.

By the end of 1934 the emergency phase of exchange control had ended. During this period the objective had been to limit the depreciation of the peso consistent with the demands of the export sector for remunerative rates of exchange. In the course of 1934 exchange control was integrated into a complete system of export and import control, and the structure then remained essentially unchanged for three years except that, with the limited recovery of export markets, official policy in the exchange market was to resist a too rapid upward revaluation of the peso. Overall, however, the effect of exchange control had been to limit the increase in local currency earnings to exporters which the fall in the value of the peso would otherwise have granted them. This effect was somewhat reduced from 1932 with the granting of differential export rates, and there was further relief for the livestock sector with the introduction of bonus payments on livestock sales in 1934.

At the end of 1937 the exchange system was reformed, and the fiscal ingredient of exchange profits was introduced for the first time. Free, free controlled and official rates were replaced by a single controlled rate with a margin of 13 per cent between the buying and selling rates. The margin was to enable the Banco de la República to 'cover its costs', the remainder being credited to the government. Twelve months later the system was extended and formalised: the margin was widened to 25 per cent, of which 23 per cent was received by the government into the Exchange Profits Fund (Fondo de Diferencias de Cambio). In 1939 the dollar replaced sterling as the parity base, and the basic exchange rates of $1. 519 (buying) and $1.90 (selling), which were formally to continue for twenty years, were adopted. Revenue received by the Fund was allocated to special expenditures, and in the late 1940s and 1950s was the main source of income for payment of subsidies to consumers, agrarian producers and some others.

The pre-1937 exchange control system embodied the principle of multiple exchange rates, but not as an explicit instrument of policy. The 1937 regime established a single controlled rate (although of course a black market continued) and a formal system of multiple rates did not appear until the 1940s. From 1944 non-traditional exports received the free market rate, and in 1947 imports were classified for the purpose of exchange allocations into three groups: necessary raw materials, consumer goods and specified capital goods in the first; goods competitive with domestic industries and luxuries; and remaining imports. In 1949 the multiple exchange rate system was established in its classic form, with three buying and three selling rates for penalised, preferred, and other transactions. During the following decade until its abandonment in 1959, the system was to become immensely complex, particularly as inflation gave rise to numerous partial devaluations and created a host of different effective rates.[42]

Apart from their direct role in generating revenue for government (i.e. by maintaining a higher weighted average selling price than the weighted average buying price), the multiple rate system was also employed to influence the price level (preferential rates for imports of necessary consumer goods and producers' goods), to shift the structure of production (penalty rates for traditional exports, preferential rates for imported capital equipment), and to assist the balance of payments (increasing preferential export rates and penalty import rates). In the absence of effective additional policy instruments to support these four objectives, it is known that the contradictions between them will require the partial abandonment of some of them.[43] In the case of Uruguay, the manipulation of rates to secure equilibrium in the balance of payments was largely neglected, deficits being met from accumulated currency reserves. The other three objectives all had clear fiscal implications, either on the revenue side, or in the pattern of subsidies implied in preferential rates for certain categories of imports.

Subsidies to consumers of basic foodstuffs (mainly meat, milk and bread) were met from the Exchange Profits Fund. *Frigorifico* losses were also met from this source, but the principal burden on the Fund until the mid-1950s was the subsidy to wheat producers (Table 4.4). During the

TABLE 4.4. Total subsidy payments financed by exchange 'taxes', 1940–52 (million pesos)

	Exchange Profits		Preferential Rates	Total
Consumption	117.8		—	117.8
Milk		58.4		
Meat		45.8		
Bread		11.8		
Agriculture	157.3		12.3	169.6
Wheat		136.4		
Livestock development		14.4		
Rice			4.3	
Manufacturing	24.4		118.8	143.2
Spinning			63.3	
Frigorífico		10.7	26.1	
Leather		1.1	12.0	
	299.5		131.1	430.6

Note: The calculation of subsidies by preferential exchange rates assumes that the basic export rate ($1.519 to the dollar) was also the 'true' rate of exchange.

Source: Israel A. Wonsewer, Luis A. Faroppa and Enrique Iglesias, 'Política de Subvenciones en el Uruguay', *Revista de la Facultad de Ciencias Económicas y de Administración*, No. 5 (1953).

mid-1950s the income to the Fund (i.e. the product of the margin between buying and selling rates) averaged about $50 million annually, but the effects of inflation and growing pressure from the rural sector for more favourable export rates had by 1959 virtually eliminated the margin and therefore the income to the Fund. The granting of subsidies payable from the Fund was never in fact related to the capacity of the Fund to meet them, and 1952 was the first year in which it was necessary to bolster the Fund with a grant from general revenue.[44] With the ending of the wheat policy in the middle of the decade the level of subsidies declined considerably but the Fund remained in deficit. During 1953–8 revenue to the Fund was $230.4 million against an expenditure of $402.6 million.[45]

The formal system of multiple exchange rates was abandoned in the Monetary and Exchange Reform Law of 1959.[46] The Reform was the response of the Nacional party, guided by rural sector interests and the IMF, to the deteriorating economic performance and complex set of trade and exchange controls which it inherited from the Colorados. The exchange rate was unified and devalued, and the controls dismantled. In their fiscal aspects, these changes were intended to form part of a comprehensive policy which included the introduction of an income tax, and which would reduce the tax burden on the external sector. As a transitional measure new trade taxes were introduced: export retentions (*detracciones*) and import surcharges (*recargos*) were levied at differential rates for preferred or penalised exports and imports. Thus in practice an essential feature of the discarded exchange rate system was retained; and moreover in the absence of effective direct taxation the 'transitional' trade taxes remained in force into the 1970s. The spread of equivalent exchange rates (i.e. the difference between the highest and lowest rates for exports and imports) calculated by Daly for 1960–2 was substantial, averaging 49 per cent of the lowest rate in the case of exports and 72 per cent of the lowest rate in the case of imports, thus implying considerable discrimination between commodities and sectors of the economy. The importance of the revenue objective was shown by the average for 1960–2 of 28 per cent between the weighted average export and import rates.[47]

Thus the effect of the 1959 Reform was in practice to increase the dependence of the fiscal system on the external sector, which by the early 1960s was providing almost 30 per cent of tax income, and still averaged 27 per cent during 1966–70 (excluding social security contributions).[48] That a government elected with strong *ruralista* support should respond by increasing the tax burden on the export sector is apparently paradoxical. The explanation was partly the greater administrative simplicity of the export retentions tax compared with that of a tax on the incomes of rural producers. Another factor was that the retentions tax was non-progressive in its burden on the rural sector, such that the *latifundistas* were taxed less heavily than they would have been by a (progressive) income tax. Even more important was the inelasticity of the tax to changes in the domestic price level, and the capacity of rural producers to press for reduced taxes in order to maintain their real incomes. Apart from the activities of pressure groups representing the rural sector, and the greater receptiveness of government after 1959 to their demands, rural producers were in a position to starve the country of foreign exchange, by the withholding of wool from the market, and by illegal sales of cattle to neighbouring countries. In thus provoking an exchange crisis, producers could secure a devaluation of the exchange rate, which increased both their real incomes and the retentions revenue of the government. The acceptability of higher export taxes in 1959 to the rural sector was largely determined by the devaluation of the peso in the Reform. Thus the fiscal needs of government coincided with the interests of the rural sector: devaluation during the 1960s increased the incomes of both, though at the cost of accelerating inflation (which tended to reduce the yield of other taxes).[49]

Diagnosis

Because of agriculture's role in providing almost all of Uruguay's exports or exportable raw materials, an explanation for the low productivity of the land has central importance for an understanding of the country's long-run economic problems. It is clear from the final section of Chapter 3 that the supply of agricultural production has shown a very low rate of increase during this century, and since 1930 the periods of more rapid growth have generally reflected changes in the composition of production rather than an increase in productivity. It bears repeating that all branches of agricultural production are characterised by low and stationary yields per hectare. The question is therefore why agriculture has failed to adopt new techniques of production to shift the agricultural supply curve outward. In the second section of this chapter it was concluded (in answer to Martínez Lamas) that although there was evidently an outflow of the surplus generated in the rural sector towards the urban economy before 1930, this transfer was voluntary and appeared to result from the greater profitability or security of urban investment. This section examines the price history of the sector during the crisis period, land concentration and land tenure, the profitability of agricultural enterprise, and constraints on technological advance, as explanations of the stagnation of recent years.

The interventionism of the period after the Second World War, marked initially by rapid industrial growth and subsequently by general stagnation, seems to add new weight to the view that the problems of the agricultural export sector might be attributed to the effects of discriminatory government policy. Such a case has been argued by Díaz Alejandro for Argentina[50] and has been alleged to apply to Uruguay also:

> Although agricultural products have been the only things that Uruguay has been unable [sic] to export in quantity, indicating this to be the efficient sector of the economy, much of the profit of crop and cattle production has been siphoned off through exchange policy and uneven taxation placing a penalty on investment in livestock and agriculture.[51]

It is true, of course, that the rural sector has not escaped taxation; few activities or social groups in a modern economy can expect to do so. Indeed, it is to be expected that part of the profits of the sector would be siphoned off, in a policy aimed at diversification and reduced vulnerability to adverse changes in external markets, since the costs of the sector are low and its contribution to the total surplus available to the community as a whole is substantial. Moreover, the sector shows a high degree of concentration in property ownership and income distribution, which in a large number of societies would attract the attention of revenue collectors. It is not sufficient therefore merely to state that much of the profit was siphoned off: criticism of fiscal policy would have to show that the effect of taxation on the sector as a whole was punitive, effectively confiscating the re-investible surplus. Alternatively it might be argued that taxes bearing on the sector were such as to produce neither beneficial changes in the structural characteristics of the sector, nor a positive response in the level of production.

Since the bulk of rural sector taxes were levied not on the income or profits of the sector but on exports—through penalty exchange rates and subsequently export retentions—the main impact of taxation on rural producers was experienced in the prices which they received for their output from exporters. Accordingly, one indicator of the weight of taxation on the sector is the way in which prices received by it moved in relation to the general price level: specifically, whether during the period of rapid industrialisation the internal terms of trade of the rural sector moved adversely. Table 4.5 presents various price indices for the rural sector for the period 1945–64. The index for domestically consumed output (column 1) shows comparatively small fluctuations against the general price level, though the initiation of the wheat policy in the late 1940s and the favourable policies of the Blanco government at the end of the 1950s are both well marked. There is certainly no evidence of a sustained adverse movement. The price index for exportable production (column 2) is more relevant to the analysis. It shows an improvement against the general price level after the war, slight recession in the late 1940s, a massive rise in 1950–1, falling in 1952 to the level of the late 1940s. From 1952 there is a clear rising trend in the internal terms of trade of rural export producers to reach a peak in 1960, with only minor setbacks. During 1961–4 prices reverted to their relative level of the mid-1950s.

A possible explanation for the behaviour of this price index is that it was determined by movements in the prices received for exported production. In other words, a growing tax burden in the 1950s would be consistent with the improving internal terms of trade if world price for Uruguay's exports were improving even more rapidly. In column 4 of Table 4.5 the internal terms of trade for producers of exportable production (i.e. beef, wool and linseed) are deflated by the general export price index. When this is done, certain trends are clearly revealed. Between 1945 and 1952, prices received by the rural sector were deteriorating in relation to the prices paid in world markets to Uruguayan exporters, a trend interrupted in 1950–1, when farm prices turned upward as a result of the great increase in world commodity prices. From 1952 to 1960 the trend was reversed: while export prices declined in almost every year, real prices to producers were generally improving, and did so continuously when deflated by the export price index. It may be that export houses and intermediaries were less efficient or more able to exert a monopsonistic control over their suppliers before 1952, such that they could capture for themselves the main share of the

TABLE 4.5. Price indices of rural sector production and exports, 1945–64
(1961 = 100)

	Farm prices of agricultural output, deflated by general price index		Export price index	2/3
	Output for domestic consumption	Exportable output (beef, wool, linseed)		
	1	2	3	4
1945	99.3	64.2	60.2	106.6
1946	86.3	66.4	79.3	83.7
1947	99.0	85.3	104.6	81.5
1948	106.1	83.3	117.2	71.1
1949	103.3	77.7	116.4	66.8
1950	96.6	95.3	124.0	76.9
1951	88.7	130.1	172.9	75.2
1952	103.9	80.0	132.2	60.5
1953	94.2	84.2	130.0	64.8
1954	96.7	87.9	128.0	68.7
1955	101.8	86.0	117.0	73.5
1956	93.7	85.8	109.4	78.4
1957	90.0	103.7	116.9	88.7
1958	94.4	94.9	101.3	93.7
1959	105.9	120.4	97.8	123.1
1960	121.1	137.3	105.0	130.8
1961	100.0	100.0	100.0	100.0
1962	94.3	89.4	99.7	89.7
1963	91.2	79.9	101.5	78.7
1964	101.3	95.6	116.0	82.4

Source: MGA–CIDE, Estudio Económico y Social de Agricultura, vol. I, pp. 182, 479.

benefit of improving export prices, and after 1952 themselves absorbed the impact of deteriorating prices. But this does not seem likely. It would appear rather that having lost out by discriminatory fiscal policy in the early years of the exchange profits regime, the rural sector mobilised effectively during the 1950s to press for consistently improving exchange rate treatment. By 1963, when the initial benefits of the 1959 Reform were largely lost to the rural sector, the tax burden on it (with export taxes imputed to agricultural producers) was still only 16 per cent of total tax revenue, compared with an overall tax ratio of 14.3 per cent of GDP.[52]

If it is difficult to make the case that rural producers as a whole were excessively burdened by taxation, it is nonetheless clear that the way in which they have been taxed has been undesirable. The conclusion of one analysis was that taxation of the rural sector 'is neither simple nor efficient nor elastic nor direct nor progressive'.[53] All of these criticisms can be made of the revenue system as a whole, but the damage done by a tax system whose only objective is to raise revenue is potentially greater when applied to a sector whose output provides almost all the economy's export earnings. Analysis of the origin of revenue derived from the rural sector for 1962–4—it appears to have changed little during the rest of the decade—indicates that 70 per cent was levied on exports of agricultural output, a massive proportion.[54] Taxes on land provided a further 16.5 per cent; on sales of agricultural production, 9.5 per cent; on inputs used in the sector, 3.5 per cent; and on incomes, 0.5 per cent.

Some characteristics of the tax on exports—the retentions tax—have been mentioned already. It had clear administrative advantages. The tax was difficult to evade, except by smuggling; liability was discharged by the retention of some part of the local currency proceeds of export transactions, so that delay in tax payment is difficult; and the tax could be varied to impose a differential burden on different commodities. However, this and the sales tax had the disadvantage that the tax liability was incurred in marketing output, in a sector whose rate of growth of output has been disastrously low. The overwhelming part of the tax burden was thus incurred by producing, rather than by owning land. In principle, since the tax was levied as a fixed sum per unit of exported production, the tax was proportional to gross income, and therefore non-progressive. In practice this general conclusion is valid, but the uneven distribution between commodities of the export tax should be noted. Wool in fact yielded in 1962–4 70 per cent of revenue on this account, and the taxation/gross value of output ratio in sheep production was 34 per cent, compared with 14 per cent for all rural production.[55] The reason for this higher burden is essentially that sheep-raising is a low-cost activity, with a comparatively low requirement for labour, materials or equipment; and that, unlike cattle producers, the prices received by producers for wool did not have to reflect the inefficiency of the industry processing its output.

An alternative and very different diagnosis of stagnation is the hypothesis that the concentration of landownership among a small number of families over an extended period of time has produced a class of wealthy and tradition-oriented agricultural producers who are not profit-maximisers, or who admit non-economic considerations into their calculations of cost and profit. This is not a fashionable view in general in development studies, and although inadequate study has been made of the *latifundista* class in Uruguay there are reasons for doubting its relevance. Certainly, there was an informed belief early in this century that in spite of the modernisation which had taken place, the landowners in general remained a conservative influence on agricultural practice, opposing ploughing and preferring to retain the land in its natural state. But the rapid growth of acreage under crops after the Second World War suggests that such a preference may have lost much of the force it once had. Indeed, shifts in the composition of production within the livestock sector as well as between livestock and arable production indicate that producers are sensitive and responsive to the price stimulus.[56] Landownership remains highly concentrated, but A. E. Solari has suggested a high degree of mobility affecting the landowning elite, compared with the relatively enclosed rural upper class of Argentina, this mobility originating in the speculative gains in land or cattle sales of some, the failure to adapt promptly to changed economic circumstances by others.[57] There is also evidence, noted in Chapter 2, of mobility between the rural and urban elites. The assumption of economic irrationality on the part of a small fixed group of agricultural producers does not therefore commend itself as a plausible hypothesis.

From the structuralist perspective one might expect to relate the inadequate supply response of agriculture to certain characteristics of the sector, especially the size of land-holdings and the prevailing forms of land tenure. The problems of the *latifundia* and of absentee landowners and unsatisfactory tenancies are frequently cited as responsible for the low productivity of the land; in view of this it is perhaps surprising that, as Brannon notes, little research has been done on the variation of land yields by farm size.[58] Nonetheless, the available evidence suggests that farm size has not been an important factor in the determination of yields. Table 4.6 demonstrates remarkably little variation in livestock production per hectare in the farm size range 50–2500 hectares. Above 2500 hectares (conventionally defined as *latifundia*) there is a slight falling away in production, though this is not caused by a lower level of investment. Evidence on wool yields also shows little deterioration on large or small farms, and in the rate of reproduction in cattle their performance may be marginally better than on medium-sized farms. Arable crops in general show a decline in yield as farm size grows, but for both wheat and linseed the difference between the most and least productive farm sizes is less than 20 per cent. Brannon also found that in general there was an inverse relation between crop yield and farm size, but that the percentage variations were small.[59]

It is almost as difficult to find support for the view that the efficiency of land use has been impaired by forms of land tenure. It is true that the CLEH–CINAM study found, in relation to livestock producers, that the technical level on large farms surveyed varied markedly with the form of tenure: of owner-worked farms, 45 per cent were 'good' and 25 per cent 'bad'; in the case of tenants the proportions were 10 per cent and 30 per cent.[60] On the other hand Brannon compared the distribution among land tenure forms of selected improvements (sheep dips, cattle

TABLE 4.6. Agriculture: yields and investment by farm size

	Farm size (hectares)				
	1–50	50–200	200–1000	1000–2500	2500+
Gross livestock production per hectare (pesos)[1]		130	135	130	115
Productive investment in livestock sector per hectare (pesos)[1,2]		489	429	388	386
Wool yield per head of flock (kilos)	3.21	3.43	3.84	4.15	4.11
Wool yield per hectare (kilos)	17.9	16.6	17.8	17.8	16.9
Wheat yield per hectare (kilos)	861	826	808	764	733
Linseed yield per hectare (kilos)	604	561	532	496	549
	1–50	50–500	500–2500	2500–10000	10000+
Rate of procreation in cattle	59.9	53.5	56.1	55.1	63.6

Notes: All data refers to early 1960s. Results for some farm sizes shown here are the result of averaging two or more farm size classes in the sources.
1. Excludes dairy production.
2. Excludes investment in housing.

Sources: Livestock production: CLEH–CINAM, *Uruguay Rural*, pp. 109–10. Wool, wheat, linseed, cattle: MGA–CIDE, *Estudio Económico y Social de Agricultura*, vol. 1, pp. 684–6.

pens, ploughs, tractors, fertilisers, etc.) with the distribution of pasture and crop land among the same farms, and concluded that 'there is little relationship between tenure forms and the amount of investment made in the enterprise'.[61] Evidence on wheat and linseed yields per hectare and on rates of reproduction in cattle, drew the conclusion that owner worked farms were not necessarily more productive than other forms of tenure; indeed, from this limited examination sharecropping emerged as marginally the most efficient.[62] The 'structuralist' view does not therefore seem to be well-founded in the case of Uruguay. Rather primitive production techniques are distributed among all sizes of farm and all tenure forms, resulting in uniformly low yields per hectare. While structural reform is likely to be a condition of the successful introduction of improved agricultural techniques, and while it might be preferable for political or social reasons that the proportion of farmers working their own medium-sized farms should be increased, it does not seem likely that the size of farms and the tenure system have by themselves been responsible for agricultural stagnation.

The remaining hypothesis to be considered is that agricultural producers have pursued profit-maximising strategies, and that they have acted rationally in failing to shift from extensive to intensive land use. It was noted earlier that net investment in agriculture (apart from mechanisation) has run at low levels in recent decades. Also, the use of cash inputs in raising yields has been very little exploited. An implication of this might be that the return on capital in agriculture is relatively unattractive compared with yields in other sectors of the economy or returns on funds held abroad. Few studies have been made of the profitability of agricultural investment, but the evidence does indeed suggest that yields are low. In livestock production the rate of profit on total investment in the early 1960s was found to be about 7.6 per cent, and in agriculture about 9.7 per cent.[63] For the livestock sector a very similar estimate, 7.8 per cent, has also been employed.[64] This modest yield does not necessarily imply the lack of a fund of savings available for reinvestment, since the concentration of land-holdings and ownership endows 1.8 per cent of livestock enterprises with 46.5 per cent of the total profit of the sector.[65]

In addition, it appears very doubtful whether the introduction of such improved techniques as have been available would have improved the rate of profit. The CLEH–CINAM study found that investment in improvements was unlikely to be profitable, especially on large farms.[66] Artificial pasture is widely regarded as the eventual solution to the nutritional problem in livestock production on those lands sufficiently fertile, since its yield in physical terms is between two and four times that of natural pasture. However, not only is the area of artificial or improved natural pasture still very small as a proportion of total available pasture, but even this has been achieved largely through the subsidised use of fertilisers and cheap ten-year credits financed by the World Bank and administered by the Plan Agropecuario.[67] It has been argued that the limited adoption of artificial pasture is explained by the very low return on capital—3.4 per cent—assuming an average pasture yield. Even assuming a greater than average grass yield, artificial pasture is a considerably more risky investment than traditional production methods, being particularly vulnerable to climatic conditions and requiring skilled management.[68] The programme of the Plan Agropecuario has also been criticised for the somewhat superficial modifications it has made to technologies developed elsewhere which have then been employed in Uruguay on a trial and error basis.[69] An analogous situation exists in the crop sector, where inadequate research has been undertaken in the selection of fertilisers, pesticides and crop strains, and their use is not yet widespread because their profitability has yet to be established. Although the general form which agricultural improvement should take is known, the adaptation of these techniques to Uruguayan conditions has not occurred: the rate of return on investment in improvements increasing land yields has not yet become sufficiently attractive to result in a shift away from traditional extensive land use patterns. A livestock producer who wishes to increase his production undoubtedly acts rationally in buying or renting more land, rather than using his existing land more intensively.

The emphasis in the preceding paragraph on the lack of profitable land-intensification technology does not of course imply that the cost structure or price history of the sector are not relevant to the question of agricultural stagnation. If the relative profitability of investment in the sector had been greater, the competition of capital for the fixed supply of land should have driven up the price of land and therefore encouraged the development of land-intensive techniques. The question arises, therefore, whether the return on capital in agriculture has been insufficient, a question which can only be considered in relation to prices and costs, and the connection between them.

The thesis of inadequate returns to capital in Uruguayan agriculture may be presented in three forms. The first argues that government policy towards the sector diminished its profitability through discriminatory price policies and that this accounts for the low level of investment in the sector. Naturally enough, this argument has been especially popular in the agricultural sector itself, but its merits as an explanation of long-run stagnation are doubtful. Government of course has had a determining influence over most prices to agricultural producers both directly, in setting crop purchase prices and through the state-owned Conaprole (dairy producers' cooperative), and indirectly, through fiscal and exchange rate policy. But Table 4.5 makes it clear that prices to the sector did not deteriorate during the twenty post-war years. The capacity of government to depress prices to agricultural producers has been limited both by the need to ensure supplies of foreign exchange from exports and of production for domestic consumption needs, and by the activities of interest groups such as the Federación Rural. The frequency with which producers in the 1950s and 1960s pressed the government for more favourable treatment, for example by refusing to sow crops or sell the wool clip, or by selling cattle illicitly in neighbouring countries, is well known. The simple conclusion is that 'prices for the agricultural sector have been improving in real terms. The slow growth of agricultural production cannot be attributed to the lack of economic incentives.'[70]

R. H. Brannon, while accepting this, has presented data for the period

1950–64 to show that prices to Uruguayan producers for their beef cattle and wool have been lower than those in other major producing countries.[71] The meaning of such a comparison is far from clear however. Apart from difficulties in obtaining price series for comparable products, and variations in internal purchasing power of the dollar, no account is taken of the costs of production nor of the burden of taxation falling directly on producers (which in the case of Uruguay is extremely low). Indeed if low prices were the cause of agricultural stagnation one would expect to find a net movement of producers out of the sector, resulting in downward pressure on the price of land.

In fact, however, the rapid rise in land prices was a notorious feature of the 1950s and 1960s, and is a basic element of the two variants of the low-profitability thesis. Unfortunately, it is extremely difficult to construct a land price series. The data available suffers from a variety of defects; prices which have been calculated for departments are simple unweighted averages; the systematic reporting of land sales has in recent years been subject to long delays; and a comparison of thirty reported transactions with the actual value of those transactions in 1964 and 1966 revealed an undervaluation (for tax purposes) in the declared price of 49.6 per cent.[72] In these circumstances it is pointless to attempt or pretend to precision in the analysis. Brannon constructed a land price index for 1940–64 based on the assumption that the rate of undervaluation in declared prices had remained constant. When compared with general price and agricultural price indices, the data indicates that land prices had increased rapidly, keeping pace until the mid-1960s with the rise in the cost of living, but rising less rapidly than agricultural prices. It would be reasonable to expect that the degree of undervaluation of recorded land prices might have increased as the inflation of land prices accelerated, such that the extent to which agricultural prices exceeded land prices is probably not significant.

More precise evidence on the evolution of land prices would be invaluable in assessing the two remaining low-profitability hypotheses. The first of these accepts that agriculture faced relatively favourable price treatment in recent decades, and the problem to be explained is therefore why the sector failed to react positively to the inducement of higher real prices.[73] An explanation which has been offered[74] is that the supply response in agriculture occurs slowly, since there is a considerable time-lag before more intensive techniques yield increased output, and the profitability of these techniques is in any case in doubt. In order to take more immediate advantage of favourable prices, therefore, producers attempt to secure more land to increase their scale of production, thus bidding up the price of land. But because 'land rent, or the interest on capital invested in land and livestock, constitute the most important elements in the cost of livestock production',[75] the rate of profit in agricultural production returns to its equilibrium level. The increase in agricultural prices has stimulated not production but the rapidly inflating market in land, rewarding speculators rather than producers. A mechanism of this kind is implied by CIDE in its analysis of the consequences of the exchange reform of 1959, which provided substantial incentives to producers of exportable commodities but failed to achieve a sustained increase in production.[76]

The third hypothesis is basically a variant of the second, but it inverts the causal connection between higher agricultural prices and higher land prices, stressing the primary role of the latter. It is clear that, in the context of the sustained and rapid inflation in Uruguay, the purchase of land proved to be a sound investment for the maintenance of the real value of assets. Land, moreover, is a liquid asset offering the prospect of speculative gains. The existence of such a market in which land is a store of value might well have implications for agricultural production in which land is a necessary factor. To the extent that it is a speculative market, land is valuable not because of the income it yields when employed in agriculture, but because of the existence of buyers willing to purchase it at a higher price in the future. In the long run, of course, the speculative value of land largely rests on its productive capacity: if there should be a catastrophic fall in the real level of agricultural prices then the price of land would eventually follow, and funds seeking a hedge against inflation would move elsewhere. However, the risk of this occurring is minimal. Landowners in Uruguay have a monopoly of the resource on which the Uruguayan economy is totally dependent, and it endowed them—certainly until the early 1970s—with formidable bargaining power *vis-à-vis* the government. It was thus possible to secure increases in agricultural prices sufficient to enhance the value of land as a rapidly appreciating asset and to provide an adequate rate of profit in agricultural production.

However, the utilisation of land as a store of value has additional implications for land as a factor of production. Investment in improvements raising the intensity of land use, even if it should prove to be profitable, involves locking up capital in depreciating assets. It also reduces the liquidity of the main asset, land, since the market in improved pasture land is undeveloped and the market value will not fully reflect its higher pasture yield. There is thus a conflict between the speculative and productive uses of land, which would exist even if there were profitable technologies available in agriculture. In the context of rapid inflation in Uruguay, it has clearly been a more secure investment to increase production by acquiring additional land, rather than by the intensification of land use which reduced its speculative value. It seems likely that the development of a speculative demand for land was on occasion fed by higher agricultural prices, but has also itself operated to push up costs and thus necessitate compensatory price increases. On this analysis the rewards of rising agricultural prices went to landowners rather than agricultural producers, and this prevented the resumption of the process of expanded reproduction in agriculture.

It would be wrong to suppose that the explanation for so deep-rooted a phenomenon as the stagnation of agriculture could be reduced to a single cause, or even an unchanging hierarchy of causes. The two mechanisms described in preceding paragraphs, by which higher real prices have persistently failed to induce a shift towards more intensive land use, have probably operated at least during the 1950s and 1960s, but they are only an expression of a more basic weakness of the rural sector. The fundamental failure of agriculture in Uruguay has been technological: a failure to develop suitable technologies to permit the profitable intensification of land use by the generality of producers. The failure is puzzling, in the sense that Uruguayan agriculture has shown itself advanced in the incorporation of some technical changes, particularly the breeding of cattle and sheep to produce increased or more appropriate yields. The explanation has several aspects, the first of which is that the introduction of improved livestock, or wire fencing, merely required the adoption of technical advances developed elsewhere. The transition to artificial or improved pasture, on the other hand, requires not only the adoption of technical advance but also its adaptation to Uruguayan conditions, involving soil analysis and prolonged experimentation with types of grass, fertilisers, insecticides, etc. Basic research on this scale exceeds the resources of individual producers. Moreover, it would have represented an unwarranted commercial risk. The relative fertility of the natural pasture, the sparseness of the population it was required to support, and the concentration of power in the small but wealthy *latifundista* class, inhibited the search for solutions to the critical constraint on sustained agricultural development posed by the limited animal-carrying capacity of the land.

Where the interests of a sector of the dominant class are frustrated by a constraint whose removal exceeds the capacity of individual members of the class, it is reasonable to expect the collective resources of the capitalist system to be utilised through the intervention of the state. Yet in spite of initiatives in this field before the First World War, most of which benefited the arable sector, the level of research and extension activity supported by the state was very low and quite inadequate at least before the 1960s. The reasons for this were partly those mentioned at the end of the previous paragraph. But it may also have been the case that the relative lack of direct political representation of the landowning class in the *batllista* system deprived the class of the level of participation in state resources which it would otherwise have had. That is not to suggest that the landowners lacked political influence; rather, their immense political weight was directed towards short-term economic objectives which carried no implications for change in the traditional and (for them) highly satisfactory rural structure. Moreover, the period of rapid industrialisation offered a new outlet for the economic surplus generated in agriculture. It is significant, therefore, that it was not until the 1960s, following the cessation of industrial growth and with a Blanco government which had attacked the *batllista* system, that the land-owners collectively invoked the assistance of the state and foreign capital in a (so far) feeble attempt at the intensification of land use.

5 Exports and the Meat Industry

I have no desire to tilt against the Beef Trust, which is very probably an excellent institution, but one that, since it openly lays no claim to a purely philanthropical policy, cannot be expected to safeguard the welfare of concerns that do not tend toward its own advancement. (W. H. Koebel, *Uruguay* [1911] p. 282.)

I. Exports

In common with the rest of Latin America, it would be appropriate to designate Uruguay's pattern of growth before 1930 as export-led. The emphasis on the urban character of *batllista* Uruguay should not conceal the fact that the growth process in this period was determined by the performance of exports, and later the export sector was crucial to the import-substitution model after the Second World War. The significance of exports has consisted not only in determining the rate of growth of the economy in the long run, but also in converting a highly favourable if limited natural resource endowment per capita into a high level of per capita income, on the basis of which the redistributive policies of *batllismo* were constructed. There is indeed a strong positive correlation between the health of the export sector, with its political and economic implications, and the fortunes of the *batllista* cause.

The vulnerability of Uruguay to the performance of its export trades is to some extent shared by all small economies. But although the major long-run obstacle to improved performance has been the stagnation of exportable production, examined in the two preceding chapters, small size has had further harmful implications. In the first place, Uruguay has accounted for only a few per cent of total world exports of its principal export commodities, and a tiny proportion of total world supply. The marginality of its position in world trade has been further emphasised by the concentration of some important trades on the British market which from 1930 became increasingly unsatisfactory; and by competition from the Argentine export sector, whose comparable but larger and superior natural resource base endowed it with a dominant position in the River Plate export trades, in terms of quantity, quality and regularity of supply.

Growth

The estimation of the growth of the value of exports (and of imports) before 1940 presents serious data problems which are discussed in the Appendix. For 1913–40 it was possible to revise the official figures and the resulting estimates are presented in Table 5.2. For the years before 1913 (Table 5.1) only a very crude adjustment could be made for 1900 and 1910. The overall picture is one of fairly rapid growth in the first decade of the century — appriximately 4 per cent annually — followed by a very sharp rise to 1913. Export values thus doubled between 1900 and 1913, though in Argentina over the same period they trebled. The volume index indicates an average annual rate of growth of 2.5 per cent in the pre-war decade (1900–3 to 1910–13).

TABLE 5.1. Commodity exports, 1895–1913

	'Official value' (million pesos)	Estimated value (million pesos)	Volume (1913 = 100)
1895	32.6		96.3
1896	30.4		86.5
1897	29.4		85.4
1898	30.3		79.9
1899	36.6		84.7
1900	29.4	32.1	72.3
1901	27.8		80.1
1902	33.7		86.9
1903	37.4		89.7
1904	39.0		93.0
1905	30.8		76.2
1906	33.4		81.3
1907	35.0		84.0
1908	40.3		98.8
1909	45.1		106.2
1910	40.9	46.7	98.1
1911	42.5		101.4
1912	48.8		111.7
1913	44.9	68.5[1]	100.0

Note:
1. Official estimate.   Other notes and source: see Appendix.

The apparent decline in the volume of exports up to the turn of the century is slightly misleading. The crisis of 1890 was followed by several years of commercial depression, but by the middle of the decade revival was evident in exports of most commodities, especially of wool. However, wool exports (the most important single commodity) declined sharply in the late 1890s, not achieving again the peak level of 50 million kilos in 1895 for a decade. Growth thereafter to 1904 was sustained by increased exports of hides and jerked beef (*tasajo*). That year marked a watershed in the export economy. For although the Blanco insurrection severely disrupted the livestock sector and produced a sharp fall in exports, it coincided with the establishment of the first meat-freezing plant. Nonetheless the contribution of frozen beef and mutton to the export boom which reached its peak in 1912 was modest, and the value of the traditional meat products, extract and jerked beef, declined. Exports of hides equally showed little dynamism. But while the cattle industry adapted its herds to the requirements of the *frigorífico*, wool exports achieved very high levels, averaging 70 million kilos in 1911–13. However, since the wool clip in these years, though markedly larger than previously, averaged only 55 million kilos, it is clear that these figures (and those for other exports in other years) are substantially inflated by a re-export trade whose exact proportions are unknown.[1]

The First World War period was marked by generally low export volumes, but high and rising prices which reached a peak in the immediate post-war years (Table 5.2). The decline in volume was mostly accounted for by wool and jerked beef. The demand of the Allies for frozen meat, hides and corned beef grew steadily as the war progressed, and with imports into Uruguay limited by problems of shipping space — freight rates between the UK and the River Plate rose by 1100 per cent between the end of 1913 and the end of 1916[2]—the peso rose above par during 1916–20. The exceptionally favourable conditions of 1919–20 were succeeded by an unprecedented collapse, as the post-war recession in the consuming countries took hold. Contraction was greatest for those commodities for which demand had been inflated by war—hides, corned beef, and beef extract. The chilled and frozen meat trades on the other hand were scarcely affected by the recession. It was these trades, moreover, which dominated export performance in the 1920s. Recovery took place during 1921–4, but thereafter until the depression the value of exports remained on a plateau even though the volume of all the principal commodities continued to rise. Between 1923–5 and 1927–9 the volume grew by over 4 per cent annually, but in value terms exports remained stationary. The depression dealt a severe blow to Uruguay's export trade. Export earnings were 30 per cent lower during 1931–4 than they had been in 1927–30, and the decline in volume was even greater. But in the recovery in the second half of the 1930s, though earnings rose to slightly higher levels than a decade earlier, the volume of exports never achieved its former level, averaging 20 per cent lower than in the second half of the 1920s. Thus revival was mainly the result of a rapid improvement in prices, while markets remained restricted.

Perhaps the most remarkable aspect of Uruguay's foreign trade up to 1940 is that even during the period of export-led growth the volume of

TABLE 5.2. Commodity exports, 1913–40

	Value (million pesos)	Volume (1938 = 100)	Price (1938 = 100)
1913	68.5	103.1	69.0
1914	59.5	73.2	84.4
1915	73.3	79.8	95.4
1916	73.9	72.2	106.2
1917	103.5	83.1	129.4
1918	121.3	90.5	139.2
1919	162.0	120.0	140.2
1920	91.4	67.5	140.6
1921	70.3	85.0	85.9
1922	67.9	92.6	76.1
1923	89.0	100.4	92.0
1924	103.6	102.7	104.8
1925	97.0	100.6	100.1
1926	94.3	112.3	87.2
1927	96.4	131.0	76.4
1928	100.8	116.5	89.9
1929	93.0	111.4	86.7
1930	100.9	140.9	74.4
1931	78.3	120.2	67.6
1932	58.3	82.0	73.8
1933	66.7	92.0	75.3
1934	70.0	72.6	100.1
1935	95.3	102.8	96.3
1936	90.2	92.3	101.5
1937	98.9	92.8	110.7
1938	96.3	100.0	100.0
1939	101.4	104.6	100.7
1940	110.5	99.4	115.4

Notes and sources: See Appendix.

exports showed signs of the stagnation which is more usually associated with subsequent decades. This occurred in spite of the introduction of new commodities with the arrival in Uruguay of the meat-packing industry. The process of expansion of export volume, not rapid before the First World War, was not fully resumed until the second half of the 1920s and was ended by the depression of the 1930s. In per capita terms there can have been very little increase. This rather weak performance was relieved by exceptionally high prices in the late 1910s, and by a period of firm prices beginning in 1934.

Since 1940 it has again been true that price trends account for most of the variation in the value of exports (Table 5.3). In volume terms the lack

TABLE 5.3. Commodity exports, 1935–70
(f.o.b.)

	Value (million US dollars)	Volume (1961 = 100)	Price (1961 = 100)		Value (million US dollars)	Volume (1961 = 100)	Price (1961 = 100)
1935		108.4	27.5	1953	269.5	119.4	129.8
1936		90.9	35.6	1954	248.8	112.9	127.6
1937		90.3	43.6	1955	183.0	90.3	116.7
1938		96.0	35.8	1956	215.7	114.8	109.6
1939		101.3	32.8	1957	136.0	67.4	116.4
1940		98.9	39.5	1958	155.4	88.6	101.1
1941	70.8	94.0	43.4	1959	108.3	63.3	98.0
1942	57.8	59.2	57.5	1960	129.4	71.6	104.0
1943	100.0	105.7	54.1	1961	174.6	100.0	100.0
1944	97.5	99.0	56.1	1962	153.4	87.6	100.2
1945	122.0	112.2	62.0	1963	165.2	93.3	101.3
1946	152.8	108.5	80.4	1964	178.9	88.8	115.3
1947	162.5	88.8	104.6	1965	191.2	99.3	110.2
1948	178.1	87.7	117.3	1966	185.8	94.8	112.3
1949	191.6	94.4	116.3	1967	158.7	86.8	105.8
1950	254.2	117.7	124.3	1968	179.2	108.5	94.5
1951	236.3	78.6	173.2	1969	200.3	111.4	103.0
1952	208.7	91.2	132.3	1970	232.7	124.8	106.7

Sources: CIDE, Estudio Económico, vol. II, tables 25 and 26; Universidad de la República, Estadísticas Básicas, tables 40 and 64; BCU, Boletín Estadístico Mensual.

of growth is quite remarkable. During 1953–6 the level of exports was sustained at a relatively high level, but this was barely 3 per cent above the previous peak period of a decade earlier and was immediately followed by a fall of one-third in the disastrous period 1957–60. Thereafter there was a slight recovery, but no evidence of any real increase until the end of the 1960s. Strengthening prices, however, did allow the total value of exports to show sustained growth through the Second World War and the late 1940s, reaching a peak with the Korean War boom. The growth of export earnings which was basic to the industrialisation policy of the period was almost entirely therefore a consequence of favourable world price trends. But in the subsequent collapse, a price fall intensified the effects of the shortage of exportable production, resulting in the acute balance of payments problems of the late 1950s. In the following decade prices showed generally greater stability, and contributed to the very slow recovery of the 1960s. However, not until 1970 was the peak volume of the early 1950s reached, and not until the commodity boom of 1973–4 were the values of twenty years earlier exceeded. In Chapter 3 it was emphasised that the lack of growth in the rural sector was a very long-run feature of the Uruguayan economy. The export record reveals a quite extraordinary degree of stagnation.

Composition and Direction

Until the 1970s, it appears that Uruguay's export commodities and markets changed little in the course of this century. In 1900, as in 1970, Uruguay exported principally the products of temperate grasslands — mainly wool, meat and hides — with a small proportion derived from arable agriculture. The main outlet for these exports was still Europe, as at the beginning of this century, with the United States absorbing only a small proportion. Nevertheless, though there has been considerable stability in these aspects of the export trade, on closer examination important shifts are revealed. The changing composition of exports is summarised in Table 5.4. Especially before 1914 the data is subject to considerable error because of the use of official prices. If the eighty-year period is looked at as a whole, certain very broad trends do emerge; for wool and meat there have been substantial fluctuations, but the combined importance of the two grew fairly steadily up to 1940, and has stabilised at about 75 per cent of total exports since then. A further category showing a long period of sustained growth is agricultural exports, which recovered from their low level during the First World War and reached a peak in the 1950s. These growth trends have been achieved mainly at the expense of hides and sheepskins, whose importance in total exports has steadily declined throughout the period.

The principal developments in the export trades up to the First World War concerned Uruguay's meat products. Although the establishment of a meat-freezing plant in 1904 introduced new export products, and initiated the process of improving the quality of the cattle herds, these developments were of limited significance before the war. Pre-war growth in these new products amounted to little more than compensation for the slow decline of the traditional meat products, extract and jerked beef. The *saladero* was confronted by growing restrictions on jerked beef in its main markets, Cuba and Brazil, and eventually, with the *frigoríficos* paying high prices for improved cattle, by difficulty in receiving adequate supplies of traditional *criollo* cattle suitable for processing. But the earlier arrival of the meat-freezing industry in Buenos Aires meant that this transition occurred there first, and during the 1890s until the eve of the war Uruguayan *saladeros* were able to secure an increased share (over 50 per cent, 1895–1907) of the total *saladero* slaughter in Argentina, Uruguay, and southern Brazil.[3] Hence the contraction in exports of *tasajo*, though continuous after 1900, was nevertheless gradual. But the confinement of the cattle industry mainly to traditional products tended to enhance the importance of wool exports and restricted cattle production.

TABLE 5.4. Composition of commodity exports, 1891–1970
(five-year averages, per cent at current prices[2])

	Meat and extracts	Hides	Wool	Agricultural products	Other	Total
1891–5	19	35	23	5	18	100
1896–1900	22	27	31	7	13	100
1901–5	20	29	33	5	13	100
1906–10	16	25	40	4	15	100
1911–15	24	20	42	3	11	100
1916–20	38	18	35	2	7	100
1921–5	33	17	32	5	13	100
1926–30	33	13	30	10	14	100
1931–5	30	13	32	9	16	100
1936–40	21	12	45	12	10	100
1942–5[1]	34	12	44	5	5	100
1946–50	21	13	45	17	4	100
1951–5	15	9	54	20	2	100
1956–60	16	8	59	14	3	100
1961–5	26	10	53	9	2	100
1966–70	31	10	44	9	6	100

Notes:

'Wool' includes spun wool and textiles; from 1942, 'meat and extracts' includes fats, guano etc., and 'hides' includes animal hair. Principal commodities in 'other' are live animals, sand and stone, and livestock by-products (before 1942).

1. Four year average.
2. Values are at official prices, unadjusted, before 1913; at 'market' prices 1913–40, adjusted 1918–25; in current dollars 1942–70.

Sources: DGEC, *Anuario Estadístico*; A. Melgar, E. Peguero, C. Lavagnino, *El Comercio Exportador del Uruguay 1962–1968* (Montevideo, Universidad de la República, Instituto de Economía, 1972); BCU, *Boletín Estadístico Mensual*.

The principal effect of the First World War on the structure of exports was the abrupt increase in the share of meat. Export of frozen beef grew fairly slowly until 1912. But in the following year a second *frigorífico* was installed, and in 1915 95,200 metric tons were exported, a figure only once exceeded before 1940. Demand for frozen beef declined later in the war, its place taken by an astonishing but short-lived increase in exports of canned beef. Wool exports, though less in volume than their pre-war peak, were sustained by higher prices.

While wool retained its position after the war as the most important single export commodity, the principal developments of note in the 1920s were the growth of *frigorífico* production and the recovery of arable agriculture. Although small quantities of chilled beef had been marketed during (and even before) the war, the perishability of the product limited its rapid development until after the war and post-war depression. From 1922, however, exports of chilled beef were at a high level, as were those of frozen beef and mutton; and the contraction of chilled exports in the protectionist world after 1931 was relatively small, and much less than for other *frigorífico* products. Increased exports of agricultural produce in the inter-war period reflected the recovery of wheat and linseed prices — the main export crops — from the abnormal conditions of the war.[4] However, climatic conditions caused considerable variation in the size of the exportable wheat surplus. The other category to expand its share of exports between the wars was the miscellaneous group, composed mainly of live cattle, sand, and animal products such as fats, bone, etc. Growth of such exports, though valuable, did not however imply either diversification away from livestock production, or the development of more highly processed or manufactured goods for export.

During the late 1930s wool prices improved sharply, while quantities exported increased, especially of washed wool. The effect of this was to reassert the importance of wool production after two decades in which export growth had been primarily associated with the meat trades. And although meat exports, especially of frozen beef, were maintained at good levels during the Second World War, wool dominated Uruguay's export performance during 1945–70. Increased wool production was only partly responsible for the growing share. Other factors were the extremely high prices which wool commanded during the Korean War boom; the growing proportion of beef production which was retained for domestic consumption, resulting in a sharp reduction in meat exports in the 1950s; and the increasing share of exports taken by wool which has been processed in some degree, especially tops. Apart from the dominance of wool and the decline of meat in the 1950s, the rise and fall of agricultural products has also been remarkable. Stimulated by very high guaranteed prices, wheat production increased dramatically in the decade 1948–58, producing substantial exportable surpluses in those years. In addition, rice, oil-seed, oil and cake contributed a much larger share to exports than before the war.

In analysing the destination of Uruguay's exports (which is summarised on the basis of uncorrected official data in Table 5.5) one encounters the full range of problems relating to data of this kind, especially the failure to use market prices for valuations, the importance of Buenos Aires as a port of transhipment for Uruguayan exports, and the re-export trade from certain European ports, especially Antwerp, to final destinations. Of these, the problem of transhipment through ports in neighbouring countries is probably the most important. The table shows that over 30 per cent of exports at the beginning of the century were directed to Brazil and Argentina. Some proportion of this trade consisted of goods in transit. For Brazil the proportion was probably

TABLE 5.5. Destination of exports, 1891–1970
(five-year averages, per cent of current value)

	1891–95	96–00	01–05	06–10	11–15	16–20	21–25	26–30	31–35	36–40	42–45[1]	46–50	51–55	56–60	61–65	66–70
UK	14.7	7.0	8.0	7.2	13.9	20.6	26.2	24.9	28.9	23.1	30.0	17.6	19.3	14.9	19.5	15.7
France	18.8	16.7	16.4	20.1	19.3	17.8	10.9	12.3	10.1	5.2						
Germany	5.6	9.9	12.0	12.9	12.1	1.7	15.3	14.9	15.0	12.4	1.4	23.0	29.4	36.4	35.4	31.0
Belgium	13.0	17.2	16.8	15.8	11.0	3.3	8.2	7.5	5.8	3.8						
Italy	1.9	2.1	2.6	3.3	7.1	9.5	4.7	6.1	8.7	4.8						
Other EEC 6	—	—	—	—	—	1.3	3.2	1.8	2.9	3.3						
Other W. Europe	2.2	2.0	2.5	2.7	4.5	7.5	1.7	1.3	2.6	6.3	8.5	9.5	8.7	10.6	9.6	15.1
E. Europe	—	0.1	0.1	0.1	0.2	—	—	1.6	1.7	3.4	—	3.4	3.7	14.8	9.3	7.7
Europe	56.2	55.0	58.4	62.1	68.1	61.7	70.2	70.4	75.7	62.3	39.9	53.5	61.1	76.7	73.8	69.5
USA	7.1	5.7	6.5	6.4	9.1	25.2	16.5	9.9	7.7	14.7	47.7	32.8	21.5	11.2	13.1	9.4
Argentina	13.8	15.4	17.6	18.2	13.5	9.2	7.5	12.8	8.3	6.9	10.1	9.9	12.8	8.4	8.5	13.2
Brazil	20.2	21.5	13.4	9.1	5.3	2.3	3.8	4.0	3.0	4.2						
Other America	2.1	1.8	3.2	3.2	3.2	1.2	1.8	1.2	0.3	1.3						
America	43.2	44.4	40.7	36.9	31.1	37.9	29.6	27.9	19.3	27.1	57.8	42.7	34.3	19.6	21.6	22.6
Other	0.6	0.6	0.9	1.0	0.8	0.4	0.2	1.7	4.2	10.4	2.4	3.7	4.5	3.9	4.7	7.8

Notes:
Before 1925 export values are substantially affected by the use of official prices, for which no correction has been made here. 'Other' includes unknown destinations, which in 1936–40 were 5.1 per cent of the total.
1. Four-year average.

Sources: DGEC, Anuario Estadístico; Universidad de la República, Estadísticas Básicas, table 40; BCU, Boletín Estadístico Mensual.

low: at the turn of the century the trade was overwhelmingly in jerked beef for domestic consumption, which accounts for the decline in Brazil's share of total exports from 1900. For Argentina, however, the proportion was very high: 89 per cent of exports to Argentina—mainly wool, hides and meat extract—were in transit to other destinations in the period 1896–1900.[5] It is likely therefore that Europe's share in Uruguay's exports in that five-year period was closer to 70 per cent than to the 55 per cent indicated in Table 5.5. This gives further emphasis to the European orientation of the export trades which has been an almost continuous characteristic of the twentieth century; only during war-time periods has the US market become very important to Uruguay.

Two further generalisations about export destinations may be made: that only in exceptional circumstances has a single country taken a commanding share of total exports—though the UK absorbed 25 per cent throughout the inter-war period; and only for a few products has a single national market been dominant. Wool was sold to Germany, France, Belgium, the UK and USA before 1914, for example, with no one market claiming more than a third of the total export. Hides similarly found markets throughout western Europe as well as in the USA. In both cases market diversification tended to be greater in the inter-war years, though during the 1914-18 war, and again in the late 1930s the USA took large shares of the wool clip. Agricultural exports before 1940 concentrated heavily on Argentina for wheat and linseed—presumably for re-export—and on Brazil for wheat flour. But the degree of concentration was greatest in the case of meat. Before 1914 exports of frozen mutton and beef went almost exclusively to Britain, and between the wars mutton continued to depend very largely on the British market. In the case of the premium meat product, chilled beef, dependence on British consumers was complete; but for frozen beef, by the mid-1920s British absorption was matched by that of France, with Belgium, Italy and Germany also taking significant shares.

After 1945 new trends in export markets became apparent. In comparison with the 1930s, though the relative shares of America and Europe are similar, the composition of the European market changed significantly. The share of Britain and the six original EEC countries—the traditional main markets—fell, to be replaced by the EFTA countries (minus the UK), Greece, Spain and the East European bloc, notably East Germany and Czechoslovakia. There was significant growth also in exports to the rest of the world, particularly to Israel and Hong Kong. By 1970 Uruguay had been forced to diversify the direction (through not significantly the content) of her export trade, through formal or informal bilateral trade relationships, in part because of problems of maintaining and assuring supply to traditional markets and because also of their tendency to retain a greater share of their domestic markets for domestic producers.

II. The Meat Industry

Since the beginning of this century the story of the meat industry in Uruguay has essentially been the establishment and growth of the frozen meat trade. The arrival of the *frigoríficos* proved to be of immense significance for the twentieth century economy. They provided a range of new exportable commodities which were largely responsible for the growth in the value of exports, especially in the two decades 1910–30. They paid higher prices for premium quality cattle, thus stimulating the process of livestock improvement and confirming the dominance within the landowning class of the modernising group of *estancieros*. They also introduced a massive concentration of foreign capital, dominated by US corporations. But whereas the USA was supplanting Britain as a source both of capital and of imports, the frozen meat trade increased Uruguay's dependence on the British market at a time when British interest in Uruguay was rapidly declining.

Not the least significance of the *frigoríficos* was the timing of their arrival, since by 1900 cattle producers were faced, as they had often been faced during the nineteenth century, with inadequate market outlets for their cattle stocks. The central problem which confronted producers was their distance from potential consumers in Europe, which prevented the export of fresh meat. Until this problem was solved, meat exports were limited to jerked beef (*tasajo*) produced by the *saladeros*, meat extract, and the export of live cattle. All these outlets were in some degree unsatisfactory.

The *saladero* was the earliest form of meat-processing establishment in the River Plate countries, dating from the late colonial period. Its characteristic product—dried salt beef—was prepared by cutting the flesh into strips, immersing it in salt, and laying it out to dry in the sun. But *tasajo* was not the only product. The *saladeros* also salted hides, and to an increasing degree during the nineteenth century made more efficient use of by-products—blood, bones and fat especially.[6] Indeed there are grounds for regarding the *tasajo* itself as another by-product, since in 1862 it formed only 28 per cent of the value of exported *saladero* output.[7] In spite of a high rate of turnover of enterprises in the industry, the number of *saladeros*—there were about twenty at the turn of the century[8]—seems to have varied little since the 1870s, and their distribution, in Montevideo and along the Littoral, reflected the importance of river transport. Large aggregations of capital were not required to establish a *saladero*, the principal equipment required being a boiler to reduce the fat, and European capital showed no interest in the industry. It is likely that the importance of the industry as an employer—the work force was estimated at 6000 in 1872[9]—had been more or less maintained down to 1900.

Although the importance of the *saladero* to the livestock industry is indisputable, absorbing 54 per cent of recorded cattle slaughter and live export in the decade 1895–1904, it is equally clear that the salting plants were a strongly conservative influence on the industry, and left it vulnerable to changes in demand. Although, as has been indicated, *tasajo* seems to have increased its share of total *saladero* output during the nineteenth century, it was nonetheless an unsatisfactory way to market beef. *Tasajo* was a fairly unpalatable product, for which a taste was most likely to be acquired under duress: the principal consumers being the slave (or, after 1886 and 1888 respectively, emancipated) populations of Cuba and Brazil. Europe was offered *tasajo*, and declined it.[10] Hence a low-value product was confined almost entirely to two traditional markets, where its position was being undermined in the final decades of the century less by the end of slavery than by US competition in Cuba, and by protection in Brazil for the *saladeros* of Rio Grande do Sul. In spite of attempts to increase the efficiency of the industry, by the beginning of this century it was only the reduced production of *tasajo* in Argentina which enabled the Uruguayan industry to survive.

Moreover, as long as the *saladero* remained the principal outlet for the cattle producers, the livestock sector remained tied to an institution which frustrated the efforts of 'progressive' landowners. For while the latter were attempting to improve the quality of cattle by the import of pedigree stock, the *saladeros* bought low-price, lean, unimproved *criollo* stock. The high proportion of final output accounted for by hides meant that the *criollo* beast, with its thick heavy hide, was ideally suited. Lean flesh was preferred because there was difficulty in drying fat adequately. And in addition, while the sheep flock totalled some 18 million by 1900, the *saladeros* could make no use of mutton.

Many of these shortcomings were also associated with the production of meat extract. Liebig's Extract of Meat Company began operations at Fray Bentos in 1865, and its near-monopoly of extract production persisted until its assets in Uruguay were sold in 1924. The volume of its cattle purchases—not less than 100,000 head annually between 1870 and 1910—opened a new outlet for cattle producers on the Littoral,[11] though their participation in the resulting income generation was surely less spectacular than that of Liebig's shareholders, mostly British, who received dividends averaging over 18 per cent annually during 1883–1903, and 23 per cent annually during the next twenty years.[12] But the general significance of Liebig's for the development of the rural economy was limited: 'the Fray Bentos plant had in fact merely added a product to the old organisation of the *saladeros*, for grease and hides continued to be the mainstays of the business'.[13] Indeed, until 1884 Liebig's also produced *tasajo*. The contribution of Liebig's to the modernisation of the cattle herds was very limited. The most important feature of their purchases was that they should be cheap. The *criollo* cattle were thus perfectly suited to their needs. the extract itself was a product of recognised quality, but never achieved market acceptance as a replacement for meat. It was demanded in Europe largely to supply the needs of armies in the field, and was therefore subject to substantial demand fluctuations. Production of extract made rather more efficient use of the same raw material employed by *saladeros*, but did not offer an adequate alternative outlet for the abundance of low-quality cattle.

The export of live cattle to Europe was a trade which originated late in the nineteenth century and never grew to importance. An initiative in 1889 to establish an exporting company did not survive the Baring crisis:[14] even had it done so, it is unlikely that it would have found sufficient quantity of improved stock to bear the high freight costs to British ports. A decade later the trade was established, but in such small quantities that the cattle were shipped from Argentine ports; and in any case the loss of the British market in 1900 because of foot and mouth disease in the River Plate countries, and competition from the *frigorí-ficos* in Argentina, spelled the end of live exports to Europe. But livestock still moved to Argentina, to meet the demand of the *frigoríficos*, and in this way the process of cross-breeding was en-couraged even before the first Uruguayan *frigorífico* began to slaughter in 1904. The export of stock to Argentina (whether or not for re-export) thus represented an intermediate stage in the modernisation of cattle-raising. It benefited primarily the *estancieros* of the Littoral, identified at least since the 1870s as in the vanguard of progress, and emphasised the divergence of interests between themselves and the *caudillo* landowners of the north. It was by no means entirely coincidental that the final rebellion of the latter came in the first year of *frigorífico* slaughter.

The first successful *frigorífico*, La Uruguaya, was formed in 1902 and began slaughter two years later. Led by Manuel Lessa, a member of the first directorate of the Banco de la República, the company had thirty-five shareholders representative of the landed and banking interests. But although the *frigorífico* was potentially the solution to the problems of the livestock sector, this was not immediately evident in practice. In its first five seasons the *frigorífico*'s total slaughter was only 65,000 cattle and 580,000 sheep. More than once the shareholders tried to interest foreign capital in the acquisition of the 'languishing establishment',[15] but not until 1911 did they find a buyer (by which time profits were being earned).[16] The reasons for the early unprofitability of La Frigorífica Uruguaya were doubtless the same as for the late appearance of the industry in Uruguay. It was not that the technology of meat freezing was novel, or that acceptance for frozen meat in the British market still had to be won. The trade from Argentina had been established since the early 1880s, and export of Argentine chilled beef began in 1901, as exportable surpluses of beef from the USA diminished. Indeed, in 1884 the River Plate Fresh Meat Company had installed a freezing plant at the Uruguayan town Colonia, facing Buenos Aires across the River Plate, but the venture was ended in 1888 for lack of suitable livestock. So after 1904, while the import of pure-bred cattle and sheep occurred on an unprecedented scale, the production of fatstock in adequate numbers was necessarily delayed.

The year 1911, in which export of chilled beef began, marked a significant stage in the development of the industry. The reluctance of the owners of La Uruguaya to risk more capital in increased capacity, and the steady decline of the *saladeros*, once more introduced the threat of overproduction. The incoming administration of Batlle y Ordóñez proposed to form a second *frigorífico*, with a majority holding by the state and a minority participation of British capital.[17] Whether demand for increased *frigorífico* capacity would have overcome conservative opposition to state participation in the industry was not put to the test. Four years earlier, US capital had entered the Argentine meat trade, dominated until then by British companies, and embarked on an aggressive drive to increase its share of the market by emphasising chilled beef and paying top prices for high-grade cattle. Competition within the Argentine industry was intense, until late in 1911 the first pool was formed to distribute agreed shares of the market; but during the competitive phase cattle prices were high and rising, and the attraction of Uruguay, where the price of cross-bred steers was stable and slightly lower in 1910–11 than in 1905–6,[18] must have increased as a low-cost source of supply. Swift and Company were the first to make an offer for La Uruguaya, but were outbid by the Argentine-owned Sansinena, in February 1911. Swift then acquired the premises of a *saladero*, and their Frigorífico Montevideo began slaughter late in 1912. In spite of the increased capacity installed by Sansinena, Swift immediately dominated the market. Cattle prices doubled between 1911 and 1913, Swift taking 58 per cent of cattle slaughtered in their first full year of production. By 1916 their share was 74 per cent.

The expansive phase of *frigorífico* development in Uruguay thus occurred as a reflection of its development in Argentina. The formative, unprofitable phase had been borne by private Uruguayan capital, while the entry of foreign capital was timed to take advantage of good supplies of improved stock at low prices. The formation of the first pool in December 1911 had not included Uruguayan producers, since Uruguay's participation in the trade was marginal. With competition in Argentina restricted by the pool, the Uruguayan cattle market now became the arena in which an improved share of the trade could be won. In 1911, 23,200 cattle were acquired for chilling and freezing, and in the next three years the figure rose to 68,500, 132,700, and 278,400.[19] Such rapid growth outside the pool strained the agreement, which was ended in April 1913. When the second pool agreement was reached in mid-1914 the Uruguayan *frigoríficos* were allocated quotas in the River Plate beef trade. The size of the quotas, however, emphasised Uruguay's marginal status in the trade. Swift's quota was 5.862 per cent, Sansinena's 2.966 per cent.[20] The mutton trade was also divided between the two plants, but as proportions of Uruguayan rather than River Plate shipments.

The operations of the beef trust and its restrictive pool arrangements caused little alarm at first. The activities of the trust in Chicago were well known in the River Plate—competing British interests saw to that[21]— but in Uruguay there were few grounds for complaint. With the outbreak of war in Europe, demand for frozen and tinned beef increased enormously. The annual average *frigorífico* cattle slaughter in 1917–19 was more than twice its level in 1914. Prices held fairly steady at a high level; the loss of the trade in chilled beef affected Uruguayan producers much less than their Argentine counterparts because the trade was scarcely established in Uruguay. The industry's capacity was further increased when the Frigorífico Artigas, a venture initiated by Uruguayan capital in 1915 but quickly absorbed by Armour of Chicago, began operations in 1917. The meat trust was denounced late in 1916 by Herrera, one of the Blanco party leaders, for discriminatory treatment against the Uruguaya plant,[22] but such conflicts seem to have been rare. Not until post-war recession in Europe put an end to the decade of immense prosperity was the meat trust identified as a harmful influence.

The collapse of demand in the meat trade in 1920–2 reflected not only the fall in purchasing power associated with the transition to peace-time conditions, but also the vast stocks of frozen and canned beef built up during the war through government contracts to the suppliers. The release of these stocks had a severely depressing effect on the market. In 1919 the Uruguayan *frigoríficos* had processed 663,500 cattle: in the next two years this figure fell to 392,600 and 275,700, and not until 1926 was the level of 1919 reattained. The price collapse followed. From 1920 average steer prices fell from a peak value of $68.4 to $45.7 and $31.8 in the two succeeding years.[23] But whereas the volume of cattle purchases did recover well, especially in the second half of the 1920s, steer prices remained weak, averaging only $38.7 in the rest of the decade. It was in these circumstances that dissatisfaction with the operation of the *frigoríficos* grew, resulting eventually in the creation of the Frigorífico Nacional. Remarkably, however, they were exempted from attack by Martínez Lamas, whose criticisms were reserved mainly for the impositions of the *batllista* state.

That the packing companies restricted competition amongst themselves by the operation of an agreed total export and quota system was well known.[24] A number of factors made this policy both desirable to the companies, and possible. It was desirable because the capacity of the market—Britain, mainly—to absorb supplies of meat was limited, such that during periods of unrestricted competition between the *frigoríficos*, when the supply of meat was greatly increased, prices fell away badly. This was especially true of chilled beef, which, if not disposed of within about forty days from slaughter, had to be frozen and sold off at a loss. It was possible, moreover, because of the highly concentrated and integrated structure of the industry. In Uruguay there were only three buyers—four after 1924, when Vestey's acquired Liebig's newly-installed freezing plant at Fray Bentos—but Swift and Armour alone acquired 78 per cent of cattle for *frigorífico* slaughter during 1920–9. The degree of concentration was less in Argentina, but from 1911 the industry was led by the US companies. The advantages of a pool agreement were emphasised by the usual form of shipping arrangements, with insulated shipping space being engaged for a certain period, normally for as long as five years.[25] In the British market the *frigoríficos* themselves sold direct to the retailer via their own cold storage capacity and stalls at Smithfield. Vestey's (Union Cold Storage Co.) in fact reached the consumer direct via their own network of retail outlets—some 2400 in the mid-1920s.[26]

The *frigorífico* pool essentially operated as a shipping conference of South American meat importers in London who allocated shipping space amongst the companies in line with the agreed quotas. Clearly it was to the advantage of the companies to share out the available insulated shipping space in this way, since freights were payable on space chartered, whether it was filled or not. An additional virtue claimed for the conference was that it reduced the likelihood of alternate gluts and shortages in the market, since each producer knew the production and shipping plans of the others. The *frigorífico* companies thus held a position of immense power in the frozen meat trade, buying cattle from the landowners and selling in Europe to retailers or even direct to consumers. They bought either at Tablada, the central cattle market in Montevideo, where cattle could scarcely be withdrawn from the market if prices were low since this would entail costs for feed or a return journey to the pastures; or they bought forward on the *estancia*. After 1924 Sansinena's participation in the Uruguayan trade rapidly diminished, leaving only Armour and Swift to compete in Montevideo. When Liebig's requested the tax concessions enjoyed by the other *frigoríficos* for the freezing plant it proposed to install, it was claimed that a new competitor would limit the power of the beef trust. In practice, however, the location of Fray Bentos tended to limit purchases for the plant to the Littoral region, and although transport costs for cattle to Fray Bentos were much lower, it was a source of grievance to *estancieros* that the Frigorífico Anglo's (Vestey's) prices were persistently lower than those of the American packers in Montevideo. Sales to the *frigoríficos* were not the only outlet for cattle producers, but the capacity of the domestic market to absorb more was limited by the fact that beef was already, in Montevideo at least, the staple item of diet.

Thus, as a British government publication observed about the *frigorífico* industry, 'the ownership of the works, in a country [*sic*] such as South America, may be said to be, of itself, the key position'.[27] The power of the *frigoríficos vis à vis* the cattle producers was contrasted in the report with the structure of the industry in Australia and New Zealand, where a far larger number of packing plants inhibited market domination. For the Uruguayan landowners the critical issue was the power of the *frigoríficos* to fix the prices at which they would buy livestock; the latter of course denied that price agreements, of the kind operated by the beef trust in Chicago, were employed. But the suspicions of the Uruguayans were echoed even in the UK:

> Agreement as to buying prices for cattle would, of course, sensibly weaken the position of the producer overseas . . . All that can be said is that, if a working agreement does or were to exist among the South American companies as to prices to be paid to the producer and as to quantities to be shipped, their ownership both of works and means of distribution would place them in an unassailable position in the chilled beef trade.[28]

Yet, at least in the case of Uruguay, the relevant question might seem to be less whether prices were formally agreed, but rather whether such agreements were even necessary for the *frigoríficos*, given the existence of a high degree of concentration in the industry and agreements on total exports and the shares for each plant.

During two periods the pool system collapsed and a 'meat war' broke out between the contending companies. As indicated above, until 1914 Uruguay was not included in the pool, and during 1912–14 (i.e. following the arrival of Swift) the cattle market was characterised by a rapid increase in both volume and price. It appears however that these happy consequences for the cattle producers owed less to the competitive model than to the market strategy of the Swift corporation: to develop the premium trade (chilled) for which top-quality cattle were required, and to secure a dominating share of the market in order to exploit installed capacity fully and in anticipation of future pool arrangements. In 1925 the companies again went to war over their respective shares of the trade, at the conclusion of which, in 1927, Sansinena had sustained substantial losses and was virtually eliminated from the export trade. But any hopes entertained by the cattle producers that competition between the *frigoríficos* would restore prosperity were to be disappointed. Sheep slaughter did increase dramatically, but there is no price information available. But in the case of cattle, only for calves was there any sign of increasing demand, and steer prices were at their lowest in 1927 since 1922. The reasons for this appear to be two-fold. First, the industry was no longer in a rapid-growth phase; indeed the British market was thought to be at risk from pressure for protection for Dominion producers.[29] Second, the real objective of the meat war in the

River Plate as a whole seems to have been to shed the marginal companies[30]—represented in Uruguay by Sansinena. The other three companies were all so strongly entrenched that losses additional to those which were being declared could hardly have been justified by the prospect of a marginal increase in market share.[31]

For livestock producers, therefore, the 1920s was a decade of disillusion and resentment with the operations of the foreign-owned *frigorífico* industry. The dispute raises important issues concerning relations between a domestic economic elite and foreign capitalist groups whose cooperation is required for the status of the elite to be maintained. Although 'collaboration' may be a useful first approximation to describe the relationship of the domestic elite with foreign capital, the long-run identity of interest implied does not preclude acute short-run periods of friction. Landowners were already aggrieved at the poor service they received from the foreign-owned railway system. Now in the 1920s they faced in addition low prices for their livestock from the *frigoríficos*. Dependent economically on foreign capital for the commercialisation of their production, the livestock producers were obliged to invoke the power of the state to act in their defence against foreign capital and to strengthen their position in relation to other domestic groups.

In 1915 Manuel Quintela, president of the Asociación Rural, had identified increased taxation on livestock producers and the operations of the beef trust as the principal dangers facing the rural sector.[32] The vulnerability which he and other rural leaders saw in the inadequate control of the sector over the state machinery was expressed in the formation of the Federación Rural in 1916 to press politically their interests. But their capacity to limit the power of the *frigoríficos* was small. In Argentina, confrontation came in 1923 over minimum-price legislation, and resulted in a resounding victory for the foreign companies. In Uruguay confrontation was avoided, though the issue—low fatstock prices—was the same. During 1923 a number of measures were proposed, including anti-trust laws and commissions to give more information on and control over the trade; but the most important was for the creation of a Frigorífico Nacional.

When state participation in the *frigorífico* industry was first proposed in 1911, the reason was the need for increased capacity in the industry, and the proposal was abandoned because of the arrival of North American capital. Now in the 1920s, ironically, the function of the Nacional would be broadly to participate in the meat trades and thus, by increased competition in the cattle market, to induce the other *frigoríficos* to adopt policies more favourable to the national interest. The proposal raised obvious political problems. The critical question in deciding the constitution of the Nacional was to determine whose interests coincided with those of the nation. In the submission of the

Federación Rural, 'The Frigorífico Nacional is an organisation intended to protect the interests of the livestock owners, which are none other than those of the nation, since it is axiomatic to say that both are joined in an inseparable amalgam.'[33] While maintaining a generally pessimistic view on the likely benefit, the livestock sector had three main preoccupations regarding the project during the extensive debates on it: first, that the necessary capital should be raised by a loan and not by a tax whose incidence might fall on themselves; second, that it should not be organised as an *ente autónomo*, subject to the same bureaucratic and inefficient direction as the rest of the public sector;[34] and third, that landowners should form a majority of the Directorate.

The project which was finally approved in 1928 was a compromise between these objectives and those of (especially) the *batllista* political group. A tax was to be levied on all live animal sales, to amortise the initial loan capital. The Nacional was not organised in the same way as other *entes autónomos*, but the livestock sector had only two-fifths' representation initially on the Directorate. This would increase as shares, based on eventual profits, were distributed to livestock suppliers. It was to compete with the other companies in export markets, but was also granted a monopoly of the supply of clean meat to Montevideo— replacing the inefficient slaughterhouses of Barra de Santa Lucía. To begin operations as soon as possible, the Nacional rented the disused plant of La Frigorífica Uruguaya of Sansinena. Slaughter began in June 1929.

The significance of the Frigorífico Nacional, at least in the pre-depression period, was perhaps more in the manner of its creation than in its operation.[35] Cattle prices became firmer at the end of the 1920s, but it is doubtful whether much credit could go to the new enterprise since demand in the principal markets was buoyant at this time. On the other hand, the new institution immediately gave notice of its intention to support the livestock producers; 'it has been the policy of the National plant to pay slightly higher prices for its cattle than that offered by the American "frigoríficos"'.[36] Perhaps because of this, Montevideo consumers, despite representation on the Directorate, found that their meat was supplied no cheaper, though inefficient retailing was alleged to be responsible.[37] In the export trades, its capacity to participate was limited in the short run by the existing conference agreement on shipping space quotas. But in any case, the depression produced radical changes in the meat export trade; and having produced an institution to cope (however imperfectly) with one problem, Uruguay now faced another far greater.

The effect of the depression and the restrictionist commercial policies of the 1930s was devastating for Uruguay's export trades in general, and especially so for meat. Total exports reached a peak value in 1930, but in 1932 were only 57.8 per cent of that peak. Recovery was not apparent until 1935, and was then due primarily to a marked revival in the price of wool and expanded purchases by the USA of canned meat. In the fresh meat trades revival was both limited and delayed. By 1935 chilled beef was only 49.0 per cent of 1930 value, frozen mutton 27.7 per cent and frozen beef 26.8 per cent. Even in 1937 (the best year of the decade) chilled beef, the most buoyant of the trades, was only two-thirds of the value and 70 per cent of the volume of 1930. This poor performance was related to Uruguay's dependence on the British market, to her marginal position in the River Plate trade, and to the demand from Dominion producers (with chilled beef exports from Australia and New Zealand now technically feasible) for preferential access to the British market. In 1930 Uruguay sold all her chilled beef, 83 per cent of frozen mutton, and 39 per cent of frozen beef to Britain; but she commanded only 9.5, 22.6 and 26.9 per cent respectively of South American shipments in that year. Uruguay was therefore much more vulnerable than Argentina in the British market, in terms of both her hold on the market—by 1932 the proportions of South American shipments from Uruguay had dropped to 5.7, 10.6 and 23.1 per cent respectively—and her bargaining strength with the British government.[38]

Out of the 'muddle . . . *ad hoc* concessions and desperate last-minute bargaining'[39] of the 1932 Ottawa Conference, preferential treatment was granted to Dominion meat exporters. Already strong in the frozen meat trades, they especially sought to reduce imports of chilled beef into the UK which reduced the marketability of their frozen meat and inhibited the development of their own chilled trade. The displacement of South American meat supplies from the British market was thus a process already under way, to be accelerated by the Ottawa Agreements.[40] The basic provision of the Agreements relating to meat was that while Australia and New Zealand were to have duty-free access (while limiting exports to the UK during 1933),[41] chilled beef from South America was to be limited to the level of July 1931—June 1932, and frozen meat was to fall to 65 per cent of the level of that period. For Uruguay these arrangements were severe; while South America's share of the British market had already contracted by 1931–2, Uruguay's share of the South American trade had also shrunk, as has been indicated. In the Roca–Runciman Agreement of 1933, whose provisions were extended to Uruguay, it was agreed that a reduction of more than 10 per cent on 1931–2 chilled beef exports would be matched by an equivalent reduction from all meat-exporting countries. The quota of the British market which Uruguay in the event received represented a 9.3 per cent reduction on the base year in each of 1933/4/5, and in the frozen trades a reduction by 1935 equal to 35 per cent.[42]

The imposition of these cuts, particularly damaging to Uruguay because of her poor performance during the base year, did not result in a diversification of meat export markets. Throughout the 1930s Britain remained the only market for chilled beef and absorbed at least 80 per cent of frozen mutton consignments. France, the other traditional market for frozen beef, restricted her imports from Uruguay after 1935; and though Italy and later Germany increased in importance, Britain continued to be at significant market in this trade. Overall, therefore, restrictions imposed by Britain condemned the meat trade to a decade of stagnation.

From free access before the depression, and quota arrangements during the1930s, the meat trade became the subject of inter-governmental contracts during the Second World War and post-war periods. Though the industry prospered during the war, complementing the British policy of expanding arable acreage at the expense of meat production, in the 1950s it encountered increasing difficulties as a result of which Swift and Armour ceased operations, and exports fell to very low levels. Although the Armour plant resumed slaughter the following year (1958) after the creation of EFCSA, the traditional *frigoríficos*, employing antiquated equipment and requiring a large throughput of cattle, were at an increasing disadvantage. Ten years after the withdrawal of International Packers Ltd, owners of the Swift and Armour installations, the Frigorífico Anglo also closed its doors, in 1967. The place vacated by these companies in the export trade has been filled by a number of small plants dispersed in the interior of the country, apparently nationally-owned but with the participation of foreign capital. The position of the Frigorífico Nacional was also progressively undermined. Its monopoly of Montevideo supply ensured for many years a high level of slaughter; but outdated plant and a process of bureaucratisation raised its costs, and its monopoly was breached by black market suppliers. Economic difficulties were aggravated by a political climate increasingly hostile to public enterprise, and by the beginning of the 1970s the Nacional had little effective importance in the cattle market or in the meat trade.

The regime of meat contracts between the governments of the UK and Uruguay was initiated within a few weeks of the outbreak of war in 1939.[43] The contracts, which stipulated prices and quantities of each type of meat, gave Uruguayan producers some security in what was now almost the only meat export market, but at very low prices; and in order to maintain cattle prices at remunerative levels, a subsidy equivalent to 23 per cent on cattle prices was payable to the *frigoríficos* during the first contract. In subsequent contracts—six were agreed during the war, five after the war—the price in sterling increased and the level of subsidies apparently fell. However, during the war Uruguay experienced a shortage of cattle in the face of domestic demand and export commitments, as a result of drought and disease, and in the mid-1940s Montevideo consumed larger quantities of mutton and prepared beef ('hot-packs') in order to ensure fulfilment of the British contracts.[44] The domestic price of beef was raised by 12 per cent in 1944, but the Frigorífico Nacional continued in deficit, to the benefit of producers and consumers.

By 1947 the restoration of alternative export markets paying prices higher than those of the UK produced a significant change in Uruguayan government policy. While the Nacional was now to have priority in acquiring cattle for home consumption, cattle prices were to be fixed in accordance with prices ruling in international markets and beef for home consumption would be priced to cover this cost. The effect of this was to produce a 34 per cent increase in the price of steers in 1947 compared with the previous year. Meanwhile, losses made by *frigoríficos* in exporting at unremunerative prices to the UK were to be subsidised from profits on sales to free markets.[45] The level of the subsidy was determined not by the difference between UK and free market prices, but by the losses declared by the *frigoríficos* themselves on sales to the UK and for home consumption. Thus was introduced the problem of subsidies to the privately-owned *frigoríficos* which became such an important issue in the 1950s. In the absence of adequate accounting techniques to check the losses declared, the Frigorífico Nacional was once more employed in the public interest as an *ente testigo*, taking the costs which it declared as a standard on which to assess those of Swift, Artigas (Armour) and Anglo. On this basis the costs of the US companies were found to be within 4 per cent of those of the Nacional, but those of Anglo were 20 per cent higher for chilled and frozen, and 25 per cent for canned beef.[46] Anglo, in fact, had made losses on its sales to free markets, as well as to the UK and the home market by the time the Fondo de Compensaciones Ganaderas (FCG) was wound up in January 1950. Although Anglo could buy its cattle cheaper, through its proximity to the producing areas, its export quota was relatively small, and in addition it had to sustain the costs of transhipping its export output at Buenos Aires. Moreover, it had a history of poor labour relations. Nonetheless Anglo's failure to earn profits in any market made a nonsense of the FCG, but even so its claims for an additional subsidy were partly met.[47] The management of the Fund was made still more difficult by the downward movement of free market prices in 1949, and the sharp increase in *frigorífico* labour costs following the establishment of the wages councils in 1948.[48]

The subsequent history of the industry, until the closure of Swift and Artigas in 1957, was one of continuous deterioration in the face of conflicting policy objectives:

High prices for livestock producers; adequate profits, which have customarily been high, for the *frigoríficos*; high wages for the work force; low prices to consumers; meat contracts which do not cover declared costs; a search for free markets whose prices, together with exchange profits, serve to plug all the holes. The pyramid does not rest on its base.[49]

The central problem of the trade was that the local currency earnings of meat exports were not sufficient to satisfy the demands of the principal participants in the trade—cattle producers, foreign-owned *frigoríficos*, and their labour force. The crisis was heightened by the diversion of exportable production to the domestic market, in which the Frigorífico Nacional still exercised a monopoly, resulting in very high and rising per capita beef consumption. But of course the underlying problem was the inadequate supply of cattle to meet the *frigorífico* industry's requirements (Table 5.6).

TABLE 5.6. Cattle slaughter, 1935–59
(five-year averages, 1935–9 = 100)

	Total slaughter	Slaughter for consumption	Per cent of total slaughter for export	Average real price of steers[1]
1935–9	100.0	100.0	41.9	100.0
1940–4	101.4	93.2	46.4	133.5
1945–9	81.1	89.0	36.1	130.9
1950–4	103.5	120.9	31.8	134.2
1955–9	82.7	114.4	19.6	170.2

Note:
1. Per live kilo for steers bought by Frigorífico Nacional.

Source: BROU, *Producción Agropecuaria*, pp. 84, 162.

In order to meet the income aspirations of the participants in the trade, a subsidy was necessary. The FCG was abandoned in 1950 because the revenue earned in the high-price markets was insufficient to compensate the losses incurred in the low-price (but large and relatively secure) UK market. But the form of the subsidy remained effectively unchanged until 1953. During that time cattle prices were established by the government—a regime modified in 1951 by the introduction of differential prices for different grades and types—and having thus raised the main component of the *frigoríficos*' direct costs government then paid to the *frigoríficos* the difference between their peso earnings and their costs plus profit. The system was clearly fallible in that government was unable to monitor the costs declared by the *frigoríficos*, except on the basis of those of the Nacional and in spite of the creation of a Comisión de Costos in 1951, and the companies had a clear incentive to inflate their declared costs and thus collect a larger subsidy. While the price differential for chilled and frozen between the UK and other markets persisted, improved exchange rate treatment was inappropriate since this (and therefore the withdrawal of the subsidy) would have diverted supplies away from the UK market, to which Uruguay had contractual obligations. However, for corned beef and extract there was no such differential, and in 1952 the preferential rate of $2.35 to the dollar was introduced for these products.

In April 1953 the regime of fixed cattle prices was abandoned. Exchange rates remained unchanged, flat-rate subsidies were payable per ton of chilled and frozen beef exported to the UK, and cattle prices were left to find their own level. In principle the system of payment of subsidies to the private *frigoríficos* on the basis of their own cost declarations was over. During 1954 it became necessary to extend the regime of flat-rate subsidies for beef exports to all markets, and the private *frigoríficos* continued to press the government for indemnification of their increasing costs—in 1954, for example, for losses resulting from higher labour costs. Not until March 1956 was there a general devaluation of exchange rates for meat exports: the rate for frozen beef then fell from the basic $1.519 to $3.10 to the dollar.

For the private *frigoríficos*, the penalty exchange rate treatment of meat exports represented the basic obstacle to profitable operations: hence their expectation that the free determination of cattle prices without improved exchange rate would result in lower prices.[50] In fact, however, cattle prices rose above the level at which they had been previously fixed; while the Nacional could meet higher prices, through the subsidy on domestic consumption and frequent subventions from the state, the private *frigoríficos* were in the market to take advantage of the preferential rate for corned beef exports, and to secure an adequate throughput of animals to reduce the burden of fixed costs.

In 1954 the meat industry entered a critical phase which exposed its basic weakness. The number of cattle slaughtered in that year was 20 per cent less than the average of the previous five years. Not until the 1960s was there any recovery, and only in the middle of that decade was the level of fifteen years previously regained. A number of additional factors were operating at this time which accentuated the long-term stagnation of the livestock industry. The private *frigoríficos*, excluded from participation in the trade for domestic consumption and therefore wholly dependent on export markets, blamed exchange rate policy which discriminated against livestock producers:

The exchange rate for meat must keep relation with that for other agricultural products. Although this year cattle prices have been remunerative for livestock producers, it is unquestionable that other forms of agricultural production have been more profitable . . . The greater part of the lands which were artificial pasture for finishing the preparation of livestock are now used for agriculture.[51]

There is no doubt that the very high guaranteed prices for cereals during the late 1940s and 1950s did deprive the livestock sector of half a million hectares. Although the subsidy to the *frigoríficos* enabled them to buy cattle at the official prices before 1953, these prices showed no tendency to increase in real terms and cattle production became relatively unattractive. However, though the loss of pasture was real enough, probably the fall in *frigorífico* slaughter in the 1950s (Table 5.7) exaggerated the fall in cattle production. Particularly for northern landowners the illicit sale of cattle across the border to Brazil had long been traditional when domestic prices were unattractive, and smuggling undoubtedly accounted for part of the apparent fall in production.[52] A further loss to the *frigorífico* industry—though much smaller—resulted from the growth during the 1950s of black market supplies to the Montevideo market. A disproportionate number of slaughterhouses were established in neighbouring departments—small, unencumbered by bureaucracy, and subject to less rigorous sanitary inspection—which were able to compete (illegally) with the Frigorífico Nacional in supplying Montevideo, in spite of the subsidy which the latter received in this trade.[53]

The inadequate supply of cattle proved fatal to the traditional

TABLE 5.7. *Frigorífico* capacity and slaughter, 1950–7
(thousand head of cattle)

	Nacional	Swift	Artigas	Anglo	Castro	Total	Proportion of capacity (per cent)
Capacity[1]	600	335	280	335	150	1700	
Slaughter							
1950	495	239	183	165	5	1087	63.9
1951	377	198	150	128	48	901	53.0
1952	437	141	116	85	52	831	48.9
1953	491	163	125	81	46	906	53.3
1954	270	82	67	52	57	528	31.1
1955	391	37	28	17	30	503	29.6
1956	352	99	86	22	52	611	35.9
1957	234	91	71	45	39	480	28.2

Note:
1. On the basis of one eight-hour shift, 250 days per year.

Source: G. Bernhard, *Comercio de Carnes en el Uruguay* (Montevideo, Aguilar e Irazabal, 1958) p. 168 (capacity); G. Bernhard, *Uruguay en el Mundo de la Carne* (Montevideo, Aguilar e Irazabal, 1967) p. 59.

frigorífico industry. Since the Nacional had priority in purchasing for domestic production, the fall in output was concentrated in the private sector. As long as cattle were available, even at prices which were uneconomic at ruling exchange rates, it had been possible for the *frigoríficos* to function by securing subsidies to ensure their profitability, using the threat of unemployment to secure the compliance of government. Now the lack of cattle exposed a cost structure heavily burdened by a fixed component. Cost estimates per ton of frozen beef, for the Frigorífico Nacional, indicate that whereas raw materials fell from 85.2 per cent to 56.6 per cent between 1942–4 and 1955–7, over the same period direct labour costs rose from 2.4 per cent to 7.3 per cent, and indirect costs from 11.0 per cent to 34.8 per cent.[54] These figures only roughly approximate the position of the private *frigoríficos*, which though they were not burdened with a bureaucracy,[55] suffered much more from excess capacity (Table 5.7). During 1956–7 an investigating commission of Congress attempted to ascertain the costs and profits of the foreign-owned *frigoríficos*. Finally, after several years punctuated by periods of idleness and threats of closure, Swift and Artigas abandoned operations in December 1957. The following year the Frigorífico Castro, a comparatively small factory which began freezing in 1948, also closed.

Excess capacity was one of the primary problems confronting the *frigorífico* industry in the 1950s; but the sudden loss of about 45 per cent of total capacity did not prove to be a viable solution, largely because of the consequent unemployment. The assets of the US companies were acquired in 1958 by the newly-formed EFCSA, whose share capital was held by the work force but which apparently financed its operations by credits raised abroad,[56] and the Artigas plant was reopened. The Castro plant also resumed operations, so that in the early 1960s the average rate of utilisation of installed capacity in the traditional *frigoríficos* was below 40 per cent.[57] The industry thus remained high-cost, while its position, and in particular that of the Frigorífico Nacional, was further undermined by larger political and economic processes at work.

In the elections of November 1958 the Blanco party, strongly representative of rural interests, emerged victorious. Its orientation characterised particularly by the Monetary and Exchange Reform Law of 1959, was to give substantial incentives to the agricultural export sector and to replace the *dirigismo* of the Colorados by greater market freedom. Consistent with this policy was the decision earlier in 1959 to end the Nacional's monopoly of the supply of meat to Montevideo though all licensed suppliers were still to employ the slaughter facilities of the Nacional. The effect of this was seriously to weaken the Nacional which, until its monopoly of supply was restored in 1964, secured less than 30 per cent of the Montevideo market.[58]

More damaging to the traditional industry, however, was the participation of new exporting groups in the meat export trade which provided severe competition for supplies of cattle. These, though recovering from the depressed levels of the 1950s, were still far from adequate. The new entrants to the trade appear to have been attracted by the comparatively generous fiscal and exchange treatment for meat exports which had been granted at the end of the 1950s in order to make the inefficient traditional industry profitable. All the plants had considerably smaller capacity than the old *frigoríficos*; indeed only a small number installed freezing equipment themselves. But in other respects the newcomers varied considerably. Many of the slaughterhouses outside Montevideo feeding the black market entered the export trade in the early 1960s. Such establishments, authorised to export, amounted to about 20 per cent of capacity in the industry in 1964 (excluding plants supplying the interior of the country).[59] In addition, a number of intermediaries entered the industry briefly in the mid-1960s, operating essentially by renting slaughter facilities, cold storage and transport. The temporary nature of many of these operations is indicated by the fact that during 1962–8 no less than 62 firms participated in the meat export trade, but the maximum number in any single year was 34.[60] Foreign capital financed a significant proportion of these ventures, such that during the 1960s 'there was an increase in the degree of external domination [in the meat export trade] compared with the previous decade'.[61]

By the late 1960s the traditional *frigoríficos* in general, and the Frigorífico Nacional in particular, were in a state of crisis: starved of the volume of cattle required for efficient production, burdened with obsolete equipment, and with government policy increasingly hostile to public enterprise. In 1967 the Frigorífico Anglo closed. The plant, offered for sale by Vestey's, was rented by the government presumably to offer some opportunity of employment, and was eventually expropriated. In 1969, the Nacional was again deprived of its monopoly of supply for the Montevideo market. In the allocation of quotas the Nacional received 15 per cent, and the Fray Bentos (ex-Anglo) plant was allocated a similar proportion. EFCSA, which during the 1960s secured some 30 per cent of the export trade, received a quota of 28 per cent of the domestic market. In 1968, however, the weakening position of EFCSA was reflected in a long strike—the first in its history—and the operation of the plant was taken over by the state in the following year.

The fundamental problem of the meat export trades—indeed, to a large extent the fundamental problem of the Uruguayan economy as a whole—has been the inadequate supply of cattle for slaughter. The problem is not simply the long-term stagnation of cattle production, but also the markedly seasonal nature of cattle slaughter, the result of the primitive nature of feeding techniques which reduces the availability of winter food. To the extent that foreign aid has permitted a greater area of pasture to be fertilised and improved, one might expect to find a reduction in recent years in the seasonal variation of number of cattle

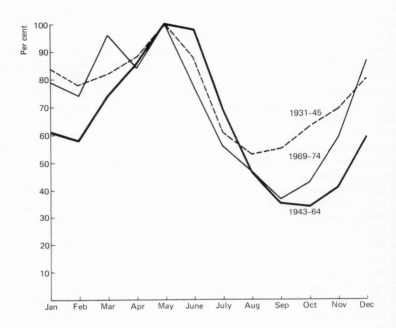

Figure 5.1. Monthly variation in cattle purchase for slaughter, 1931–45, 1943–64, 1969–74
(monthly totals as per cent of May total)

Notes: 1931–45 refers to sales of steers only (the largest and least stable category) at Tablada; 1943–64 refers to sales of all cattle at Tablada; 1969–74 refers to slaughter of all cattle by *frigoríficos* and factories.

Sources: 1931–45, MGA, *Plan Agropecuario Nacional*, p. 169; 1943–64, MGA–CIDE, *Estudio Económico y Social de Agricultura*, vol. II, p. 329; 1969–74, BCU, *Boletín Estadístico Mensual*.

slaughtered. Though Figure 5.1, in which monthly slaughter totals are expressed as a percentage of the peak month (May), is inexact for a number of reasons, it is clear that the degree of variation in 1969–74, though less than in 1943–64, was greater than in 1931–45. The damaging implication of this seasonal variation is not only that Uruguay needs to maintain a far larger capacity in the meat industry than is warranted by the total annual slaughter, but also that Uruguayan meat tends to disappear periodically from world markets, thus reducing its acceptability.[62]

Uruguay has seen its participation in world meat exports diminish sharply. This has been particularly the case for canned meat. During 1934–8 Uruguay accounted for 18.2 per cent of world exports; by 1959–61 the proportion had fallen to 1.7 per cent, and to 1.1 per cent in the decade 1962–71. During the same periods, participation in world exports of carcase beef and veal fell from 7.5 per cent before the war to 4.0 per cent (1959–61), recovering somewhat to 5.1 per cent in 1962–71. The improved performance reflected in part the recovery of the livestock sector from the crisis of the 1950s, but also was the result of declining domestic per capita beef consumption, from 79.3 kilos in 1959–61 (in 1952 it had been 90.2 kilos) to 65.9 kilos in 1963–71.[63]

The long decline of the traditional *frigorífico* industry, and its virtual elimination by the beginning of the 1970s, called into question the role of the Frigorífico Nacional in the meat trade. At the time of its creation its essential function was to compete in the cattle market with the foreign *frigoríficos*, thus breaking their monopsonistic position. The Nacional's monopoly of the supply of Montevideo was granted in order to ensure it a commanding position in the market, and to raise the efficiency and sanitary conditions of the domestic meat supply. Taking over the premises of the Sansinena Company enabled the Nacional to begin operations immediately, but condemned it to the employment of physical plant which was antiquated then and remained deficient.[64] Though the Nacional quickly established itself in the market, it was unable to prevent a fall in the price of cattle in the early 1930s. In 1934, with the price of steers at 67 per cent of the 1930 level, a subsidy was introduced for cattle producers, financed from exchange profits.[65] Until 1936 the operations of the Nacional showed a profit; but as the market price of cattle recovered, the subsidy to producers was ended in 1937 and was replaced by a subsidy to cover the losses incurred every year after 1939 in supplying Montevideo's meat requirements.

How far did the Nacional achieve the objectives which were prescribed for it? Basically it was given the contradictory functions of ensuring adequate prices to cattle producers while meeting domestic demand for meat at prices which it did not determine. A policy of high cattle prices appears to have been pursued, in that the Nacional generally paid higher average annual prices than its competitors[66]— though since its obligation to supply the domestic market forced it to buy cattle throughout the year, including the spring months when prices reach their peak and export activity is reduced, this result is not altogether surprising. The weakness of its position resulted from its dependence on subsidies to cover losses on supplies of meat to Montevideo, sold at politically determined prices. In addition, in common with the rest of the public sector, its administration was increasingly overloaded from the late 1950s by an inflated bureaucracy.[67]

In a larger sense, the Nacional was charged with the function of protecting the national interest against the operations of foreign capital in the meat trade. To the extent that cattle producers received a higher average price for their output than they would have done if the Nacional had not participated in the market, this may have been achieved. On the other hand, if cattle prices were such that, at ruling taxes and exchange rates, it was not profitable for the foreign companies to operate, then they could either withdraw from the market to obtain more favourable treatment, or press the government to cover the losses which they declared. These were in fact the strategies employed during the 1950s, when strongly though the Nacional attacked the costs declared by the foreign companies, its role as *ente testigo* in the industry was outflanked by the economic power of the companies and the indifference of government. Ultimately, it is doubtful whether the Nacional had any decisive impact on the structure of the industry. The principal factors determining that were largely beyond its control. The stagnation of the livestock sector, the level of the prices in world markets, and the increasing relative inefficiency of the traditional *frigorífico* plant, were the principal reasons why foreign capital deserted the traditional industry. When it reappeared under new forms in the 1960s, it decisively undermined the position of the Frigorífico Nacional.

6 Imports and Industrialisation

> Protection to industry, through the imposition of higher customs duties on competing foreign products, is right and proper when these products are consumed directly by the public. But when the output of one industry is required and utilised by the rest of national industry . . . protection ceases to be protection as such and becomes a sinecure for a particular company. (Comment of Unión Industrial Uruguaya on an application by a glass bottle factory for increased protection, *Diario de Sesiones de la Honorable Cámara de Representantes*, 1911, vol. CCXIII, p. 200.)

I. Imports

Because of Uruguay's dependence on foreign trade flows for much of its fiscal income, trade has tended to be better served by official statisticians than other aspects of economic activity. For this reason—and in spite of the deficiencies of the data which are discussed in the Appendix—the analysis of imports is significant not only in view of their high per capita level, but also because they provide indirect evidence on the changing structure of domestic production. Uruguay's very small size has imposed severe limits on the process of industrialisation, but *batllista* policies implied diversification of the economy such that proportionate to its size Uruguay was by 1930 one of the most highly industrialised countries in Latin America. Industrial growth increased demand for imports but changed their composition. Natural and tariff protection reduced the import of consumer non-durables, since early enterprise tended to concentrate on production of wage goods. The equipment and materials required for such production, however, were generally not available or did not lend themselves to local production, so that imports became relatively more concentrated on these goods, and much less with meeting the demands of consumers directly.

From the beginning of this century, in conditions of relative price stability, expenditure on imports grew steadily to reach a pre-war peak of about $52.3 million in 1912 (Table 6.1). In that period imports approximately doubled, a similar rate of increase as for exports. Domestic recession in 1913 and the onset of war had a severe effect on

TABLE 6.1. Commodity imports, 1899–1938
(million pesos)

Year	1 'Official value'	2 Estimated value	3 Volume 1913 = 100	4 Price 1913 = 100
1899	25.7	23.0	64.7	76
1900	24.0	23.9	58.8	87
1901	23.7	25.3	65.2	83
1902	23.5	25.0	66.0	81
1903	25.1	25.6	65.8	83
1904	21.2	28.1	71.6	84
1905	30.8	31.2	79.3	84
1906	34.5	35.5	85.3	89
1907	37.5	37.8	85.9	94
1908	37.5	38.5	90.4	91
1909	36.9	41.2	98.9	89
1910	40.8	43.7	98.3	95
1911	44.8	49.0	111.3	94
1912	49.8	52.3	116.5	96
1913	50.4	46.8	100.0	100
1914	43.2	39.6	85.5	99
1915	40.6	36.1	70.1	110
1916	52.9	42.4	66.0	137
1917	66.6	54.8	83.5	140
1918	100.8	63.7	72.4	188
1919	113.2	90.1	85.9	224
1920	132.5	97.9	70.7	296
1921	93.9	113.4	89.3	271
1922	81.9	80.0	79.9	214
1923	102.1	85.9	85.0	216
1924	81.8	90.2	94.9	203
1925	95.4	82.3	100.0	176
1926	74.1	82.1	111.8	157
1927	81.8	85.0	123.5	147
1928	94.0	89.8	130.6	147
1929	93.3	95.6	134.4	152
1930	93.9	97.8	127.4	164
1931	114.1	110.7	114.3	207
1932	68.8	77.5	89.5	185
1933	67.7	64.2	81.6	168
1934	61.4	55.1	79.1	149
1935	59.5	58.9	84.4	149
1936	66.4	74.0	103.4	153
1937	80.2	79.2	101.3	167
1938	74.6	115.7	107.1	231

Note: Columns 2–4 are expressed as three-year moving averages. Other notes and sources: see Appendix.

the country's import trade. But though the import bill recovered rapidly from a low of $36.1 million in 1915 to $113.4 million in 1921, in real terms (i.e. deflated by the export price indices of the USA and UK, which shared some 45 per cent of the Uruguayan market) the recovery of imports was irregular and only partial. Not until the prosperous years of the late 1920s did the quantum of imports exceed the level of the pre-war boom, but in the ensuing slump imports sharply contracted, by more than 40 per cent between the peak of 1929 and the low point of 1934. And in the revival of trade in the second half of the 1930s, as with exports, the value of imports regained the level of a decade previously while in volume terms they lagged 15–20 per cent below the level of the late 1920s. Thus although the revival of world commodity prices after the depression allowed a slight increase in export earnings from a much reduced volume of exports compared with pre-depression years, the increase in import prices and the devaluation of the peso reduced the capacity to import over the same period. During the Second World War the import trade was depressed by low export prices and problems of supply, but thereafter the volume of imports grew rapidly to a peak in the early 1950s, an increase of 150 per cent over the level towards the end of the war (Table 6.2). The decline in export earnings of the 1950s was not fully reflected in a reduced supply of imports until 1958, as currency reserves were employed to finance payments deficits. Indeed, imports

TABLE 6.2. Commodity imports 1942–70
(million US dollars, c.i.f.)

	Value	Volume 1961 = 100	Price 1961 = 100		Value	Volume 1961 = 100	Price 1961 = 100
1942	60.5	54.5	53.5	1957	252.2	111.2	109.2
1943	61.2	46.4	63.5	1958	142.7	63.8	107.7
1944	68.5	47.4	69.6	1959	175.7	82.6	102.4
1945	93.4	62.8	71.6	1960	215.1	107.1	96.7
1946	144.8	82.9	84.1	1961	207.7	100.0	100.0
1947	214.7	112.2	92.1	1962	228.6	115.5	95.3
1948	208.2	111.1	90.2	1963	175.0	84.8	99.4
1949	184.2	98.1	90.4	1964	195.2	95.1	98.8
1950	210.6	118.9	85.3	1965	145.4	71.4	98.1
1951	310.7	146.5	102.1	1966	164.2	82.1	96.3
1952	238.4	109.0	105.3	1967	171.4	86.2	95.7
1953	204.7	99.7	98.9	1968	157.4	76.9	98.5
1954	272.4	141.0	93.0	1969	197.3	96.6	98.3
1955	236.5	112.5	101.2	1970	230.9	100.6	100.5
1956	208.5	94.4	106.4				

Sources: Universidad de la República, Estadísticas Básicas, tables 37 and 64; BCU, Boletín Estadístico Mensual.

recovered strongly at the end of the decade in response to trade liberalisation measures which were intended to restore incentives to the export sector. The crisis in the supply of imports was thus delayed until the mid-1960s by when exports were slowly recovering. At bottom (1965–7), the supply of imports was 35 per cent below its peak fifteen years earlier, a level which by 1970 had still not been exceeded.

In the long run the level of supply of imports is determined by the performance of exports. Changes in the composition of imports are determined by a variety of factors, of which the trade and exchange regime and income growth and distribution are of major importance, as well as short-run fluctuations in the supply of foreign exchange. Table 6.3 presents a summary classification of imports by end-use for 1899–1910, 1924–40 and 1942–70. While the Appendix discusses its limitations, it should be emphasised here that variations in the source material or classificatory index for the three periods make it hazardous to compare them too closely.

In the period from the turn of the century to 1910, the share of consumer goods as a whole was already tending to diminish slightly. In the case of consumer durables, where import substitution is unlikely to be significant in the early stages of industrialisation, the proportionate increase was modest, though well marked in personal transport equipment and domestic appliances. Among non-durable consumer goods the pattern was mixed. Foodstuffs and tobacco tended to increase their participation (especially unprocessed, i.e. fruit and vegetables), but beverages in particular and clothing declined, as a result of competitive domestic production. Among intermediate goods, the boom in construction activity in the pre-war decade—both residential and infra-structural—is clearly evident in imports of iron, timber and cement for construction. The apparent decline in raw materials for industry, however, is misleading. Included in that category are imports of non-breeding cattle, presumably required to supplement domestic supply for slaughter or fattening, and they diminished sharply in the course of the period analysed. If these imports are excluded, industrial raw materials maintained their position almost exactly in the four successive three-year periods. Capital goods for agriculture show little variation except for a sharp increase in 1905–7; this resulted in part from higher imports of breeding sheep and cattle associated with the installation of the first *frigorifico*, but even more from imports of fencing wire and posts needed to make good the damage done in the civil war of 1904. Industrial equipment doubled its share of the import bill between 1899–1901 and 1908–10; and although this was from a very small base, such an increase is consistent with the growth of manufacturing activity in the period. Indeed the increase may have been even greater, since part of the unenumerated imports admitted free of duty (see Appendix) were destined for manufacturing activities, including paper, match and textile

TABLE 6.3. Composition of imports by end-use, 1899–1970
(three-year averages, per cent)

	Consumer non-durables	Consumer durables	Fuels and Lubricants	Raw materials, for			Capital Goods			Unclassified	
				Agriculture	Industry	Construction	Agriculture	Industry	Transport		
1899–1901	38.1	4.4	7.8	2.1	35.7	5.8	4.4	0.9	0.5	0.3	100
1902–04	38.7	4.0	9.1	2.0	33.1	6.7	4.8	1.0	0.5	0.1	100
1905–07	32.1	5.1	8.3	2.2	36.1	7.9	5.9	1.3	1.1	0.1	100
1908–10	35.2	5.5	10.4	2.5	30.2	9.2	4.3	1.8	0.8	0.2	100
1924–26	22.7	6.8	22.5	1.0	26.7	10.1	3.1	2.9	4.1	0.1	100
1927–29	18.6	6.7	26.8	1.2	24.9	10.5	2.8	3.1	5.4	0.1	100
1930–32	20.7	3.0	34.7	0.5	25.2	9.0	1.5	2.5	2.9	0.1	100
1933–35	20.6	1.8	34.7	1.2	29.8	5.6	1.4	1.6	3.3	0.1	100
1936–38	18.4	4.4	28.0	0.7	31.9	6.7	2.5	3.4	4.0	0.1	100
1939–40[1]	19.6	3.0	26.5	0.7	34.5	6.3	2.1	4.3	2.9	0.1	100
Raw Materials				Metallic	Non-metallic						
1942–44	18.2	1.7	17.4	8.0	42.6	5.8	1.1	4.1	0.6	0.3	100
1945–47	14.9	3.2	8.6	7.4	44.6	7.9	1.3	7.6	4.2	0.2	100
1948–50	11.9	4.7	11.7	8.8	33.6	7.0	3.9	14.4	3.6	0.3	100
1951–53	8.9	4.2	13.8	8.9	32.1	6.5	3.8	14.3	7.3	0.2	100
1954–56	8.0	3.1	15.7	9.4	34.4	6.5	2.5	14.8	5.4	0.1	100
1957–59	7.9	1.9	21.1	10.7	38.7	4.5	1.2	10.2	3.6	0.3	100
1960–62	7.2	3.8	14.4	12.8	36.8	3.0	3.5	11.6	6.2	0.3	100
1963–65	8.1	2.0	14.8	11.4	38.6	2.6	3.5	11.9	6.8	0.6	100
1966–68	7.6	0.5	19.2	10.5	42.5	2.2	2.2	11.4	3.3	0.4	100
1969–70[1]	7.0	1.1	13.7	13.0	38.0	2.0	4.3	15.1	5.2	0.7	100

Note: 1. Two-year average. Other notes and sources: see Appendix.

factories. But the category most understated by the incomplete enumeration was probably transport equipment, since the railway companies accounted for more than half of such imports.

Whereas the growth of imports to 1910 was regular, so that the changing composition reflected principally income growth modified slightly by protectionist policy, the inter-war period was marked by a boom in the volume of imports in the late 1920s, followed by an abrupt fall at the beginning of the 1930s and the introduction of direct controls on commodities traded. These fluctuations had unmistakeable repercussions on the composition of imports. During the 1920s, the major change in the structure of imports compared with pre-1910 was the sharp drop in the level of consumer non-durables, while durable consumer goods slightly increased their share. Most of the fall was accounted for by import substitution in beverages and clothing, but the share of toiletries and other non-durables also contracted. A startling increase between the periods occurred in the case of fuel, reflecting the country's almost complete dependence on imported supplies. Coal was the most important component of the fuel bill in the early 1920s, but demand for coal remained stationary over the inter-war period as a whole. Consumption of fuel oil increased,[1] but the principal cause of the dramatic rise in fuel imports was the growth of road transport. Imports of petroleum alone grew from 24 million litres in 1924 to 122 million in 1931: in the 1920s experiments were made with alcohol as a substitute in an attempt to reduce this massive import bill.[2] The behaviour of raw material imports in the 1920s in Table 6.3 conceals contradictory trends. The increased value of intermediate goods for construction was clearly the result of the high level of activity in the sector, creating an expanded demand which import-substituting industries—cement, for example— were unable to fill. The reduced level of agricultural raw materials, on the other hand, largely resulted from reduced imports of sheep dip because of domestic production beginning in 1911. The category of industrial raw materials also shows a sharp reduction compared with the pre-war period, and this is true for all sub-categories except for those materials of chemical origin. A major part of the reduction was the result of import substitution through domestic production of intermediate textile and paper products.[3] In the import of capital goods it is quite clear that the expansion of domestic productive capacity continued in the 1920s, even though there was no general strengthening of protectionist legislation. The rapid adoption of road transport is evident in the very large imports of transport equipment, but imports of industrial equipment also grew steadily through the 1920s to a peak in 1929.

The rapid fall in total imports at the beginning of the 1930s, and the introduction of controls, produced substantial shifts in Uruguay's import trade which reflected the relatively high level of industrialisation already achieved by 1930, and the priority which industry's require ments could command in the period of retrenchment. The share of consumer goods in general, and durables in particular, declined. The most important decline came in the personal transport category, i.e. motor vehicles, though there was some revival in the late 1930s. The increase in the share of non-durables in the first half of the decade was entirely due to the importance of food imports. The only other group to show an important increase in the depression was fuels. In quantity terms the levels of 1929–31 were not reached again in the following decade, and when the La Teja oil refinery of ANCAP began production in 1937 imports of refined fuels could be much reduced. In the short-term, however, the depression exposed Uruguay's complete dependence on overseas fuel sources; at the peak in 1932, fuel comprised no less than 38 per cent of the import bill. The contraction in the level of domestic demand during the depression years resulted in substantial excess capacity in industry, with very low imports of industrial equipment and construction goods in consequence. The increase in imports of raw materials was led initially by foodstuffs for processing, but from 1934 almost all industrial raw material groups participated. Within that category there was a shift of some importance towards less highly processed materials. Excluding edible raw materials, the share of processed goods in total industrial raw material imports fell from 68 per cent in 1924–6 to 61 per cent in 1933–5, and to 51 per cent in 1939–40.

After the Second World War, with the restoration of more normal supply conditions, the composition of imports became increasingly determined by economic policy considerations subject to the constraint of stagnating export earnings. Consumer goods were reduced to very low levels, with some increase in the share of durables occurring during the Korean War boom and a decade later following the abolition of import controls. The import of industrial equipment rose to a high level during the period of rapid industrial growth, but declined substantially during the stagnation period. The post-war wheat policy resulted in a much higher allocation of foreign exchange to agricultural equipment, especially tractors, in the early post-war years. The elimination of the tramways of Montevideo at the beginning of the 1950s, newly acquired from their British owners, and the consequent growth of urban transport by bus, resulted in increased imports of transport equipment, as did the attempt to introduce modern motive power on the railway system. Finally, the reduced importance of construction materials is an eloquent indicator of economic stagnation.

Changes in the origin of Uruguay's imports are summarised in Table 5.4, and again it is necessary to emphasise the provisional nature of the information presented. However, the transit trade from Argentina is considerably less of a problem than in the case of exports to Argentina: at the turn of the century only about 25 per cent of imports from Argentina were regarded as in transit at Buenos Aires. In broad terms,

TABLE 6.4. Imports by source, 1891–1970
(five-year averages, per cent of current value)

	1891–5	96–00	01–5	06–10	11–15	16–20	21–5	26–30	31–5	36–40	42–5[1]	46–50	51–5	56–60	61–5	66–70
UK	31.5	26.9	25.9	29.7	24.3	18.4	18.6	15.7	18.5	18.6	8.5	15.6	12.3	7.0	10.0	6.2
EEC 6	36.6	35.8	37.6	41.5	32.4	8.0	22.8	27.7	23.1	23.8	0.1	12.8	23.5	19.5	24.5	18.6
Other W. Europe	8.9	7.8	6.2	5.4	16.2	6.7	5.2	4.4	3.9	4.5	3.3	6.3	7.5	8.8	7.0	7.3
E. Europe	—	—	—	—	—	—	—	0.6	4.8	2.7	—	0.8	0.7	6.6	1.5	2.6
Europe	77.0	70.5	69.7	76.6	72.9	33.1	46.6	48.4	50.3	49.6	11.9	34.5	44.0	41.9	43.0	34.7
USA	6.2	8.0	9.1	9.7	5.2	28.2	23.8	29.1	13.9	12.1	29.7	28.7	21.2	19.6	17.3	15.0
Argentina	7.0	13.7	13.7	7.3	12.6	21.7	11.6	9.7	12.7	7.3						
Brazil	8.3	6.4	6.1	5.0	7.6	14.0	10.2	6.1	9.1	7.6	52.1	32.2	29.5	33.7	28.9	33.7
Other America	1.6	1.4	1.6	1.1	1.2	2.3	5.9	4.9	10.6	16.4						
America	23.1	29.5	30.5	23.1	26.6	66.2	51.5	49.8	46.3	43.4	81.8	60.9	50.7	53.3	46.2	48.7
Other	—	—	—	0.4	0.4	0.8	1.9	1.9	3.4	7.1	6.3	3.6	5.3	4.7	10.8	16.5

Notes: Before 1940 official prices were used for the valuation of imports, and infrequent changes in these prices implies that these proportions represent volume more nearly than value.
1. Four-year average.

Sources: As Table 5.5.

the import trade before the First World War was dominated by European suppliers, with the UK the most important source. But British exports to Uruguay were heavily weighted towards her traditional commodities: in the decade 1901–10, 70 per cent of the total consisted of textiles, iron and steel, and coal, and in the inter-war years the UK could only command a generally steady but diminished share of the market. Moreover, the share fell sharply when total imports increased in the late 1920s. The shift in fuel consumption from coal to oil and derivatives, and the growth in road transport, were fundamental factors enabling the USA to maintain during the 1920s the massive increase it had won during the war. The reduction in the share of the USA in the 1930s was partly to the benefit of the UK, and followed the introduction of explicit bilateralism. Latin America and Caribbean countries increased their share markedly, especially in the new demand for crude oil, while Japan and the Soviet Union were other non-traditional sources of supply to assume importance. Since the Second World War the pattern of diversification has proceeded further. The USA and UK have continued to diminish in importance, while other Western European countries have maintained their position. In the late 1950s, when export earnings were at their lowest point, the socialist bloc countries developed an important trade; but this diminished after 1960 when the incoming Blanco administration brought a number of bilateral trade and payments agreements to an end. A most remarkable increase in non-traditional sources of supply came during the 1960s with the growing share of Africa, Japan and the Middle East in the import trade.

II. Industrialisation

1875–1930

The first phase in the industrial development of Uruguay came to an end with the depression of the early 1930s. In comparison with the growth rate achieved subsequently, progress in the early years was slight. Probably for this reason the period has been very little studied,[4] and the poor statistical materials add to the difficulties.[5] Nonetheless there are grounds for attaching particular significance to the period. The stimulus to industrialisation presented by the conditions of the 1930s could hardly have met a positive response without a previous stage of preparation during the years in which Uruguay pursued predominantly liberal trade policies, and in which the dynamic sector of the economy was based on export markets. Certainly the ideology of protection was widely proclaimed, especially by *batllistas*, before and after the First World War, and it is important to assess how far it was able to modify an economic system which had largely been formed by the interests of the commercial and agricultural sectors; and what kinds of industries were established and the conditions for their survival.

The earliest tariff legislation designed to have a significant protection-ist effect dates from 1875. This doubled the basic import tariff of 20 per cent on articles competitive with domestic production—mainly foods-tuffs and clothing—and the rates were further raised in 1886. In 1888, a general tariff of 31 per cent was established, with considerably higher rates for imports competitive with domestic production, especially of foodstuffs and clothing. Concessions were also granted on the import of raw materials and machinery at this time. The commodities whose production was thus encouraged were nonetheless limited in range. By 1912, however, when the Ley de Materias Primas was enacted, there had been a considerable growth of manufacturing under protection. The significance of the 1912 legislation was the consolidation and extension of tariff concessions which had previously been granted on an *ad hoc* basis, and the introduction of the classification 'Raw Materials' in the tariff schedule.[6]

These concessions had been negotiated during the previous two decades by a variety of industries, and marked the introduction into Uruguay of large-scale enterprises producing for the domestic market. Whereas manufacturing (apart from the processing of animal products by Liebig's and the *saladeros*) was largely confined previously to workshop activities, by the turn of the century the factory had been introduced. In 1891 and 1894 two ventures proposing the extraction and refining of sugar were granted tariff concessions on the import of raw sugar and molasses. By 1900, however, the latter company, which had been taken over by Belgian interests, was in liquidation; the Uruguayan company of Félix Giraud was rescued by legislation in 1900 and 1906 which reduced the duties on other inputs, subsidised the cultivation of sugar-beet for five years after 1906, and gave modest and diminishing fiscal concessions to the Refinería Nacional de Azucar. Other industries were evidently more successful. In 1898 protective duties were granted on paper products, and by 1925 the Fábrica Nacional de Papel had a labour force of 400. In 1898 and 1900 two companies were granted tariff concessions on the manufacture of textiles. Almost immediately they merged and, as Salvo, Campomar y Cia., built a new mill in 1905 employing over 500. This was the pioneer textile enterprise in Uruguay, and was soon followed by others, among them 'La Uruguaya' in 1907, and Alvarez Lista y Cia. in 1909. In older established industries, such as footwear, clothing and furniture, there was a move to larger-scale production. But the limited size of the market also induced a process of concentration, notably in soap production and the monopoly of alcohol distillation. The legislation of 1912 and the negotiation of tax privileges added further industries, and by the First World War production of cement, glass and sheep dip amongst others had also begun.[7] Unfortunately it is impossible to estimate the growth of manufacturing production before 1914. Import data is diffcult to interpret, partly because many imports for manufacturing industry were admitted free of duty and their nature left unrecorded in the source material (see Appendix). However, Table 6.3 does record an increase in the proportion of imports accounted for by industrial capital equipment between 1899–1901 and 1908–10, and industrial raw materials maintained their share.

A surprising feature of the early history of Uruguayan industry is that a substantial proportion of these industrial initiatives preceded not only the growth period associated with the frozen meat trade and the new investment in railways, trams and the port in the decade before 1914, but also the redistributive, urban-based policies of Batlle y Ordónez. In 1883 it had been observed that 'It is much to be regretted that Montevideo makes such slow progress in its import trade, thereby denoting the poverty of the population, the inference being that any accumulation of wealth is entirely confined to the successful *Estancieros*.'[8] By the 1890s this situation was evidently being modified by massive and mainly urban-based immigration which supplied both a labour force and a rapidly-expanding domestic market for manufacturers.

Though evidence is somewhat sparse, it is likely also that immigration provided many of the early entrepreneurs.[9] Some may have brought capital with them, but a more usual process of accumulation was probably from the profits of modest initial investments. Antonio Barreiro y Ramos arrived from Galicia in 1871 and opened a bookshop. By 1880 he was also publishing books, and in 1894 established a printing press.[10] Luis Podestá, a migrant from Italy in 1854 aged fourteen, established a flour mill in 1872 and subsequently founded the Banco Italiano del Uruguay.[11] By 1890 there were also immigrant entrepreneurs engaged in the production of soap, furniture and tobacco products, operating a dyeworks, and doubtless in a variety of other primitive industries. Manufacturing activity by native-born Uruguayans may indeed have been unusual. José Borro, who in 1908 established a cigarette factory, later drew the comment that 'he is one of those industrialists, Uruguayan by birth, who is an example to us, since the idea seems to be well-established here that the pleasures of success are reserved for foreign initiative because of the inadequacies of our own'.[12] It must be stressed that though many entrepreneurs were foreign by origin they were almost entirely resident in Uruguay. Examples of foreign capital manufacturing for the domestic market before 1914 were very rare. The unsuccessful venture of Belgian capital in sugar production has been noted. One of the few others was the British company William Cooper and Nephews, which responded to protective legislation of 1911 by establishing a subsidiary to produce sheep dips for the Uruguayan market.[13]

The effects of the First World War on industry were on balance probably beneficial. The most general result of the difficulty in securing imports was to reinforce the ideology of self-sufficiency. Protection by high freight rates and physical shortages of competing imports aided many of the newly established industries, and some, like the hat manufacturers, even found new markets in other South American countries. More significant was the effect of war-time protection on the manufacturing section of the state-owned Instituto de Química Industrial. IQI was established in 1912 to advise on the better utilisation of domestic raw materials and to give technical assistance to industry. At the instigation of its North American director, Latham Clarke, and in the absence of any domestic manufacture of basic chemicals, IQI began in 1915 the commercial production of a variety of chemicals.[14] But most industries depended to some extent on imported materials, and there must have been many others like the ironworks of Angel Pozzoli which by 1916 was working at only 50 per cent of pre-war capacity.[15] The fact that the number of firms surviving in 1936 which had been founded in 1915–19 was no greater than those founded in 1910–14 (Table 6.5) may suggest either that war-time conditions were not propitious for new enterprise, or more probably that the rate of eventual failure among war-time ventures was high.

TABLE 6.5. Average annual number of industrial enterprises founded which survived in 1936

1850–9	1	1910–14	150	1931–2	477
1860–9	4	1915–19	150	1933–4	760
1870–9	11	1920– 4	239	1935–6	872
1880–9	21	1925– 6	326		
1890–9	33	1927– 8	390		
1900–9	92	1929–30	487		

Note: Construction, extractive industries and public utilities are included.

Source: *Censo Industrial de 1936* (Montevideo, 1939) p. 49.

Certainly the restoration of normal trading conditions after the war permitted the inflow once more of raw materials and machinery, but also of competitive goods. For some industries the early 1920s was a painful period, but the number of manufacturing establishments continued to grow. A survey of industry in 1929 found that of 7681 establishments, 60 per cent had originated since 1921,[16] though about a quarter of the latter had disappeared by 1936 (Table 6.5). The decade preceding the depression was characterised in general by the consolidation of industries previously established, rather than the introduction of new industries which had been a feature of the pre-war period. The industrial structure revealed by the census of 1930, which is the earliest year for which there is systematic information of the composition of manufacturing production, was dominated by foodstuffs, beverages, clothing, leather and wood products, and construction materials (Table 6.6). Much of this production, particularly in the foodstuffs and leather products groups, had a very high raw material content and was destined for export.[17] For the industrial sector as a whole the proportion of final value added in manufacturing was 40 per cent; with the exclusion of the foodstuffs group, perhaps half of whose production was accunted for by the *frigoríficos*, the proportion rises to 54 per cent. Manufacturing was thus largely confined to 'traditional' industrial groups; and although as early as 1914 a number of large-scale plants had been established in a variety of industries, by 1930 the average manufacturing enterprise still employed fewer than nine personnel.

Secondary manufacturing grew almost entirely on the basis of the

TABLE 6.6. Structure of manufacturing industry, 1930
(per cent of total)

	Employment	Gross production	Value added
Foodstuffs	33.4	44.9	25.5
Beverages	4.9	7.0	9.9
Tobacco	2.1	3.4	4.1
Textiles	4.6	3.8	4.3
Clothing	9.5	7.5	10.0
Wood products	8.1	5.6	8.0
Paper products	1.4	1.3	1.0
Printing	5.5	2.5	3.6
Stone, sand and cement products (construction materials)	6.7	5.8	8.0
Leather products	6.9	6.0	6.6
Rubber products	0.3	0.2	0.4
Chemicals	3.0	3.6	4.2
Metals	7.2	4.5	7.0
Transport equipment	4.7	2.9	5.5
Electrical equipment	0.6	0.4	0.7
Optical surgical and precision equipment	0.4	0.2	0.4
Other	0.9	0.5	0.7
Total	100.0	100.0	100.0

Note: The 1930 census was partially published in 1933; the classifications published in 1939 were adjusted to be comparable with the industrial groups of the 1936 census.

Source: *Censo Industrial de 1936*, p. 55.

domestic market. Even hat producers, who found export markets during the First World War, were confined to the domestic market in the 1920s, and even there the position was not secure. Less traditional industries were harder hit. The cement factory at Sayago, established immediately prior to the war, was taken over by US interests in 1919 and suffered severely from overseas competition in the 1920s, in spite of the high level of construction activity during the period. The debate over protection in the 1920s mainly centred on the woollen textile industry, which following rapid growth during the war was in acute difficulties by the middle of the decade, and received additional protection in 1926.[18] Table 6.7 indicates the growth of the principal woollen textile imports: The protection was clearly not prohibitive, as some critics argued.

TABLE 6.7. Woollen textile imports, 1900–39
(five-year averages, thousand kilos)

	'Casimires'		'Paños'	
	Wool and cotton	wool	Wool and cotton	wool
1900–4	130	127	23	38
1905–9	217	211	10	37
1910–11[1]	216	147	19	23
1915–19	85	106	9	12
1920–4	87	180	28	14
1925–9	156	227	38	28
1930–4	95	105	12	31
1935–9	118	131	1	4

Note: 1. Two-year average.

Source: DGEC, Anuario Estadistico.

It is difficult to determine how substantial or how effective the protectionist policies were. There were no quantitative restrictions at all, protection being exercised through certain tax advantages (for example, exemption from property taxes), but mainly through variations in the basic revenue tariff of 31 per cent established in 1888. Standard rates for commodities competitive with domestic production were 44 per cent, 48 per cent and 51 per cent, but particularly in the case of foodstuffs, beverages and tobacco, specific duties were levied which for some commodities exceeded 200 per cent of their value.[19] Raw materials and machinery required by domestic producers were granted concessionary rates. In addition to the basic tariff structure there were additional taxes which by the late 1920s added as much as 20 per cent to the total revenue derived from imports (and therefore might add substantially to a protective duty). The tariff percentages were calculated not on the market values of imports but on their official *aforo* (i.e. officially determined) values. This device of fixed prices was adopted to prevent revenue losses by underdeclaration of prices; but since the *aforos* were changed only infrequently, the real level of protection could differ substantially from the apparent level.

An indication of the overall level of protection is given by the ratio of taxes derived from imports to the estimated value of imports (Table 6.8). The Uruguayan data shows a dramatic fall in the apparent incidence of tariffs, from about 30 per cent per-war to about 12 per cent in the immediate post-war period. Proportionately similar declines are recorded for Argentina and Peru. Rising world prices, which were responsible for the declining yield of the effectively specific duties, were an alternative source of protection for Uruguayan producers, but of declining significance as the domestic price level also rose and war-time trade restrictions were eased. Pressure to revise the *aforos* resulted in a revaluation which came into effect from 1923, but the new values were deliberately set below market prices in most cases, and the overall tariff incidence stabilised at about 24 per cent in the second half of the 1920s. This level, though significantly higher than for Argentina or Peru, was substantially less than the pre-war figure, and represented a proportionately greater decline than that recorded for Argentina. A likely explanation for the falling ratio of import revenue to imports would be the effect of import substitution in causing a shift away from high tariff competing imports to low tariff inputs for domestic industry. If this did occur, one would expect to find an increasing proportion of imports receiving concessionary tariff treatment. The little evidence available suggests the reverse, however: the proportion of low tariff imports fell from 22.4 per cent of imports at *aforo* values in 1915–17 to 19.2 per cent in 1927–30, while the overall tariff incidence remained constant.[20]

More precise conclusions about the level of protection are not warranted by the available evidence. It is clear that the revenue tariff in Uruguay before 1930 was very high, and was manipulated for protectionist purposes. However, the system adopted was rigid, since although tariff levels could be and were varied, changes in world prices were the major determinant of the level of tariff protection. Prohibitive tariffs were few, and probably confined to some alcoholic beverages and matches. With no data for manufacturing production it can only be hazarded that industry grew in the course of the 1920s, but increased its share of the domestic market only in the range of traditional manufactures. If Uruguay had not developed a more substantial manufacturing sector by 1930 it was not, as is often implied by the literature on outward-directed growth, because protection had not yet been adopted as a policy principle.

TABLE 6.8. Incidence of import tariffs, Uruguay,
Argentina and Peru, 1903–30
(import revenues as per cent of imports valued at
market prices)

	Uruguay	Argentina	Peru
1903	35.6		22.8
1904	30.0		
1905	30.1		
1906	33.0		
1907	30.7		
1908	30.1		
1909	28.4		
1910	29.7	20.1	25.4
1911	28.2	19.2	
1912	28.7	18.5	
1913	34.4	17.7	
1914	33.6	16.2	
1915	27.7	13.7	
1916	25.9	12.6	12.1
1917	18.2	11.2	8.8
1918	18.7	7.8	10.4
1919	11.2	7.5	9.6
1920	13.3	7.5	9.8
1921	11.0	9.4	11.3
1922	15.9	11.7	14.9
1923	16.1	12.3	16.9
1924	17.7	13.6	17.7
1925	22.1	15.2	17.6
1926	23.4	15.3	17.7
1927	23.8	15.5	17.6
1928	24.2	17.4	20.4
1929	24.1	17.3	21.3
1930	23.2	16.7	

Sources: Uruguay: Table 6.1; Pedro Dondo, Los Ciclos
en la Economía Nacional: Evolución de las Rentas Públicas
(Montevideo, 1942); Mario La Gamma et al., 'Desarrollo
de los Ingresos Públicos Nacionales', Revista de la
Facultad de Ciencias Económicas y de Administración,
Year 1 (1940).

Argentina: Carlos F. Díaz Alejandro, Essays on the
Economic History of the Argentine Republic (New Haven
and London: Yale University Press, 1970) p. 282.

Peru: Rosemary Thorp and Geoff Bertram,
'Industrialisation in an Open Economy: A Case-Study of
Peru, 1890–1940', in Rory Miller, Clifford T. Smith and
John Fisher, Social and Economic Change in Modern Peru
(Centre for Latin American Studies, University of
Liverpool, Monograph No. 6, 1976) p. 61. 'Import
revenues' includes duties plus surcharges.

This is not to deny the influence which groups such as the Federación Rural, Cámara Mercantil de Productos del País, and Cámara Nacional de Comercio, with interests in the free flow of goods to and from the country, would have exerted to restrict the growth of protectionist barriers. But the very existence of trade barriers as substantial as those erected by 1914 suggests that theirs was not a determining influence. The ideology of protectionism in Uruguay has a long history. In 1880 the Liga Industrial began the publication of a journal which campaigned for protection.[21] Though it did not survive the decade, the Liga was succeeded in 1898 by the Unión Industrial Uruguaya, which from 1914 was administered and directed by the Cámara de Industrias.[22] The protectionist cause was also served by intellectuals better than was that of the free traders. For example, although Eduardo Acevedo expressed criticisms, they were directed not at protection in principle, but at the margin of protection enjoyed by industry; already by 1903 production of alcohol, beer and matches had become monopolies, and the likelihood that protection would be permanent implied a lack of stimulus to improve quality or lower prices.[23] And there were others, the most notable being Pedro Cosio and Juan Carlos Quinteros Delgado, who stressed the advantages of protection. Though free trade might be appropriate to countries whose industrial status was secure, they noted that such countries had not hesitated to protect their own industries, and that even Britain by 1920 had modified its traditional free trade policy. Protection was the key to industrial autonomy. However, the advantages of such autonomy were defined in a somewhat curious way. Little stress was laid on the vulnerability of an economy dependent on a limited range of exports, though Acevedo had noted the inflexibility of the economy revealed by the decline of the *tasajo* trade at the end of the nineteenth century. Diversification was not the objective, nor was import substitution the means to that end; import substitution was an end in itself. Calculations were made of expenditures on imports which could be saved if certain commodities were produced domestically;[24] the country would then be freed of 'the enormous tribute paid for our purchases abroad'.[25] By thus economising on its income spent abroad, the nation could create more employment (enhancing its attraction for immigrants) and make better use of its under-utilised natural resources. Rarely was it argued that industrialisation might diversify the structure of exports;[26] the problem was perceived as the size and composition of the import trade, and the task was to reduce the import bill.

The only significant intellectual opposition to protectionism came from Julio Martínez Lamas in 1930. His argument was based on the belief that industrial growth had occurred at the expense of agriculture, raising agricultural costs in favour of the urban sector and resulting in the stagnation of agriculture. Where the protectionists were anti-import, Martínez Lamas was pro-export: ' . . . this independence, or the capacity to be self-sufficient, does not consist, here or anywhere else, in avoiding purchases from abroad, but in selling there as much as possible—more, much more, than it is necessary to buy there.'[27]

It is not necessary to dwell on the limitations of the arguments employed both for and against protection. The significant points about the debate are firstly, that the protectionists reflected government policy which was in general strongly in support of national manufacturing; but secondly, there was no concerted industrial policy, there were few state initiatives in this sector, and the most important of them, the creation of ANCAP, did not come until 1931. The paradox was clearly apparent in the thought and policy of the dominating influence of the period, Batlle y Ordóñez. One might expect that industrialisation would have been a corner-stone of the urban-based policies executed and inspired by him. Indeed he is frequently credited with an active role in encouraging industrial growth,[28] and he was strongly protectionist in his writings on the subject.[29] Yet his achievement was limited to the granting of protection to individual industries and a law consolidating the regime of preferential tariffs on industrial inputs—the Ley de Materias Primas of 1912. Policy responded to individual initiatives, rather than creating a basis for more general industrial growth. Just as protectionist policies preceded the era of Batlle, so it was the export and construction boom of the pre-war decade, rather than specifically *batllista* policies, which were the foundation of industrial growth before 1930. It is not hard to find reasons why policy was not more forceful. Weighty interests were ranged against the protectionist cause. The supply of entrepreneurship in industry seems to have been somewhat limited. But above all, the average tariff level was very high; and in the absence of quantitative trade restrictions, the degree of protection necessary to make domestic production of a wider range of commodities competitive with imports would have placed an additional burden on consumers which would have been unacceptable in pre-1930 conditions.

1930–70

The quarter-century which elapsed between the world depression and the onset of stagnation in Uruguay was marked by the rapid growth of manufacturing industry. While the livestock sector made only a very limited recovery from the slump, and during this period devoted an increasing proportion of its output to satisfy domestic demand, industry showed a remarkable dynamism which is indicated by the growth in participation of the industrial product in GDP (Table 6.9). In spite of the lack of quantitative estimates of production before 1930, it is safe to regard the depression at the beginning of the 1930s as a discontinuity which divided a decade of relatively slow growth in a limited range of industries from a period of rapid growth and industrial diversification.

TABLE 6.9. Ratio of industrial product to GDP, 1930–70
(per cent)

1930	12.5	1955	22.0
1935	14.8	1960	23.1
1940	17.7	1965	22.9
1945	18.9	1970	23.0
1950	20.3		

Sources: Millot, Silva and Silva, *Desarrollo Industrial*, table 23; Universidad de la República, *Estadísticas Básicas*, table 12; BCU, *Boletín Estadístico Mensual*.

Nonetheless, even by 1930 Uruguay had one of the more highly industrialised economies in the region, exceeded only by Argentina and Mexico,[30] and this early growth was a basic condition of the positive response made by Uruguayan industry to the disruption of the international economy. Although in the late 1920s the landowning class showed more political strength—and secured power in 1933—the urban orientation of policy during the *batllista* period had created an important if small group of manufacturers whose interests (and significance for the economy of Montevideo) could not be ignored. In addition the industrial capacity existing at the time of the depression, almost certainly under-utilised, made possible a rapid response when domestic demand revived.

Evidence on the way in which industrial production grew between 1930 and 1955 is not unanimous. Contemporary material includes occasional official estimates of industrial production, and the industrial census of 1936 which makes that year a bench-mark for studies of industrialisation.[31] The publication of the census results was valuable in addition for the presentation on a comparable basis of the findings of the 1930 census. There is more or less satisfactory census material also for 1948 and 1955.[32] Annual series for industrial production have been estimated by Teichert for 1936–51 from a variety of sources,[33] and more authoritatively by BROU in the estimates of GDP for the period since 1935.[34] The BROU data indicates that the end of the Second World War sharply divided a period of industrial stagnation (0.5 per cent annual growth 1935–45) from a decade of rapid growth (7.7 per cent 1945–55). Such a view of the process of industrialisation in Uruguay, if correct, would bear important implications which run contrary to a widely accepted interpretation of the nature of the process in the rest of Latin America: briefly, that depression and war, by disrupting economic and political relations between centre and periphery, have had a generally stimulating effect on industrial growth in the region.[35] The reasons for the lack of industrial growth during 1935–45 might include a lack of protectionist policy, or inadequate export earnings, or the inability during war to import inputs and equipment; and the industrial spurt after 1945 would reflect the stimulating effect of the revival of world trade in peace-time.

In fact, there is contemporary evidence to suggest that the BROU data has underestimated growth during 1935–45. For example, the BROU estimate indicates an enormous fall of 28 per cent in the level of industrial output between 1937 and 1939, even though ANCAP's oil refinery—by far the most important industrial development of the decade—was inaugurated in 1937 and by 1939 had more than doubled its first year's output.[36] An official industrial production index found that production in 1938 was 13 per cent above the 1936 level, and 23 per cent greater in 1939.[37] Thus there are doubts about the reliability of the BROU estimates, and they have in fact been recently reworked and extended back to 1930, yielding results which are more trustworthy.[38] The revised data suggests that during 1930–6 the rate of growth of manufacturing averaged 3.3 per cent accelerating in the late 1930s to average 12.7 per cent (1936–8), slackening to 2.3 per cent during the Second World War, and finally a decade of sustained growth at 6.1 per cent until 1955 (Table 6.10).

The impact of the world crisis made itself felt in Uruguay in the course of 1930. The effect of the decline in export earnings was to restrict the capacity to import and to contract the level of domestic demand through the direct loss of income and the decline in government revenue. The

TABLE 6.10. Growth and composition of industrial product, 1930–55 (per cent of total, and annual interval rate of growth, 1936 prices)

	1930		1936		1938		1945		1955
Traditional	71.3	3.0	70.3	7.5	64.0	2.0	62.3	5.6	59.4
Dynamic	28.7	3.9	29.7	24.1	36.0	3.0	37.7	6.9	40.6
Total	100.0	3.3	100.0	12.7	100.0	2.3	100.0	6.1	100.0
Traditional excluding meat and textiles	43.0	5.0	47.4	9.0	44.3	0.7	39.6		
Dynamic excluding metal and petroleum industries	22.3	3.8	23.0	6.4	20.6	4.0	23.0		

Note: Industries classified as 'traditional' are food products, beverages, tobacco, textiles, clothing, wood, furniture and leather products; the remainder are 'dynamic'.

Source: Millot, Silva and Silva, Desarrollo Industrial, p. 169 and table 1.

effect on industry was potentially severe, and although there are no complete production estimates for the early 1930s it is very likely that the level of manufacturing production fell. For example, output of beer and safety matches fell until 1933, and of cement until 1935;[39] electricity sold to industrial users was 15 per cent less in 1933 than in 1930,[40] and there was certainly increased unemployment. Nonetheless, the effect of policy was to moderate the force of the slump on industry. With the introduction of exchange control in 1931, the peso was stabilised at an over-valued rate, so that manufacturers were shielded from the full increase in the cost of imported inputs; and the imposition of import controls and higher tariffs in the same year protected producers from the competition of imported goods. The measures were designed of course to meet an emergency, but it would be quite wrong to suppose that the protectionist effects were incidental or unlooked-for. Indeed, even before the crisis developed the government was considering two proposals to raise the level of protection, and the severity of the crisis was seen to some extent as a reflection of the failure to have done so earlier.[41] The industrial effort was further strengthened by the creation in late 1931 of ANCAP, a public corporation having a monopoly in the production and/or sale of cement, alcohol and petroleum products.

Thus, increased protection for domestic producers was almost an inevitable response from the *batllista* government in power until removed by the *coup* of 1933. If policy could do little more than moderate the effects of the depression, it is noteworthy that in spite of the difficulties experienced by other industries, two new textile companies—Industria Lanera del Uruguay and Textil Uruguaya— were formed in 1932–3, contributing to the impressive growth of this industry up to 1936.[42] More surprising than the reaction of the *batllistas*, however, was the continuation of protectionism by the Terra regime, the basis of whose support was the landowning class. The depreciation of exchange rates by the regime certainly redistributed income in favour of export producers, and increased industrial costs; but the weakness of the trade union movement until the late 1930s was a factor permitting downward pressure on the real wages of labour,[43] and the purchasing power of the middle class market was probably less affected. Moreover, the structure of trade and exchange controls, discriminating in favour of domestic industry, was consolidated. The explanation for the continuity in industrial policy is unlikely to have been a large–scale mobility of capital between the livestock and industrial sectors at this early stage, when the small enterprise was still typical in manufacturing, but more simply that the sector was too important as a source of income and employment to be neglected, particularly because of its concentration in Montevideo.

The growth of manufacturing during 1930–6 was largely confined, as we have seen, to the latter half of the period. Apart from clothing, whose output was mysteriously smaller in 1936 than in 1930, all sectors of industry showed expansion except those which were linked to the badly depressed construction industry. The decline in construction activity, estimated to have fallen by 1933 to 40 per cent of its 1930 level,[44] was especially severe in the private sector where it was affected by the decline in new investment. Industrial growth, in fact, depended in the first half of the 1930s on increased utilisation of installed capacity, rather than the creation of new capacity. Imports of industrial machinery throughout the 1930s remained below the level of the late 1920s, except for heavy equipment towards the end of the decade (Table 6.11), which was doubtless related to state initiatives in the construction of the ANCAP oil refinery and of the Rincón del Bonete hydro-electricity installation on the Río Negro. But while industrial equipment declined from 3.1 per cent of total imports (1927–9) to 1.6 per cent (1933–5), and construction materials from 10.5 per cent to 5.6 per cent, the combined share of industrial materials and fuels and lubricants rose from 51.7 per cent to 64.5 per cent (Table 6.3). Trade controls were evidently employed to restructure imports in order to sustain the level of manufacturing output.

The brief period 1936–8 marked the culmination of the revival. The very high rates of growth recorded, which affected all sectors of industry, were in part the continuation of an accelerating growth trend, but in part also the result of the commissioning of the ANCAP oil refinery. If this new development is excluded, the growth of the dynamic group of industries is reduced from 24 per cent annually to 8 per cent. Both meat and textiles were depressed in these years—reflecting the failure of the British market to recover in the first case, and probably problems of

TABLE 6.11. Imports of industrial equipment, 1924–40
(three-year averages, by volume, 1927–9 = 100)

	Total imports (volume)	Industrial machinery				
		Less than 100 kilos	100–500 kilos	500–1000 kilos	Over 1000 kilos	Electric motors
1924–6	79	61	61	69	69	80
1927–9	100	100	100	100	100	100
1930–2	85	58	52	74	70	106
1933–5	63	31	24	34	49	37
1936–8	80	90	58	52	163	69
1939–40[1]		67	43	33	155	73

Note: 1. Two-year average.

Source: Table 6.1; DGEC, Anuario Estadístico.

over-expansion in the second—and with their exclusion the performance of the traditional industries was very strong (Table 6.10). In general
the picture remains one of growth rather than diversification, since the
only important new industry to be established at this time—apart from
oil refining—was the manufacture of rubber tyres by FUNSA. The
ANCAP refinery, however, represented a decisive step towards national
autonomy in fuel supply, and a substantial saving of foreign exchange.

Throughout the 1930s the industrialisation process could be regarded
as a response to the emergency of the depression. Though the *batllista*
Colorados were traditionally protectionist, the justification for increased protective barriers in 1931, and the reason for their maintenance
after 1933 by a regime which was promoted by the rural sector, was the
fall in export earnings, the depreciation of the peso, and the depressive
effects which these would have had on the domestic economy in the
absence of government policy to sustain the level of demand. The logic
of this policy might entail that with the revival of exports in the later
1930s, and with upward pressure on the value of the peso, the growth of
domestic manufacturing would be resisted by the rural sector and by
importers. On the other hand, the consolidation of industry in the 1930s
and the growth of employment in the sector gave increased force to its
claims for protection; and when the peso was revalued at the end of
1937, making competitive imports cheaper, the continuation of import
controls and exchange budgeting shielded the interests of the industrial
sector.

Nonetheless, and in spite of favourable political changes in the early
1940s, it has been argued that the decisive adoption of industrialisation
in preference to competing economic strategies did not come until 1947
and the presidency of Luis Batlle.[45] The overthrow of the 1934
constitution in 1942, renewed interest in redistributive social policies,
and the creation of new state corporations, were evidence of the gradual
restoration of the *batllista* forces. The new militancy of trade unionism
reflected and sustained the urban orientation of policy. On the other
hand, the diversion of wool exports from Europe to the USA with whom
a commercial treaty was signed in 1942, appeared to strengthen the case
for a return to a more liberal and non-discriminatory trading system
after the war. But the meat industry remained tied to the British market,
and Uruguay's traditional commercial connections with Europe were
reasserted at the end of the war when trade with the USA abruptly
declined.

The performance of the economy during 1938–45 was weak, with the
rate of growth of GDP scarcely exceeding population growth. Industry
continued to grow more rapidly than the rest of the economy, but at a
much reduced rate (Table 6.10). Not until the final two years of the war
were there signs of the dynamic industrial growth which would
characterise the post-war decade. Though the slow growth of aggregate

domestic demand, unaided by redistributive measures to extend the size of the mass market until the early 1940s, was doubtless a factor, the poor performance was much more the consequence of external constraints and the drought of 1942 which devastated the rural sector. Indeed, if the meat industry and oil refining are excluded—the first closely linked to a single controlled export market, the second experiencing severe difficulties in the supply of crude oil which halved its product between 1940 and 1943—the performance of industry appears much more respectable. Textiles, for example, were affected like other industries by the recession of 1942–3 occasioned by the drought, but nonetheless the product of the industry in 1945 was more than double its pre-war maximum. But such growth was exceptional. It is hard to escape the conclusion that although problems in the supply of imports of consumer goods during the war did strengthen the arguments of protectionists against those who saw Uruguayan industry as 'artificial', still a necessary condition of the growth of industry in the short term was the restoration of peace-time world trade. In 1942–4 an average of US$2.5 million was spent on imports of industrial equipment, 4.1 per cent of total imports; by 1948–50 the proportion was 14.5 per cent (Table 6.3). Increased incomes, increased import capacity, and a more defined industrialisation policy are only partial explanations of the change. The timing of industrial growth in a small economy lacking a domestic capital goods sector depended in addition on the availability of industrial equipment supplies from the centre countries.

The industrial recovery from the low levels of activity in 1942–3 led into a period of sustained and quite rapid growth of industry until 1956–7. In the ten years after the war, the rate of growth averaged over 6 per cent with the dynamic industries continuing to increase their share of the total product, though rather slowly. This interpretation of post-war industrial growth, based on the re-estimation of the BROU data, conflicts with the traditional view held by CIDE that during the Second World War the rate of growth of the dynamic industries was negative, but was extremely rapid and nearly three times the rate of the traditional industries during 1945–54.[46] Accepting the revised estimates for 1945–55, it is clear that all industries participated in the growth process with the exception only of leather goods.

Growth appears to have been particularly rapid among the small new dynamic industries, such as machinery, electrical goods and basic metals. Among the larger dynamic industries, fuels, chemicals and transport equipment all registered above average growth. Yet by 1955 the combined contribution of these three industries and construction materials totalled only 22 per cent of the industrial product. Output in fact was still dominated by food processing, beverages and textiles, whose combined share of the product in 1955, some 47 per cent, was unchanged since 1945. Thus the post-war decade evidently saw a process of industrial diversification, but the bulk of output still came from the traditional group.

The conditions of the period were favourable to an expansion of industry. The restoration of the *batllista* faction of the Colorados, and the cultivation by Luis Batlle of a populist style of leadership, produced an expanding domestic demand through higher wages, increased social benefits, and increased public employment. But underlying the mood of optimism were three critical factors which in the short term facilitated an industrial policy but served to limit its scope and duration. Firstly, the apparatus of trade and exchange controls and differential exchange rates was easily adapted to produce a pattern of subsidies and protectionist barriers. The structure of domestic production was in fact reshaped fundamentally by policy weapons operating on the external sector, rather than by domestic fiscal instruments, integrated industrial credit policies, or an industrial development bank. Secondly, the opposition which might have been expected from the landowning class to the multiple exchange rate system elaborated in 1947 and 1949 was reduced by an extraordinary period of export growth, which saw the value of exports double between 1945 and 1950. Thirdly, the accumulation of foreign currency reserves and the high level of wool prices during the Korean War enabled Uruguay (for a limited period) to finance the heavy import requirements of industrialisation.

By the mid-1950s the value of industrial production had doubled in real terms in little more than a decade. In the following fifteen years the stagnation of the industrial sector was almost complete. Not until 1964 did the manufacturing product reach the level of 1957 again. Growth was renewed during 1968–70, but the three succeeding years all saw a contraction in output, and the level in the peak year 1970 was only 14 per cent above that of the mid-1950s. It is difficult to find a coherent pattern in the growth performance of individual industries in this period. If industrial stagnation was induced by the decline in the rate of growth of national income, or if it was the consequence of a diminishing capacity to import the necessary materials for industry, then in general one would expect the dynamic group of industries to have performed worse than the traditional industries, since the income elasticity of demand for the output of the former is greater, and its import coefficient for the supply of raw materials tends to be higher.[47] However, although in practice there were substantial fluctuations in the performance of individual industries, the trend before 1955 of an increase in the importance of the dynamic group continued in the early years of the stagnation. Its share of total industrial product grew from 40.6 per cent in 1955 to 48.3 per cent in 1960, but then began to decline sharply to 42.2 per cent in 1963.[48] In fact, the main causes of these changes were sharp fluctuations in the performance of food processing and textiles, whose participation in total industrial product fell from 39.0 per cent in 1955 to 31.8 per cent in

1960, reviving slightly to 1963. During 1955–60 the combined product of the two industries at constant prices fell by 15 per cent, largely it would seem because of problems of raw material supply from agriculture and the livestock sector, in both of which output was contracting in the second half of the 1950s. Thus the stagnation of rural production had adverse consequences for industry not only in terms of a decline in foreign exchange receipts, but also in a reduced supply of raw material inputs.

For the 1960s, information on the performance of manufacturing industry is incomplete and less easy to interpret.[49] After 1967 there was no published production data for six industrial groups (including basic metals, machinery, and transport equipment). Table 6.12 summarises industrial performance during the crisis period to 1969–71. Apart from a year of growth in 1964 industrial output as a whole remained stationary, with the gross value of output in 1967 only 1 per cent greater than in 1960. The evidence suggests that the tendency for the dynamic

TABLE 6.12. Gross volume of production of manufacturing industry, by sector, 1955–71
(1960 = 100)

	1955	1960	1965	1969–71
Foodstuffs	116.3	100	115.7	129.7
Beverages	96.3	100	111.0	165.0
Tobacco	74.3	100	118.8	130.9
Textiles	118.5	100	116.4	94.1
Clothing	85.8	100	122.3	111.9
Wood	156.6	100	69.5	n.a.
Furniture	113.1	100	104.8	n.a.
Paper	45.4	100	112.7	132.3
Printing	70.6	100	82.1	89.4
Leather	127.7	100	126.5	n.a.
Rubber	59.0	100	47.7	49.2
Chemicals	83.1	100	97.6	127.6
Oil	102.4	100	119.3	116.4
Non-metallic minerals	70.9	100	89.4	124.7
Basic metals	110.0	100	82.1	n.a.
Metal products	117.4	100	89.1	58.7
Machinery	84.4	100	69.0	n.a.
Electrical equipment	82.3	100	100.4	74.4
Transport equipment	104.4	100	127.0	n.a.
Other	45.4	100	90.0	n.a.
Total	95.7	100	104.0	113.3

Source: Universidad de la República Estadísticas Básicas, table 25; BCU, Indicadores.

industries to grow more slowly than the rate for industry as a whole was sustained beyond 1963. During 1963–7, only paper, chemicals and non-metallic minerals among the dynamic group were growing, while oil refining, metal products, machinery and electrical equipment all declined. In the period of growth from 1967 to 1970 important traditional industries—especially foodstuffs, beverages and tobacco—did well, and paper and construction materials also grew. But textiles and clothing did not share in the growth of wage-good industries, and metal products and electrical goods also declined.

Characteristics of Industry 1950–70

In spite of the industrial stagnation of the previous fifteen years, in 1970 Uruguay was still one of the relatively more industrialised economies in Latin America.[50] Nonetheless, the process of industrialisation occurred in conditions which are unusual in the Latin American context, essentially because the market is high-income, but small, and with zero or negative growth. Only Argentina and Venezuela have a higher per capita income than Uruguay, but in terms of total GDP Uruguay ranked only ninth among the countries of the region at the beginning of the 1970s, producing 1.3 per cent of the regional GDP.[51] Moreover, population growth, although it was the lowest in the region, exceeded the rate of growth of national income. Manufacturing industry therefore faced a market which has grown very slowly in terms of household units, and the average real income available to these units has declined.

An additional market characteristic which determines the profile of domestic demand is the way in which income is distributed. Information on the size distribution of income in Uruguay before the 1970s is very limited. There is a generally held belief that the distribution of income has been more equal than in the rest of Latin America, reflecting the importance of the middle sectors in the social structure and the promotion of the urban sector. However, although there is a very wide variation between the minimum-inequality and maximum-inequality distributions (Table 6.13) in the estimates of pre-tax income made by households for 1963, the corresponding Gini coefficients are high: 0.45 and 0.57 respectively. The data for 1968 implies a more equal distribution than either of these, but it is not known how comparable the estimates are. A summary examination of available estimates for other countries in the region suggests that while income in Uruguay in the early 1960s may have been more equally distributed than in Peru, Colombia or Brazil, it was less equal than in Costa Rica, Argentina or Puerto Rico.[52] A feature of the distribution is the high proportion of income—and the comparatively small variation between the two estimates—which accrued to the seventh, eighth and ninth deciles in

TABLE 6.13. Estimates of size distribution of household incomes, 1963 and 1968 (income share to percentile of recipients)

	0–20	20–40	40–60	60–80	80–90	90–100	Total
A	4.6	8.6	14.0	22.7	16.2	33.9	100
B	3.0	6.3	10.8	19.1	15.0	45.8	100
C	16.5		35.5		48.0		100

Sources: A and B, minimum and maximum inequality distributions of pre-tax income, 1963 in CECEA, *Plan, Compendio*, vol. I, p. 166. C, based on household survey data, 1968, reported in H. Chenery *et al.*, *Redistribution with Growth* (London, Oxford University Press, 1974) p. 8.

Uruguay. This group composed mainly of skilled and white-collar workers, technical and clerical employees and small businessmen, received between 34 and 39 per cent of pre-tax income, a much higher proportion than in Argentina, and suggesting the importance of the middle sector market in Uruguay.

The categories of 'traditional' and 'dynamic' industries which were used in the previous section to describe the process of industrial growth are rather crude groupings. Perhaps the most important analytic properties of dynamic industries are the higher income and growth elasticities of industries producing capital equipment, intermediates and consumer durables, compared with the characteristic wage goods of traditional industries, such as foodstuffs, clothing and basic household equipment. But the groups may be distinguished in other ways which are important in assessing the nature of industrial development in Uruguay. The most important derive from the nature of the technology used in the two groupings. In general, the dynamic industries are likely to employ more complex and capital-intensive technologies, either because of the technical sophistication of the final output, or because the factor proportions and size of consumer markets in the equipment-producing centre countries dictate the development of such technologies and enforce their adoption in the periphery. A number of important consequences stem from this technological differentiation. One such is that foreign capital is likely to participate more actively in the dynamic than in the traditional sector, since its ownership of the technology allows it to earn a monopoly rent, as well as facing more rapid growth potential.

The capital intensity of the technology is likely also to produce a more favourable demand profile for the dynamic sector by increasing the participation of upper income groups in the distribution of income. However, the technology also imposes indivisibilities in the production process, so that the coexistence of workshop or artisan activities with factories which is typical in traditional industries is less likely to occur in the dynamic group. The importance of economies of scale in large-sized production units employing relatively advanced technologies may in addition result in above average excess capacity and very high cost production.

While similar generalisations to these have been made about recent industrialisation in Latin America as a whole, it is clear that the unique characteristics of Uruguay mentioned at the beginning of this section have made this a case apart. At the comparatively high level of per capita income reached in the mid-1950s, it is unlikely that demand for the output of traditional industries was sufficiently dynamic to sustain a continued process of rapid industrial growth. But the non-traditional industries faced not only a shrinking supply of foreign exchange for inputs, but in particular an extremely small, high-income, consumption-oriented market.[53] Given the problem of technical indivisibility in this sector, it is likely that the rapid-growth industries of the 1950s would have particular problems of excess capacity and very high cost, combined with a high level of concentration and monopoly power. Their vulnerability to a stagnating national income and declining export receipts would predictably be very great, and this seems to be borne out by the evidence. In spite of the deficiencies of Table 6.12, a number of the dynamic industries—rubber, basic metals, metal products, machinery, electrical equipment—evidently experienced a sharp contraction in output in the 1960s. Apart from the somewhat mysterious growth of paper production, it is noticeable that the non-traditional industries which maintained their growth have been chemicals (which includes wage-good production such as soap and matches), non-metallic minerals (supplying the construction industry which has been sustained by speculative real estate investment), and transport equipment (which consists mainly of very small enterprises engaged in repair and maintenance activities).

Two other characteristics of industrial production should be borne in mind, though to a large degree they are shared with the rest of Latin America. Demand for Uruguay's industrial output was almost entirely domestic, and only a tiny proportion of this output consisted of investment goods. The only precise calculation of these features of Uruguayan industry relates to 1963, but the proportions would have varied little up to 1970. In 1963 only 10.5 per cent of industrial output was exported, comprising about 65 per cent of the value of exports.[54] These proportions are somewhat misleading, however, since 95 per cent of these exports consisted of Uruguay's staples—meat, wool, hides and linseed oil—which had received some degree of processing. By 1970 probably only about 10 per cent of exports could be regarded as manufactures—mainly textiles and leather products—rather than processed primary products, and although it has been a feature of the post-1973 economic strategy to increase the value of such exports, the dependence of Uruguayan manufacturing industry on the domestic market has historically been almost total. Less than 1 per cent of industrial production for the home market in 1963 was composed of capital goods, with final consumption and intermediate goods accounting for 54.9 per cent and 44.5 per cent respectively. The imbalance reflects not so much the disincentive to potential producers of equipment of advantageous rates of exchange for imports of equipment during the rapid growth phase of industry, but more the extremely limited domestic demand for capital goods, especially, but certainly not exclusively, those embodying capital-intensive technologies.

The domestic orientation of industrialisation meant that the growth of manufacturing made only a minor contribution to the export capacity of the country before the 1970s. The direct impact of industrial growth on the balance of trade has been made through the demand for imports. The process of import substitution does not of course mean that the demand for imports falls. The share of consumer goods in the import bill is likely to contract, but as industrialisation proceeds the level of imports will increase because of growing demand for non-substitutable industrial inputs. However, substitution may be expected to occur in terms of a reduction in the ratio of commodity imports to GDP, and in the ratio of imported industrial inputs to industrial product. Even so, other factors than industrialisation may intervene to disturb these ratios, including import restraints imposed for balance of payments reasons, or problems of world supply, or the relaxation of import restraints resulting from an export boom. In Uruguay the overall import coefficient has passed through several clear phases in the post-war period. In the mid-1940s commodity imports were about 8 per cent of GDP, having been held at a low level during the war. The release of pent-up demand and very high export earnings increased the ratio to 18 per cent in the early 1950s, falling to 13 per cent by the end of the decade, and to 10 per cent in the mid-1960s. By 1970 it had increased slightly to 12 per cent. Table 6.14 summarises additional material on the relationship between imports and industrialisation. Comparing columns A and B it is interesting to observe that during periods of import growth the share of 'industrial inputs' remained steady or declined slightly, but increased as a proportion of total imports during periods of declining imports. Column D indicates that in the early post-war years of industrialisation, industry showed a high growth elasticity of demand for imports, until the early 1950s. This was associated with the great increase in imports of industrial equipment during the 1940s. From 1951 to 1959 the ratio of industrial imports to industrial product fell continuously: additional units of industrial output required smaller increases in foreign currency expenditure. It increased briefly as a result of the liberalisation of imports by the Blanco administration, but resumed its decline from 1962.

TABLE 6.14. Imports and industrial growth, 1942–67
(three-year averages)

	A Total commodity imports at 1961 prices (1961 = 100)	B Per cent of 'industrial inputs'[1] in imports	C Industrial product (1961 = 100)	D Ratio of imports of industrial inputs to industrial product (1961 = 100)
1942–4	30.5	72.1	50.1	60.5
1945–7	72.7	68.2	59.5	112.1
1948–50	96.8	68.5	70.1	130.7
1951–3	121.0	69.1	84.8	135.5
1954–6	115.2	74.3	99.4	118.0
1957–9	91.6	80.7	102.7	97.5
1960–2	104.6	75.6	100.9	107.7
1963–5	82.8	76.7	103.6	84.1
1966–7[2]	78.5	82.9	105.4	82.1

Notes:
1. Raw materials, fuels and lubricants, and capital equipment.
2. Two-year average.

Sources: Tables 6.2 and 6.3; Universidad de la República, *Estadísticas Básicas*, tables 12, 38; CIDE, *Estudio Económico*, table 27; Millot, Silva and Silva, *Desarrollo Industrial*, table 23.

An additional aspect of industrialisation with implications for the balance of payments is the role of foreign private capital. Unfortunately, there is very little information on foreign investment in Uruguay on which to base an assessment of its significance. The traditional sectors in which foreign capital had been important before the Second World War were public utilities (almost all British) and meat packing (US and British). By 1950 most of the public utilities had been acquired by the state, and it is generally believed that in the immediate post-war years there was little foreign capital available for export to Latin America. Nonetheless, as Table 6.15 shows, the net disinvestment of the 1930s was followed in the 1940s by a rapid increase in the book value of US direct investments in Uruguay. Moreover, more than three-quarters of the increase between 1942 and 1948 was financed by an inflow of capital, rather than from retained earnings, but the capital financed increased capacity in existing establishments, rather than new enterprises.[55] By 1950 the value of direct US investment had further increased to US$ 55 million.[56] In the absence of information on the industrial composition of this total, it is difficult to assess its significance. However, most of the increase is probably accounted for by the two meat-packing companies. Swift increased its capitalisation from $5.0 million (pesos) to $7.5

TABLE 6.15. Direct private investment by the USA in Uruguay, 1929–60 (million US dollars)

	1929	1936	1940	1943	1948	1960
Manufacturing	15.6	7.6	5.7	16.8	28.1	20
Distribution	5.1	2.9	2.5	2.8	6.0	4[1]
Petroleum	3.2	3.4	2.4	3.3	5.0	
Miscellaneous	4.0		0.3	1.3	1.3	23
Total	27.9	13.9	10.9	24.2	40.4	47

Note: 1. 'Trade'.

Source: UN, ECLA, *Foreign Investments in Uruguay* (E/CN.12/166/Add. 6, 2 May 1950) p. 6; (1960), US, Department of Commerce, *Survey of Current Business*.

million in 1945, and Artigas from $5.0 million to $7.0 million in 1945, and to $14.0 million in 1950.[57]

Though there were examples of foreign enterprise in manufacturing activity, it is very unlikely that foreign capital financed a significant part of Uruguay's industrialisation, at least before 1950. Rather, the capital was generated domestically, in the early period up to about 1950 largely on the basis of undistributed profits earned in industry itself.[58] Institutional forms of mobilising private savings were not an important source of industrial finance. During the rapid growth phase of industry, probably from the late 1940s, it appears that the high level of profitability of manufacturing was able to attract the surplus being earned in the livestock sector, thus reducing the traditional conflict of interest between the urban industrial bourgeoisie and the landowning class. Solari noticed in the early 1950s that 'the urban character of the rural upper class has increased in recent years through the growing participation of large landowners in the direction of large industrial enterprises, banks, etc.'[59] The same theme was taken up by Trías, who identified certain landowning families with particular industrial interests, though not on a systematic basis: '. . . these few examples serve to illustrate a fact of enormous importance in the history of Uruguay. The clear division between landowners and industrialists and bankers in the 1920s and 1930s has been giving way gradually but increasingly to an ever closer union of interests.'[60]

The prosperity of the rural sector at the end of the Second World War and during the Korean War, and the mobility of capital between sectors, evidently permitted the financing of industry from mainly domestic sources. In 1950 US direct investment in Uruguay stood at US$55 million, 1.2 per cent of the total in Latin America as a whole. In 1957, when the period of rapid industrialisation had reached its peak, US investment had only increased marginally, to US$57 million (0.8 per cent of the total).[61] In the following two years there was a net disinvestment by the USA of US$12 million, representing the withdrawal of US interests from the traditional *frigorífico* industry. By 1962, US capital in Uruguay represented 0.6 per cent of the total in Latin America, and 1.3 per cent of the total in manufacturing in the region. Clearly, Uruguay was of marginal and diminishing importance to US investors—the main source of foreign capital—during the period of industrial growth. Indeed, by the time US foreign investment in Latin American manufacturing began to grow rapidly in the 1950s, the stagnation of Uruguayan industry made it a very unattractive proposition. Not surprisingly, Uruguay's participation in US investment in the 1960s continued to shrink. In 1968 Uruguay shared 1 per cent of US direct investment in Latin America manufacturing with Paraguay, Ecuador and Bolivia. Probably the most attractive industry to US investors by then was meat packing, in new, small-scale and dispersed plant; but the bulk of foreign capital entering Uruguay in the 1960s went to the more profitable sectors of the economy, especially banking.

The use of technologies developed abroad also implies a burden on the balance of payments, either in direct payment of fees or in the acquisition of new equipment embodying the technology. It is impossible to say how heavy this burden has been, though one would not expect it to be proportionately as great as in those countries where industrial growth has been maintained, and where the dynamic group of industries is well developed. In other words, it is largely because of the low rate of industrial investment, and the very poor performance of the non-traditional industries that Uruguay has escaped some of the manifestations of technological dependence. It is certainly not through the development of a national and autonomous technological capacity. It is true that before 1930 there was important industrial research activity, much of it centred on the Instituto de Química Industrial, a public corporation.[62] But by the 1950s there was very little industrial research undertaken in the country, a lack which motivated proposals for the establishment of a technical assistance centre for industry. Such a centre was never established, but the proposals did result in a report assessing the technological needs of industry.[63] The needs were defined as the capacity to solve specific technical problems in production processes, and to develop new industrial products using Uruguayan raw materials. The possibility of developing new technologies of production adapted to Uruguayan conditions was apparently not considered specifically. However, one example—evidently isolated—was quoted of a foreign-owned plant managed by Uruguayan nationals which had succeeded in adapting an imported technology to local conditions of very small market size, displacing imported equipment with domestic capital goods. The general conclusion of the report on the technical competence of Uruguayan industry was that it varied inversely with the age of the capital equipment. The technical level of post-1945 industry was found to be good, whereas the failure to modernise pre-1940 plant condemned these establishments to high cost production using outdated techniques. Moreover, 'in some of these older industries, even when there is some knowledge of new improved methods, there could be more understanding of the need for technical advances. In industries with no real domestic competition, and with foreign competition excluded by tariff barriers, a manufacturer can have a guaranteed sale for his products whatever their price and quality.'[64]

The implication that competitive forces in Uruguayan industry are not well developed finds some support from data on industrial concentration in 1968. Establishments employing more than 100 persons in that year numbered 208, which was 0.71 per cent of all industrial establishments employing at least one person, and produced 50.2 per cent of the gross value of industrial output.[65] If workshop establishments employing 1 to 4 persons are excluded, the proportion would probably increase to approximately 57 per cent. This estimate compares with 51.5 per cent of total output of factory establishments (i.e. employing at least 5 persons) produced by large enterprises in 1964;[66] but the exclusion of the public sector in the estimates for that year reduces the apparent participation of large plants, notably through the omission of ANCAP whose oil-refining activities amounted to some 5 per cent of total industrial output. This level of industrial concentration is quite high, but not exceptionally so in comparison with other Latin American countries.

Obviously the 1968 data is not properly comparable with that for 1964, but part of it, relating to the number of large plants per industry, has been included in Table 6.16. Comparing the final two columns of the table, there are inexplicable discrepancies between the sources on the existence of large plants in the chemicals and machinery sectors. Nonetheless, it is possible to extract some general conclusions on the nature of industrial concentration. First, the majority of large enterprises were found in the basic traditional industries, notably textiles, foodstuffs, beverages and clothing. The first three of these also had a high proportion of total output (between one-half and three-quarters) produced by large establishments. Other traditional industries were dominated to a far lesser degree by large plants. In the clothing industry they produced less than 20 per cent of the sector's output, and there were no large plants at all in wood products and furniture making. On the other hand, only in the tobacco products and leather goods industries among the traditional group did the average large establishment account for more than 5 per cent of the industry's output, a conclusion confirmed also by the 1968 data.

Perhaps surprisingly, the dynamic industries were characterised to a

TABLE 6.16. Characteristics of private sector factory industry, by industrial sector, 1964

	Output per worker[1]	HP per worker	Machinery per worker[1]	Per cent of output from Small establishments[2]	Large establishments[2]	No. of large establishments[2,3]
Foodstuffs	137.2	3.15	53.2	12.9	65.0	34
Beverages	136.5	1.53	86.5	12.5	50.1	13
Tobacco	346.8	2.19	125.8	—	43.7	4
Textiles	88.2	2.61	90.6	5.2	75.7	50
Clothing	51.8	0.50	13.1	28.9	18.6	16
Wood	53.7	7.05	40.7	47.7	—	—
Furniture	55.2	1.03	13.2	45.4	—	—
Paper	92.5	11.30	122.2	4.0	64.9	4
Printing	82.5	1.48	78.2	19.4	27.8	9
Leather	83.5	8.09	61.4	12.4	62.0	4
Rubber	108.5	n.a.	134.8	7.3	92.7	4
Chemicals	175.0	4.98	108.6	28.8	—	19
Non-metallic minerals	80.7	7.59	57.3	12.2	43.0	16
Basic metals	168.8	8.67	55.3	30.9	58.4	5
Metal products	51.7	3.59	45.9	27.4	40.6	10
Machinery	56.9	3.89	50.1	8.2	42.8	—
Electrical equipment	68.3	2.14	38.9	14.4	39.6	7
Transport equipment	50.7	0.91	43.7	22.7	37.9	10
Other	62.6	1.86	57.8	58.2	5.7	2
Total	101.5	3.04	64.1	15.5	51.5	207
Traditional	112.5	2.64	62.6	12.2	60.5	
Dynamic	84.6	3.67	66.3	22.1	32.9	

Notes:
1. Thousand pesos at 1963 prices. Machinery valued at replacement cost.
2. Small = 5–19 employed, large = 100 +.
3. 1968; includes public sector establishments, oil refining is excluded.

Sources: (1964) Instituto de Economía, *Estructura Industrial del Uruguay*, vol. I (Montevideo, Universidad de la República, 1972); (1968) *Censo Económico Nacional: Industrias*.

far lesser degree by large plants. In 1964 less than one-third of output was produced in plants employing over 100 persons, and approaching a quarter of output in small establishments—in marked distinction to the distribution of output in the traditional group (Table 6.16). Only in rubber, paper and basic metals was the bulk of output produced by large establishments, and these were also the industries in which the concentration of output among a small number of plants was most clearly evident. The *a priori* view that dynamic or non-traditional industries incorporate more advanced technology which requires large plant size for its efficient utilisation, and which leads to the concentration of output and monopolistic control of sectors by a few establishments, does not seem to be supported. On the other hand the classification of industries as 'traditional' or 'dynamic' is in many ways a crude proceeding, since there are few industrial sectors which do not contain in some degree the demand and supply characteristics of both.

This point is emphasised by the data in Table 6.16 on capital intensity. It is true that horsepower per worker in the dynamic group is substantially greater, and machinery and equipment marginally greater, than in the traditional group. But what is most striking is the range of variation between the clothing industry and transport equipment on the one hand, and tobacco or leather and paper on the other. In the context of Uruguay, at least, it is evidently a myth to suppose that traditional wage-good industries are likely to be less capital-intensive, smaller scale, and with lower labour productivity than the dynamic group. But while these categories and the industries composing them are heterogeneous to a high degree with respect to size, mechanisation and productivity, Table 6.17 reveals a positive association for manufacturing industry as a whole between the size of establishment (measured by persons employed), machinery per head, and productivity. However, in comparison with a sample of other Latin American countries, the size of establishment in Uruguay does not appear to be the cause of very marked variation in the other factors.[67] Nor, surprisingly, does the degree of excess capacity increase with plant size; while there is very little difference between small and medium establishments, large plants have a markedly lower level of unutilised capacity as a proportion of total potential production (Table 6.17). Traditional industry produces 61 per cent of its output in large plants (Table 6.16), so predictably excess capacity is lower in such industries, at 48.1 per cent than in the dynamic group (52.3 per cent).[68] Nonetheless, this is largely the result of the importance of food processing in the industrial structure, which has a comparatively high utilisation rate; if food is excluded, the dynamic group—in spite of the supposed problem of technical indivisibilities—makes fuller use of installed equipment than does traditional manufacturing.

While the industrialisation process in Uruguay showed a number of peculiar features, the crisis which became apparent in the second half of the 1950s was not dissimilar to the more general crisis of import substitution in Latin America as a whole. The early growth of manufacturing resulted from the comparatively high income level of the population, and the concentration of population growth in Montevideo, the only centre of mass consumer demand. The further contribution of immigrants was to supply industrial enterprise. The significance of

TABLE 6.17. Characteristics of private sector factory industry, by size of establishment, 1964

	Employment	%	Output[1]	%	Output[2] per worker	Index	HP per worker	Index	Machinery[5] per worker	Index	Unused[3] capacity
Small[4]	22988	21.0	1715.6	15.5	74.6	100.0	2.56	100.0	44.6	100.0	53.6
Medium[4]	38069	34.8	3670.0	33.1	96.4	129.2	2.89	112.9	65.8	147.7	54.2
Large[4]	48245	44.1	5708.1	51.5	118.3	158.6	3.39	132.4	72.0	161.4	43.3
Total	109302	100.0	11093.7	100.0	101.5		3.04		64.1		49.7

Notes:
1. Million pesos at 1963 prices.
2. Thousand pesos at 1963 prices.
3. Unrealised production as per cent of potential production.
4. Small = 5–19 employed; medium = 20–99; large = 100 +.
5. Thousand pesos at 1963 prices, replacement cost.

Source: Instituto de Economía, *Estructura Industrial del Uruguay*, vol. I.

batllismo was primarily to extend the size of the market by redistributive policy, while acceding to demands for protection generally instigated by individual producers. The result by 1930 was, in comparison with the rest of the region, a highly developed, highly protected manufacturing industry. When resumed in the late 1930s and the decade after the Second World War, industrial growth continued to be based exclusively on the production of consumer goods for the domestic market. The exercise of trade and exchange control permitted the closure of the market to competing goods from outside, and the subsidised though irregular import of capital goods and·the embodied technology. Small market size, which also discouraged the participation of foreign capital, condemned import substitution to a rapid exhaustion of its growth potentialities. If *batllista* policy reduced the external competitiveness of Uruguayan industrial production by raising labour costs, it is hard to see this as an important explanation of the failure to explore potential export markets. Production costs were also raised by the gross under-utilisation of installed capacity and by the inefficiency engendered by a small number of firms dominating a captive market. The severe crisis in the rural sector provoked both supply and demand problems and exposed the fragility of the industrialisation model. However, the realignment of economic policy following the exhaustion of import substitution, attempted at the end of the 1950s, was frustrated by the continued command of the state machinery by the political parties. It was not finally achieved until the advent of the military.

7 Public Utilities and Public Corporations

I congratulated the President on the success of his *coup*, and his Excellency laughingly replied that he was sure we British would be pleased. I acknowledged that we had every reason to be, and that the hostility manifested for so long towards our companies would now doubtless be a thing of the past. I have never seen Dr Terra so care-free and gay . . . (Michell [Montevideo] to Foreign Office, 3 April 1933, FO 371 A3292/175/46.)

I. British Investment and Public Utilities

Anglo-Uruguayan Relations

It would be difficult to over-emphasise the importance of Britain's commercial and financial relationships with Uruguay as a formative influence on the economic structure of the country. Few other nations were absorbed so completely into Britain's informal empire in the nineteenth century. Indeed, it was British mediation at a critical stage in relations between Brazil and Argentina which promoted independence for Uruguay in 1828. Although Britain intervened no further in protecting Uruguay from the attentions of her two neighbours,[1] as late as 1885 Palgrave, British Minister in Montevideo, assured the Uruguayan government of 'effective support' (*apoyo efectivo*) in relations with Brazil and Argentina: and in 1911 the Foreign Office moved hastily to assure the Uruguayans that nothing more than 'good offices' had been offered.[2]

The importance of Uruguay to British interests in the early nineteenth century, apart from its role as a buffer state, was its strategic location on the estuary of the River Plate, thus commanding the great river systems—and trade routes—into the interior of the continent. Early fantasies of great wealth waiting to be exploited were not realised, but from the last quarter of the nineteenth century there was to be abundant compensation. The growth of exports of primitive pastoral commodities made Uruguay an attractive market for British enterprise, and enabled the country to sustain, with few lapses, the highest per capita foreign debt of any South American country. By the eve of the First World War

Britain had over £46 million invested in Uruguay. Almost all the country's foreign debt was held in London. The railway system—the second largest per capita and largest by land area of any South American country—was owned and operated by British companies. Public utilities in Montevideo were British monopolies or dominated by British capital: gas, water supply, trams, telephones. Britain was still the principal source of Uruguay's imports, and half the foreign shipping tonnage entering Montevideo was British.[3] In banking and insurance British companies held commanding positions. British capital was also represented in Liebig's, in land companies, and (least successfully) in gold mining. Not only was this adoption of the Uruguayan economy by British capitalists extremely lucrative:[4] it was a form of tutelage, with social and political as well as economic implications for the autonomy of the country.[5]

In 1913 British investments in Uruguay had virtually reached their peak. But for at least a decade a number of influences had been operating which threatened the position of British enterprise in the country, in particular by weakening the system of alliances with domestic social groups. Fundamental factors were the rigidity in the composition of British exports to Uruguay and the emergence of France, Germany and the United States as alternative sources of loan funds and imports. With New York anxious to supplant London in the foreign loan business, the British companies became somewhat more vulnerable than they had been when their treatment by the Uruguayan government might determine the success or failure of a loan. Uruguay was thus integrated into an imperial system which even before 1914 was under challenge; the existence of rival imperialist powers in principle offered Uruguay a degree of flexibility in its relations with Britain which would have been impossible in the nineteenth century. It is an historical irony, therefore, that one of the most important expressions of the loosening ties of dependence on the UK before 1914—the modest and diminishing share of exports to the British market—should have been so dramatically tightened by the growth of the chilled and frozen beef trade in the 1920s for which the UK was the main market. This commercial vulnerability intensified by restricted world trade conditions in the 1930s and 1940s, gave British interests a new sanction in their relations with the Uruguayan government.

Nevertheless there were also important internal developments at the turn of the century which resulted in tension between British capital and the host country. The period up to the First World War was characterised by rapid export growth, and a degree of diversification as import substitution occurred in a range of consumer-goods industries. This growth enabled Uruguay to sustain a higher rate of net immigration after the decline of the 1890s and the estimated population in 1914—1,223,000—was some 30 per cent greater than in 1900.[6] For

British capital, growth of the economy implied generally more profitable operations and expansion of capacity in some utilities but also sharper conflicts over tariff rates and the quality of service. This was true in relations both with landowners investing heavily in refined stock to take advantage of *frigorífico* prices; and with consumers in Montevideo, who found some of the utilities reluctant to expand and improve their services to keep pace with the rapid growth of the city. Dissatisfaction expressed by consumers was matched by the growing discontent of labour. The radicalisation of working-class aspirations in the late nineteenth century, associated with mass immigration and an open door policy towards those who were politically unacceptable elsewhere, found a focus in the British companies, like the railways and tramways, which were the largest industrial employers in the country. Moreover, the fact that 'the British section of the staff . . . form the bulk of the higher paid staff'[7] did little to endear the companies to their Uruguayan personnel, who saw their chances of promotion to more responsible and remunerative administrative posts diminished by this policy.

It is clear, therefore, that although Batlle y Ordóñez was identified by the Foreign Office as the source of all hostility to British-owned assets in Uruguay, and that he did much to obstruct their peaceful and profitable operation, nonetheless he was fundamentally expressing an antipathy towards British influence felt by a range of social groups for a variety of reasons. Before 1900 the domestic bourgeoisie had found itself in conflict with the *círculo orista*—the financial sector committed to the convertibility of the peso, led by the London and River Plate Bank and the Banco Comercial. Although the latter group was strengthened by the collapse of the Banco Nacional in 1891, the establishment of the Banco de la República in 1896 was a victory for the domestic capitalist class requiring credit for expansion, while the London and River Plate Bank had eventually to retire its bank-notes from circulation. Unlike Argentina, Uruguay did not have inconvertible paper currency regimes (except at moments of crisis), for which the strength of financial and trading interests, and the relatively smaller attraction of Uruguay to foreign investors, were doubtless responsible. But as the foundation of the state bank shows, the ranks of livestock producers, *saladero* owners, domestic manufacturers and wholesale and retail traders were growing stronger, relative to those—and the British were amongst them—whose interests were served by stable peso values and high interest rates.

The period during which Batlle's influence was the dominant force in Uruguayan politics extended virtually from the turn of the century to the depression. His role was to express the frustrations experienced by emerging capitalist and working classes in a small dependent country at their subordination to foreign capital, and to use the resources of the state to challenge the position of the British companies. In view of the notoriety which his policies aroused, it is important to note how his 'anti-imperialism' was circumscribed. It is certainly true for example that Batlle was prepared to exploit the ambition of US capital to supplant the position of the British, in floating loans, granting railway concessions, or stimulating the development of road transport. *Batllismo* was thus not opposed to the import of foreign capital— quite the reverse—but sought it as a means of limiting the power of foreign capital already located in the country, in defence, fundamentally, of the domestic capitalist class.

Nor was Batlle's anti-imperialism, if directed specifically against British imperialism, necessarily an expression of anti-British sentiment. During his first administration the Foreign Office expressed disapproval of Batlle for his aggressive settlement of the 1904 rising, his refusal of attempts at conciliation, and rejection of *coparticipación* in favour of party government—all of which would have restored tranquillity, and given those with 'the greatest stake in the Country, and the most real interest in its prosperity and welfare'[8] a voice in government. There was friction also over the affair of the *Agnes Donahoe*, a Canadian sealer arrested for fishing in territorial waters in 1905, whose owners' claim for compensation was eventually met by a secret payment in 1909, while Batlle was in Europe. The invective lavished by successive British representatives on Batlle, and the frequency (and ill-concealed hopefulness) with which his assassination was predicted, should not conceal the remarkable correctness with which Uruguay's financial affairs were conducted. Budgets were balanced, and debt obligations in London were promptly met.[9] However much his British critics might attribute this regularity to his ministers of finance, the recuperative powers of the *campo*, or his good luck, it is clear that Batlle was not tempted either to inflate the national debt—as President Idiarte Borda had done during revolutionary troubles in the 1890s—or to give British bondholders the least cause for complaint. Had Batlle intended a hostile policy towards Britain, the outbreak of war in 1914 and Uruguay's declaration of neutrality would have been the opportunity for some separation from the British system, particularly in view of the growth of German assets in the country and her expanding trade in the pre-war decade. But on the contrary, it was reported that Batlle's attitude to Britain gave every cause for satisfaction.[10] And if this euphoric appreciation should be discounted somewhat, it remains the case that it was the British companies and the commanding position enjoyed in particular by the public utilities, which were at the centre of Batlle's hostility.

The operation of public utilities by private enterprise, and in particular by foreign capital, is subject to certain peculiar conditions. In general, utilities require large fixed capital assets. They operate as *de facto* monopolies and may indeed be granted concessions guaranteeing a monopoly. Their product is consumed very generally within the society, and the terms on which it is made available may have widespread effects on the efficiency of the economy or on the welfare of the society. Their pricing policies may therefore assume special significance. If the tariff is high and the product of low quality, the criticism aroused is likely to be much greater than would be the case for the product of a competitive industry. Public hostility is likely to be greater still if the utility is not owned by nationals, partly because it is politically easier to focus criticism on a non-national group.

In Uruguay, with almost no national capital (private or public) in the public utility sector at the turn of the century, there was substantial criticism of the price of services to the consumer, the quality of services, and the profitability of the companies. Hostility was manifested in a variety of ways during the *batllista* period: by strikes, on occasion with official support or sanction; by taxes or similar financial penalties; by delaying or refusing to sanction tariff increases; by the promotion of competing companies or competing industries; and by negotiations for purchase by the state or the threat of expropriation without compensation. The treatment of specific utilities and its consequences are examined separately. But the general point can be made that political hostility to foreign-owned utilities, unless it forms the basis for prompt intervention or expropriation, may have negative results. By discouraging new investment the service is unlikely to be improved, while a further characteristic of public utilities—their capacity to sustain long-term capital consumption—may conceal disastrous long-run consequences for the host country.

Railways

In common with railway enterprise in a number of other South American republics, and with other public utilities in Uruguay, the pioneer installation was the initiative of Uruguayans and British residents in the country. Even before the first length was opened in 1869, however, British capital had been raised; and in 1876 ownership of the 200 km linking Montevideo with Durazno was transferred to the Central Uruguay Railway (CUR), the company which was to dominate the Uruguayan railway system. By then the North Western Uruguay Railway (NWUR) had begun construction of its line from Salto. For a decade thereafter progress was slow, but the investment boom of the 1880s produced an astonishing growth of construction (Table 7.1), total track open actually doubling between 1889 and 1891. The main line of the CUR crossed the Río Negro in 1887, and its Northern Extension reached Rivera from Paso de los Toros in 1892. The NWUR had also reached the Brazilian border at Cuareim in 1887, and the completion of the Midland Uruguay Railway's (MUR) main line in 1890 linked the

TABLE 7.1. Kilometres of railway open to traffic, 1869–1939

	Km opened	(With profit guarantee)	Total
1869	20	—	20
1870–4	260	—	280
1875–9	60	—	340
1880–4	37	—	377
1885–9	300	(235)	677
1890–4	858	(850)	1535
1895–9	159	(53)	1694
1900–4	276	—	1970
1905–9	192	(190)	2162
1910–14	396	(371)	2558
1915–19	80	—	2638
1920–4	—	—	2638
1925–9	72	—	2710
1930–4	124	—	2834
1935–9	175	—	3009

Source: DGEC, *Anuario Estadístico*.

CUR at Paso de los Toros with the main cities of the Littoral, Paysandú and Salto. Other lines completed by 1891 included the Uruguay Northern to the Brazilian border at Artigas, the North Eastern of Uruguay (leased by the CUR) to Minas, and the Central's Eastern Extension as far as Nico Pérez. By the mid-1890s two-thirds of the British-owned mileage was complete, the remainder—mostly extensions—following by 1914.

Two prominent characteristics of the system were its density of track per square kilometre, and the radiation of the lines from Montevideo. Both were inherent in the objectives for which the railways were built, and both had adverse effects on the Uruguayan economy. Though it is hard to escape the conclusion that the first railway in Uruguay was built out of enthusiasm for the progress which the railway was believed to represent, as early as 1872 a government commission was formed to study the appropriate railway network, and its report formed the basis of the Ley de Trazado Géneral de Ferrocarriles of 1884. Besides establishing the framework of concessions and privileges, the law of 1884 laid down the radial design of routes (later amplified by the law of 1888) which were to be built, stretching from Montevideo to the Littoral and the Brazilian border. For government, the railways were to secure the border and to assure the dominance of central authority over the regional power of *caudillo* landowners. And while a substantial internal traffic of wool and hides as well as passengers and general merchandise was expected, the decisive consideration for the dominant commercial interests was to draw through Montevideo a transit trade from Rio Grande do Sul, Argentina and Paraguay. One of the earliest railway concessions, granted to the North Western in 1868, was intended solely to convey international traffic to navigable waters at Salto. The system was thus built in the expectation of a traffic much greater than could be generated internally. The failure of those expectations, as Brazil and Argentina extended their own systems and improved their own ports, left Uruguay with an onerous burden.

That burden, of a railway system with substantial excess capacity, was borne in terms of deficient service, high freight rates, and payment by the government of guaranteed interest to the companies. By the end of 1907, some $12.4 million had already been paid to the companies in respect of guarantees on $27.0 million invested in guaranteed lines.[11] But the manner in which the guarantee was calculated further contributed to the railway problem. The law of 1884 established that 7 per cent (reduced to $3\frac{1}{2}$ per cent in 1891) would be guaranteed by the government on the construction costs of lines built under the conditions of the law, subject to a maximum construction cost of £5000 ($23,500) per kilometre. In practice the cost of construction on all lines was assumed to be £5000.[12] The companies therefore maximised the guaranteed return on their capital by minimising actual construction costs and maximising the length of their routes.[13] In practice this meant avoiding earth-works where possible, either by allowing numerous gradients, or by diverging from the direct route to avoid obstacles. Apart from contemporary comment, a comparison of track characteristics with Argentina gives some indication of the extent to which this occurred (Table 7.2). The result was a network, somewhat over-extended in length,[14] of sinuous

TABLE 7.2. Railway track characteristics, Uruguay and Argentina

	Total track length (km)	Per cent of track curved	Per cent of track graded
Uruguay (1893)	1450	29.7	74.6
Argentina (1916)	33822	10.0	69.7
Argentine North East Railway (1916)	1210	14.8	63.9
Entre Ríos Railway (1916)	1091	17.9	62.7

Note: A comparison of this kind needs to be made cautiously, especially because of geographical and track gauge variations. The ANER and ERR were both, like the Uruguayan system, built to standard gauge.

Sources: (Uruguay) Juan José Castro, *Estudio Sobre los Ferrocarriles Sudamericanos* (Montevideo, La Nación, 1893) pp. 88–96. (Argentina) Ministerio de Obras Públicas, Dirección General de Ferrocarriles, *Estadística de los Ferrocarriles en Explotación 1916* (Buenos Aires, 1924) table 6.

and undulating lines on which slow trains offered an infrequent and expensive service.[15]

High freight rates were the most frequent source of complaint about the British-owned railways throughout their history. Likely though it is that they were interested in immediate dividends rather than the long-term gains to be derived from tariff policies stimulating the development of the interior, still there were other reasons why rates were high. For example, the deficiencies of track construction limited the capacity of trains because of the gradients, and the low density of rolling stock increased the costs of assembling trains. The seasonal nature of much of the traffic also raised costs. But the main problem was excess capacity (Table 7.3):

> As the economic frontiers of Uruguay were coinciding more and more with its limited political frontiers, while it was losing the hinterland of the River Plate and the interior rivers which it had served as intermediary throughout the nineteenth century, the English railway was abruptly halted in its expansion and condemned to confine itself to the República Oriental.[16]

TABLE 7.3. Rail traffic and capacity per route kilometre, Uruguay and Argentina, 1912

			Rolling stock	
	Passenger-kms per km	Ton-kms per km	Passenger capacity per km (seats)	Freight capacity per km (tons)
Uruguay[1]	45.4	120.4	3.0[2]	19.8[2]
Argentina	85.8	264.3	5.6	55.2

Notes:
1. 1912/13.
2. CUR and associated companies only.

Sources: (Uruguay) DGEC, *Anuario Estadístico*; Central Uruguay Railway Company of Montevideo Limited, *Report of the Directors to the Proprietors*. (Argentina) *Estadística de los Ferrocarriles*.

Frustrated in their attempt to secure a significant international traffic, the railways found the domestic traffic in the thinly populated interior slow to develop. In competition with traditional forms of transport, they had relatively little difficulty in securing the traffic in exportable production. For example, for wool and hides Barrán and Nahum estimate the freight from Rivera to Montevideo (567 km) at 5–6 per cent of price in Montevideo in 1897.[17] For wheat, however, the incidence of the freight was twice as great. The spread of the railway did not result in the growth of agricultural colonisation and arable production, though the prevailing pattern of landownership, and the lack of suitable public lands for the attraction of immigrant colonists, were more crucial factors in the failure. In the development of the cattle-raising industry the contribution of the railway was very limited. Not until the beginning of the century did cattle arrivals in Montevideo by rail exceed those on the hoof; the increasing adoption of rail transport owed most to the effect of the *frigorífico* in raising prices for improved cattle. Even so, rail transport was less than satisfactory. The *Revistas* of the Asociación Rural and Federación Rural were filled with horror stories of losses due to delays and bad handling. The general manager of Frigorífico Swift estimated that only 38 per cent of arrivals by rail at Tablada were in good condition, while 12 per cent were seriously bruised.[18]

Thus, by the beginning of the twentieth century, the deficiencies of the railway service were not yet a cause of anti-imperialist sentiment, but rather of antagonism on the part of the domestic economic elite—the landowners. Even the British Minister in Montevideo, while obliged to defend its interests, would soon draw attention to the 'narrow and parochial-minded policy' of the CUR.[19] The fundamental complaint directed at the railways concerned their high tariffs. The law of 1884 permitted the state to reduce tariff rates only when the rate of profit exceeded 12 per cent.[20] Unable to demonstrate that this rate was reached, the government could only appeal to the railways from time to time for a reduction.

The issue came to a head during the First World War, when operating costs increased sharply due to the high price of coal and the effects of labour legislation. Moreover, in 1917 the forty-year concession of tax privileges and exemptions to the CUR came to an end. To meet these additional charges the CUR raised its rates, in the face of protest but at a time of export prosperity. However, late in 1920 the company announced a further increase averaging 34.7 per cent to cover the continuing high cost of materials, but coinciding with the post-war depression in the livestock sector. The increase was almost universally condemned. In extensive debates on the issue[21] the inadequate controls which the state could exercise over the companies was revealed in terms of the costs they declared and the authenticity of their claims for guarantee payments. Having failed in its attempt to show that freedom from state intervention in the fixing of tariffs was one of the privileges of the CUR which had expired in 1917, the government then offered a new guarantee in exchange for lower rates. The offer was rejected, leading the British Minister to observe regretfully that the 'unyielding attitude of Mr. Bayne [general manager of the CUR] has not helped matters'.[22] The CUR thus retained its freedom to set its own tariff rates, even to levels 'perhaps unequalled in the rest of the civilised world'.[23] Indeed, legal confirmation of this right enabled the CUR to force the issue of state purchase of its assets after the Second World War. In April 1945 a tariff increase of 30 per cent was proposed: 'Grindley [general manager of the CUR] tells me that his railway's tariffs have already been raised some 90 per cent, on an average, since the war began, and the still further increase now mooted is more intended to frighten the Government than anything else.'[24]

An alternative strategy to reduce the power of the British railways was to oblige them to compete. Even in 1888, in the full flood of enthusiasm for British capital, it had been possible to argue the principle of state railway operation.[25] But not until Batlle's second administration were effective steps taken. In 1912 a permanent fund for the construction of state railways was established with a proposal for 500 km of light railways, but in practice the initiative seems to have depended on the willingness of US enterprise to become involved. The Uruguay Railway Company (the Farquhar syndicate) was granted a concession for new construction in 1912, and the Panamerican Transcontinental Railway in 1909 took over the concession for a line from Colonia to San Luis. The actual track built was very limited, and in 1920 these and other ailing fragments were grouped together in the Administración de Ferrocarriles y Tranvías del Estado (AFTE). Some new construction was undertaken by the state in the inter-war years, but the eventual 700 km, dispersed among isolated lines, functioned essentially as feeders to the CUR, and lacked independent access to Montevideo; and AFTE persistently earned deficits. Indeed, it would have been very surprising had it done otherwise. The basic problem in the railway system as a whole was unused capacity, for which the land tenure system, and the obstacles it posed to the extension of arable production, were more to blame than the railway tariff.

Acquisition of the British lines, rather than their duplication, had evidently become policy by the end of the First World War. Though the hostile attitude of Batlle to the railways was obvious, no serious negotiations for purchase by the state seem to have occurred until 1918–20, during the period of post-war prosperity. In 1923 an Argentine syndicate was reported to be acting as intermediary in the transaction,[26] and in June 1931 provisional agreement had been reached on the price and terms of purchase of the CUR,[27] but the deal was cancelled with the depreciation of the peso and the issue was not reopened until the end of the Second World War.

In the event, the only positive competitive pressure which the government could bring to bear was the development of alternative transport systems. During Batlle's first administration an attempt was made to revive river shipping which had declined substantially during the late nineteenth century;[28] and the Western Extension of the CUR having failed to realise expectations because of the competition of coastal shipping to Montevideo, was obliged to reduce its rates.[29] But road transport was to offer the effective challenge. At the beginning of the century the state of the roads was 'primitive, not to say deplorable', for lack of investment and the fact that 'landowners are averse to having roads, as they prefer to keep their great stretches of pasture land in their natural state'.[30] The interest of the CUR, and of the landowners, lay in public expenditure improving the very poor state of access roads to the stations; but Batlle, in laws of 1905 and 1912, proposed a national system of roads. In spite of the growing adoption of road transport in the 1920s, however, most construction was limited to Montevideo and the immediate area. By 1928 only 610 km were built, extending from the capital to San José, Florida, Minas and Maldonado,[31] such that only the short-distance traffic of the CUR was affected.[32] Nonetheless, the competition of roads built on routes parallel to the railways had a considerable impact on rail traffic from the mid-1920s. The CUR introduced faster trains, lower tariffs, and even a fleet of motor lorries owned by a subsidiary company, La Uruguaya.[33] By 1930 the railways were still holding their own, but 'the road-building schemes in this Republic have assumed so comprehensive a nature, and have been pushed forward with such energy and persistence, that there is every reason to suppose that the future will witness a rapid expansion of road transportation'.[34] And having failed to sell their assets to the state in 1931, 'the early thirties found these lines resorting to drastic revision of rates to regain traffic'.[35] The effect of the depression was to slow the growth of road transport, with restrictions on the import of new vehicles. In any case, by 1933 there were still only 1800 km of roads completed; none had crossed the Río Negro, and the system fell far short of the 3145 km of national and 2329 km of interdepartmental roads proposed by the Comisión de Trazado General de Caminos y Ferrocarriles in 1923.[36] Nonetheless the area served included the region supplying Montevideo with fruit, vegetables and dairy produce, as well as the wheat-growing district of the southern Littoral and wool producers to the north and east. The Second World War also reduced the import of road transport equipment, but by 1949 6770 km of roads were completed, and the competitive position of the railways had been undermined.[37] In that year the railways passed into the ownership of the Uruguayan government.

Thus the power of the British-owned railways was curbed, but a massive price was paid. Competition from roads, the expectation of selling up, and difficulties in securing exchange for remittances, had discouraged new investment. Track, rolling stock and workshops were all antiquated. Of 147 locomotives owned by the CUR group (which since 1937 had included the other British companies), only 14 had been built after the First World War.[38] In the 1950s the railways required a complete re-equipment but priority had to be given to motive power and in other departments the process of capital consumption continued. Moreover the road system, conceived as a competitor to the railways, experienced similar problems of under-investment and was not adapted to the requirements of an integrated transport policy. 'Departmental and local roads are, in general, in bad condition, which impedes and increases the cost of conveying agricultural and livestock products to main roads or railway stations.'[39]

Water Supply

The provision of water to consumers in Montevideo provides a comparable example of the effects on a host country of a social service monopolised by foreign private capital. The elements of the case are the high capital costs of the service and the very high profits received by the Montevideo Waterworks Company (Cia. de Aguas Corrientes); and the reluctance of the company to improve the service and lower its tariff. The negotiating position of the Uruguayan government was based on its capacity to sanction a competing service, or to acquire the company; its weakness was the increasing urgency of improved service. The issue which dominated relations with the company—apart from the water tariff—was the construction of additional pipe-lines to increase capacity.

The original concession to provide a piped water supply from the Santa Lucía river, some 60 km from Montevideo, was granted in 1868 to a Uruguayan syndicate led by Enrique Fynn. Service began in 1871, with a concession granting a monopoly and a monthly subvention of $4600 (£11,700 p.a.) for twenty years. The enterprise did not yield an adequate return, in spite of the tariff of $0.40 per cubic metre to private consumers, and was sold to the British company in 1879. Even before the original concession expired there was dissatisfaction with the quality of the water, which was consumed direct from the river, and in 1889 the company agreed to install filtration and purification works. It was then able to secure a provisional renewal of the original concession which expired in 1891. The company retained its tax privileges but lost its monopoly rights, but was to enjoy the same privileges as any future competitor. Indeed the company invoked the last provision in 1894 in order to defeat a proposal by José Carrera (a former employee) who offered a scheme supplying much cheaper water in exchange for a monopoly. Nonetheless there was growing discontent and street demonstrations at the price of water—unchanged at 40 cents—and meter rents.[40] In 1900 a commission was named 'to see if a new and low cost water service was possible, and having come to an adverse conclusion and without technical and financial resources to study the matter further it presented a proposal to continue the concession of 1867'.[41] The company offered to reduce its tariff by between 26 per cent and 32 per cent in return for 'an arrangement which secures the stability of its relations' with the government for 30 years—a new monopoly presumably—but the offer was rejected.[42]

Clearly, the elements of conflict existed already by the time of Batlle's, first presidency. In 1905 the company's attempt to sell its assets to the government fell through, and the time was then propitious for Carrera to revive in 1906 (with presidential approval) his ambitious Zabala Canal project, which besides supplying water would have the additional virtue of providing passenger transport over its 106 km at half the rate charged by the CUR.[43] Even the British Minister, called upon to defend British interests, confided to London that 'no doubt it will reduce the price of water, which in Montevideo is high'.[44] In the event, though the concession for the canal remained current for several years, the British company evidently received sufficient assurances in an agreement with the government in 1907 to persuade it finally to install a second pumping main. In return the company conceded a tariff reduction to 28 cents to be made when the number of private services should reach 15,000, and to 24 cents and 20 cents with succeeding increments of 5000.[45] That the first of these reductions became effective in December 1908, with the others following at intervals of 26 months and 19 months, is sufficient indication of the extent to which the company's service had fallen behind the growth of Montevideo. Nor did these concessions jeopardise the prosperity of the company. Since 1889 it had paid an ordinary dividend averaging over $5\frac{1}{2}$ per cent; in 1909 it paid 8 per cent, and maintained that dividend throughout the next twenty years. In the circumstances the 'spontaneous' reduction of the tariff to 18 cents in 1918 was not excessively generous.

The prevarication which preceded the installation of the second main pipe was reproduced in the 1920s for the third, though over a more extended period. In 1920 the Zabala concession was granted to a British financier but the waterworks company, which was then involved (as in 1905) in abortive negotiations for the sale of the company to the government, decided not to oppose the concession. In the event its confidence that Edwin Steer would not raise the necessary US $14.5 million was justified. But until the collapse of the Zabala plan in 1923, and unless the government guaranteed the terms of an eventual acquisition (which Batlle had been threatening at least since 1911), the company declined to proceed with the third pumping main which it had proposed to lay in 1920. In 1923 the company renewed its proposal, in the context of an increasingly inadequate service: pressure was not sufficient to maintain continuous service to all consumers, new urban construction outstripped the capacity of the service, such that in the mid-1920s a third of the population of the capital still relied on collecting rainwater.[46] The proposal was extensively debated by the legislature, and not finally approved until 1928. The agreement guaranteed compensation to the company when it should eventually be acquired, and secured progressive rate reductions as the number of services was extended. It was strongly opposed by the *batllistas* who pressed for immediate expropriation of the company, but the majority report of the special commission of the House of Representatives, while stressing the urgency of the problem and its solution, took the opportunity to answer a traditional *batllista* argument.[47]

Thus the Montevideo Waterworks Company maintained intact its monopoly. That its service was seriously deficient until the 1930s is evident from the universal condemnation of it, not least—in private—from those who were obliged to defend its interests. In 1931 the third pumping main was completed, and although the depression ended its remarkably high dividend record, by 1936 it was paying 4 per cent to stockholders, and 5 per cent plus bonuses during the Second World War. In 1936 agreement was reached with the government by which an exchange quota for remittances was guaranteed, in return for minimum annual expenditures by the company on extensions. Its eventual acquisition by the state, in 1949, was for £3.06 million, little short of the company's own valuation at the end of 1945 of £3.28 million.[48] Stockholders received £170 per £100 stock.[49]

Tramways

In 1897 a British company, known locally as the Sociedad Comercial de Montevideo (registered after 1904 as the United Electric Tramways of Montevideo), acquired three of the horse-drawn tram enterprises—a fourth was added in 1905—and immediately proposed electrification. The proposal was initially refused because of the duration of the concession requested, but within weeks of Batlle taking office in 1903 it was granted and the first electrified service was inaugurated in 1906. Two years earlier a German company, La Transatlántica, had acquired two tram lines, and electrification followed. The two companies, with 280 route kilometres and 5000 employees by the mid-1920s, had a profound impact on the city in opening up suburban areas for residential construction, while land values in favoured parts of the capital increased a hundredfold.[50] In 1905 the trams had conveyed 27 million passengers; in 1910 the total increased to 63 million, and at the next five-year intervals to 78 million and 119 million. At their peak, in 1926, the trams provided 155 million passenger journeys.[51]

In that year La Transatlántica—now owned by the Cia. Hispano-América de Electricidad of Barcelona—was absorbed by the Sociedad Comercial, and ownership passed from UET to Atlas Electric and

General Trust. It was an unfortunate moment to acquire a tram company (though not as unfortunate as 1948). Passenger journeys fell to a stable average of about 120 million during 1928–35, and to barely 100 million on the eve of the Second World War. There was in fact a brief resumption of profitability; during 1913–24 only two dividends had been declared by UET, but between 1925 and 1932 Atlas (whose principal asset was the tramways of Montevideo, still conventionally known as the Sociedad Comercial) distributed nearly 4 per cent annually. But from 1933 onwards shareholders received nothing. Indeed, compared with other British-owned public utilities, including the Montevideo Gas and Dry Dock Company and the Montevideo Telephone Company, the financial performance of the trams—though not necessarily their service—was the worst.[52] Like the CUR but unlike the Waterworks, the trams faced very effective competition, from road transport; but unlike the CUR, the tram company had accepted a concession which allowed it neither to adjust its tariff nor to operate a road transport fleet itself. Also, the company enjoyed extremely bad relations with the municipal government of Montevideo, and with its work force.

In the latter, the tram company was not alone. As the largest industrial employers in the country, the railways and tram companies were inevitably a focus for union activity. But for the CUR, the test of strength came in 1908 during the government of Williman who was well disposed to the foreign companies. The strike involved 3500 railway workers, lasted 41 days, and ended in failure. The CUR's resources were massive: £25,000 was spent in combating the strike, and 'every assistance, moral and physical, was given by the civil and military authorities'.[53] For the CUR the money spent was an investment: 'We eliminated from the staff the whole of the agitators and everybody who had taken an active part in the affairs of the extinct Union'.[54] It was a major defeat for the union movement, as well as for the railwaymen.

By 1911, when the first major tram strike occurred, Batlle was back in office. The two-week strike of 3000 workers was successful in raising wages and establishing the nine-hour day, and the company complained of the half-hearted action of the police.[55] Worse, the municipal government proposed to fine both companies over £450 for each day that they failed to provide (because of the strike) a service. The same year six buses began to compete with the trams; the Sociedad Comercial claimed, unsuccessfully, that they infringed the terms of its concession. However, the primitive state of the streets in Montevideo rescued the companies. The buses were retired within a few years, and there was no effective competition to the trams until their reappearance in 1926.

By then relations with the municipality had deteriorated still further. While other public utilities were able to accommodate higher labour costs by raising their tariff, the tram companies had concessions which fixed the level of the tariff. In 1918 a claim supported by strike action for wage increases of 20 per cent was conceded in part, with a promise of full settlement if a tariff increase should be approved. In 1920 a 10 per cent wage increase was accepted, again with the offer of a further increase when a revised tariff should be sanctioned. Two years later, following a 21-day strike, the tram companies were temporarily taken over by the municipal government and a wage increase was paid, though the tariff remained at the level of the original concession. In 1923, however, the companies defeated the municipal government in the law courts over the issue of the fines levied at the time of the 1911 and 1918 strikes;[56] and in 1926 a legal action against the city for the intervention of 1922 was also successful.

During these skirmishes, the operation of the tram companies—though unprofitable—continued to grow. The introduction of buses in 1926, however, had an immediate impact which was intensified by the refusal of the municipality either to allow the tram companies to run buses themselves, or to permit the physical integration of the two tram enterprises now controlled by Atlas. Not until 1933 was this achieved, but by then over 500 buses, with the benefit of certain tax exemptions and in spite of a higher tariff than the trams, had taken 40 per cent of the urban transport business.[57] Indeed, by the terms of their concessions the tram companies had been obliged to meet part of the costs of road paving, the absence of which had been the principal barrier to a competition which was now proving ruinous.

The depression, however, in driving Uruguay into a closer bilateral relationship with a dominant country, offered opportunities for exacting more favourable treatment. The Protocol to the Anglo-Uruguayan Trade and Payments Agreement of 1935, paragraph 2, committed the Uruguayan government to grant 'such benevolent treatment' to British-owned public utilities, 'as may conduce to the further economic development of the country, and to the due and legitimate protection of the interests concerned in their operation'.[58] Atlas had made clear the sort of benevolent treatment they wanted for their tram company in 1933. Four days after the *coup d'état* of 31 March which dissolved the 1919 constitution and dispersed the *batllistas*, Atlas proposed to the national government a loan of US $1 million, repayable over fifteen months, 'on the understanding that the new concessions to La Sociedad Comercial de Montevideo would be granted before it matured'.[59] The loan contract was signed on 20 April 1933, allowing the physical absorption of the former La Transatlántica enterprise and cancelling certain claims of the municipal government against the company.

In its central objective, to buy out the bus owners and thus restore its monopoly of public transport in Montevideo, Atlas did not succeed. A government commission in October 1933 proposed a consortium between the municipality and the Sociedad Comercial, subject to the acquisition by the latter of the bus interests. Like the tram company, the government was anxious to see the installation of trolley-bus lines which would consume power generated by the Río Negro hydroelectricity works, then under construction. Negotiations dragged on while the bus owners, in spite of pressure from national and municipal government, refused to give way. In 1937 they formed a cooperative—CUTCSA—and the following year were granted a limited and circumscribed concession, but one which defeated the ambitions of the tram company, either to secure a monopoly or to receive a guaranteed return on its capital. Shareholders were warned in successive annual reports that the accummulating arrears of depreciation and renewals made it unlikely that they would ever receive a profit from the tramways of Montevideo. Finally, in 1948, a purchase price of £1,814,000 was agreed with the government of Uruguay, against a book value of £4.4 million.

II. Batlle y Ordóñez and the Public Corporations

A feature of the Uruguayan economy in the period before 1930 was the growth of the public sector. The list of enterprises which were organised as, or converted into, *entes autónomos* during the *batllista* period is remarkable, especially in view of the very limited nature of state participation in the economies of other dependent countries at this time. In seeking the special conditions which gave rise to the phenomenon of *batllismo*, a deep division of opinion exists between those who attribute the achievement to the distinctive and original ideology of Batlle and his disciples, and those for whom *batllismo* represents the outcome of a particular set of class relationships in a somewhat peculiar political context, at a time of rapid economic growth.[60] A version of the latter view has been outlined in Chapter 1; but it would be absurd to deny the singular nature of Batlle's social and economic thought. In it the economic functions of the state were a dominant theme, and were expressed concisely in his presidential message accompanying an early and highly significant proposal.[61] The state, it was argued, might provide a service or a product where to do so would increase the national income or secure a more equitable distribution of it. This might arise in conditions of private monopoly, or to increase public revenue, or to reduce a drain on foreign currency.

However, an understanding of the nature of *batllismo* lies essentially in what was achieved (and equally, what was not attempted), rather than in statements of ideology. The hostility towards foreign capital was not disguised; but as the first half of this chapter has shown, the deficiencies of the public utilities owned by British capital had long been notorious and were experienced by all economic and social classes. Batlle's contribution was to express the widespread dissatisfaction with British enterprise, at the end of the expansive phase of British imperialism, often supported by the United States. Although in the event only certain kinds of port services and insurance business were wrested from British companies and absorbed into the public sector, there seems no reason to doubt that attempts to purchase the major utilities were whole-hearted, and that they failed because of a deteriorating economic position in both 1921 and 1931.

Batlle's relations with domestic capital were very different. On the one hand the growth of the public sector in infrastructural activities—port, electricity, railways—or in the production of intermediates—chemicals, and later cement and alcohol—enhanced possibilities of the profitable employment of domestic capital. On the other hand, although the state assumed monopoly powers in a variety of activities it neither displaced domestic capital nor pre-empted industrial sectors likely to attract domestic capital. The extension of the public sector was thus consistent with the policy of the Banco de la República—nationalised at the beginning of Batlle's second administration—in expanding the supply of credit to meet the growing requirements of commerce and industry. It also accorded with the concession of tax privileges to protect incipient manufacturing activities, and the Raw Materials Law of 1912. In the aspiration to meet the government's expenditure requirements out of surpluses earned by state corporations, the role of the public sector was consistent with Batlle's fiscal ideas, in particular to minimise taxes on productive activity.

The role of the state in the economy was thus largely complementary to that of the domestic private sector. In promoting urban industrial and commercial activities, in the context of (though not at the expense of) rapid export growth, Batlle championed the small capitalist class and associated urban groups on which his power was effectively based. *Batllismo* did not create these classes, or effect a fundamental realignment of their interests; the growth of manufacturing, of arable agriculture for the domestic market, of an identifiable working-class movement, were all clearly evident by 1900. The rise of the middle sectors in Uruguay was partly a function of the relative weakness of commercial interests, in losing the transit trade, and of the rural sector, in transition from primitive to modernised capitalist forms of production: but decisively, it was a function of immigration. Politically, Batlle was able to exploit the weakness of the rural sector in general, and of the Blanco party in particular, to identify the Colorado party with these urban groups and to extend to them formal political rights in the constitution which was accepted in 1917 and came into force two years later. An alliance was created consisting fundamentally of groups which had no direct participation in the flow of income generated by the dominant economic activity, the production and export of livestock products.

Within the alliance there remained substantial internal conflicts, in particular between petty capitalists and workers. Some of the most characteristic features of *batllismo*—the growth of the state sector, the expansion of education—found common ground, but in labour and social welfare legislation *batllismo* appears to have advanced working-class interests in opposition to those of urban employers. The explanation of this apparent contradiction is two-fold. Firstly, Batlle's labour legislation did not run far ahead of trade union demands, but generalised what had been achieved only by the most highly organised workers. In that sense the *batllista* initiative consisted less in devising radical measures of protection for labour—limitation of hours of work, compensation for injury, minimum wages—than in converting working-class demands into part of the political programme of the Colorado party. Nonetheless the labour laws did increase conflict within the urban economy. Although the largest employers were foreign companies—public utilities and *frigoríficos* especially—domestic capital was strongly opposed to government interference in labour matters.[62] Hence the second and more fundamental explanation of the alliance of conflicting groups is that while seeking to promote their common interest, the *batllistas* also recognised the inevitability of social conflict and changed its nature to suit their own purpose. One of the great paradoxes of *batllismo* is that while supporting the working class in the achievement of its aims—'every strike is justified and it would be ideal if all could be successful'[63]—it also denied the necessity of social classes and the utility of class conflicts.[64] By appropriating the aims of the working class and converting them into legislative achievement or aspirations, *batllismo* not only fatally weakened working-class political and economic institutions, but also established itself as a multi-class political force, and invested in the apparatus of the state the power to mediate in conflicts arising within the urban economy. The extension of state authority in this sphere enhanced the role of the political process and consolidated the dominance of the Colorado party.

Equivalent functions were performed by the growth of the public sector of the economy. While the profitability of private capital was generally heightened by state involvement in complementary activities, employment possibilities were also increased, especially for the middle classes, in the administration of the state corporations, for whom equivalent employment in the British-owned public utilities was blocked.

The development of State enterprises and services ensured employment for the developing middle classes, for which the educational system was extended to provide the necessary preparation of the personnel which the public administration would later recruit. The dependent upper middle classes rose with the development of the State . . .[65]

The expansion of the state sector in the economy occurred generally in response either to the failure of existing private capital in an industry, or to the development of a new industry. In a number of instances it took the form of consolidating a position, by declaration of a full monopoly or complete nationalisation, which the state had already achieved before the *batllista* period. Radical initiatives to displace existing private interests were rare. In the financial sector, the Banco de la República was nationalised in 1911 not by expropriating existing private share-holders—there were none—but by reversing the intention when the bank was established in 1896 eventually to admit the participation of private capital. The following year the state did take over private interests in the Banco Hipotecario, but only following disclosure of malpractice and speculation in its bonds by the bank's directors. The state monopoly of services in the port of Montevideo was envisaged in the law creating the Administración Nacional del Puerto de Montevideo in 1916, and became effective a decade later, but the state had participated in port services since the opening of the port in 1909. State operation of railways began with the acquisition in 1915 of the moribund Ferrocarril y Tranvia del Norte from private owners who were in no sense reluctant.[66] Monopoly by the state of electricity supply (except for the concessions held by the tram companies) was secured for Montevideo in 1905, and extended to the rest of the country when the Usinas Eléctricas del Estado (UEE) was created in 1912; but in this case also public sector participation began when the assets of the private company passed to the municipal government of Montevideo on the liquidation of the Banco Nacional, its owners, in 1896. State particip-ation in the *frigorífico* industry was proposed by Batlle, in the face of conservative opposition, but the plan was not pressed once US capital had arrived to increase capacity in the industry in 1912.

Nonetheless there were some fundamental initiatives. In 1912 the Instituto de Química Industrial (IQI) was established. With educational and advisory responsibilities to the private sector as well as to government, IQI was a classic illustration of the role of the public sector in supporting private capital. During the First World War production of certain chemicals was begun to meet local requirements while imports were restricted. In the 1920s superphosphates were produced and their use by arable farmers encouraged by credits. Lack of information on soil characteristics reduced their usefulness, however, and so for a brief period IQI conducted free chemical analyses of soil.[67] There were also experiments in the early 1920s to develop a motor fuel based on domestically produced alcohol in place of rapidly growing imports of refined fuels.

These attempts to expand domestic consumption of industrial alcohol were also linked with another departure from orthodoxy, the proposal to secure a state monopoly in the production and sale of alcohol. After fluctuations in the level of protection available to domestic distilleries, high tariffs were imposed at the beginning of the century, and production grew from an annual average of 2.4 million litres (at 96 per cent equivalent) in 1901–3 to 3.0 million in 1910–12.[68] This somewhat leisurely growth was accompanied by an increasing concentration of the industry in the hands of the French industrialist Meillet who made 'an immense fortune';[69] and in 1912 Batlle proposed that the protected, private, foreign-owned monopoly should be replaced by a state industry. Meillet, with the backing of the French government,[70] declined the terms of expropriation. The level of protection was immediately reduced, such that the import component in the total supply of alcohol increased between 1910–12 and 1918–20 from 30 per cent to 90 per cent; but Meillet shifted his alcohol interest from production to trade, and dominated imports. In 1921 Batlle renewed his attempt to secure a state monopoly, but again it foundered on the refusal by Meillet to accept the government's valuation of his distilleries. Not until the creation of ANCAP in 1931 did state participation in the industry begin.

The only other major attempt to oust private capital also concerned foreign interests but in this case—the creation of the Banco de Seguros del Estado—it was rather more successful. One of the first proposals of Batlle's second administration was a state monopoly of insurance business on the grounds of its profitability, the need to subsidise from his profitable business certain forms of socially desirable insurance, the loss incurred by the nation in the remission of profits by foreign companies, and by some evidence of very limited competition between the companies. Especially in fire and marine risk the market was in fact dominated by foreign companies, which since 1906 (when of the 33 companies, 20 were British and only two Uruguayan) had paid higher levels of tax than their domestic competitors.[71] On the grounds that the declaration of a monopoly without compensation would deprive the British companies, which wrote about three-quarters of insurance in the country,[72] of the value of the good-will they had earned, the Minister of Foreign Affairs was warned that 'legal and Diplomatic claims will probably be preferred against the Uruguayan government'.[73] The validity of such claims was rejected by the government, on the grounds that the legislation would not discriminate against foreign capital, but the threat seems to have been effective. The Banco de Seguros opened for business at the beginning of 1912 with a monopoly of fire, life and workmen's compensation risks, but the monopolies were not to become effective until some future date. The local representative of Standard Life believed that diplomatic pressure was responsible for this victory.[74] However, the Banco de Seguros immediately secured a commanding share of the market, offering lower rates than its competitors and in the mid-1930s it had two-thirds of fire insurance and three-quarters of life and marine business without needing to invoke its monopoly powers.[75] While losing business to the state corporation the British companies nonetheless enjoyed good relations with it, apparently securing from it a substantial reinsurance business.[76]

By the conclusion of Batlle's second term of office, the public sector had been extended to include a considerable variety of activities. The initial capital, and funds required for major new investments, was generally raised by the issue of public debt specifically for the particular corporation. At the end of 1915 a total of $23.9 million (£5.1 million) had been raised for industrial and financial activities in the public sector, and by 1930 a further $10.4 million—both figures excluding railways.[77] It is not easy to determine the exact distribution of these loans between the domestic and foreign capital markets, but particularly during and after Batlle's second administration there was a growing tendency to place public issues domestically. In 1910 only 6 per cent of the debt in circulation was internal, compared with 17 per cent in 1915 and 36 per cent in 1930.[78] Thus the initial capital of the Banco de la República was raised in London in 1896, the construction of the port of Montevideo was financed externally, and as late as 1914 a loan to permit the acquisition of the Banco Hipotecario was made in London. In addition most of the railway construction by the state during the 1920s was financed in New York. But the initial capital of the port administration (1915), the Banco de Seguros (1911) and the Usinas Eléctricas (1912) was found in Montevideo—some $9 million—and the $5 million capital of the Frigorífico Nacional (1928) was also raised domestically. Thus a significant part of the growing surplus generated in the livestock export sector was being channelled into government loans, and clearly the incursion of the state into directly productive activities did not dismay those who controlled the allocation of the surplus. Nor is there evidence that domestic risk capital wished to challenge any of the state (or foreign-owned) monopolies. On the contrary, by 1920 only eighteen companies had made public issues which were quoted in that year on the Montevideo stock exchange, the largest (apart from commercial banks) having an authorised capital of no more than $1 million.[79]

The variety of industries and services for which state corporations were created, and the varying motives for their creation, make it difficult to assess the performance of the public sector in general. Criteria which might be used for assessment include the flexibility of the supply response to changes in the level or nature of demand; the efficiency of the corporations; and the use made of surpluses which were earned. The laws creating the corporations rarely spelled out what policy should be pursued on these questions. The UEE, for example, was given a monopoly of electricity supply in 1912. It was required to obtain the approval of the government in setting its tariff. Ten per cent of annual profits were to be retained as a reserve fund, the remainder in each department of the country to be employed in increasing capacity or lowering the tariff (in proportions to be determined by the government) with payment of a fixed annual sum to the department of Montevideo.[80] The laws of the other corporations contained similar provisions.[81] The *batllista* ideology was well developed in explaining the necessity or the preferability of state enterprise in certain sectors, but less strong in indicating appropriate commercial policies for such organisations.

In practice, the directorates tended to be 'conservative in expansion, in borrowing, and in reducing rates',[82] at least into the 1930s. Hanson's general conclusion to his study of public enterprise is that far from suffering a loss of efficiency due to the lack of competition, the directorates 'sought to demonstrate beyond a doubt the efficiency of their administration'; and while complying with labour legislation, their reaction to the increased financial burdens imposed 'not infrequently . . . resembled those of a private enterprise protecting its interests'. Perhaps most surprising of all, in view of the doubts commonly expressed by the conservative classes about public enterprise, and of the history of the public corporations after 1950, was their capacity to earn surpluses sufficiently large that they could make significant contributions to the general revenue of the state. Hanson estimates that in the period 1912–33 some 25 per cent of gross earnings of the public corporations were thus employed.

Within the general picture of financial orthodoxy and prudent management in the pre-depression years there were substantial variations. The Banco de Seguros actively sought new business, and without invoking its grant of monopoly powers in the major risks, it managed to achieve a dominant position over its private competitors. Its rates were marginally below those of its competitors—not least because of the tax exemptions it enjoyed—but profits earned were used to strengthen the bank's reserves or directed to government revenues rather than to benefit consumers. The UEE also tended to gauge the efficiency of its service by its financial record, giving rise to frequent complaints that the extension of the service to interior towns occurred unnecessarily slowly. But in Montevideo (where actual or potential demand was heavily concentrated) electricity to both domestic and industrial users was cheap compared with the tariff to consumers in Buenos Aires,[83] while supply grew steadily. From a total of 19.9 million Kwh in 1912–13, consumption in Montevideo had increased to 55.9 million a decade later, and reached a pre-depression peak of 126.1 million in 1930–1.[84]

The generally high level of financial and commercial competence in the public sector was achieved in spite of the fact that from the beginning the public corporations were also required to meet political objectives prescribed for them. They supported the political system by enormously extending the scope of public employment for which nominations could come only through the political parties. The importance of this was only partly electoral, though at the turn of the century probably a quarter or more of registered voters were employed by the state.[85] More significantly, patronage on a much larger scale legitimised and strengthened the two traditional parties which otherwise lacked a coherent basis for their authority rooted in the identifiable interests of distinct social groups. The *batllista* alliance itself, the most potent political force in the first thirty years of the century, was composed of relatively weak (and in some degree conflicting) groups, and could only have prospered in the context of a political system which had found for itself a means of sustenance not directly dependent on the dominant sector of the economy. That means of sustenance was the machinery and apparatus of the state, and of course depended on the level of demand for public employment. Although the pork-barrel pact of 1931 and the collegiate constitution of 1951 were landmarks in the growth of a politicised bureaucracy, it is wholly erroneous to suppose that the phenomenon is at all recent.

> Those who know the ante-rooms of the National Council, of the Ministries, and of the public corporations, are well aware of the numerical importance of candidates for jobs. Daily more than a thousand people go there, and to the homes of high officials, seeking a place. The giving of jobs is, in practice, the most important function of government.[86]

It is extremely difficult to assess the implications of *empleomania*—the demand for public posts—on the public sector before 1930. Hanson makes no direct reference to it, but implies that, in their concern for efficiency, the corporations were not excessively bureaucratised. Under the constitution of 1919 the directorates were appointed by the National Council,[87] and could hardly resist pressure to make new appointments in spite of the formally autonomous nature of the corporations.[88] The ambivalent role of the public sector was indicated by Juan J. Amézaga, soon to become president of the Banco de Seguros:

> Without specialised staff and competent employees, the national organisations must necessarily fail. If from the political point of view autonomy is a guarantee imposed by the essential needs of the democratic organisation of the country, from the technical point of view it is a necessity imposed by the very nature of the new functions of the State.[89]

The satisfactory financial record of the corporations is a fairly clear indication that their autonomy could be protected or—less likely—that the demand for posts was exaggerated. It was even possible on a few occasions to suppress a public service. When the Tranvía del Norte was closed by AFTE in 1926 with the loss of 103 jobs, the question arose in the legislature of the fate of these employees. The precedents cited suggested that they should continue to receive their salaries from the government until new and equivalent posts could be found for them. A leading *batllista* expressed the view that 'If a government like ours, which has so many public corporations available, cannot quickly fix up sixty unfortunate individuals, it is a government which does not know how to administer.'[90]

Redundancies on such a scale were extremely rare. Public employment was growing in the 1920s and unquestionably gave ample scope for government and opposition political groups to place their supporters in public posts, under the version of *coparticipación* which was practised during the period of the first collegiate constitution. The exact scale of public employment is difficult to assess: indeed in 1924 a census of public employees was decreed, covering central government and the corporations.[91] Perhaps the government regarded the enumeration of posts which it made itself in budgets with some suspicion. Nonetheless, a count of the posts budgeted for in 1924/5 gives a total for central government of 30,100 (of which the armed services were 10,800). Public corporations and dependencies employed a further 7100, and departmental administration 5500. Public employment thus totalled 42,700 (excluding day-labourers) in the mid-1920s, some 7 per cent of the total active population. Central government totals for 1930/1 and 1931/2 were 30,000 and 30,300, but in these years Public Health (which employed 1800 in 1924/5) was for some reason excluded, which explains the apparent lack of growth. With allowance made for this, public employment must have totalled at least 45,000 by 1930.[92]

After fifteen years in which the public sector had largely been confined to activities legislated to it during the presidencies of Batlle, the end of the 1920s saw a further expansion. In 1928 the Frigorífico Nacional was created as a semi-public corporation. Significantly, in view of the fact that the economically dominant rural interests would be directly affected by the functioning of the *frigorífico*, control of it was partly wrested from the political system; the rural interest groups secured the right to nominate members of the directorate, and it was intended that the Nacional should raise share capital. In 1931 UEE was finally authorised to construct and operate as a monopoly a new telephone system replacing the poor service provided by the two private companies. Much more remarkable, however, were the circumstances in which the Administración Nacional de Combustibles, Alcohol y Portland (ANCAP) was brought into being in October 1931. It has been shown already that it was a long-established objective of the *batllistas* to secure a state monopoly in the manufacture of alcohol. In 1921 state participation also in cement production was proposed, but nothing came of the initiative in spite of the high level of consumption resulting from the expansion in the 1920s of residential construction and public works.[93] In addition, Uruguay's effectively complete dependence on fuel imports and lack of domestic refining capacity was proving particularly onerous. By the beginning of the 1930s over one-third of imports was composed of fuels and lubricants compared with little more than 10 per cent before the First World War (Table 6.3), and the contraction in the capacity to import during the depression emphasised the country's vulnerability. Moreover, the trade in fuels, like the production of alcohol and cement, was dominated by foreign capital.

ANCAP represented a very substantial incursion by the state into manufacturing industry, and as such was opposed by the more conservative elements of the opposition. To secure its acceptance the *batllistas* within the ruling Colorado party made a deal with a sector of the Nationalists, which became notorious as the pork-barrel pact (*pacto del chinchulín*). The *batllistas* conceded that *coparticipación* should be institutionalised to the extent that directorates of public corporations should be appointed by the Consejo Nacional de Administración (CNA) in the same proportion as the parties were represented in the CNA, and new public employee appointments were to be made from lists of applicants drawn up by the parties. The politicisation of the bureaucracy was thus greatly accelerated; though paradoxically the supporters of the pact among the Nationalists would claim in its defence that administrations in future would be less political than those reflecting the previous dominance of the Colorados.[94]

The political alliance which produced the pact, and the 1919 constitution in which it operated, were overthrown by the *coup d'état* of Gabriel Terra in 1933. The *coup* was unquestionably linked to the severe deterioration in the economy as a result of the depression, and the predictable difficulties which any administration would have found in coping with the situation. But Terra found support in Herrera, leader of the Nationalist group which had not been a participant in the pork-barrel pact, and which, more significantly, had close ties with the landowning class; and it was on this alliance that the new regime was built. Ironically, however, there is little evidence that the 1931 pact was used to shelter its electoral supporters from the effects of the slump: public employment did certainly increase, but so too did the scope of the public sector. Indeed, in its attempts to balance a budget which was strained by the loss of revenue derived from trade taxes, the government was generally restrictionist. After 1933, however, it would seem that the price to Terra of *herrerista* support was admission to the spoils of office. The budget of 1937 enumerates 39,400 posts in central administration,[95] a substantial increase over the 1931/2 total which can be estimated at 32,500. The tendency after 1933 to increased central control over the public corporations—a tendency criticised by S. G. Hanson[96]—was certainly not an attempt to control an abuse of their autonomy. Gallinal wrote of the 'bureaucratic avalanche' after 1933, apparently with good reason.[97]

The adoption by the new regime of the techniques of government practised by its predecessor should not be allowed to disguise the class basis of the new governing alliance, but it does reflect the extent to which the traditional political system (from which the new regime was drawn) depended for its sustenance on its own patrimony. Predictably, therefore, there was little attempt to reduce the range of activities undertaken in the public sector (whereas this was attempted following the rout of the political system in 1973). However, the state corporations were attacked in the Baltar Law of 1936, which set aside all concessions giving them the right to institute state monopolies. The principal result of this legislation was to deny ANCAP the exclusive right to import and refine crude oil in its La Teja refinery which began processing in 1937, and in 1938 the international oil companies concluded a secret agreement with ANCAP, by which they received quotas for the distribution of products in the domestic market, and imported crude oil to cover their quotas to be processed by ANCAP. Opposition from the private sector and foreign interests may account also for the failure of ANCAP's cement division to begin production until the mid-1950s, though production of alcohol did begin in 1934 with the acquisition of the privately owned distilleries.

Greater national autonomy in energy supply through public sector projects was achieved not only in the refining of oil—imports of refined fuels ceased in 1950—but also in the installation of hydro-electricity generating capacity. Proposals to exploit the hydro-electricity potential of the Río Negro, which bisects the country from east to west, had been current since before the First World War.[98] Since the mid-1920s Terra had himself been an advocate of the project, but not until 1936 were tenders invited for the construction contract, which was awarded to a German consortium the following year. Construction was interrupted by the Second World War, and it was in 1946 that the Rincón del Bonete generating station finally began production. Fifteen years later a further station on the Río Negro at Rincón de Baygorría, was commissioned. Both oil refining and hydro-electricity generation had important direct import-substitution effects, and increased capacity was essential to industrial growth. Energy sold by UTE on its industrial tariff reached a peak of 64.5 million Kwh in 1930, a level not reached again until 1936, but by 1939 sales to industry exceeded 100 million Kwh.[99]

In 1938 Hanson expressed the opinion that 'the next expansion of the State in industry would be occasioned by absolute necessity, i.e. such industries as the railways and tramways might find it financially impossible to continue without more favourable treatment from the government'.[100] The prediction was essentially correct. The growing profitability of industry and the relative decline of the livestock sector tended to strengthen the *batllista* wing of the Colorados while the influence of the *herrerista* nationalists waned. The restoration of *batllismo* received formal confirmation in the peaceful *coup* of 1942, and in 1947, with the accession of Luis Batlle to the presidency, *batllismo* was once more the governing faction of the Colorados. To what extent the *batllistas* might have wished to resist British pressure that the government should acquire the unprofitable and depreciated British public utility companies is unclear. But if the traditional ambition to secure public ownership of the utilities was insufficient, British control of the blocked sterling balances, combined with the freedom to fix railway tariffs, was decisive. The Anglo-Uruguayan Agreement of 15 July 1947 transferred 10 per cent of the accumulated balance (£1.7 million) to a multilateral account. A further £1.8 million was allocated to the purchase of the tram company, for which negotiations were already well advanced. The remainder was assigned to purchase of the railways and other utilities, and the repatriation of debt bonds held in London.[101] Prices eventually agreed were £3.06 million for the waterworks and £7.15 million for the railways. There may have been some consolation for the Uruguay negotiators in 'burning the fingers' of speculators in CUR shares in London, who expected between £8 million and £10 million. The Montevideo Gas and Dry Dock Company was left as the only survivor of British public utility enterprise.[102]

Thus in the later 1940s the public sector was substantially enlarged by the formation of new enterprises on the basis of the British companies. During the next quarter century the sector was deeply affected by inadequate new investment, the general economic decline, and political reaction to the decline. The high level of financial and administrative competence reached before 1930 was lost as deficits mounted and service deteriorated. Essentially, the fortunes of public enterprise mirrored those of the traditional political system. In 1952, in the euphoria of rapid industrial growth and unprecedented export values, the second collegiate constitution had been introduced and *coparticipación* in the public corporations further refined: directorates were now to be composed of members of the majority and minority parties in the ratio 3 + 2. But with economic decline from the middle of the decade, the corporations were increasingly politicised while their economic structure deteriorated. From its inception the public sector had always been supportive of the political system; but acceptance of it by the conservative classes depended on its performing other functions, notably the efficient production of goods and services where private domestic capital was unable or unwilling to accept the risk, or which increased the profitability of private capital. From the mid-1950s these functions were increasingly neglected as the political parties sought to protect themselves. Moreover, the corporations had traditionally served primarily the industries and population of Montevideo, but the urban alliance itself lost strength with the end of rapid industrial growth and the growing control of landed and commercial capital.

Because of the diversity of the state sector, including social and economic infrastructure, processing of primary products for export, and secondary manufacturing, the crisis was experienced with differing degrees of intensity. In general, the symptoms were mounting operating deficits and a lack of new investment. On the supply side, the crisis was especially severe on the corporations operating depreciated capital assets, especially those which were inherited from the private sector: railways, municipal transport, and the Frigorífico Nacional. Increased maintenance needs and unused capacity in industries with high fixed costs raised total costs, which were further inflated by the armies of bureaucrats occupying the central offices of the corporations. Revenue was affected by political pressure to restrain increases in the tariffs of those corporations providing services directly to the public. But revenue was also reduced by the growth of competition in the private sector—the case of the railways—and by reductions in the level of service due to a financial inability to maintain ageing capital equipment in serviceable condition.

The only reasonably complete data on the financial performance of the public sector is confined to 1955–63, a period divided by the introduction in 1959 of the monetarist-inspired reforms of the Blanco administration. However, the shift in policy relating to the state sector made only a small impression on the total operating deficit of the public corporations, which fell from $312 million in 1957 to $254 million in 1959, but by 1963 was approaching $500 million (all at 1961 prices).[103] The share of the public sector in total investment tended to decline after 1955, while the overall rate of investment as a proportion of GNP has also been declining (except briefly at the beginning of the 1960s). The reasons for the decline relate partly to the failure of the public sector to produce an investible surplus, but also to the politically derived need for government to expand its consumption expenditures, especially on salaries. In order to meet the shortfall in public saving—or, arguably, permitting the government to continue to consume a high proportion of its income—international loan and aid agencies have been important sources of finance, particularly for infrastructural projects. Road construction and installation of electricity-generating capacity attracted a high proportion of Uruguay's long-term foreign loans, amounting to approximately 46 per cent of outstanding loans at the end of 1968.[104] Loan agencies are notoriously reluctant to finance public sector projects likely to be competitive with the private sector. The only major exception to this practice in Uruguay has been loans made by the Inter-American Development Bank to the cement and oil-refining divisions of ANCAP.

8 The Economic Crisis 1955–1970

That Uruguay should have moved forward is natural, because all nations progress, and it would be shocking if it, or any other society, should find itself at the same level as sixteen years ago. (Julio Martínez Lamas, *Riqueza y Pobreza del Uruguay* [1930] p. 194.)

Stagnation

The growth of the Uruguayan economy in the post-war period might have appeared, by the mid-1950s, to give every cause for satisfaction. The development of Uruguay had been based since the last century on world demand for products which Uruguay was by nature fitted to produce at low cost—meat, wool and other animal products—and the prosperity of the country was the result of the high ratio of the value of exports to population. In 1956, when per capita income reached its maximum value, Uruguay enjoyed the highest per capita income of any Latin American country,[1] and it is likely that it had held this position throughout the first half of this century. Moreover, the post-war decade of rapid growth saw substantial modifications to the vulnerable model of export-led growth which broadly fits the Uruguayan economy before 1930. The period 1945–54 was above all a decade of rapid industrial growth, during which the product of manufacturing industry averaged an annual growth rate of 6 per cent.[2] High export values were achieved during the period, but this resulted from a sharp rise in export prices during the Korean War period rather than an increase in exported production. The annual rate of growth of per capita incomes during 1945–55 of about 3.4 per cent[3] was achieved on the basis of the domestic market.

Diversification and import substitution were characteristic of agriculture as well as industry in this period. Under the stimulus of high guaranteed prices, the average area under cereals increased from 1.0 million hectares in 1944–5—1948–9 to 1.4 million and 1.6 million in succeeding five-year periods. The objective of a greatly increased area devoted to arable farming was of very long standing, and was fulfilled to an unprecedented degree in the post-war decade. As a result, in the 1950s Uruguay once more had exportable surpluses of wheat.

Another traditional objective of public policy was achieved in 1948 when a group of British-owned public utilities—the most important of them being the railway companies—was acquired by the state in exchange for the partial liquidation of Uruguay's blocked sterling balances in London. While the wisdom of this purchase was highly questionable, the transfer to national ownership of the principal foreign-owned enterprises (apart from the three *frigoríficos* and the Montevideo Gas Company) had symbolic significance. Moreover, external indebtedness and the penetration of foreign private capital in manufacturing industry retained relatively modest proportions in the first half of the 1950s. Additionally, the period of economic growth was accompanied by the further extension of labour and social security legislation, notably the institution of wages councils from 1943, and family allowances (1950).[4]

It can thus be argued that by 1955, on the eve of the crisis, Uruguay had enjoyed a decade of rapid economic and industrial growth, accompanied by a far greater degree of diversification and national autonomy than had been possible previously. Nonetheless, although the contrast with Uruguay's experience since 1955 may seem abrupt, the performance of the Uruguayan economy in the post-war decade was itself far from convincing. It depended to a very great extent on favourable, but temporary, external conditions—the accumulation of foreign exchange reserves during the Second World War, sustained high commodity prices after the war, and the relative autonomy of all the dependent economies (particularly those linked to European metropoli) while the post-war disruption of the international economy lasted. The erosion of these favourable factors, and the accumulating distortions which accompanied the process of expansion and diversification, were already evident in Uruguay in the early 1950s. To a considerable extent this was an experience shared with other Latin American countries which adopted the strategy of import-substituting industrialisation. It is the severity of the subsequent crisis which has been unique to Uruguay.

The central characteristic of the period after the mid-1950s was the stagnation of production (Figure 8.1). Following the rapid growth of the post-war years, deceleration was evident during 1954–7. Thereafter, GDP at constant prices was not exceeded in absolute terms by a significant margin until 1966; but in 1967 GDP was again at a lower level than it had been in 1957, ten years earlier. This extraordinary record of economic decline necessarily had a severe impact on the value of production measured in per capita terms, in spite of a rate of growth of population which, at about 1.3 per cent was the lowest in Latin America. Table 8.1 indicates very clearly the marked deterioration which began in the second half of the 1950s, and which resulted in a negative rate of growth of per capita income for the period 1955–70. Indeed in only six of the fourteen years between 1957 and 1970 did the growth of

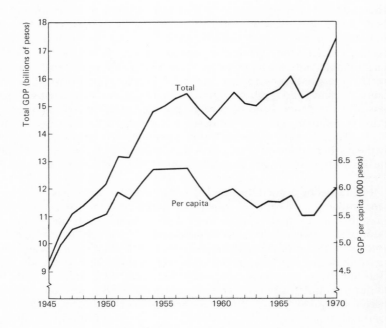

Figure 8.1. GDP at constant (1961) factor cost, total and per capita, 1945–70

Sources: BROU, *Cuentas Nacionales*, pp. B165–7; BCU, *Indicadores*.

production exceed the growth of population; and in 1970 per capita GDP at constant prices was reduced to the level which had been reached in the early 1950s.

Stagnation was accompanied by shifts in the sectoral composition of production (Table 8.2). During the period of rapid industrial growth up to the mid-1950s, the secondary sector increased its share of GDP dramatically. Primary and tertiary activities both grew at the rate of 4 per cent in this decade, each thus showing a proportionately equivalent reduced share of GDP. During 1955–60, when GDP showed no growth at all, the primary sector contracted still further. In the course of the 1960s there was a tendency for these changes to be reversed. The tertiary sector in particular, and the primary sector, increased their participation during the decade. For the period as a whole, however, the most significant shift was undoubtedly the reduced participation of primary activities and the growth of the secondary sector.

Table 8.1. Average annual rates of
growth of GDP, total and per capita, at
constant (1961) factor cost, 1945–70
(per cent)

	Total	Per Capita
1945–50	5.4	4.0
1950–5	4.2	2.7
1955–60	0.0	—1.5
1960–5	0.8	—0.6
1965–70	2.2	0.9
1945–55	4.8	3.4
1955–70	0.9	—0.3

Source: As Figure 8.1.

Table 8.2. Composition of GDP by sectors, at
constant (1961) factor cost, 1945–70
(per cent)

	Primary	Secondary	Tertiary
1945	18.0	21.7	60.3
1950	17.6	24.9	57.5
1955	16.6	28.0	55.4
1960	14.3	29.2	56.5
1965	15.9	26.9	57.2
1970	14.8	27.1	58.2

Source: As Figure 8.1.

The important components of the primary sector in Uruguay are
agriculture and livestock production; fishing makes a relatively insignificant contribution, while extractive industries are included in
manufacturing. The growth of the sector up to 1955 was fairly well
sustained at the rate of 4 per cent annually, but this was succeeded by a
five-year period of equally sustained, and almost as rapid, contraction.
The 1960s were marked by substantial fluctuations round a trend rising
from the low level of the late 1950s to a peak in 1966, when the figure for
1955 was exceeded for the first time by a significant margin. Agriculture
was principally responsible for these variations, livestock production
being relatively stable. Value added in agriculture grew annually by 6.9
per cent between 1943–5 and 1953–5, and contracted annually between

1953–5 and 1963–5 by 2.6 per cent (at 1961 factor cost). During the same periods the growth of the product in the livestock sector was 3.1 per cent and 1.0 per cent respectively. Both sectors are vulnerable to adverse weather conditions which account in part for the sudden falls in production in 1959–60 and 1967–8. The evolution of the agricultural sector was also heavily influenced by active government support beginning in the second half of the 1940s, and the reduction of that support a decade later. Overall the product of the primary sector grew very slowly, by 1.3 per cent per annum between 1945–9 and 1965–9 so that the product per capita over this period scarcely remained constant. Since Uruguay was entirely dependent on this sector for its exportable production, its stagnation had grave results.

Whereas in the primary sector the downturn began in 1955, in the secondary sector growth continued, slowly after 1954, until 1957. The value of the sector's product then declined until 1963, and the subsequent revival was slow. Not until 1970 was the level of 1957 exceeded. Comparing the growth rates of the products of manufacturing and construction between these dates, it is apparent that while manufacturing was relatively stable throughout the period, construction was almost continuously depressed. Thus, during the period of rapid growth 1945–57, manufacturing product grew at 7.0 per cent per annum with construction almost keeping pace at 6.4 per cent. From 1957 to 1963, however, although both sectors had negative rates of growth, construction contracted at the annual rate of 7.4 per cent, compared with 0.9 per cent in the case of manufacturing. Finally the period of slow growth from 1963 to 1970 was again more marked in manufacturing, which grew at 2.7 per cent compared with the stagnation of the construction sector (0.9 per cent).

The tertiary sector of the economy consists of a variety of activities whose common characteristics are not obvious, so that it is of limited usefulness to treat them together; nor is the sector satisfactorily disaggregated in the national accounts of Uruguay. However the collective importance of these activities in the Uruguayan economy is undoubted, accounting for not less than 55 per cent of the GDP of Uruguay in any year during 1945–70. In the rapid growth period to the mid-1950s they grew at a slower rate than the economy as a whole; in the subsequent period of stagnation, however, though the rate of growth was reduced, the sector performed better than the rest of the economy and maintained a nearly constant per capita product. Before 1955 the product of commerce, banking and financial services, and government services, was not disaggregated in the BROU's *Cuentas Nacionales*— together they comprised over 80 per cent of the tertiary sector product. During the 1960s this proportion declined to 72 per cent (1969–70) mainly as a result of the shrinking product of commerce from the high level of 1955–7 and the comparatively healthy growth of other components of the sector, especially public utilities and, to a lesser extent, housing.

The process of economic stagnation was accompanied by changes in the utilisation of the national product, summarised in Table 8.3. The most significant of these was a substantial decline in the investment coefficient. Unfortunately there is no data available on the rate of investment before 1955. Thereafter, gross domestic fixed investment as a proportion of GDP at constant market prices declined from an average of 17.6 per cent (1955–7) to 11.2 per cent (1964–6). The only interruption of the downward trend, which had begun in 1958, occurred during 1960–2, when the coefficient rose to 15.8 per cent. The subsequent decline was abrupt, and was relieved only by a slight rise at the end of the decade to 14.0 per cent (1970).

Evidence on the composition of investment supports the view that the reason for the revival of investment at the beginning of the 1960s was the availability of imported capital goods as a result of the policy changes of 1959. Investment in machinery and equipment, as a proportion of gross capital formation (GDCF) at current prices, fell to below 20 per cent in 1958–9 from an average of 34 per cent in 1955–7, but during 1960–4 averaged 41 per cent. Estimates of investment at constant (1961) prices, moreover, indicate that the principal source of variation in the level of capital formation was changes in investment in machinery and equipment. The investment 'boom' of the early 1960s had no visible effect at all on the level of construction, which persistently contracted.[5]

The participation of the public sector in the process of capital formation was low, declining from 22.9 per cent of GDCF (1955–6) to 17.7 per cent (1960–1) and 17.8 per cent (1965–6), but rising to 22.4 per cent (1969–70).[6] Equivalent ratios for Latin America as a whole were 29.1 per cent (1960–1) and 36.3 per cent (1969–70).[7] The relative proportion of capital expenditure on construction was much greater in the case of the public sector than of the private sector. The latter was responsible for an annual average of 85 per cent of investment in machinery and equipment during 1955–7 and 1962–5; this proportion fell to 66 per cent during 1958–9, when import restrictions were severe, and rose to 90 per cent during 1960–2 when these restrictions were modified or removed.

The falling trend in per capita product since 1957 must have been accompanied either by rising unemployment or a declining average level of productivity, assuming that the active proportion of the population remained constant. This is, unfortunately, an area in which data collection was particularly deficient. On the size of the work force, available estimates do not suggest a diminution. The 1963 census found that 39.0 per cent of the total population was economically active (employed, unemployed, or seeking work for the first time),[8] compared with 38.0 per cent estimated by CIDE for 1957.[9] The latter source, on

TABLE 8.3 Gross Domestic Product and National Income, 1955–70
(million pesos, 1961 prices)

	Consumption		Gross Domestic Fixed Investment	Inventories	Exports	Imports	Gross Domestic Product	Terms of trade effect	Net income of foreign factors	Gross National Income
	Private	Government								
1955	12821	1763	3135	19	1914	2814	16838	320	−53	17105
1956	12596	1759	2895	−34	2470	2555	17131	183	−49	17265
1957	13698	1804	2970	213	1636	3017	17304	165	−47	17422
1958	12336	1794	2152	44	2232	1877	16681	−134	−39	16508
1959	12106	1752	2261	243	2028	2176	16214	−329	−34	15851
1960	12934	1794	2488	336	2008	2758	16802	−24	−41	16737
1961	12536	1828	2753	318	2467	2623	17279	0	−70	17209
1962	13087	1913	2810	−71	2118	2975	16882	188	−85	16985
1963	12691	1889	2327	133	2211	2283	16968	77	−108	16937
1964	13444	1962	2049	61	2296	2498	17314	320	−176	17458
1965	12383	2113	1951	41	2939	1906	17521	31	−172	17380
1966	13228	2301	1919	167	2606	2113	18108	444	−217	18335
1967	12747	2294	2165	89	2432	2362	17365	177	−292	17250
1968	12560	2485	2010	−11	2784	2186	17642	−76	−287	17279
1969	13587	2488	2568	−23	2781	2688	18713	158	−323	18548
1970	14454	2783	2745	−12	2928	3304	19594	87	−270	19411

Sources: Universidad de la República, Estadísticas Básicas, table 10; BCU, Producto e Ingreso Nacionales, (1977), p. 7.

the basis that there had been no reduction in the active proportion of the labour force during 1955–61, argued that there was some increase in unemployment during the period, and also a reduction in the average product per unit of labour.[10] It seems very likely that this process occurred during the crisis period as a whole, but it must be borne in mind that the lack of regular data on unemployment, and the questionable meaning of available unemployment figures, make precise judgements impossible. In any case, the mass exodus of population, especially from the second half of the 1960s onwards, renders them almost meaningless. The best figures are probably those of the 1963 census, in which 9.7 per cent of the active population (10.3 per cent of the active population for which there was information), were either unemployed or seeking work for the first time. For Montevideo, which in 1963 contained 48.6 per cent of the total active population, the rate of unemployment was very similar at 9.6 per cent;[11] while later estimates for the capital indicated unemployment rates of between 7 per cent and 9 per cent.[12]

The only safe conclusion to be drawn from these figures is that in spite of emigration, open unemployment took on massive proportions during the 1960s. Although there are no estimates for unemployment during the growth decade 1945–55, it is likely that the rate at least doubled during the crisis period. In addition, disguised unemployment and under-employment were certainly on the increase. The practice of holding jobs of less than full-time status, sometimes in multiple or in combination with one or more pensions, is widely believed to have become more general. There was also an increase in the numbers employed in the public sector, particularly in the early years of the crisis. During 1955–61, while employment in the private sector grew at the annual rate of 0.9 per cent, public sector employment was growing at 2.6 per cent (and the number of government pensions granted at 5.9 per cent),[13] but public sector investment in real terms declined at the annual rate of 3.5 per cent.[14] Thus, while the rate of unemployment increased during the crisis, one reaction was to increase employment in the low productivity public sector. According to the 1963 census over 66,000 persons, 7.0 per cent of the active population, were employed in government services, excluding services to the public (transport and public utilities, social, health and education services, etc.).[15] With the inclusion of these services and other state enterprises, 193,800 persons (21.1 per cent of the employed population) were estimated to be employed in the public sector in 1961. In the same year 278,000 persons were receiving state pensions; so that in total 471,800 persons—about 23 per cent of the total population of ten years or over—was directly (though not necessarily wholly) dependent financially on the state.[16]

Such an expansion in the level of state activity might be expected to require the government to secure an enlarged share of the national product. This requirement is reflected in the rapid growth which occurred in general government consumption expenditure, mainly on wages and consumable goods and services. As a proportion of GDP at current prices, general government consumption increased continuously from less than 10 per cent in the second half of the 1950s to almost 16 per cent at the beginning of the 1970s.[17] However, this increase was not accompanied by a sustained increase in the proportion of national income accounted for by general government current income. Over the period 1955–65 increased government consumption was achieved by allowing the proportion of income consumed to grow rapidly, largely at the expense of the proportion saved which by the mid-1960s had been converted to a substantial deficit (Table 8.4). Thus government was unable to match its increased consumption requirements by increasing its current income, but instead did so initially by altering the composition of its expenditure, and after 1961 by allowing total current expenditure to exceed its income. Increasing fiscal deficits incurred by government were also accompanied by substantial operating deficits in the rest of the public sector.

TABLE 8.4. Proportionate size of general government current income and composition of current expenditure, 1955–65 (three-year averages)

	Current income (per cent of GDP at current prices)	Current expenditure (per cent at current prices)					
		Consumption	Transfer payments	Subsidies	Public debt interest	Saving	Total
1955–7	25.8	37.0	35.3	13.9	2.4	11.5	100
1958–60	23.9	39.4	38.9	17.6	2.1	2.0	100
1961–3	27.3	46.2	42.5	11.2	1.4	—1.4	100
1964–5[1]	25.8	54.1	39.3	11.2	1.4	—5.9	100

Note: 1. Two-year average.

Source: Universidad de la República, Estadísticas Básicas, tables 2 and 4.

If unemployment was one of the main indicators of internal disequilibrium in the Uruguayan economy, a process of rapid inflation was certainly the other. The index of consumer prices demonstrates a rising trend throughout the period 1945–50 to 1965–70 (Table 8.5). Inflation has essentially been a post-war problem, since although prices were rising consistently in the decade 1935–45, the increases were modest, not exceeding 7 per cent until the final year of the decade. During 1945–55 the rate of increase of prices reached a maximum of

TABLE 8.5. Average annual rate of
increase in consumer price index,
1946–70
(five-year averages)

1946–50	5.5
1951–5	11.1
1956–60	23.4
1961–5	30.7
1966–70	66.1

Sources: DGEC, *Indice de los Precios del
Consumo*; BCU, *Boletin Estadistico
Mensual*.

over 14 per cent in 1951 and 1952, but declined to below 10 per cent in
1955 and 1956. During the period of economic stagnation the rate of
inflation increased to severe proportions which far exceeded the
comparatively modest increases in the price level up to 1956. Three
phases in the inflation can be detected. The first reached a peak in 1959
and 1960 with annual increases of about 40 per cent in the price level.
The rate then fell to 10 per cent in 1962, following the introduction of a
'classic' IMF stabilisation package, but thereafter accelerated steadily to
a peak of 125 per cent in 1968. In June that year the imposition of wage
and price controls succeeded in reducing inflation to below 20 per cent in
1969 and 1970. But with the relaxation of controls and public spending
restraints during the election year of 1971 inflation once again
accelerated, with annual inflation rates approaching 100 per cent in the
early 1970s.

The external situation was dominated by four factors: the failure of
export earnings to regain the level achieved in the early 1950s; a
persistent tendency to run a deficit on the balance of payments current
account; the loss of gold and currency reserves; and the growth of
international indebtedness. The evolution of export earnings up to 1970
is given in Table 5.3, and three distinct phases are apparent during the
1950s and 1960s. During the early 1950s current receipts were very high,
averaging US$244 million for the five years 1950–4. The second phase
was of decline to 1957–60, when average receipts fell to US$132 million.
The third phase, covering the decade 1960–70, saw a slow but sustained
recovery, which by 1970 produced export receipts in excess of US$200
million for the first time since the mid-1950s (though of course in per
capita terms there had been a substantial reduction). The high export
prices caused by the commodity boom at the time of the Korean War
represented for Uruguay the culmination of a rising export price trend
which had begun at the end of the 1930s. It would be quite wrong,
however, to suppose that the rapid decline of export earnings after 1954

merely resulted from the loss of exceptionally favourable world prices. There was in addition a dramatic fall in the volume of exports, and in spite of sustained recovery in the 1960s, the export quantum of the first half of the 1950s had still not been reached by 1967. The real crisis of exports was therefore a reduced supply of exportable production.

Current expenditure abroad generally moved in sympathy with receipts, but at a higher level, thus producing a current account deficit almost continuously after the late 1940s. Although both these characteristics appeared to be reversed during 1964–6, it should be noted that an accumulated current account surplus for those years of US$130.5 million must be set against accumulated unidentifiable payments (errors and omissions) for those years of US$191.2 million. The relationship between receipts and payments was closest during the period of trade and exchange controls which ended in 1959. Receipts reached peak values in 1950, 1953 and 1956, payments in 1951, 1954 and 1957. The net balance on current account is shown in Table 8.6. Clearly the 1950s was the significant period, when initially the effort to industrialise, and subsequently the failure of exports, gave rise to an accumulated current account deficit of over US$350 million.

TABLE 8.6. Balance of payments current account: accumulated net balances, 1946–70
(million US dollars, five-year totals)

1946–50	+ 20.1
1951–55	− 134.8
1956–60	− 219.3
1961–65	− 15.5
1966–70	+ 20.7

Sources: Universidad de la República, Estadísticas Básicas, table 35; BCU, Indicadores.

The chronic tendency to run a current deficit was supported in part by the reduction of gold and currency reserves, and in part by increased borrowing abroad. The declining level of net reserves is indicated in Table 8.7. During the Second World War current account surpluses and an inflow of foreign capital created a strong currency reserve which was not seriously weakened until the early 1950s, but deterioration thereafter was rapid. In addition, the level of external obligations increased very greatly, particularly in the decade 1955–65 (Table 8.8). Assets during this period fell slightly, such that there was a substantial net increase in liabilities. The principal areas in which external indebtedness

TABLE 8.7. Net gold and foreign currency reserves, 1946–70
(million US dollars, end of year)

1946	293.1
1950	311.8
1955	141.1
1960	83.1
1965	56.0
1970	32.4

Sources: Universidad de la Republica, *Estadísticas Básicas*, table 49; BCU, *Boletín Estadístico Mensual*.

TABLE 8.8. Total assets and liabilities with non-residents, 1950–70
(million US dollars)

	Assets	Liabilities	Net assets
1950	279.5	111.9	167.6
1955	246.5	181.1	65.4
1960	238.0	286.7	— 48.7
1965	225.8	480.8	—255.0
1970	222.2	508.9	—286.7

Sources: Universidad de la República, *Estadísticas Básicas*, table 41: Instituto de Economía, *Estudios y Coyuntura 2*, table 24.

increased were loans to government by international organisations and foreign banks; suppliers' credits; and borrowing by the private banking sector from foreign banks.

Diagnosis

In the previous section, the economic crisis was defined as the loss of dynamism in the mid-1950s and the absence of economic growth thereafter. From the perspective of the 1970s, that might seem an unduly restrictive appreciation of the nature of the crisis. Some contemporary characteristics of the Uruguayan economy—for example, the erosion of living standards, the reduced scope of the public sector, the growth of foreign ownership in land and banking, the immense increase in foreign debt—might well be regarded as problems of greater significance, and must also be associated with the nature of the political crisis in the country. These features of Uruguayan development have not simply arisen as a direct consequence of the lack of growth in the domestic economy. They are also reflections of the way the international capitalist economy has evolved in the post-war period, and are shared in some degree with other dependent Latin American countries. Nonetheless, the absence of economic growth was the overriding characteristic of the economy at least during 1955–75; it aggravated the manifestations of dependence; and it is the phenomenon which most stands in need of explanation. It is a commonplace that such an extended period of economic decline must have deep-rooted historical causes, but they are the subject of earlier chapters.

Two factors appear to have played a primary role in causing the downturn in the 1950s, while other mechanisms emerged subsequently to perpetuate stagnation. The first factor was the deterioration of the external sector, which was the result of two elements: firstly, the declining value of exports, and secondly an inelastic demand for imports. Production of exportable commodities has been subject to long-run stagnation; but an additional problem in the early 1950s was the effect of government support for arable production in diverting land away from livestock production (the source of about 80 per cent of export earnings). Between 1945–9 and 1955–9 cultivated acreage increased by 575,000 hectares, mostly at the expense of pasture land; and although this represented only about 3 per cent of the total pasture area, the loss to the livestock sector was considerably greater than this since in general the lands converted to arable use were the fertile areas of the Littoral and western region, with the highest animal-carrying capacity. As a consequence, although exports from the expanded arable sector increased, this was achieved at the expense of the traditional, low-cost export sector. A more serious loss to the volume of exports resulted from the diversion of exportable production to meet domestic demand, such that a declining proportion of agricultural and livestock production was available for export (Table 8.9). This effect was particularly severe in the case of beef, apparent per capita consumption increasing from 72.1 kilos (1948–50) to 87.6 (1951–3) and 79.4 (1954–6).[18] The fall in export volume further aggravated the effects of declining world price levels. At the height of the Korean War boom (1950–2), the export price index averaged 143.3 (1961 = 100). This declined in successive three-year periods to 124.7 (1953–5), 109.0 (1956–8), and 100.7 (1959–61).[19] The effect of price and quantity trends was to reduce the value of Uruguay's commodity exports by 43 per cent between 1950–2 and 1957–9.

By the mid-1950s, however, when the decline in export proceeds began to be felt, the structure of imports was substantially different from that of a decade earlier (Table 6.3). Rapid industrial growth in this period was based on the progressive substitution of imports of consumer goods by domestic production, such that the share of non-durable

TABLE 8.9. Proportion of agricultural and livestock production
exported, 1935–70
(per cent, by volume)

	Agriculture	Livestock	Total
1935–40	23.9	54.0	46.4
1947–9	28.1	35.4	33.6
1950–2	23.3	40.4	35.7
1953–5	28.0	37.5	34.4
1956–8	25.4	30.7	29.0
1959–61	12.5	30.9	26.4
1970	11.3	39.2	29.8

Sources: CIDE, Estudio Económico, vol. I, p. II 19; CIDE, Plan Nacional
de Desarrollo 1973–1977, vol. I, p. 267.

consumer goods in total imports fell from 14.9 per cent in 1945–7 to 8.0
per cent in 1954–6. In the same interval capital equipment for industry
increased its share from 7.6 per cent to 14.8 per cent and fuels and
lubricants from 8.6 per cent to 15.7 per cent. Throughout the post-war
period raw materials accounted for at least half of the import bill. The
structure of imports had thus become closely geared to the needs of a
rapidly growing industrial sector, with producers' inputs forming the
bulk of imports and capital equipment increasing its share of the import
bill. The ratio of total imports to industrial production increased rapidly
in the immediate post-war period, rising from 0.29 in 1944–6 to a
maximum of 0.41 in 1948–50. By the time imports reached their
maximum value in 1951 industrial production was already growing
more rapidly, so that the ratio of imports declined persistently
throughout the 1950s reaching 0.27 in 1954–6 and 0.18 in 1958–60.[20]
However, from 1956 onwards, with imports falling sharply and
industrial production almost stationary, the composition of imports
shifted again. The share of consumer non-durables remained more or
less the same, but that of durables began to diminish, a process relieved
only by the brief period of trade liberalisation at the beginning of the
1960s. A more significant decline occurred for industrial capital
equipment, to barely 10 per cent in the late 1950s. Proportionately
greater cuts were experienced by other capital goods. Imports of fuel and
raw materials, on the other hand, increased their share of the total. Thus
the reduced level of foreign exchange earnings restricted the supply of
imports—indeed, induced a contraction—and although this resulted in
some further reduction in the level of imports for consumers, the process
of import-substituting industrialisation had already by the mid-1950s
caused imports of non-durable consumers' goods to approach an
irreducible minimum. Imports of raw materials, fuels and lubricants had

to be maintained in order to sustain industrial production at its existing level, and the main impact of the deteriorating import capacity was thus felt by imports of capital equipment.

It is unlikely, however, that import difficulties were themselves a main cause of the almost complete cessation of industrial growth after 1957, which was the second factor causing stagnation. In the long run, of course, since the domestic manufacture of capital goods is almost negligible,[21] the import of machinery and equipment was necessary for sustained industrial growth. But estimates made in 1963 suggest that manufacturing industry was producing only one-half of the potential production of its installed capacity,[22] and utilisation can hardly have been much greater in the late 1950s, notwithstanding the brief revival of investment at the beginning of the 1960s.

Changes in the level of demand for industrial output, and the structural characteristics of industry itself, are the most convincing explanation of the ending of industrial growth. Both agricultural production and construction activity reached peak values (in real terms) before the downturn in industry occurred, and the effect of the sharp recession in each was particularly severe for industry in terms of reduced supply of raw materials and contraction of demand. But the pattern of industrial growth of the previous decade was itself the critical factor leading to stagnation. As import substitution proceeded, and in the absence of significant export markets for industrial products—the import coefficient in the supply of industrial goods fell from 18 per cent in 1948–50 to 8 per cent in 1957–9[23]—it became progressively more 'difficult' to sustain rapid industrial growth. The structure of protectionist policy and the absence of domestic raw materials (apart from the reduced output of the rural sector) impeded the development of backward linkages; while the limited domestic market and dependence on technology developed abroad made new industries increasingly high cost. Rapid industrial growth in the post-war decade was marked by the establishment of new industries with typically high income elasticities of demand. When further industrialisation encountered difficulties and aggregate damand declined, the effect on such an industrial structure was correspondingly severe.

Though the rural sector in the 1960s did achieve some growth following the decline of 1955–60, and industry managed a limited revival at the end of the 1960s, the basic conditions of the crisis—the stagnation of the primary and secondary sectors—remained constant. The distortions resulting from the crisis, however, introduced new mechanisms which determined the distribution of the burden of stagnation and contributed to its continuation. The most important of these was the acceleration of inflation in the crisis period. While the economy grew rapidly in the post-war decade on the basis of domestic demand for industrial production, it is not altogether surprising that the price level should show a fairly gentle upward trend. After 1955, however, a new set of factors operated. Stationary or declining levels of production in manufacturing industry implied lower productivity and higher costs. The sustained decline in per capita income intensified competition between social groups to maintain their real income levels. The persistent trade deficit of the 1950s, financed primarily by the depletion of reserves which permitted the maintenance of overvalued exchange rates, resulted in a succession of devaluations in the later 1950s and throughout the 1960s, which in the absence of effective measures to reduce or control the size of the public sector deficit created additional inflationary pressure.

The distortions implicit in this experience contributed to important shifts in the allocation of resources. The public sector, vulnerable to pressure to absorb labour displaced from employment elsewhere in the economy, and unable to secure a sufficient share of the national income, reduced the proportion of its total expenditure allocated to capital projects, with adverse effects on the efficiency of public services. The private sector, in a situation of increasing uncertainty, and with declining profitability in manufacturing industry, also reduced its level of fixed capital formation. While investment in productive activities declined, new openings were found for the utilisation of the economic surplus. The banking sector experienced a period of very rapid growth, the number of banks owned wholly or principally by Uruguayan nationals increasing from 30 in 1954 to 45 in 1959 and 50 in 1962,[24] but declining from the middle of the decade as a result of amalgamations and spectacular failures. The latter helped to reveal the role of the banks in channelling savings into speculative investments in luxury housing, land, and the stockpiling of imports and exportable production, and into foreign currencies. These are classic reactions to the process of chronic inflation, which further weakened the productive base of the economy while accentuating the inherently inflationary struggle on the part of different social groups to maintain incompatible real income levels. The levels were incompatible because per capita incomes were declining, and they were declining not because of inflationary distortions—damaging though they were—but because of the failure of the economic strategy which had been adopted after 1947, and the long-run absence of growth in the rural sector.

The Policy Response

Economic stagnation dealt a blow to *batllista* Uruguay which eventually was to prove fatal. It was the loss of dynamism in the economy which began the process leading to the political crisis. It may be that some form of political crisis was inevitable, given the weakening position of national bourgeoisies throughout Latin America at the close of the import-substitution era, and the emergence of new forms of dependency. But had it been possible to sustain the rate of growth of real per capita incomes at 2 or 3 per cent per annum beyond the mid-1950s for so long would the onset of the crisis have been deferred. The political elite seem rarely to have stated the necessity of sustained economic growth as an object of economic policy.[25] But the redistributive consensus politics of post-war Uruguay were premised on economic growth—though not necessarily themselves growth-inducing—as completely as were the politics of the pre-depression decades under Batlle y Ordóñez. The reaction of policy-makers to the cessation of growth is therefore of great interest.

Throughout the 1950s there was no major revision of the economic strategy which began to be implemented in the late 1940s. The distortions in the economy which were evident by 1955 were not so pressing that demand for change was irresistible, nor so severe that *ad hoc* measures could not contain their adverse effects. Exchange reserves were still adequate to meet the continuous trade deficits. And though public expenditure persistently exceeded revenue, the annual rate of increase of prices to consumers averaged only 11 per cent during 1951–5. But to these signs of disequilibrium in the first half of the 1950s were added, in the second, the onset of stagnation and the exhaustion of currency reserves. In spite of these pressures, the Colorado government re-elected in 1954 maintained its overall strategy, in which 'the protection and encouragement of our manufacturing industry is the fundamental element in our economic life and the social peace we enjoy'.[26] Luis Batlle also took the opportunity to castigate rural producers for their dependence (except in the case of wool) on subsidies and to affirm the importance of the multiple exchange rate system. In September 1955, however, there was a devaluation of the rate applicable to almost all imports and some exports, and in the following year trade and exchange controls were strengthened to restrict the level of imports and to permit an increasingly bilateralist commercial policy. Also in 1956 negotiations began with a group of New York banks for a loan of US $30 million, but the loan was not made, apparently because the Uruguayan government was unwilling to meet the conditions demanded.[27] The accelerating depreciation of the currency heightened social tensions. Strikes were frequent, and almost certainly more damaging than they had been earlier in the decade. Wool exporters, with the advantage of a non-perishable commodity, withheld production from the market to secure more favourable exchange rates; and the supply of foreign currencies to importers became increasingly restricted and irregular. In October 1957, indeed, the exchange market was closed for a time.

The policy orientation of the Colorados was finally abandoned with the Exchange and Monetary Reform Law of December 1959. Political opposition had increased from 1957 onwards, and was mounted most effectively by the rural exporting sector. Its capacity to provoke exchange crises by withholding production from the market, or by clandestine export to Brazil, further undermined an economy whose bases were in any case unsound. The dissatisfaction of rural producers found political expression in the Liga Federal de Acción Ruralista, and its decision to support the Blanco party *lema* in the elections of 1958 was a decisive factor in the defeat of the Colorados. The first Blanco government in this century, taking office in March 1959, did not however do so with a coherent doctrine or set of prepared measures. Subsequently, Blanco policy at this time was said to have been orientated towards four objectives: financial reforms and recovery, commercial freedom, monetary stability, and economic and social development.[28] But policies were slow to emerge, and it was not until the end of 1959, almost six months after the arrival of a team of IMF officials, that the Reform Law was promulgated.

This package of stabilisation measures was an event of great significance, highly controversial at the time and subsequently, and yet it had little long-term importance.[29] It did not, of course, create the economic problems of the country, as its political opponents claimed; but equally, its prescriptions were largely irrelevant to those problems. Its ideology was that of the free market and the competitive model, a reaction against *dirigismo* and state intervention in the economy which was regarded as having distorted the structure of prices and production. Its objects were therefore to re-establish internal and external equilibrium by creating a free exchange market and single exchange rate, dismantling trade and exchange controls, and reversing the trend to bilateralism. These measures were accompanied by a restriction of the money supply and a substantial devaluation: the free commercial market rate $4.11 to the dollar (pre-Reform) was raised to $11.06. To minimise the difficulties of the transitional period, export taxes (*detracciones*), import surcharges and advance deposits against imports were introduced in what was intended to be a temporary regime. The levels of the taxes, surcharges and deposits were variable according to the nature of the commodity traded, such that an essential characteristic of the multiple exchange rate system was reproduced. A few months later, in September 1960, the par value of $7.40 to the dollar was agreed with the IMF, the Uruguayan quota with the Fund was raised from US$15 million to US$30 million, and the way was now open for the inflow of dollar credits.

The Reform Law was, in a sense, an inevitable development. It was clear by the late 1950s that the import-substituting industrialisation strategy implemented by the Colorados was played out, and that attempts to extend its life by further manipulation of trade and exchange controls could only be effective in the very short run. The need for external assistance was evident in the approaches made by the Colorado government to the IMF, even though they were unsuccessful. Given the predilection of the Uruguayan political elite for making the minimum changes required to avert immediate crisis, to the Blancos a *rapprochement* with the IMF must have seemed the obvious move. It was open to the criticism that it delivered up the country to imperialist penetration, and contributed to a regressive redistribution of income. On the other hand, the IMF could offer a coherent (if fallacious) formula for the country's economic development, an asset the Blancos did not have; the redistribution of income in favour of the landed interest rewarded the powerful conservative class whose support for the Blancos had been instrumental in their electoral victory; and at least some of the policy changes required by the Fund—fixing a par value for the peso, unifying the exchange rate, for example—were nominal rather than real.

Thus the IMF offered to the Blancos a solution to the immediate problem of the balance of payments crisis, at a price which favoured the dominant rural interests of the party, and which still allowed the Blancos to win the next elections, in November 1962. Indeed, the economy showed signs of revival at first. Following the disastrous year of 1959, when floods inundated large areas of the country disrupting rural production, GDP grew by 3.6 per cent in 1960 and 3.0 per cent in 1961. Merchandise exports revived somewhat, achieving in volume terms the highest level for five years in 1961, though this was no more than the average level of 1945–55, and was not to be reached again until the late 1960s. In 1959 and 1960 central government achieved budget surpluses (though the public sector as a whole remained in deficit), and the rate of increase of the consumer price index fell from 39.3 per cent in 1959 to 10.9 per cent in 1962.

Even in the short term, however, the Reform demonstrated serious inadequacies. After a decade in which imports had been regulated by physical controls and thus related, however crudely, to a set of priorities and to the supply of foreign exchange, the removal of controls in 1960 produced a surge in the level of imports, particularly of durable consumers' goods and capital equipment. The accumulated current account deficit during 1960–2 totalled US\$160 million. The liberalisation of the foreign trade regime permitted the expression of an inelastic demand for imported goods which had formerly been repressed.

The Reform might have retained some coherence if the improved export performance of 1961 had been sustained. However, it has been argued in Chapter 4 that while total farm output is basically elastic to price changes, higher output prices tend to result in rising costs. In any case, continued inflation with lagging exchange rate adjustment served to erode the income redistribution in favour of the rural sector, with the real price of exportables falling sharply after 1960 (Table 4.5). It ca also be argued that the presence of deep-seated structural problems in the rural sector made the Reform simply irrelevant as a long-term solution to the stagnation of rural output.

A further significant factor during the Reform period was the growth in external indebtedness, in which suppliers' credits to importers—freely negotiable as a result of the Reform—were a major part. The fundamental weakness of the Reform was not that it sacrificed economic growth in the interests of a reduced rate of inflation, as happened with stabilisation packages elsewhere in Latin America,[30] but simply that the necessarily incomplete restoration of market forces in the exchange market and the abolition of controls failed to eliminate the causes of disequilibrium in the balance of payments.

Though the Exchange and Monetary Reform Law was the characteristic expression of Blanco economic policy, an important potential initiative during the Blanco administration was the elaboration of a ten-year National Plan.[31] CIDE (Comisión de Inversiones y Desarrollo Económico) was created in 1960 with the task of coordinating public sector investment projects. With the commitment to produce national plans as vehicles for foreign aid under the Alliance for Progress, the resources of CIDE were strengthened and its task widened to the preparation of a comprehensive report on the problems of the Uruguayan economy, which was published in May 1963.[32] At the beginning of 1964 CIDE was reconstituted as the Consejo Inter-ministerial de Desarrollo Económico, and its Plan was published in May 1965.

Although the Plan itself and its recommended reforms were almost totally ignored by successive governments, the work of CIDE was of immense value. The 1963 report was the first serious diagnosis to be made of the Uruguayan crisis. Its findings were, however, less novel than the data and analysis which were marshalled in support. At the beginning of the 1960s Uruguay was extraordinarily deficient in the basic statistical materials required for rational economic policy-making. The population census of 1963 was the first to be taken in Uruguay since 1908. In 1962 a group was established to elaborate a set of national income accounts, which were published in definitive form in 1965 and covered the period 1955–63.[33] Until that time, estimates of national income were confined to isolated and individual attempts based on inadequate statistical material. Apart from these basic materials, CIDE was also responsible for a number of reports on sectors of the economy. To the dispassionate and persuasive diagnosis of the crisis made in these publications was added the intellectual authority of its technical secretary, Enrique Iglesias.

CIDE's diagnosis was fundamentally structuralist and 'developmentalist' in character. The problem of inflation was regarded as primarily a consequence of stagnation and the resulting social conflicts, and of deteriorating terms of trade, rather than due to expansionist monetary policy.[34] The stagnation itself was rooted in the problems of manufacturing industry, which had exhausted easy import-substitution possibilities and was limited by a small domestic market, and in 'the weak reaction of rural production to the stimulus of prices alone'.[35] The Plan proposals included a set of targets for the ten-year period, notably an average increase in per capita income of 4 per cent; a three-year programme designed to lay the basis for rapid growth; and a one-year stabilisation plan to reduce the rate of inflation and eliminate the non-structural causes of instability. The entire programme followed the pattern of indicative planning by outlining proposed public sector investment spending, which would increase its share of total capital expenditure especially during the three-year period, and by ranking private sector projects according to the priority they assumed in the light of public sector spending. No increase in the scope of public sector activity, at the expense of the private sector, was anticipated. The economy was to remain 'mixed', with the role of the price mechanism in the private sector enhanced. The proportion of investment to be financed by foreign borrowing was to fall from the pre-Plan level of 16 per cent (1960–3) to less than 1 per cent in 1974;[36] foreign capital was only to be employed when strict conditions relating to the level of domestic saving and the balance of payments situation were met.

The significant area of the Plan did not lie, however, in the projected growth rate, nor in the creation of a Plan framework acceptable to the Committee of Experts of the OAS which secured Uruguay's eligibility for further foreign aid. The important proposals contained in the Plan were a set of structural reforms, whose implementation was repeatedly stressed as indispensable to the success of the Plan. Reform was to extend to agrarian structures, seeking to eliminate inappropriate farm unit sizes or forms of tenure which obstructed the introduction of new technologies; to the tax system, reducing the proportion justifiable only in terms of the revenue it produced, and improving the administration of the fiscal system; to the financial system, creating a separate Central Bank and permitting the Banco de la República a more specialised role as a development bank; and to public administration, improving both the quality of its services to the public, and its ability to conduct and coordinate economic policy. Fundamental changes were also recommended in the social security system, in export and industrial promotion, and in the various sectoral plans. These reform proposals derived directly from CIDE's earlier diagnosis of the structural problems of the economy. Their far-reaching nature, and insistence in the Plan on the necessity for their introduction, made the Plan a manifesto for reform as much as a programme for development.

An economic plan even of the indicative type is inherently a political document, both in its ideology of centrally guided development and in ts implications for established interest groups and the structure of economic power. The Plan attempted to resolve this problem by allowing an area of choice which was 'political', while emphasising that the Plan itself was a 'technical' instrument.[37] The political area included the decision to adopt planning, the creation of confidence in the nation's future, and the securing of effective collaboration from the private sector.[38] With a positive political response, the Plan could be adopted as a technical and realistic device for achieving economic growth and a just distribution of its benefits, employing efficiency and rationality as the objective' criteria for reform.

The implication, however, that inefficiency and irrationality were basic obstacles to the development of Uruguay was a fundamental flaw in the structuralists' case for development by reform. Efficiency and rationality are objective criteria only within an agreed set of social values and political preferences, and this condition did not apply in Uruguay. The Blanco government was obliged to create a planning machinery by the terms of the Alliance for Progress, and by the domestic political need to demonstrate a concern for the future. But the stress laid in the Plan on the necessity for political leadership to adopt planning as a basic policy technique clearly suggests what events were subsequently to reveal: that the political parties had no intention of implementing the Plan or its reforms. To do so was directly against the interests of the parties themselves, of the bureaucracies they controlled, of the private sector in general, and of the landed interest and the commercial-financial system in particular. The centres of economic and political power within Uruguay had no interest in the introduction of an effective planning process, and were able to prevent it.

In 1962 the Blanco government which had introduced the Exchange and Monetary Reform Law was re-elected to office. By 1962, essential features of its economic strategy were becoming untenable, though for electoral purposes they had to be retained. But in 1963, the peso was devalued from $11.04 to $16.50 and a new exchange market was created, mainly for non-commercial transactions, in which the rate was not supported by BROU. The over-valued exchange rate before 1963 had been effective in securing a degree of price stability, but at the cost of large trade deficits, growing speculative pressure against the currency, and heavy foreign borrowing. With the election won, the pressure to abandon the Reform no longer had to be resisted.

The economy during the second Blanco administration was marked by continued stagnation and accelerating inflation; by substantial fiscal and public sector deficits; and by the growth of financial speculation operating through the enlarged banking sector which resulted in an estimated capital flight of US$246 million during 1962–7.[39] The current account deficits sustained during the years of trade liberalisation of the first administration, on the other hand, were eliminated by further devaluations of the peso in the official market and the manipulation of import controls. Although there was no formal breach in relations with the IMF, and indeed agreement was reached on refinancing the external debt in early 1966, economic policy during the mid-1960s was marked by a limited return to trade and exchange control practices and the absence (except for the publication of the National Plan) of any new policy initiatives.

The elections of 1966 were fought almost exclusively on the question of constitutional reform. The economic situation did not become an issue in the campaign; but the result of the elections, which restored the Colorados to power in a one-man presidential constitution, marked a significant stage in the response of government to the crisis. The significance derived partly from the elections, since the restoration of a single president in place of the nine-man presidential committee strengthened the executive against the pressures exerted by the political process. This reform was thought to forestall the possibility of a *coup* but, ironically, it made possible the 'unannounced' *coup* effected by Pacheco Areco after his succession to the presidency on the death of President Gestido in December 1967. But underlying these institutional changes, the deterioration of the economic position made a change in the orientation of economic policy inevitable.[40] Inflation had accelerated steadily since the early 1960s, and exceeded 70 per cent in 1966 a stabilisation programme could not be long delayed. Even more pressing was the accumulation of foreign debt obligations arising from the high level of external credits in the first half of the 1960s, with US$96.8 million in interest and amortisation on public sector borrowings falling due for payment in 1967.[41]

However, stabilisation was not immediately attempted by Gestido on coming to office in March 1967. Until shortly before his death Gestido resisted a *rapprochement* with the IMF, relying instead on his non-political background and reputation for capable administration to secure mass support for 'developmentalist' policies. The attempt ended with the devaluation in November 1967 of the peso, from $98 in the official market to $200.[42] This reversal was the result not only of inherited economic problems and the growing opposition of the private sector to further exercises in interventionist economic policy, but also to successive periods of drought and flood during the year which reduced the volume of exportable agricultural production, accelerated the inflationary process by increasing food prices, and stimulated speculative activities in the exchange market. The accession of Pacheco Areco to the presidency confirmed the new orientation, though its features did not become fully apparent until the middle of 1968. In April 1968 a further devaluation of 25 per cent was effected, and a general freeze on wages and prices was decreed in June in order to halt an inflationary process which had seen an increase of 180 per cent in the consumer price index during the previous twelve months. The wages councils were replaced by the Comisión de Productividad, Precios e Ingresos (COPRIN), which regulated the freeze. Control over wages was supplemented by a repressive policy towards trade unions, including the arrest of union leaders and the prohibition of strikes and demonstrations. The power of the executive, already augmented by the reform of the constitution in 1966, was further strengthened by the semi-permanent imposition of emergency security measures. The economic strategy remained largely intact until its own contradictions, particularly the increasingly over-valued exchange rate, and the requirements of the election campaign of 1971, forced its relaxation and abandonment. It was a very significant stage in the development of the crisis and requires careful analysis, not least because this interval of enforced 'stability' was accompanied by a revival of growth.

The strategy adopted in 1968 bore a certain similarity to that introduced in 1960 by the Blanco administration. In both cases the devaluation of the currency greatly increased rewards to landowners and exporters, and also increased government revenue, while reducing real wage levels. However, the wage freeze which confirmed the redistribution of income in 1968 had not been possible at the beginning of the 1960s, when the *batllista* mode of government was still dominant. The confrontation with organised labour was unprecedented, and in spite of wage adjustments which were permitted late in 1968 the average real wage that year fell to 86.5 (base 1961) compared with 101.7 in 1967.[43] The antagonism between government and labour was not reduced by an increase in the wage index to 102.3 in 1969, nor by the commitment of the regime to exchange stability following a scandal which accompanied the devaluation of April 1968.

The policies of Pacheco were remarkably successful not only in halting the extremely rapid inflationary process but also in achieving faster rates of economic growth than at any time since the mid-1950s. The consumer price index increased by 125 per cent in 1968, but by only 21 per cent in 1969 and 16 per cent in 1970. Growth of GDP in real terms was −4.1 per cent in 1967 and 1.6 per cent in 1968, but over 5 per cent in each of the two succeeding years. In general in Latin America stabilisation programmes have been accompanied by a reduced rate of economic growth (although both Chile and Argentina were also more successful in maintaining growth rates in 'second-round' stabilisations in the second half of the 1960s),[44] and it is of obvious importance to explain why the Uruguayan experience differed so sharply.

IMF-inspired stabilisation programmes were undertaken at this time in the expectation of short-run stagnation followed by long-run growth. Growth would result from the removal of inflation-induced distortions, savings and investment would be encouraged, speculation discouraged, and foreign capital would flow in. However, growth would be preceded by a period of stagnation resulting from the curtailment of credit and public spending, and the effects of devaluing an over-valued exchange rate on real incomes and industrial costs. Such an analysis assumes an inflation based on excess demand. But in Uruguay inflation was accompanied by a stagnation of output, and the stimulation of demand by expansionist monetary policies permitted social groups to contend for greater shares of a stationary national income, rather than creating a demand-led growth process. Hence the reduction in the level of aggregate demand did not automatically entail adverse consequences for growth; in fact, contraction in the level of activity was very brief, and revival came as wage adjustments were permitted from September 1968 onwards.

In any case, the explanation for the success of the *pachequista* policies should be sought primarily in two other directions. Firstly, the export sector responded very strongly to higher domestic prices resulting from the devaluation, the effect of which was strengthened by improving world prices in 1969–70 and magnified by recovery from the climatic difficulties of 1967. As a result, export earnings in 1970 were not only higher than in any year since the early 1950s, but also 47 per cent greater than in 1967. Secondly, *pachequismo* represented a clear break with previous economic policy-making, and the private sector responded with confidence to the new policies. The traditional political groups who had presided over the *batllista* policies of social consensus were generally confined to Parliament and excluded from the executive branch of government. The government's success in confronting organised labour and the radical left—though not the Tupamaros—encouraged the view that monetary stability would be matched by political and institutional stability on terms which would allow private capital to prosper. In addition to the rural sector, industry showed a marked revival with output growing at an average annual rate of 5 per cent during 1968–70. Gross fixed investment was higher in real terms in 1969 and 1970 than in any year since 1962.[45]

Though relative price stability lasted into 1971, with an increase in the price level that year of 24 per cent, the dynamism of the economy did not last so long. In 1971 and 1972 GDP in real terms contracted by 1 per cent annually, and by 1972 the objective of price stability was also lost. The reasons for the failure of the model are to be found partly in its own limitations, and partly in the transitional character of Pacheco's government. As to the first, it is clear that inflationary pressures were not eliminated, but rather suppressed through the non-orthodox use of price controls. The level of demand remained high through continued expansion of the money supply and public sector deficits. In 1968 central government spending had been cut and the deficit almost eliminated, but spending then rose from 13.2 per cent of GDP in 1968 (the lowest in the decade) to 19.7 per cent in 1971 (the highest).[46] Active demand was also evident in the external sector, where the current account surplus of 1968 became a deficit in each of the following three years, in spite of the devaluations of 1967–8 and the recovery of exports. The consequent pressure on the peso revealed a further departure from orthodoxy, in the commitment of the government to maintain the value of the peso at the rate established in April 1968.

This commitment, which was responsible for the re-emergence during 1970 of currency speculation, reflected a contradiction in Pacheco's strategy. Having looked to private capital to support his arbitrary rule, backed by a politically impassive military and implemented by *técnicos*, while ignoring the political groups and confronting organised labour, Pacheco was still forced by the strength of the tradition of constitutional government to operate within the framework of an electoral system. Hence stable exchange rates were maintained in order to minimise increases in the cost of living, but at the cost of currency speculation, increased foreign debts, and the erosion of the real income gains secured by landowners and the export sector. Stabilisation was further jeopardised by increased public spending—interest-free loans to public employees, for example—during the months preceding the elections of November 1971. Though Pacheco's nominee, Juan María Bordaberry, was successful in those elections, the economic model could not be used again. Within a month the peso was devalued, and following the expansionist measures of 1971 the rate of inflation exceeded 70 per cent in 1972 (and in each of the three succeeding years). The volume of exports contracted sharply in 1972, though the effects of this were counteracted by an upward surge in the level of world prices. Nonetheless, in 1972 as in the previous year, there was a fall in the level of GDP. But the performance of the economy was overshadowed by the heightening of the political crisis and the military *coup* of 1973, which brought to an end the transition phase initiated by Pacheco.

9 The Military Regime since 1973

The constitution of the Republic establishes a democratic and republican political system as the form of government of the country. Uruguay has reaffirmed this principle in a very clear and decisive manner in November 1971, which assures the coexistence of different political positions and, fundamentally, the possibility that they should be expressed freely. (Presidencia de la República *Plan Nacional de Desarrollo 1973–1977*, 2nd ed. (1977), vol. I, p.20.)

The Coup

Although the events which led to the military *coup* of June 1973 have been outlined already in the conclusion to Chapter 1, it is impossible to embark on the main theme of this chapter—an analysis of the economic strategy implemented since 1973—without some assessment of the forces which produced the *coup*. The behaviour of the military in the year preceding their takeover was marked by a number of confused and contradictory aspects which are relevant to an understanding of their subsequent strategy. Indeed, the *coup* appears to have been somewhat hesitant in its timing and more especially in the ideological orientation of its authors. On the other hand the increasing scale of political intervention by the armed forces during that year made the *coup* itself predictable. Moreover, the emergence of similar authoritarian military regimes in Chile and Argentina in the 1970s—and in Brazil a decade earlier—indicates that the crisis requiring a reorganisation of the state may be characteristic of dependent capitalist societies at a certain level of development of their relations with the international economy. However, the following account does not seek to generalise beyond the case of Uruguay.

The origins of the military intervention, it is clear, lay in the long-run political crisis following the breakdown of the import-substituting industrialisation model, and the inability of the political system to restructure the ruling alliance within the dominant class. For a decade the crisis was contained by the use of redistributive *batllista* policies, which frustrated the renewal of the process of accumulation but secured a degree of social consensus. In the late 1960s, however, these policies ceased to be viable, and the crisis entered a new phase with the attempts of Pacheco to reduce the authority of the traditional political groupings, and to strengthen the position of the capitalist class within the executive while attacking organised labour. Having thus won the confidence of the capitalist class, it was then lost at the beginning of the 1970s by the operation of factors which serve to identify *pachequismo* as an intermediate regime, and which further deepened the crisis. They included Pacheco's reversion to traditional political practices, especially inflated government expenditure, in anticipation of the 1971 elections; his inflexibility in the face of certain demands from the export sector, notably for exchange rate adjustment, and the re-emergence of speculative activities; the growth of the left-wing political alliance, the Frente Amplio; the inability of the regime to eliminate or even contain the Tupamaro guerrilla movement; and the loss of external confidence in the conduct of economic policy and in internal security.[1]

The election result in 1971 defeated Pacheco's ambitions for a second presidential term but—amidst allegations of electoral fraud—allowed him to be succeeded by his vice-presidential candidate, Juan María Bordaberry. In spite of its 18 per cent of the officially recorded vote, the performance of the Frente Amplio was weaker than predicted. To permit the new party to contest the elections without additional official harassment, the Tupamaros declared a truce during the election period. The truce coincided with the transfer of responsibility for internal security from the police, discredited and humiliated by the success of guerrilla operations and in particular the mass escapes of Tupamaro prisoners from jail, to the armed forces. In the interval preceding the resumption of guerrilla attacks in April 1972, it is evident that the military laid an effective basis for their own counter-offensive, aided by the declaration of a state of internal war and by betrayal of the movement by a disaffected Tupamaro leader. By late 1972 the guerrillas had been eliminated as a serious force, but their influence was far from being at an end. Information passed by them to the armed forces on the level of corruption implicating leading political figures served to undermine the confidence of the military in the political process. This, and growing awareness by the military of the extent of contacts between the Tupamaros and other political groups, contributed to discredit the political establishment in its relations with the armed forces during the second half of 1972.

But the military at this stage of the process were divided by substantial differences of ideology, and probably only a zeal to root out corrupt figures in civilian life was a common denominator. The issues on which the military divided were whether to operate within or outside the constitution, and the desirability either of a strategy promoting social change (the *peruanista* faction) or of imposing a development model akin to that of the Brazilian armed forces. The first of these issues was resolved early in 1973. The influence of the constitutionalists was steadily undermined by evidence on the way in which those in power—and who had been sustained in power by the success of the armed forces—had profited from their position. It was further weakened by counter-attacks from political figures which were taken to impugn the honour of the military. The position of Bordaberry in attempting to maintain sufficient political support for his administration to function grew doubtful. The critical point was reached in February 1973, when the military denied his right to make ministerial appointments which did not have their approval. Bordaberry backed down, and having failed to protect the authority of the nation's institutions he was thereafter dependent on military support. The *coup* then developed rapidly. In February the role of the armed forces in decision-making was institutionalised in the military-controlled National Security Council (COSENA). Control of the more important public corporations was secured in April. By then the attack on the legislature had begun, and it was its refusal to permit charges of subversive association to be brought against a senator which gave the armed forces the occasion they sought to dissolve the legislature, at the end of June. The full range of repressive measures was then unleashed, with the arrest of leading political figures of all parties, trade unionists, and members of the university, which was occupied by the army in October. Bordaberry was retained as president, possibly to disguise the unconstitutional nature of the regime but more probably to inhibit the emergence of presidential ambition within the ranks of the military high command. A nominated Consejo de Estado was announced in June to replace the legislature, but the twenty-five nominations were not in fact made until the end of 1973.

The *coup* ended a period of almost ninety years in which the Uruguayan military, in contrast with practice elsewhere in Latin America, had remained politically passive.[2] Even in 1933 it was the police which provided the show of force necessary for Gabriel Terra's *coup*. The explanation for the withdrawal of the armed forces from an active political role over so long a period lies in their traditional loyalty to the Colorado party, in the domination of government by the Colorado party, and in the lasting peace between the parties achieved early this century. The military thus developed along professional and technical rather than political lines, and did not have strong family connections with the political parties. The electoral defeat of the Colorados in 1958 and the subsequent elevation of Blanco officers disrupted the relative political homogeneity of the military. But more urgent reasons for the changed role were the emphasis in US military aid programmes on anti-insurgency techniques in the 1960s, and the much-increased use of the armed forces to suppress social and labour unrest, especially after 1968.

During the regime of Pacheco the security forces became practised in many of the brutalities which have since been employed to sustain the military in power. As early as 1970 an investigating commission of the Uruguayan Senate found that the use of torture by the police was 'normal, frequent and habitual'.³ During the period of the *coup* the target of the apparatus of repression broadened from suspected Tupamaros and strike leaders to include, on a systematic basis after the *coup*, political dissidents, trade union militants, and all suspected of Marxist leanings. Arbitrary arrest, torture and 'disappearances' have served to eliminate all effective opposition. Newspapers and journals which criticised the new regime—inevitably they included *Marcha*, the only Uruguayan periodical of international standing—were closed. Control by the executive over the educational system was greatly extended in 1972 and completed after the *coup*. Those who were suspected of left-wing sympathies were deprived of their posts in the bureaucracy, the public sector and education. For Uruguay in the mid-1970s the melancholy record was claimed of having the highest ratio of prisoners of conscience to total population of any country in the world. The disregard of human rights by the regime aroused particular concern in the USA and led to the suspension of military and economic aid programmes in 1976–7. A recent report of the Inter-American Commission on Human Rights provides documentation on the brutalities of the regime.⁴

While the strength of the *golpista* faction of the armed forces (i.e. those in favour of a military *coup*) was evident by early 1973, the dominant ideology of the faction remained in doubt until considerably later. The position of the *peruanista* reformists—as of the *golpistas*—was strengthened by revelations of corruption among the powerful, and late in 1972 they brought pressure to bear on the government to grant general wage increases. The firmest evidence of a reformist faction came with the publication in February 1973 of two military communiqués, nos. 4 and 7, which promised (amongst other objectives) the elimination of unemployment, oppressive foreign debt, corruption, subversion, and monopolistic practices, and the introduction of export incentives, land redistribution, policies to promote a more equal distribution of income, fiscal reform, and reorganisation of the diplomatic service.⁵ The random listing of policy aims suggests that the communiqués were simply an expression of intent with no basis in a coherent and systematic analysis of national problems. They caused brief uncertainty within the ranks of the left as to the possibility of collaboration with a reformist military regime. But as a manifesto aimed at securing support within the officer ranks they evidently failed. Nothing more was heard of the *peruanistas*, and the logic of the *coup* meant that reformist proposals, many of which had been put forward by the Frente Amplio and were therefore tainted by Marxist association, were insupportable. But the conservative faction seems to have had little to offer either beyond an expressed admiration of the Brazilian achievement. In these circumstances a five-year plan prepared by the governing conservative faction of the Colorado party, published in April 1973 but attracting little attention at that time, was taken up and adopted by the military regime in August to form the basis of its economic strategy.

The Military Regime

The regime formally designates itself as *cívico-militar*. The civilian component is comprised of the president, the Consejo de Estado, and the heads of ministries. The powers of the president are nominal. Bordaberry retained the office until 1976, when disagreement over proposals for a return to some form of constitutional government caused the military to remove him, and he was replaced by Aparicio Méndez. The only effective centre of civilian authority has consisted of the group of *técnicos* who conduct economic policy from the Ministry of the Economy and Finance and the Central Bank. The only outstanding individual has been Alejandro Végh Villegas, who was appointed Minister of the Economy in July 1974 to superintend the implementation of the new economic model, and who since his resignation in September 1976 has been a member of the Consejo de Estado.

Military participation in government is exercised formally through COSENA and a council of commanders in chief, as well as key positions in the executive and the direction of the principal public corporations. The decision to retain a titular civilian presidency may reflect an anxiety among senior officers to prevent the emergence of a Pinochet or a Videla, but the post of army commander-in-chief, rotated annually, confers a pre-eminence which was employed by General Gregorio Alvarez to further presidential ambition during 1978–9. There is no doubt that the effective exercise of the political function is confined to a very small group of senior officers and those civilians whom they have selected to hold office. The decision in August 1973 to adopt the five-year plan as the basis of the government's strategy was taken at a conclave of twenty civilian and military leaders, and guidelines for the implementation of the strategy have been agreed at similar meetings, generally at annual intervals. The repression of conventional forms of political expression has meant that there is no effective opposition or free comment on government policy.[6]

A feature of the enclosed nature of the decision-making group and the low level of political output has been the difficulty encountered by the private sector in giving effective expression to its views. As will be seen in the following section, the economic model has sought the consolidation of the capitalist system, but at the same time has entailed severe difficulties for major and traditionally powerful sectors of the capitalist class. They have found the ruling groups apparently impenetrable. Both the Asociación Rural and the Cámara de Industrias have failed in their attempts to exert a significant influence on policy, and indeed in 1975 the president of the Federación Rural was arrested for voicing criticisms of the regime's economic policy. Moreover, Végh Villegas in speeches during 1974–5 went out of his way to criticise the conduct of pressure groups.[7] It seems therefore that the capacity of traditionally dominant groups to influence the political process, which had been exercised quite directly during the early years of the Pacheco regime, has now receded. Their lack of representation also poses more fundamental questions concerning the identity of the interests represented by the regime, and the latter's capacity to construct an alliance among the favoured groups within the capitalist class which would be capable of sustaining a hegemonic role if the armed forces should withdraw from active political participation.

The existence of tensions within and between the ruling military and civilian groups has been ill-concealed. They have concerned the personal ambitions of some senior officers, the implications of the high level of military spending for the economic model, and the implications of the economic model for national autonomy. The most urgent question, however, relates to the future political role of the military and the need to legitimise the regime by recourse to an electoral process of some form. After 1973 the repression of political life extended beyond Marxists and radical dissidents to include the political system as a whole, tainted by subversion and corruption. The Blanco and Colorado parties, though tolerable as non-class-based institutions, posed a threat to the regime because as instruments of mass mobilisation and lacking ideological definition they invited the penetration of Marxist ideas. Yet some form of representative political process may be regarded as essential to the long-run survival of the capitalist state, given the diverse structure of interests within the capitalist class, and it is unlikely that even the most conservative officers see the present level of political involvement of the military as capable of being maintained indefinitely.

The issue became critical at the end of 1975 when, in response to the need to decide whether or not the elections scheduled for 1976 should take place, Bordaberry proposed their indefinite postponement and an extension of his term of office. To rehabilitate the parties and permit elections would in his view have left the door open to subversion. The proposals were countered by Végh, who argued for the gradual restoration of representative government. The military should return to their traditional role as 'supreme arbiter of the Nation' and permit limited political expression. In its absence, a resumption of Marxist activity would be inevitable, while a continued political role for the military ran the risk of deepening internal division within the armed forces, leading either to the suicide of the military government or the emergence of a military *caudillo*.[8] The military response was to announce in May 1976 that there would be no early resumption of political activity—hence no elections—and in June to dismiss Bordaberry.

Their longer-term plans were announced by Aparicio Méndez on his inauguration in September. All those who stood for office in the 1966 or 1971 elections as candidates for Marxist or 'pro-Marxist' parties, or who have been tried for subversive activities, are deprived of all political rights until the beginning of the 1990s. Those who were candidates of any other party or were members of the national executive of a party, are deprived of all political rights except the right to vote, also for fifteen years. The effect of the decree is to eliminate an entire generation of politicians, estimated to number as many as 15,000,[9] as punishment for their role in permitting the growth of subversive forces. The two traditional parties have been exonerated, however. In October 1976 it was announced that there would be a presidential election in 1981 but with only one candidate. He is to be selected, according to a decision reached at the end of 1977, by the Blanco and Colorado parties acting jointly, provided that the nomination carries military approval. Parliamentary elections were promised for 1986. Clearly, the transition to representative government, however slow, limited and controlled, poses delicate problems for the regime. By rehabilitating the traditional parties under new leadership, the intention is evidently to seek the legitimation of the transitional regime by the appearance of some continuity with the pre-1973 political structure, while utilising the undefined class orientation of the parties to inhibit the emergence of a popular political movement. Those who are expected to seek the presidential nomination include Végh Villegas, who is believed to have the backing of the US embassy, and former army commanders Gregorio Alvarez and Julio César Vadora. To emphasise the very limited nature of the political 'opening' which may be expected, however, the creation of a Ministry of Justice in 1977 to control the judiciary and the Electoral Court gave institutional form to the total domination of the executive branch of government.

Economic Strategy[10]

The attraction of the *Plan Nacional de Desarrollo 1973–1977*[11] for the armed forces was two-fold. First, it offered a reasonably coherent guide to policy in an area in which they were entirely inexperienced; and second, the plan embodies principles of economic liberalism which offered the best guarantee of consistency with the anti-Marxist ideology which united the military. The Plan proposals centred round the greater use of the price mechanism, in opposition to the interventionism of the import-substituting industrialisation period. The role of the entrepreneur was underlined as necessary to the functioning of the market economy, and the profitability of private investment was to receive greater emphasis as an instrument for the fulfilment of the Plan's objectives.[12] No increase in the size of the public sector was envisaged; the emphasis would be instead on improving its efficiency. To permit market forces to operate more freely, the degree of openness of the economy was to increase. This was consistent with the central growth strategy of the Plan, which was to expand and diversify the export trade, particularly of more highly processed or manufactured national raw materials. Foreign capital should receive the same treatment as domestic capital, except that a 'dynamic attitude' was required to attract foreign capital into advanced technology industries or those, like fishing or tourism, in which rapid development was seen as essential.[13] Income redistribution would be left to occur naturally as a result of the process of economic growth itself.[14]

Attention was drawn in the Plan to certain features or problems of the transitional period, which undermined or appeared to contradict the principles of the new model. Inflation, which at the end of 1972 had reached 95 per cent was the most severe of these (Table 9.1). The Plan declared 'the incompatibility of a rate of inflation above 20 per cent and sustained growth in the long and even medium term',[15] and it was

TABLE 9.1. Annual change in prices, real wages and means of payment, rate of unemployment, 1970–8

	Rate of change in consumer price index, Montevideo		Index of real wages			Unemployment in Montevideo	
	Year average (per cent)	Year end (per cent)	Year average 1968 = 100	Year end, av. 1968 = 100	Rate of change of M1 year end	per cent of labour force	Labour force as per cent of population
1970	16.4	20.9	110.0		12.7		
1971	23.9	35.6	115.7		54.2	7.1	38.0
1972	76.5	94.7	95.9	83.5	57.0	7.7	37.5
1973	97.0	77.5	94.3	90.2	75.6	8.9	37.7
1974	77.2	107.2	93.5	85.7	62.9	8.1	38.6
1975	81.4	67.1	85.2	83.0	52.2		
1976	50.5	39.9	80.2	76.6	61.6	12.9[1]	42.1[1]
1977	58.2	57.3	70.7	71.0	40.2	11.8[1]	43.4
1978		46.0					

Note:
1. Average of two half-years. Data for other years is a half-yearly figure.

Sources: Universidad de la República, Estadísticas Básicas; BCU, Boletín Estadístico Mensual; DGEC, Encuesta de Hogares.

intended that this reduced rate should be achieved in 1974 or 1975. Wages and central bank credit were identified as the principal autonomous inflationary factors, with short-run policy instruments competent to bring them under control. The role of COPRIN in controlling some prices, and especially in administering a wages policy, was thus defended. So too was the regime of tax rebates (*reintegros*) on non-traditional exports, as a transitional measure.

At the San Miguel conclave in August 1973 the proposals of the Plan were ratified, with the central principle stated as 'the objective of the Government to restore to the price system its guiding function in the allocation of resources'.[16] Guidelines were laid down for the instrumentation of the Plan. A Law of Industrial Promotion was already under study, and in contravention of the liberal principles of the Plan, a proposal to establish a regime for the promotion of foreign investments was approved. In mid 1974 Végh Villegas was appointed by the military to be Minister of the Economy, to superintend the implementation of the new economic model. By then the economic position of the country had deteriorated still further, as the impact of the oil price rise in late 1973 made itself felt. The visible trade balance, carried into surplus in 1973 by the massive increase in export prices (Table 9.2), was sharply reversed by the addition of US $100 million to the oil import bill. Although central government expenditure and the budget deficit were both relatively low in 1973, and the level of liquidity contracted sharply, in 1974 the effect of imported inflation was supplemented by a deficit in central government spending equal to 4.4 per cent of GDP (Table 9.3). To the long-term task of restructuring the economy along the lines laid down by the military was added that of reducing the large trade gap and the fiscal deficit.

TABLE 9.2. Indices of exports and imports, 1970–6
(1961 = 100)

| | Exports | | Imports | | Terms of trade |
	Volume index	Price index	Volume index	Price index	
1970	124.8	106.7	100.5	100.5	106.2
1971	114.1	103.2	118.0	90.6	113.9
1972	93.0	125.9	114.9	88.6	142.1
1973	103.7	180.8	120.7	113.6	159.2
1974	121.7	179.4	102.4	228.9	78.4
1975	159.3	138.3	109.7	244.2	56.6
1976	228.3	141.6	122.2	231.3	61.2

Source: BCU, *Boletin Estadistico Mensual*.

TABLE 9.3. Central government income and expenditure, 1971–7
(million new pesos)

| | Income | Expenditure | | Gross saving | Deficit | Deficit as per cent of | | Expenditure as per cent of GDP | Per cent of deficit financed by Central Bank credit |
	1	Current 2	Investment 3	1-2	1-2-3	Expenditure 4	GDP 5	6	7
1971	103.1	142.8	1.9	−39.7	−41.6	28.8	5.7	19.7	87.5
1972	167.5	185.7	13.7	−18.2	−31.9	16.0	2.6	16.1	93.3
1973	370.2	372.2	34.3	−2.0	−36.3	8.9	1.4	16.0	57.4
1974	587.9	709.4	80.1	−121.5	−201.6	25.5	4.4	17.1	46.5
1975	985.5	1203.8	145.0	−218.3	−363.3	26.9	4.3	16.1	26.2
1976	1721.7	1808.0	239.4	−86.3	−325.7	15.9	2.6	16.3	53.1
1977	2937.6	2795.9	382.3	141.7	−240.6	7.6	1.2	16.0	66.0

Sources: BCU, Boletín Estadístico Mensual; BCU, Producto e Ingreso Nacionales (1977).

Stabilisation

In spite of the priority attached in the Plan to the rapid reduction in the rate of inflation, it was evident in Végh's economic programme that neither the need to stabilise nor the deterioration in the world economy should be allowed to interfere with the overall economic strategy. Unlike the programme of 1968, with which Végh had also been associated, stabilisation in 1974 was not to be achieved by the shock treatment of a freeze and controls, but rather by a process of gradual adjustment. The principal reason given by Végh for the change in approach related to the large public sector deficit in 1974, necessitating further expansion of the money supply and therefore additional inflationary pressures to be expressed.[17] There were certainly other reasons, however. One was the adoption of the practice of mini-devaluations of the exchange rate in 1972 which obviated the need to protect export sector incomes through a drastic cut in the rate of inflation. Another was the intention to let markets function freely, which was plainly incompatible with the extensive exercise of price controls, particularly if, as with COPRIN after 1968, their use became integral to the stabilisation effort rather than a transitional measure.

Accordingly, the central weapons in the anti-inflation policy from 1974 onwards were restrictions on the rate of growth of the money supply and the containment and restructuring in favour of investment of public expenditure. In 1974 credit contracted sharply (Table 9.4), but central government spending and the size of the deficit both increased. Although approximately 96 per cent of items in the cost of living basket were subject to price control in the second half of 1974, it does not appear that control was used at this period as an instrument to suppress inflation. However, in April 1975 certain basic features of policy were suspended, constituting a pause in the gradualist approach (or alternatively a limited adoption of shock measures). With the rate of inflation over the previous twelve months reaching 100 per cent, the balance of payments fully exposed to the effects of the oil price rise, and difficulties encountered in negotiations in March with the IMF over a further stand-by credit, it was decided to hold wages, prices and the exchange rate at their existing levels. Agreement was reached with the IMF on the terms of the credit in May.

Though the effectiveness of the measures was quickly apparent, the reasons for the change in approach are in doubt. Végh did not conceal his limited aspirations for the new tactics.

I do not believe in price control as a fundamental element in the fight against inflation . . . The backbone of the anti-inflationary strategy is monetary containment. It must be so since there is no effective way of combating inflation other than the slowing down of the rate of

TABLE 9.4. Domestic money supply, 1971–7
(million new pesos, end December)

	Means of payment M1	Annual Growth M1 (per cent)	M1 at constant (1968) prices	M1 plus time and foreign currency deposits M2	Annual growth M2 (per cent)	M2 at constant (1968) prices	Ratio of foreign currency deposits to total time and f.c. deposits (per cent)	Ratio of M2 to GDP
1971	120.1	54.2		176.6	51.5		15.9	24.0
1972	188.6	57.0		285.1	61.4		30.1	23.0
1973	331.2	75.6	45.8	505.8	77.4	74.4	22.5	19.6
1974	539.5	62.9	36.0	858.0	69.6	65.0	32.1	18.6
1975	821.4	52.2	32.8	1596.5	86.0	79.3	42.9	19.1
1976	1327.0	61.6	37.8	3280.1	105.5	126.6	56.2	26.2
1977	1860.1	40.2	33.8	4969.1	51.5	172.6	67.3	24.2

Sources: BCU, Boletín Estadístico Mensual; BCU, Producto e Ingreso Nacionales (1977).

expansion of the quantity of money. Price control has a supporting role to play in the first phase of the process, so that monetary restriction does not achieve its results through excessive unemployment.[18]

The explanation is not wholly convincing, since the published estimate of unemployment for 1974 did not show an increase over the previous year, while the very high levels of unemployment in 1976–7 have not been taken to justify any modification of the economic strategy. In a later discussion Végh agreed that having begun to implement appropriate monetary and fiscal measures, shock measures to reduce inflationary expectations were justified. It would moreover permit the consolidation of 'a structure of relative prices which was considered adequate and which harmonised the legitimate interests of the consumer with the necessary profitability of the productive sector'[19]—although the central government deficit showed virtually no improvement in 1975, and there were therefore further inflationary pressures in the pipeline. But an interval of relative stability had obvious attractions at this stage, since a number of factors impairing the functioning of the price mechanism—including subsidies to consumers, low house rents and low public utility tariffs—had been substantially rectified. At the end of September 1975 the sequence of mini-devaluations was resumed, and price and wage increases followed at the end of the year. The effect of the 'pause' was certainly to moderate the rate of price increase, and accelerate the decline in real wages. Inflation, at 67 per cent by December 1975, showed a marked decline compared with 1974.[20] Real wages averaged 87.0 during January – May 1975 (1968 = 100) fell to 77.3 in October, and recovered only to average 80.8 in the first five months of 1976.[21]

The increased degree of price stability was sustained into the first half of 1976, with the price index in June less than 9 per cent above that of December 1975. The inflationary process thereafter acquired a new momentum, with an increase of 66 per cent in the following twelve months. Price controls, most of which had been lifted in early 1976, were reimposed in March 1977 by Valentín Arismendi, who had succeeded Végh as Minister of the Economy and Finance the previous October. While the fiscal performance showed a marked improvement over the previous two years, credit to the non-bank private sector in real terms grew by 30 per cent in 1976, compared with 10 per cent and 21 per cent in the previous two years.[22] An additional and novel factor contributing to monetary expansion in 1976 was the improvement in the external sector resulting in a substantial addition to the gold and foreign exchange reserves (Table 9.5). Both of these expansionary factors operated again in 1977, with real private sector credit up by 38 per cent and a further gain in the level of international reserves, but the annual rate of increase of M2 was nonetheless the lowest in any year since 1971. During 1978

TABLE 9.5. Gold and foreign currency reserves and import ratio, 1971–8
(million US dollars)

	Total gold and currency reserves 1	Total imports 2	1/2 (per cent)	Total gold and currency reserves 3	3/2 (per cent)
1971	181	325	55.7		
1972	203	305	66.6		
1973	240	398	60.3		
1974	232	634	36.6		
1975	218	717	30.4	392[1]	54.7
1976	315	785	40.1	496[1]	63.2
1977	459	987	46.5	757[1]	76.7
1978	453				

Note:

1. From December 1975 the gold held by the official banks was revalued at US$90 per ounce troy.

Sources: 1 and 2, IMF, International Financial Statistics; 3, BCU, Boletín Estadístico Mensual.

the price level rose by 46 per cent, and at the beginning of 1979 the regime again announced that stabilisation was its main objective for the year. The methods by which this is to be achieved include the reduction of total government spending, which is expected to bear particularly heavily on public investment expenditure; lower interest rates, to reduce the high rate of inflow of foreign currencies; and advance announcement of official exchange rate changes to reduce the level of speculation. Nonetheless the stimulus to demand of a high level of tourist expenditure contributed to an increase of over 27 per cent in the consumer price index in the first five months of 1979.

Both stabilisation and restructuring in the context of a regime dedicated to the greater utilisation of the price mechanism and private incentives for resource allocation have required a programme of financial reforms. Among the more important of these have been measures to increase total tax revenue both to finance the budget deficit and to compensate for the declining yield of fiscal impositions on exports and imports as a result of trade liberalisation; and to restore financial incentives to savers and improve the allocation of credit. In the first category, the efficiency of tax collection was improved and a number of unproductive taxes suppressed. Also, taxes on personal income, inheritance and company dividends were eliminated. New developments have included the concentration of the tax base more heavily on a value-added tax and consumption of fuel, and the introduction of a tax on the potential yield of land (IMPROME). In the second category, interest rate ceilings were raised from late 1974 to permit positive real rates of return and end the necessity for credit rationing.[23] This, and the freeing of the financial exchange market, have been reflected in the rapid growth of time and foreign currency bank deposits. Treasury bonds bearing variable interest rates have been issued, and provision made for the private sector also to issue adjustable bonds in an attempt to stimulate the domestic capital market. The importance of interest rates as regulators of economic activity have been emphasised since the second half of 1976 in the use of open-market operations to regulate the supply of credit.[24]

It is clear that the inflationary process has not yet been brought under control. Rates of price increase remain high, and it has been necessary periodically to give anti-inflation measures temporary priority over other objectives. Nonetheless it should not be assumed that the stabilisation programme has failed, in part because the regime has been able to utilise increases in the price level to achieve another of its objectives, a major decline in real wages. But in a more general sense, it is erroneous to divorce the objectives of stabilisation and restructuring. Whether or not price stability is a pre-requisite of sustained growth (in suggesting that it is, the Plan was perhaps excessively influenced by Brazilian experience after 1964), stability is not a necessary condition of a restructuring programme. On the contrary, it would be more accurate to describe the strategy since 1974 as an attempt to impose a political, social and economic model which will secure stability, as well as higher rates of growth and accumulation. Inflation then becomes a short-term problem when its effects slow down the rate at which the new model can be imposed. The important question, therefore, blurred by the implication in monetarist doctrine that price stability as such is desirable, concerns the kind of economic model which the regime in Uruguay seeks to achieve.

Restructuring

The long-term economic strategy of the regime may be defined as an attempt to secure the closer integration of the Uruguayan economy with the world economy. By increasing the degree of openness of the economy the structure of domestic prices is to be brought more in line with international prices, thus reversing the policy of protection for non-traded goods of the import-substitution period. The implication of this strategy for economic growth is that the growth process is to be led by the export of commodities in which Uruguay has relatively low costs of production. To secure the necessary increase in investment the supply of domestic and foreign savings is to be increased, and by depressing consumption while reducing the level of protection the market should allocate the funds to the traded goods sector. The role of the price mechanism for resource allocation is, as we have seen, an article of faith for the regime. To that extent the inspiration of the model is economic liberalism. Nonetheless, there are a number of fundamental interferences with the market mechanism, some a stubborn and continuing legacy of earlier interventionism, others introduced since 1974 as instruments of the restructuring, such that there is room for doubt whether liberalisation is an adequate description for the changes in the management of the economy since the *coup*. This doubt translates into further uncertainty about the unity and coherence within the regime of civilian and military aspirations for the economic and social development of the country.

Summarising the effects of the restructuring programme, GDP at constant prices grew continuously in the six years 1973–8 at an annual average rate of 2.8 per cent (Table 9.6). While the rate of growth was very low, this was the first such period of sustained growth since the early 1950s. Gross fixed investment increased as a proportion of GDP from 10.9 per cent in 1973–4 to 16.5 per cent in 1976–7. Government consumption expenditure has shown little consistent variation in real terms; but private consumption has been hit very severely, declining from 77.3 per cent of GDP in 1973 to 62.8 per cent in 1977. While it has been policy to encourage voluntary savings, the principal explanation for the fall in consumption must be found in the quite dramatic cut in real wages. Between the election year 1971 and 1977 the fall was 40 per cent, with the greatest declines in 1972 and 1977 (Table 9.1). In spite of falling consumption, manufacturing output grew by an average 5 per cent annually over the four years 1974–7. Quite clearly it was the external market which stimulated the major part of this growth. By 1976–7, when the visible trade deficit produced by the oil crisis had been closed, the ratio of total trade to GDP had reached 41 per cent, compared with 31 per cent during 1970–2.

It is evident from the abbreviated data in the previous paragraph that there have been significant shifts in the structure of the Uruguayan economy since 1973. The fall in real consumption and the expansion of exports are particularly noteworthy. Neither of these effects is attributable to 'liberal' policy, nor will their achievement necessarily facilitate the conversion of the economy away from interventionism. The decline in consumption, based in turn on the decline in real wages, has been the product of wage controls imposed on a labour force which has historically been highly organised but since 1973 almost entirely defenceless. Accompanying the fall in real wages has been the growth of unemployment in Montevideo (Table 9.1). Although the data for Montevideo may exaggerate national unemployment, and the size of the

TABLE 9.6. Gross National Income and Gross Domestic Product, 1970–8 (thousand new pesos, 1961 prices)

	Gross Domestic Expenditure					Exports	Imports	GDP	Terms of trade effect	Net income from abroad	Gross National Income
	Private consumption	Government consumption	Gross Fixed Investment	Change in inventories	Total						
1970	14454	2783	2745	-12	19970	2928	3304	19594	87	-270	19411
1971	14611	2595	2871	176	20253	2718	3567	19404	316	-260	19459
1972	14559	2249	2341	209	19358	2526	3171	18713	710	-291	19132
1973	14594	2711	2017	441	19763	2554	3448	18869	1218	-242	19845
1974	14333	2892	2134	206	19565	3123	3232	19456	-420	-203	18833
1975	14265	2749	2919	—	19933	3766	3379	20320	-1194	-318	18808
1976	13571	2867	3191	-245	19384	5049	3585	20848	-1510	-342	18996
1977	13535	3099	3800	-56	20378	5065	3886	21557	-1337	-287	19933

Composition and rate of growth of GDP (per cent)

	Private Consumption	Government Consumption	Gross Fixed Investment	Change in inventories	Trade balance	GDP	Rate of growth
1970	73.8	14.2	14.0	—	-1.9	100	4.7
1971	75.3	13.4	14.8	0.9	-4.4	100	-1.0
1972	77.8	12.0	12.5	1.1	-3.4	100	-3.6
1973	77.3	14.4	10.7	2.3	-4.7	100	0.8
1974	73.7	14.9	11.0	1.1	-0.6	100	3.1
1975	70.2	13.5	14.4	—	1.9	100	4.4
1976	65.1	13.8	15.3	-1.2	7.0	100	2.6
1977	62.8	14.4	17.6	-0.3	5.5	100	3.4
1978							2.5

Sources: BCU, Formación Bruta de Capital (September 1978) p. 9; BOLSA, Review, XIII, no. 5/79 (1979) 316.

economically active population has been increased by the fall in real family incomes, probably a further 5 per cent are employed less than thirty hours per week and the size of the labour force has been diminished by the massive emigration of the early 1970s.[25] The regressive redistribution of income during this period is shown in Table 9.7, from which it emerges that the benefits of the redistribution have been concentrated in the second decile of income receivers. A notable aspect of this process, in its political dimension, is that unlike the case of Chile there was no mass working-class involvement in either of the radical political movements—Frente Amplio and Tupamaro guerrillas—which preceded the military *coup*. The decline in living standards should therefore perhaps be seen as a technical adjustment inspired by an ideology which extols the businessman and private sector profitability, as well as being an attack on working-class collectivism.

TABLE 9.7. Income distribution, 1973–6
(percentiles of Montevideo household incomes)

	Top 10%	10%	30%	30%	Bottom 20%
1973[1]	25.3	15.8	31.6	20.2	7.1
1976[2]	24.7	20.0	31.0	18.3	6.0

Notes: 1. First half. 2. Second half.

Source: DGEC, *Encuesta de Hogares*, quoted in *El Día* (Montevideo), 8 August 1977.

The centrepiece of the new model, and the area in which the achievement has been greatest, has been the growth and structural change of the industrial and export sectors. The industrial strategy of the Plan sought 'fundamentally the expansion and diversification of exports of industrial products',[26] and although there is no available breakdown of industrial output by market, there can be no doubt that the crushing of the domestic market and deployment of incentives for exporters has been effective. Between 1973 and 1977 the industrial product grew in real terms by 22 per cent,[27] a modest enough rate of growth by international comparison, but quite impressive in the Uruguayan context. Sectors showing the lowest rates of growth were typical wage-goods; beverages, tobacco, footwear and clothing. Those with the highest growth included non-metallic minerals, rubber products, electrical equipment and textiles—industries which have all participated in the growth of non-traditional exports (though this is true equally of footwear). The new industrial policy has been organised under the Law of Industrial

Promotion of 1974, which grants credit facilities and tax exemptions to industrial projects which are deemed to be of 'national interest'. This status, which may be granted to existing as well as new enterprises, may be acquired on a number of grounds, including greater efficiency, use of raw materials of national origin, and employment creation. In practice the most important appear to have been the growth and diversification of exports. Of the eighty-three projects approved by the end of December 1977, export earnings in the first five years of production were expected to yield US$130 million in excess of investment requirements in foreign exchange of US$80 million.[28]

Exports have been characterised by rapid growth since 1972, a result of very high prices for traditional exports, especially beef, during 1973–4, and an expanding volume of non-traditional exports since 1975. The distinction between traditional exports (basically beef and wool) and the non-traditional group lies essentially in the inability of the latter to compete in the world market. To enable them to do so, they have been eligible since 1968 for tax rebates (*reintegros*), which have effectively subsidised the new export industries and enabled them to penetrate new markets. The importance of the rebates may be seen in terms of the ratio of their value to the value of exports, which averaged 1 per cent during 1969–72, but reached nearly 13 per cent in 1975 (or approximately one-half of the central government current expenditure deficit). Non-traditional exports increased their share of total exports from about 25 per cent in 1972–3 to 55 per cent in 1976–7 and 64 per cent in 1978. Principal among such exported commodities were rice, leather goods, fish, textiles, cement, malted barley, citrus fruit, motor vehicle tyres and glass and ceramic products. The diversity of Uruguay's export trade in recent years has been impressive. It has been promoted by treaty arrangements with Brazil (1975) and Argentina (1974). The contribution of the latter has in fact been almost negligible but the Brazilian market is of fundamental significance, absorbing 15 per cent of total exports in 1975–6, of which 73 per cent were non-traditional. The US market, also, which took only US$7 million of Uruguayan exports in 1972, was worth US$59 million in 1976, largely as a result of the rapid growth of footwear and leather goods. The EEC, with one-third of exports in 1975 and 1976, has retained its traditional position as the most important regional market, notwithstanding the ban on imports of Uruguayan beef during 1974–7.

In spite of the impressive export performance of recent years (Table 9.8) there is room for doubt whether it can be sustained. First, the US government imposed countervailing duties on imports of Uruguayan textiles and leather goods in 1978 and although they were withdrawn at the beginning of 1979 the USA is clearly suspicious of Uruguay's export regime. It is true that the *reintegros* are seen as a transitional measure designed to give exporters temporary assistance in achieving efficient

TABLE 9.8 Summary balance of payments, 1971–8

	1971	1972	1973	1974	1975	1976	1977	1978
Visible exports	197	242	328	381	385	565	612	686
Visible imports	203	179	249	434	496	537	680	757
Visible trade balance	—6	63	79	—53	—111	28	—68	—71
Total net services and transfers	—57	—44	—42	—65	—92	—102	—29	
(net interest and profit)	(—22)	(—24)	(—25)	(—43)	(—71)	(—72)	(—68)	
Long-term capital	51	19	15	25	122	62	21	
Basic balance	—12	38	52	—93	—81	—12	—76	
Short-term capital	51	7	15	123	37	100	207	
Errors and omissions	—51	—20	—30	—82	—6	—10	42	

Sources: IMF, *International Financial Statistics*; BCU, *Boletin Estadistico Mensual*.

production and/or market acceptance, that over the last three years they have been reduced by some 30 per cent, and are scheduled to be withdrawn completely by 1983. Nonetheless—the second point—it is extremely doubtful that the export effort could be maintained if the subsidy were to be substantially reduced.[29] There is a danger that some of the new export industries will become as dependent on state protection as were some of the home market industries, or—if the liberalisation model is finally adopted—that the rate of growth of exports will fall and the degree of diversification decline.

The third point is that in spite of the diversification which has occurred, the agricultural base of the export trade remains emphatic (about 85 per cent in 1977). Exporting is, therefore, still tied to a source of supply which in the livestock sector has historically shown a very low rate of growth, and which in all sectors is vulnerable to climatic conditions. The problem was experienced in acute form in 1977 by the tanning and leather goods industry, the most important of the non-traditional exporters, whose rate of expansion was restricted by a shortage of raw material in spite of importing 400,000 hides from the USA.[30] It is interesting to notice therefore that while exporters were benefitting from subsidies, the sectors producing exportable output or raw materials experienced a continuous and sharp adverse movement in the internal terms of trade after 1974. The situation of the livestock sector in particular was very severe by 1977. Decapitalisation was evident in the decline of the size of cattle stocks and in a 20 per cent reduction in the area under improved pasture between 1974 and 1977. The sector was suffering from low world prices for its exported output, and from internal price controls designed both to restrict the rate of increase of food prices and ensure cheap supplies of raw materials to the industries manufacturing for export. Moreover, the effect of subsidies paid to non-traditional exports was to depress the exchange rate applicable to traditional exports. There is no doubt that until the policy was reversed in August 1978 the rural sector suffered severely from the new combination of liberalisation and interventionism.

Such discrimination against the sector until 1978 is difficult to interpret, not only because the long-term success of the economic model depends on increased agricultural output (the sectoral product was in fact lower in 1976–7 than in 1970–1), but also because the landowning class might expect to be a major participant in the new alliance of dominant class interests to be expressed in the reconstructed state in the 1980s. The abolition of price controls on meat, cattle, wheat, flour and bread in August 1978, while contributing to the surge in the level of consumer prices, represents a major step in the programme of liberalisation. Tariff levels on foodstuffs for domestic consumption and on equipment and inputs for the rural sector, have been reduced or in some cases eliminated completely. The Frigorífico Nacional is to be closed and its cold-storage facilities sold to the private sector. This radical departure from the interventionist agricultural policy of the previous five years was greeted with acclamation by the rural sector and by advocates within the regime—notably Végh Villegas—of an accelerated liberalisation. The sector continues to receive less advantageous exchange rate treatment for wool and meat by the existence of subsidies on non-traditional exports, but this should also be redressed as the *reintegros* are progressively eliminated. It appears therefore that the exclusion of the rural sector from the group of interests favoured by the regime should be interpreted as a feature of the transition to the new model rather than a long-term policy of discrimination.[31]

The sector of the capitalist class which has suffered most severely from the new model is the industrial bourgeoisie producing for the domestic market. While the intention to reduce the very high tariff levels of the import-substitution era constitutes the longer-term threat to the survival of the sector, it has been affected in the short-term by the high rate of emigration and the sharp fall in real wage levels, with private consumption diminishing by 15 per cent of GDP in four years. At the conclave of Solís at the end of 1977 the decision was taken to dismantle the protectionist structure over a period of five to eight years. Implementation of the decision began in 1979, with tariffs on imports competitive with domestic production reduced from 150 per cent and 110 per cent to 100 per cent and 90 per cent. On foodstuffs and non-competing imports the tariff is set at 35 per cent. By 1985 it is intended that the maximum tariff and tax burden on all imports shall be reduced to 35 per cent.

There is no doubt that foreign capital was expected to play a major part in the construction of the export-oriented industrial economy. The privileges which became available to foreign capital by the Law of Foreign Investment of 1974 appear to have had their origin not in the

National Plan, but in the conclave at San Miguel in October 1973. While the authors of the proposal are not known, it is interesting that the Law was criticised by Végh in 1975 as a discriminating and illiberal measure.[32] Végh claimed that new foreign investments were tending to reject the advantages of the Law because the obligations they entailed were too onerous. In the absence of general information on direct foreign investment in Uruguay, it is difficult to verify the claim. But there is a widely held belief that the participation of foreign capital in industry since 1974 has been very limited, and confidential information on the operation of the 1974 regime confirms that the number of contracts has been small, for a relatively insignificant volume of investment, and that they show no special preference for the dynamic sectors of industry. The essential provision of the Law is for a bilateral contract (*Contrato de Radicación*) to be negotiated between the government and investor, which specifies the valuation of the capital and the terms on which remittances may be made. By the end of 1977 sixteen enterprises had signed contracts with an agreed capitalisation of approximately US$15 million. Three of them were banks, while other activities represented include a dry dock, manufacture of surgical thread, foodstuffs (Nestlé), locks, and photocopiers (Xerox). In nine cases the company was already operating in the country; one of these proposed to open a new plant. In the remaining seven cases, five intended to establish themselves by the acquisition of an existing plant. Only four of the sixteen are believed to have a direct interest in exporting. The contracts are of course secret, but what is known of them suggests that in at least some cases foreign capital has secured extremely generous treatment.

In view of this, it seems unlikely that foreign capital has decided to abstain from the advantages to be secured under the Law; but rather, that in spite of the achievement of internal peace and security, the small and stagnant domestic market of Uruguay was little more attractive to direct foreign investment in the 1970s than it had been in the 1950s. The Law of Foreign Investment has had little impact in attracting new capital, in spite of the increasingly cheap labour supply, the export subsidies, and the fact that the privileges of the Law are additive to those of the Law of Industrial Promotion. The greatest concentration of foreign capital occurs in financial intermediation, in which 'it is estimated that foreign capital at present dominates 80 per cent of the country's banking resources.'[33] It is true that foreign capital has had some participation in non-traditional exports—the largest firm in the leather industry is foreign-owned, for example—but it is probably national capital, in the main, which has benefited from the growth of exports.

The Foreign Investment Law has therefore been largely irrelevant as an instrument for restructuring the economy. As far as the securing of international support is concerned—in which its authors evidently placed their faith—multinational enterprise showed little interest. Eventually the unexpectedly rapid growth of exports[34] reduced the requirement for direct investment to promote new export activities and once the effects of the oil price rise were felt, the need was for short-term financial assistance. The decision was taken in 1974 to maintain the fundamentals of the new economic strategy, in spite of deteriorating world conditions, using the relatively high level of gold and foreign currency reserves to attract a massive inflow of loans to finance the trade gap. The import regime was liberalised to the extent required to permit an expanding supply of capital goods and raw materials needed to sustain a higher rate of investment and growth. Quotas were removed on imports of consumer goods, but the increase in their supply was limited by the imposition of prior deposits. The essence of the strategy, however, was to secure external support and the effect was to produce an abrupt increase in the level of external indebtedness (Table 9.9). In 1974 and 1975 loans were contracted on hard terms, resulting in a sharp rise in debt service obligations. Since, then, however, the repayment profile has improved, easing the short-term service problem.

During 1974 the instability of the economy was emphasised not only by the trade gap but also by a deteriorating fiscal performance. The fiscal policy of the regime has had as its principal objectives to reduce the ratio of government spending to GDP while altering its composition in favour of investment, and to reduce the level of the budget deficit. As Table 9.3 shows, these aims, complementary to each other and necessary to short-term stabilisation and long-term restructuring, have proved elusive. Throughout the period the share of total central government spending allocated to investment increased, from 10.1 per cent in 1974 to 12.0 per cent in 1977. But the ratio of total spending to GDP, though slightly lower in 1975–7 compared with 1974, did not indicate an important reduction in the burden of public spending. At 16.0 per cent, the ratio in 1977 was higher than for any year during 1965–70. The financing of current expenditure out of income also proved impossible until 1977. The difficulty lay both in the stagnation of government income, and in restraining current spending. On the revenue side, the reduction of taxes on trade and the suppression of other taxes was barely compensated by increases elsewhere, due to the effects of declining consumption on sales taxes and depressed world agricultural product prices on the minimum land yield tax. The deficit left by inadequate revenue, traditionally financed by credits from the official banks, was covered to a growing extent by Treasury Bond issues up to 1975, but in 1977 only a third of the deficit was met in this way.

Government spending has proved extremely difficult to contain. In spite of declarations that the size of the enormous bureaucracy was to be reduced, the achievement has been largely confined to the dismissal of those suspected of left-wing sympathies, and the loss of security of

TABLE 9.9. External indebtedness, 1971–8
(million US dollars)

	World Bank			BCU		
	Total external public debt, beginning of year	Interest and amortisation payments	Debt service as per cent of export of goods and services	Total external debt, beginning of year	Interest and amortisation payments	Debt service as per cent of export of goods and services
1971	267.0	56.6	22.3	564.5	146.2	57.8
1972	290.8	107.2	34.3	674.2	152.3	48.7
1973	324.4	93.8	22.6	771.2	240.3	57.9
1974	344.1	156.1	31.0	717.9	162.6	32.3
1975	516.0	228.0	41.1	956.1	295.1	53.2
1976	614.5			1034.8	228.6	32.5
1977				1139.5	173.0	19.6
1978				1311.0		

Note: The World bank calculation excludes unguaranteed suppliers' credits and short-term reserve liabilities. However, both calculations include all dollar-denominated government bonds sold to the private sector. Although these have been taken up by non-residents, especially from Argentina, attracted by the favourable rate of interest, an unknown proportion of such bonds is held by Uruguayan residents.

Source: World Bank, Latin America and the Caribbean Regional Office, *Economic Memorandum on Uruguay* (December 1977), table 4, 2, p. 1; BCU, *Endeudamiento Externo del Uruguayo* (August 1978).

tenure of those who remain. Wages in the public sector have not declined more sharply than the national average. Indeed, although the regime is dedicated to the diminution of the state sector, the only important enterprise to be hived off so far has been the urban transport system AMDET, formerly owned by the municipality of Montevideo. Apart from such evidence that the regime's practice is a long way distant from its supposed liberal principles, the explanation of sustained high central government expenditure appears to be the very high level of spending on the armed forces and other security services. This has resulted from their growing size and level of remuneration. In 1973 budgetary provision was made for the army to double its numbers, and in 1976 the manpower of the armed forces and police was estimated at 45,000,[35] more than 3 per cent of the economically active population. Since 1972, when a state of internal war was declared, the incomes of members of the armed forces have been automatically increased by 40 per cent above their peace-time level, and this level has in turn been raised substantially in real terms, in spite of opposition principally from Végh. It is notable, for example, that in a speech made in 1975 to the Instituto Militar de Estudios Superiores (IMES), Végh emphasised two points: that experience of government confirmed his belief in the value of economic theory (of which the armed forces have limited knowledge); and that the budget deficit posed greater problems than the oil crisis and the balance of payments.[36] The military were not so impressed as to reduce the scale of their spending, which on the basis of two unofficial estimates made in 1976 accounted for at least 49 per cent of total central government expenditure.[37]

The appropriate level of remuneration for the armed forces was only one of the factors giving rise to disagreement between Végh (and the liberal faction in the government) and the military high command. A second, mentioned already, was his persistent support for the view that there should be a limited resumption of political activity by the traditional parties during a transitional phase leading to the full restoration of liberal democratic forms of government. The third and most fundamental area of disagreement has concerned the general validity of liberalisation and the new economic model. Whilst the model has achieved a degree of success, notably in export growth and modest but positive rates of growth of GDP, it has done so at an enormous cost in terms of lower living standards, greater inequality, increased foreign debt, mass emigration, and the exclusion of some sectors of the capitalist class. It is certain that some of the military leadership have been considerably more sensitive to these costs than have the liberals,[38] either through family connections, or through nervousness about their ability to contain social discontent in a future period of democratisation. Concern at the fall in living standards, and the effect of it on domestic producers, has also been expressed within the Consejo de Estado.

In spite of the liberal ideology of the model, the application of economic liberalism in post-1974 policy has been distinctly uneven. In 1977 it was observed that although advances had been made in the financial sector, 'Progress has been much slower as far as the allocation of resources is concerned.'[39] It is clear that there has been a struggle over the issue of liberalisation between the *técnicos* and other components of the regime, both military and civilian. Since 1978, however, the pace of liberalisation has accelerated. First, a timetable has been established for ending the transition period, with a terminal date (1983) for the regime of *reintegros* and a date (1985) by which following a series of equal annual reductions the tariff level will be fixed and substantially equalised for all categories of imports. Second, in what Végh has described as 'a milestone in the economic history of Uruguay',[40] liberalisation has been extended to the rural sector and food marketing. Third, all price controls were lifted in March 1979 except on a very limited range of foodstuffs (but including milk), pharmaceuticals and medical and educational products and services, and in April it was announced that employer's social security contributions are to be cut by up to 50 per cent.[41] With the operation of market-determined prices now increasingly extended to the 'real economy', demands for more effective stabilisation measures and a halt to the further erosion of real wage levels may become more pressing.

Conclusion

The military *coup* was fundamentally a response to the long-run crisis of hegemony within the domestic capitalist class. Its timing was dictated by the unprecedented strength of radical or revolutionary political movements in 1971–2 which threatened the survival of the capitalist system in Uruguay. Policies of stabilisation and restructuring, on the basis of a closer integration with the international capitalist economy and with massive external financial support, won acceptance among the military as a way out of the crisis which was intensified by the oil price rise in 1974. The military regime and its new economic model secured the support of the capitalist class as a whole since it guaranteed the principle of the private ownership of the means of production. However, such support can only be provisional: the resolution of the crisis of the capitalist class requires that conditions be established which encourage the profitability of at least some sectors of the class and the resumption of the process of accumulation. Moreover, although the concentration of power in the armed forces relieves the domestic capitalist class of the structural necessity to organise a ruling alliance, such that it is possible for public policy to be shaped in the interests of relatively small fractions of the capitalist class, the withdrawal of the military and resumption of a representative political process appears to require an established hierarchy of dominant class interests. The conduct of the regime since 1973 therefore provokes questions about the rationale and viability of its model, and the identity of the interests it favours.

The logic of the process appears to be to use the present exceptional period to restructure the capitalist class, such that the favoured fractions of it will be sufficiently strong to ensure their domination over other sectors at the end of the political and economic transition period in the mid-1980s. While the visible hand of the military forces the submission of the subordinate classes, the invisible hand of the market price mechanism—guided during the transition period by a continuing interventionism—is expected to reallocate resources on such a scale that the new mode of accumulation will sustain and legitimate itself after the political opening. The principal beneficiaries of the reallocation effected so far have been the group of industries producing non-traditional exports, and the banking sector through its intermediation in the export trade and de-control of interest rates. The exclusion until 1978 of the landowning class must be regarded as a transitional feature, in view of the importance of the sector to the model in producing raw materials for the export industries. Its purpose was probably in part to stimulate the growth of processing industries by the cheapness of price-controlled raw materials, and in part to express the subordination within the new hierarchy of the rural sector to the export industries. The sector of the dominant class which has no place in the new model is protected industry producing for the domestic market, whose strength derives from earlier decades of import-substitution policy and which, as a predominantly nationally owned sector with a clear interest in defending the level of real wages, is more able to legitimate its hegemony by alliance with subordinate classes. The contraction of the market since 1974, while severely affecting domestic industry, nonetheless leaves open the possibility of its recovery if an improvement in real wages should accompany the opening of the political system. For the *técnicos*, therefore, a schedule for the dismantling of tariff protection was an urgent requirement, and its achievement a major victory.

In spite of the tensions and contradictions within and between the components of the regime, it is thus possible to detect a rationale in the new model. The likelihood of successful implementation, however, is questionable. The regime has accentuated the vulnerability of a small economy by seeking to bring the structure of domestic prices more closely in line with world prices and thus establish a closer integration with the world economy. The reasons for doing so may broadly be grouped under two headings: firstly, to enlist international support for the model, and secondly, to employ the price mechanism (in the long run) to allocate resources in order to promote their more efficient utilisation. The first of these has had generally disappointing results.

Foreign capital has been willing to underwrite the model with loan funds, but direct investment has been very limited, especially if tourist developments at the resort of Punta del Este are excluded. In spite of the fall in real wages, Uruguay does not have either the supply of abundant cheap labour, nor—of course—the domestic market, which would attract multinational enterprise to establish itself. As to the second, it is as yet impossible to judge the efficiency of the price mechanism in reallocating resources because the restructuring so far achieved has been largely the result of policy-induced price distortions. Nonetheless, it is intended that by the 1980s resource allocation shall be substantially determined by the market, and even in the context of the widespread appeal of monetarist doctrine in the 1970s there seems to be an extreme and somewhat naive faith in market forces in Uruguay. There is a clear risk that a world recession, or protectionism by the USA, or even adverse domestic weather conditions, could have disastrous effects on the fragile export-led growth model. It should be borne in mind too that factor mobility is inevitably diminished in a small, very slow-growth economy with a rapidly ageing labour force.

While the social costs of a weak market response to the new model are presumably acceptable to the regime in the short term, the political opening in the 1980s implies that the export-oriented economy must establish a degree of legitimation that at present seems unlikely. Future social stability rests not only on the growth and greater efficiency of the export industries, such that they can sustain the new orientation against the claims of competing fractions of the dominant class, but also on their capacity to create new sources of employment and reverse the downward trend in real wages. The very high level of unemployment in 1979 in the leather goods industry,[42] a consequence of improved world prices for unmanufactured hides and the de-control of prices to the rural sector, is an ominous indicator, especially as this is the most significant of the non-traditional export industries. In spite of the regime's sustained attack on trade union militants, and of its attempts to orient labour towards official 'unions', the eventual popular reaction to the model will be harsh. For that reason the regime is nervous about what may be entailed by any political opening. It may well prefer to postpone the restoration of a representative political process rather than retreat from its liberalisation programme. In any event there is no prospect that the present economic model can create the ideological consensus necessary for the restoration of the generally benign exercise of bourgeois democratic power which prevailed in the pre-1968 period.

The specific features of Uruguay's economic and social structure have determined throughout this century that its dependent status should be experienced in an exceptional form. Those features are its small size, national ownership of natural resources, and high level of resource-based exports relative to population resulting in a comparatively high wage labour force. During the decades in which the *batllista* ideology predominated, the urban, redistributive orientation of policy permitted a somewhat autonomous pattern of development to emerge under conditions of social and institutional stability. In that period Uruguay developed as a highly politicised, literate and vocal society. Within the limitations imposed by size, its cultural and sporting attainments were remarkable. Equality and humanity were widely held values. That Uruguay is dead. In its place is a regime whose most evident success has been to create a silence broken only by the voices of its own spokesmen. The irony of its economic model is that in attempting to secure the possible advantages of a deepened form of dependency it seems likely to achieve only an accentuation of the economy's vulnerability.

Appendix
Foreign Trade Data

For the period up to 1940, the statistical material relating to Uruguay's foreign trade suffers from numerous defects. The most important of these relates to the method of valuation used. In common with other Latin American countries, and in order to prevent the loss of customs revenue due to under-declarations of value, the Uruguayan authorities employed a set of official prices (*aforos*) for most, though not all, imports; and this practice survived until 1940. The official values were enshrined in the Ley de Aduana of 1888;[1] the valuation commission was supposed to meet annually to revise the values, but had not met once by 1903, and the system became an absurdity with the rise in world prices during 1915–20. In 1923 a new set of official values was elaborated. Its basis was prices at the quayside in Montevideo, minus (for all except luxuries) 25 per cent, and provided that the increase on the old *aforo* did not exceed 40 per cent.[2] No general revaluation occurred thereafter, until declared values came into use in the 1940s.

The valuation of exports until 1913 was also made on the basis of official prices, though the explanation for this was presumably statistical convenience rather than to maximise revenue. Changes in these prices were introduced rarely, and in different years for different commodities. The increase in actual export prices during the First World War persuaded the Dirección de Estadística to publish export data for 1913 onwards at 'market prices', and the published data therefore purport to be real export values. However, calculation of the prices implicit in these values reveals that over certain periods fixed prices continued to be used to calculate export values. For example, the implicit price of wool and hides remained constant during 1917–20, and for most meat products during 1917–25. In the extreme case, the implicit price of corned beef exports changed only once during 1917–32. Moreover, during 1913–16 the prices of all exported commodities appear suspiciously well-rounded.

Thus, the valuation of recorded trade flows is a central problem in the analysis of Uruguay's foreign trade. The only previous attempts to revise the published data in line with real prices were contemporary efforts made under the direction of Julio Martínez Lamas,[3] and later by a commission set up in 1931. Little is known of the way in which the

275

revisions were made, so that it seemed desirable to prepare a set of alternative estimates, based mainly on US and UK data of their trade with Uruguay. The limitations of such an exercise are well known.[4]

It should be remembered, however, that the problem of prices is only one source of error in the data. The major factor contributing to the under-valuation of trade flows was the incidence of contraband. It is impossible to estimate its quantitative importance, but illicit trading with neighbouring countries was common throughout the nineteenth century and has continued to flourish. Acevedo regarded this as less significant than the entry of contraband imports through the port of Montevideo as goods in transit.[5] At the turn of the century, tobacco merchants estimated the contraband trade at a million kilos per year, which was substantially more than recorded imports of tobacco.[6] The comparatively light fiscal burden on exports implies that undervaluation because of contraband was probably much greater for imports than it was for exports, though Cosio estimated the illicit sale of cattle to Brazil at 150,000 head per annum.[7]

Notes to Tables

Table 5.1 Commodity Exports, 1895–1913

Official values, and the estimated value for 1913, are from DGEC, *Anuario Estadístico*. Estimated values for other years are crude adjustments of official figures using market prices for exportables where available. The volume index is calculated on the basis of thirteen principal export commodities (comprising 92 per cent of total export value in 1913) weighted by 1913 prices.

Table 5.2 Commodity Exports, 1913–40

The raw data is from DGEC, *Anuario Estadístico*. In the value series, the problem of valuations at fixed official prices is especially severe for 1918–25, and the data for these years has been adjusted on the basis of price data for wool, hides and cattle in Ministerio de Industrias, *Anuario de Estadística Agrícola*. The effect of these revisions is to increase the values for 1918–21, and to reduce them for 1922–5. These estimates, and the value data for other years, must be regarded with caution, since the use of official prices was not completely eliminated in compiling export data until 1933. The export volume index is calculated on the basis of sixteen commodities (88 per cent of total exports in 1938) weighted by 1938 prices.

Table 6.1 Commodity Imports, 1899–1938

The 'official value' series consists of the *aforo* valuations for 1899–1912 and 1934–8. The *aforo* values for 1913–33 were scrutinised and, in most cases, adjusted by various authorities, and these revisions (summarised in BROU, *Sinopsis Económica y Financiera*, p. 79) have been incorporated here. The estimates of import values are based on f.o.b. values of US exports to Uruguay and UK exports to Uruguay, converted to pesos at annual average exchange rates, and scaled up from the proportions of total imports from these countries indicated in Uruguayan sources, as if all Uruguayan imports came from the USA and UK. The volume series was elaborated by deflating the value estimates by an 'import price' index, which is in fact the weighted average of UK and US export price indices adjusted for exchange rate changes. The estimates are presented as three-year moving averages, to reduce the effect of time lags. The method of estimation depends on the accuracy of the recorded values in the exporting countries, and of the proportion of total imports from different sources in the Uruguayan data. An inherent error is that the import estimates are f.o.b., not c.i.f. (though Platt has observed 'a tendency in the 1900s for British manufacturers exporting to Latin America to agree a c.i.f. price in place of f.o.b.'.[8] A major potential source of error, the consignment of goods to Buenos Aires for transhipment to Montevideo, is a factor difficult to assess. Uruguayan sources record this as trade with Argentina: if British statistics did so also, these estimates would be unaffected. Data sources are US Department of Commerce, *Foreign Commerce and Navigation of the United States*; UK, *Annual Statement of the Trade of the United Kingdom with Commonwealth and Foreign Countries;* and DGEC, *Anuario Estadístico.*

Table 6.3 Composition of Imports by End-Use, 1899–1970

The classification of imports up to 1940 was made according to the CUODE system. No attempt was made to adjust official valuations which remained fixed over long periods, the only systematic revaluation occurring in 1923. A small number of revaluations of particular imports occurred in other years, and some were even recorded at declared values. The classification therefore approximates more closely to the volume of imports, at 1888 prices (1899–1910) and 1923 prices (1924–40), than to the value. For 1899–1910 the classification embraces all the commodities enumerated in the source, about 850. However, other imports, about 6.6 per cent of total imports in this period, were admitted free of duty for public offices, public utilities and manufacturing industry: these imports were enumerated according to the identity of the importer rather than the nature of the commodity, which is unknown. For 1924–40 about 450 of the most important commodities were selected for classification from an enumeration in the source covering some 5000 commodities. The commodities classified here were 81.7 per cent of total imports during the period. The advice in making this classification given by Rosemary Thorp and Geoff Bertram is gratefully acknowledged. Data sources are: 1899–1910, 1924–40, DGEC, *Anuario Estadístico*; 1942–67, CIDE, *Estudio Económico*, vol. I, table II, p. 53; Universidad de la República, *Estadísticas Básicas*, table 38; 1968–70, Presidencia de la República, *Plan Nacional de Desarrollo 1973–1977*, vol. I, p. 487.

Notes

Chapter 1 The Ideology of Batllismo 1870–1970

1. See Nicos Poulantzas, 'The Capitalist State: a Reply to Miliband and Laclau', *New Left Review* no. 95 (1976) 71–5; and *Fascism and Dictatorship* (London; New Left Books, 1974) pp. 83–8.
2. Aldo Solari, *El Desarrollo Social del Uruguay en la Postguerra* (Montevideo: Editorial Alfa, 1967) pp. 151–2.
3. See, however, E. V. K. Fitzgerald, E. Floto and A. D. Lehmann (eds.), *The State and Economic Development in Latin America* (Centre of Latin American Studies, University of Cambridge, 1977).
4. Fernando Henrique Cardoso and Enzo Faletto, *Dependencia y Desarrollo en América Latina*, 6th ed. (Buenos Aires: Siglo XXI, 1973) ch.3.
5. The analysis in this section draws heavily on the seven volumes of José Pedro Barrán and Benjamín Nahum, *Historia Rural del Uruguay Moderno*, (Montevideo: Ediciones de la Banda Oriental, 1967–78).
6. Juan E. Pivel Devoto and Alcira Ranieri de Pivel Devoto, *Historia de la República Oriental del Uruguay*, 3rd ed. (Montevideo: Editorial Medina, 1966) pp.351–2.
7. Alberto Zum Felde, *Proceso Histórico del Uruguay*, 5th ed. (Montevideo: Editorial Arca, 1967) p.215. 'The principal element adopted by the urban and intellectual presidential style of Herrera is party traditionalism. The intellectual, aristocratic Herrera becomes a *caudillo*, a *gaucho*, in order to rule.'
8. Milton I. Vanger, *José Batlle y Ordóñez of Uruguay: The Creator of his Times, 1902–1907* (Cambridge: Harvard University Press, 1963).
9. Barrán and Nahum, *Historia Rural*, vol. IV, part 4.
10. Material on the origins of the Federación Rural is to be found in *La Federación Rural: Su Origen y Desarrollo* (Montevideo: Talleres Gráficos, 1916).
11. *Censo Municipal del Departamento y de la Ciudad de Montevideo 1889–90* (Montevideo, 1892) pp. 259–60.
12. Debate on the petition of La Algodonera Uruguaya for higher tariffs on competing imports, 30 January 1913. (*Diario de Sesiones de la Honorable Cámara de Representantes* [DSHCR], 1912–13, vol. CCXXII, 462.)
13. See, for example, *DSHCR*, 1915, vol CCXLIV, 109 ff.; and *Revista de la Federación Rural*, vol II, nos. 14, 15 (1919), etc.
14. 'We shall advance no further in social and economic legislation: we shall reconcile capital with labour. We have been hurrying; now we shall halt. We shall not sponsor new laws of this kind, and we will even stop those under consideration by the legislature.' President Viera to the National Convention of the Colorado party, 1916, quoted in Benjamín Nahum, *La Epoca Batllista 1905–30* (Montevideo: Ediciones de la Banda Oriental, 1975) p.81.
15. The Foreign Office reached the same conclusion: 'Your recent reports

280   A POLITICAL ECONOMY OF URUGUAY SINCE 1870

lead me to conclude that dominant faction are determined to exploit crisis as pretext for eliminating foreign interests.' (Cable to Michell [Montevideo], 28 December 1931. FO 371 A6791/6546/46.)

16. Under the constitution of 1919, the executive was divided between the president, with responsibility for internal security and foreign affairs, and a nine-member Consejo Nacional de Administracion.

17. Martin Weinstein, *Uruguay: the Politics of Failure* (Westport, Conn. and London: Greenwood Press, 1975) p. 73.

18. Armed forces included, public corporations excluded.

19. Quoted in *Boletín del Ministerio de Hacienda*, xx, no. 10 (1933).

20. 'The labour legislation of the country, already very advanced, has left little to the initiative of the new government.' Presidential Message to the General Assembly, 15 March 1936, quoted in Julio Millot, Carlos Silva and Lindor Silva, *El Desarrollo Industrial del Uruguay de la Crisis de 1929 a la Postguerra* (Montevideo: Universidad de la República, Instituto de Economía, 1973) p. 86.

21. FO 371 A4658/94/46, Michell (Montevideo) to FO, 25 June 1932.

22. FO 371 A6791/6546/46, FO Memorandum, 18 November 1931.

23. See Alberto Couriel, 'El Ascenso del Poder Económico al Poder Político', in *Frente Amplio*, Cuadernos de Marcha no. 53, (Montevideo, 1971), and Carlos Real de Azúa, 'Política, Poder y Partidos en el Uruguay de Hoy', in Luis Benvenuto *et al.*, *Uruguay Hoy* (Buenos Aires: Siglo xxi, 1971) pp. 188–9. There are also remarkable and significant indications of continuity between the post-1968 regime and that of 1933. César Charlone, Minister of Finance under Pacheco Areco, held the same office under Gabriel Terra, whose Minister of the Interior, Alberto Demicheli, was appointed provisional president of the republic by the armed forces in June 1976.

24. Universidad de la República, Instituto de Economía, Uruguay: *Estadísticas Básicas*, (Montevideo, 1969) tables 2 and 4.

Chapter 2 Population and Society

1. UN, ECLA, *Latin America and the International Development Strategy: First Regional Appraisal* (E/CN. 12/947, 1973) vol. i, p. 7.

2. Alberto Cataldi, *Población y Fuerza de Trabajo* (Montevideo:.CIDE, n.d.); J. J. Pereira and R. Trajtenberg, *Evolución de la Población Total y Activa en el Uruguay 1908–1957* (Montevideo: Universidad de la República, Instituto de Economía, 1966) table ii.62; E. M. Narancio and F. Capurro Calamet, *Historia y Análisis Estadístico de la Población del Uruguay* (Montevideo, 1939), quoted in Juan Antonio Oddone, *La Formacion del Uruguay Moderno*, (Buenos Aires: Editorial Universitaria de Buenos Aires, 1966) p. 57.

3. Ana M. Rothman, 'Evolution of Fertility in Argentina and Uruguay', *International Population Conference, London 1969*, vol. i (Liége: International Union for the Scientific Study of the Population, 1971) p. 716.

4. *Censo Municipal 1889–90*, pp. 259–60.

5. Estimate of 48 per cent by E. Acevedo, quoted in Oddone, *Formación*, p. 23.

6. By Néstor Campiglia, quoted in *Marcha*, 17 August 1973.

7. Aldo E. Solari *et al.*, *Uruguay en Cifras* (Montevideo: Universidad de la República, 1966) pp. 11–12, based on Cataldi, *Poblácion*. The 1975 census figure is the final result, reported in *El País* (Montevideo), 4 January 1979.

8. DGEC, *Encuesta de Emigración Internacional 1976* (Montevideo, 1977) p. 17.

9. Pereira and Trajtenberg, *Población*, table II.60.

10. ECLA, *Latin America and the International Development Strategy*, vol. I, p. 7.

11. Rothman, 'Fertility', p. 723; Pereira and Trajtenberg, *Población*, p. 135.

12. Pereira and Trajtenberg, *Población*, p. 134.

13. Henry J. Bruton, *Principles of Development Economics* (Englewood Cliffs, N. J.: Prentice-Hall, 1965) p. 267.

14. Robert H. Cassen, 'Population and Development: A Survey' *World Development*, vol. IV, (1976) p. 806.

15. Solari, *Desarrollo Social*, p. 21; Centro de Estudiantes de Ciencias Económicas y de Administración (CECEA), *Plan Nacional de Desarrollo Económico y Social 1965–74, Compendio*, vol. I (Montevideo, 1966) p. 24.

16. As early as 1972, *Marcha* (4 August) was able to name over 200 members of the cultural elite who were employed outside Uruguay. *Marcha*, the only Uruguayan paper of international reputation, was itself closed down by the government in 1974.

17. DGEC, *IV Censo de Población, II de Vivienda, 1963, Fascículo I, Demografía*, table 1.

18. ECLA, *Latin America and the International Development Strategy*, vol. I, table 1.

19. Preliminary data from the 1975 census indicates a slight fall in the population share of Montevideo, from 46.3 per cent (1963) to 44.5 per cent.

20. Solari, *Desarrollo Social*, p. 32.

21. Oddone, *Formación*, p. 62; Néstor Campiglia, *Migración Interna en el Uruguay*, (Montevideo: Universidad de la República, 1968) pp. 15–16.

22. The death rate in Montevideo in 1963 was in fact rather higher than the national average, presumably reflecting the concentration there of medical facilities and its attraction therefore of the very sick from the interior. See Solari *et al.*, *Cifras*, p. 35, and Rothman, 'Fertility', p. 719.

23. *Censo 1963, Fascículo IV, Migración Interna*; analysis of the 1959 survey is in Campiglia, *Migración Interna*.

24. Campiglia, *Migración Interna*, pp. 48, 56. This is also the conclusion of Centro Latinoamericano de Economía Humana (CLEH)–CINAM, *Situación Económica y Social del Uruguay Rural* (Montevideo: Ministerio de Ganadería y Agricultura, 1964) p. 397.

25. Julio Martínez Lamas, *Riqueza y Pobreza del Uruguay* (Montevideo: Palacio del Libro, 1930) p. 186. The phrase, though striking, is inexact, since no long-term increase in the level of cattle production has occurred.

26. Campiglia, *Migración Interna*, table 50.

27. Solari, *Desarrollo Social*, p. 37.

28. See, for example, Solari, *Desarrollo Social*, ch. 10.

29. John J. Johnson, in *Political Change in Latin America: The Emergence of the Middle Sectors* (Stanford: Stanford University Press, 1958), deliberately adopted the terms 'sectors' or 'groups' rather than 'class' since 'they do not fulfil

the central condition of a class: their members have no common background of experience' (p. 3). It is perhaps easier to accept the statement than the justification for it.

30. See, for example, Antonio M. Grompone, *Las Clases Medias en el Uruguay*, 2nd ed. (Montevideo: Ediciones del Río de la Plata, 1963), esp. p. 21; and the comments of Alfredo Errandonea, 'Apuntes Sobre la Conformación de las Clases Sociales en el Medio Rural Uruguayo', *Uruguay: Poder, Ideología y Clases Sociales*, Cuadernos de Ciencias Sociales 1 (Montevideo, 1970), 31.

31. On rural poverty and the impact of modernisation, see Barrán and Nahum, *Historia Rural*, esp. vol. ii, pp. 333–49.

32. Errandonea, 'Conformación de Clases Sociales', 39, gives a contemporary estimate of 6000.

33. Barrán and Nahum, *Historia Rural*, vol. iii, pp. 217–22.

34. It has been suggested that the *ruralista* movement of the late 1950s, led by Benito Nardone, which was an important factor in the Blanco election victory of 1958, expressed the dissatisfaction of the rural middle class (especially the arable sector) not only with urban-oriented policy but also with the domination of the rural social system by an elite which it had been unable to penetrate. See Errandonea, 'Conformación de Clases Sociales', 39–40.

35. This analysis follows the discussion of rural social structure in CLEH–CINAM, *Uruguay Rural*, pp. 461–73. See also Aldo Solari, *Sociología Rural Nacional*, 2nd ed. (Montevideo: Biblioteca de Publicaciones Oficiales de la Facultad de Derecho y Ciencias Sociales de la Universidad de Montevideo, 1958), and Ministerio de Ganadería y Agricultura – CIDE, *Estudio Económico y Social de la Agricultura en el Uruguay*, vol. i (Montevideo, 1967) ch.9.

36. The estimate of MGA – CIDE was that almost two-thirds of the land was controlled by 3000 enterprises. (*Estudio Económico y Social de Agricultura*, vol. i, p. 781.)

37. Solari, *Sociología Rural*, pp. 503–14, 'Vertical mobility appears to be very rare in our rural society' (p. 511). The lack of continuity among large landownerships, compared with the *minifundios*, was also noted by CLEH–CINAM, *Uruguay Rural*, p. 465.

38. Quantitative estimates of class structure, including that of Grompone, are reviewed by Carlos Rama, *Las Clases Sociales en el Uruguay* (Montevideo: Ediciones Nuestro Tiempo, 1960), p. 107.

39. Ibid., p. 111. The estimate is by Rama for 1958.

40. Aldo Solari, 'Sistema de Clases y Cambio Social en el Uruguay', *Estudios Sobre la Sociedad Uruguaya*, vol. i (Montevideo: Editorial Arca, 1964) p. 123; and *Desarrollo Social*, p. 68.

41. *Censo Municipal 1889–90*, pp. 247–56.

42. 48.1 per cent of immigrants were males aged between 15 and 50, compared with 17.7 per cent of nationals.

43. G. W. Rama, 'Las Clases Medias en la Epoca de Batlle', *Tribuna Universitaria*, no. 11 (1963) 58.

44. This classification assumes that the occupation of 'labourer' (20.5 per cent of the total) can be allocated to the secondary sector. It is likely that most of these labourers were employed in construction activities.

45. G. W. Rama, *El Ascenso de las Clases Medias*, Enciclopedia Uruguaya, no. 36 (Montevideo, 1969) 116.

46. Per capita income expressed in dollars of 1961 purchasing power has been estimated by Luis Carlos Benvenuto, *Breve Historia del Uruguay*, (Montevideo: Editorial Arca, 1967) pp. 78, 93–4, as US$238 (1901–5), US$255 (1906–10), and US$326 (1911–15). The estimates are based on an assumed ratio of exports to GDP of 15 per cent. The export values used appear to be the official figures, which present a number of problems (see Chapter 5). Nonetheless the estimates may be accepted as orders of magnitude.

47. G. W. Rama, 'Las Clases Medias', 65.

48. DGEC, *Censo Económico Nacional 1968: Industrias*, pp. 2, 13.

49. See Solari, 'Movilidad Social en Montevideo', *Estudios*, pp. 85–112.

50. The phrase forms the theme of the diagnosis of Uruguay's problems in Herman E. Daly, 'An Historical Question and Three Hypotheses concerning the Uruguayan Economy', *Inter-American Economic Affairs*, xx (1966).

51. Simon G. Hanson, *Utopia in Uruguay* (New York: Oxford University Press, 1938) p. 126.

52. *DSHCR*, 1913, vol. ccxxiii. They included carpenters and workers in cigarette, marble and match production—the last since 1901. In flour mills, paper production, bakeries and *saladeros*, however, the working day was from 12 to 18 hours.

53. As with all retirement pension schemes in Uruguay, additional years of service would reduce the age of retirement qualification by an equivalent number of years.

54. Eduardo Acevedo, *Anales Históricos del Uruguay* (Montevideo: Barreiro y Ramos, 1936) vol. v, p. 676; vol. vi, p. 601. The most complete survey of public health and hospital facilities is in *El Libro del Centenario del Uruguay 1825–1925* (Montevideo, Capurro y Cia., 1925) pp. 623 ff.

55. J. R. Hay, *The Origins of the Liberal Welfare Reforms 1906–14* (London: Macmillan, 1975) p. 15.

56. Gaston V. Rimlinger, 'Welfare Policy and Economic Development: A Comparative Historical Perspective', *Journal of Economic History*, xxvi (1966) 556, 570.

57. Gordon C. Bjork, *Journal of Economic History*, xxvi (1966) 572.

58. Pedro Cosio, *DSHCR*, 1916, vol. ccxlvii, 118. The tram companies and *frigoríficos* alone recruited 862 new workers as a result of the new law.

59. Virgilio Sampognaro, *L'Uruguay au commencement du XXe siècle*, (published for the Brussells Exhibition, 1910) p. 341.

60. DGEC, *Anuario Estadístico*.

61. *DSHCR*, 1926, vol. cccxxviii, 126–56.

62. See Chapter 7, note 90.

63. The municipal census of Montevideo, 1930, found a population of 655,000. The growth of the national labour force is based on Pereira and Trajtenberg, *Población*, p. 181.

64. The annual average of house-building licences issued (in thousands) was 3.5 (1906–9), 3.8 (1910–14), 1.3 (1915–19), 4.5 (1920–4), 7.3 (1925–9) (Intendencia Municipal de Montevideo, *Boletín: Censo y Estadística* [1946]).

65. *DSHCR*, 1913, vol. ccxxvi.

66. Oddone, *Formación*, p. 57.

67. The number of persons receiving a retirement pension, as a proportion of the male population of 55 and over, grew from 4.0 per cent in 1919 to 17.2 per

cent in 1929 and 31.7 per cent in 1934. The pension system has been the principal factor in making activity rates among the older male population probably the lowest in the world. In 1957 they were 91.0 per cent (45–54), 67.1 per cent (55–64), and 24.5 per cent (65 and over). (Pereira and Trajtenberg, *Población*, tables ii.74 and ii.72.)

68. In his presidential message to the legislature in 1914 accompanying the proposal to establish an old-age pension fund, Batlle specifically argued that the scheme would make Uruguay more attractive to immigrants. See Efraín González Conzi and Roberto B. Giúdice, *Batlle y el Batllismo*, 2nd ed. (Montevideo: Editorial Medina, 1959) p. 323.

69. For example, Daly, 'Historical Question'; David C. Redding, 'The Economic Decline of Uruguay', *Inter-American Economic Affairs*, xx (1967).

70. Pereira and Trajtenberg, *Población*, table ii.60; table 2.2. 'Uruguay, with a life expectancy comparable with that of economically developed countries, nonetheless has the lowest normal retirement age for the most important group of workers . . . in comparison with the age of retirement in operation in the 57 countries included in a study of the ILO' (Oficina International del Trabajo, *Informe al Gobierno de la República Oriental del Uruguay sobre Seguridad Social*, (Geneva, 1964 p. 19.)

71. Hanson, *Utopia*, p. 171.

72. José Pedro Antuña, *Reglas Tendientes a la Extensión, Unificación y Consolidación del Sistema de Seguros Sociales* (Montevideo: 1939) p. 118.

73. Julio E. Kneit, *La Previsión Social en el Uruguay*, vol. i (Montevideo: Universidad de la República, Facultad de Ciencias Económicas y de Administración, 1964) p. 143.

74. Hanson, *Utopia*, pp. 150–3.

75. CECEA, *Plan, Compendio*, vol. ii, p. 397.

76. DGEC, *Anuario Estadístico*.

77. Hanson, *Utopia*, pp. 154–5.

78. Of 224 pension beneficiaries in 1912, only 6 qualified by 90 years' service plus age; 3 were at least 50 with 30 years' service, 38 had seen their posts suppressed, 47 had been dismissed without cause, and 130 were unfit for further service. (Hanson, *Utopia*, p.166.)

79. Eduardo Acevedo Alvarez, *La Economía y las Finanzas Públicas Después del 31 de Marzo* (Montevideo, 1937) p. 286.

80. Hanson, *Utopia*, pp. 180–1.

81. Comisión de Inversiones y Desarrollo Económico (CIDE), *Plan Nacional de Desarrollo Económico y Social 1965–1974* (Montevideo, 1965) p. RS 11.

82. The average pension in real terms paid by the Caja Industria y Comercio declined from 100 (1963) to 66.0 (1965) and 39.4 (1968), recovering slightly to 47.9 (1970). (Instituto de Economía, *Estudios y Coyuntura 2* (Montevideo, 1973) p. 67, based on data from Banco de Previsión Social.)

83. OIT, *Seguridad Social*, pp. 42–4.

84. Kneit, *Previsión Social*, vol. ii, p. 282.

85. OIT, *Seguridad Social*, p. 45.

86. In the Caja de Jubilaciones y Pensiones de Profesionales Universitarios a survey found that only 17.8 per cent of pension receivers had one pension; 45.5 per cent received two and 32.2 per cent received three. A single person was receiving five. (Solari, *Desarrollo Social*, p. 53.)

87. CIDE, *Estudio Económico del Uruguay: Evolución y Perspectivas*, vol. ii (Montevideo, 1963) p. ii 196.

88. CIDE, *Plan Nacional*, p. RS 23.

89. In a number of industries it appears that debts to the pension funds might be built up to relieve short-term liquidity problems, or as a bargaining factor to bring pressure to bear on central government. For example, in February 1962 the Frigorífico Anglo expressed opposition to a proposal to freeze the debt to the pension fund of another *frigorífico*, EFCSA, on the grounds that it had been created deliberately, and would penalise those which had maintained payments. However, the Anglo was itself in debt to the family allowances fund, but claimed that certain tax rebates had been paid unsatisfactorily in government bonds. (Cables from Frigorífico Anglo to Consejo Nacional de Gobierno and Senate, February 1962.) Contributions by employees as well as employers were withheld by large companies also in the textile and metal-making industries (Niko Schvarz, *Marcha*, 19 September 1969). Rapid inflation offered an additional incentive to run up large debts. Large companies were in a strong position, since attempts to enforce payment of arrears threatened important sources of employment.

90. OIT, *Seguridad Social*, p. 57.

91. CECEA, *Plan, Compendio*, vol. ii, pp. 400–1.

92. Small enterprise lacks bargaining power in negotiations with the pension funds, and could defend itself less successfully in the courts; but the chances of undiscovered evasion of contributions are better.

93. Héctor Rodríguez, *Nuestros Sindicatos*, 2nd ed. (Montevideo: Centro Estudiantes de Derecho, 1966) p.14.

94. Carlos M. Rama, *Obreros y Anarquistas*, Enciclopedia Uruguaya, no. 32, (Montevideo, 1969), p. 25.

95. Carlos M. Rama, 'La "Cuestión Social" ', *Montevideo Entre Dos Siglos 1890–1914*, Cuadernos de Marcha no. 22 (Montevideo, 1969) p. 64.

96. Francisco R. Pintos, *Uruguay: de la Liberación al Afianzamiento de la Burguesía* (Montevideo: Ediciones Pueblos Unidos, 1966) p. 209.

97. Alfredo Errandonea and Daniel Costabile, *Sindicato y Sociedad en el Uruguay* (Montevideo: Biblioteca de Cultura Universitaria, 1969) pp. 185–8.

98. Rodríguez, *Nuestros Sindicatos*, p. 18.

99. Errandonea and Costabile, *Sindicato y Sociedad*, p. 73. No source is given for this estimate, which is completely at variance with a total of almost 34,000 members of working-class associations (28,000 in Montevideo) listed by union affiliation in DGEC, *Anuario Estadístico* 1922–3, part 6. The Oficina Nacional de Trabajo is reported by Hanson, *Utopia*, p. 144, to have estimated union membership in 1929 at 25,000.

100. C.M. Rama, *Obreros*, p. 28.

101. Rodríguez, *Nuestros Sindicatos*, p. 18.

102. Neither the Socialist nor the Communist party has been a serious electoral force in Uruguayan politics. In ten national elections between 1925 and 1942 their combined share of the poll averaged 3.2 per cent (maximum 6.9 per cent in 1932). In the six elections between 1946 and 1966 the average increased to 6.0 per cent (maximum 7.3 per cent in 1946).

103. Quoted in Carlos M. Rama, 'Batlle y el Movimiento Obrero y Social', in *Batlle, Su Vida, Su Obra* (Montevideo: Editorial 'Acción' 1956) p. 46.

286 A POLITICAL ECONOMY OF URUGUAY SINCE 1870

104. Carlos Real de Azúa, 'Emilio Frugoni', *Antología del Ensayo Uruguayo Contemporáneo*, vol. I (Montevideo: Universidad de la República, 1964) pp. 111–12. Frugoni, already a declared socialist, had been nominated by the Colorados as a candidate in 1905, but withdrew. *El Día*, 16 February 1905.)

105. Socialist manifesto, quoted in C. M. Rama, 'Movimiento Obrero', p. 47.

106. C. Rama, 'Cuestión Social', p. 74.

107. Errandonea and Costabile, *Sindicato y Sociedad*, p. 135; Ministerio de Industrias, *El Salario Real 1914–1926* (Montevideo: Imprenta Nacional, 1927) p. 59.

108. Eugenio Gómez, *Historia del Partido Comunista del Uruguay* (Montevideo: Editorial Elite, 1961) ch. 3; Ulises Graceras, *Los Intelectuales y la Política en el Uruguay*, (Montevideo: Cuadernos de El País, 1970) pp. 84–6.

109. Gómez, *Partido Comunista*, p. 79.

110. *DSHCR*, 1941, vol. CDXLII. quoted in Millot, Silva and Silva *Desarrollo Industrial*, p. 119.

111. Errandonea and Costabile, *Sindicato y Sociedad*, p. 143.

112. Rodríguez, *Nuestros Sindicatos*, p. 82.

113. Centro Estudiantes de Derecho, *C.N.T.: Declaración de Principios, Programa y Estatutos* (Montevideo, 1967).

114. Jorge Ures, 'La Relación Clase-Voto en Montevideo', *Revista Uruguaya de Ciencias Sociales*, I, no. 1 (1972) 12.

Chapter 3 Agrarian Structure and Performance

1. Preston E. James, *Latin America*, 3rd ed. (New York: The Odyssey Press, 1959), describes Uruguay as 'a transitional land between the Humid Pampa and the hilly uplands and plateaus of Brazil' (p. 367). For a detailed summary of the geological structure, based on the work of the Instituto Geológico del Uruguay, see CLEH–CINAM, *Uruguay Rural*, pp. 36–7.

2. CLEH–CINAM, *Uruguay Rural*, p. 39; MGA–CIDE, *Estudio Económico y Social de Agricultura*, vol. I, p. 215.

3. Solari *et al.*, *Cifras*, p. 160.

4. CLEH–CINAM, *Uruguay Rural*, pp. 16–41. The decline in the cultivated land area since 1956 means of course that the boundaries of these zones—especially 4, 5 and 6—have shifted somewhat.

5. The data for 1913 was based on information relating to 1912–14. The degree of inequality it reveals is also analysed in Mercedes Quijano, 'El Batllismo: Su Política Fiscal y la Burguesía Agraria Entre 1900 y 1930', *Enfoques Sobre el Período Batllista*, Cuadernos de Ciencias Sociales, 2 (1972) 46–52, where it is presented as data for 1918.

6. This analysis does not support the conclusion of CLEH–CINAM, *Uruguay Rural*, which believed that the origin of the *latifundia–minifundia* problem lay in two processes: the splitting-up of small farms, and the growth in size of large farms (p. 42). The first has certainly occurred, but there is no evidence for the second.

7. Solari, *Sociología Rural*, pp. 288–90.

8. CLEH–CINAM, *Uruguay Rural*, p. 44.

9. Ibid., p. 106. 'Enterprise' is defined as the total area 'in which certain

functions are fulfilled by a single permanent work force' (p. 101).

10. MGA–CIDE, *Estudio Económico y Social de Agricultura*, vol. I, p. 781.

11. CIDE, *Estudio Económico*, vol. I, p. II 32, classifies owner-operated farms (and no others) as being without tenure problems.

12. *Marcha*, 7 May 1954.

13. Between 1918 and 1925 the proportion of arable producers who were tenant farmers fluctuated in the range 38 per cent to 42 per cent. (Ministerio de Industrias, *Anuario de Estadística Agrícola*, 1924–5.)

14. *DSHCR*, 1921, vols. CCXCV–CCXCVII.

15. Ministerio de Ganadería y Agricultura, *Plan Agropecuario Nacional*, (Montevideo, 1947), pp. 8–9.

16. Ministerio de Ganadería y Agricultura, *Recomendaciones Para el Desarrollo Agrícola del Uruguay*. Informe de la Misión Técnica auspiciado por el Banco Internacional de Reconstrucción y Fomento y la Organización de las Naciones Unidas Para la Agricultura y la Alimentación (Montevideo, 1951).

17. On the early history of colonisation, see Isaac Morón, *Problemas de la Colonización en el Uruguay* (Montevideo, 1945); Carlos A. Viera, 'La Experiencia Nacional en Materia de Colonización y la Ley No. 11, 029 de 12 de enero de 1948', *Revista de Economia*, vol. II (1948); and María Teresa Montañes, *Desarrollo del la Agricultura en el Uruguay*, (Montevideo, 1948) pp. 110–14.

18. MGA–CIDE, *Estudio Económico y Social de Agricultura*, vol. I, p. 711.

19. Julio Castro, 'Colonización y Desalojos', *Marcha*, 17 June 1957; Eduardo J. Corso, 'La Colonización se Hace con Tierras', *Marcha*, 27 January 1961.

20. *Marcha*, 17 September 1954.

21. MGA–CIDE, *Estudio Económico y Social de Agricultura*, vol. I, pp. 712–13.

22. Ibid., vol. I, p. 679.

23. Agricultural census figures for the total agricultural population are as follows (in thousands): 1937, 342; 1946, 433; 1951, 454; 1956, 414; 1961, 390; 1966, 328; 1970, 318. Since 1956 rural population has been defined as the agricultural population on farms of one hectare or more. It is not known what criterion was employed before 1956.

24. Ibid., vol. I, pp. 261–2. The population census of 1963 indicated a rural population of 507,000, but the urban/rural distinction is in this case 'based on that established by the Law of Populated Centres (21.4.1946) which grants the right to departmental governments to authorise their formation' (Solari *et al.*, *Cifras*, p. 45).

25. From 238,000 in 1951 to 200,000 in 1961: BROU, *Producción Agropecuaria* (Montevideo, 1966) p. 10.

26. 1955 estimate from CIDE, *Estudio Económico*, vol. I, p. II, 108.

27. Martínez Lamas, *Riqueza y Pobreza*. This work is analysed in detail in Chapter 4.

28. Sources are Ministerio de Industrias, *Anuario de Estadística Agrícola*, 1918–19, and 1924–5.

29. The 1951 census found 138,000 employed in arable production, compared with the 1948 figure of 84,000 in MGA, *Recopilación de la Estadística Agropecuaria del Uruguay* (Montevideo, 1950).

30. Martínez Lamas, *Riqueza y Pobreza*, pp. 214–18.

31. A. Boerger and G. Fischer, 'El Problema Agrícola de la República

Oriental del Uruguay', *Revista del Ministerio de Industrias*, x, no. 63 (1922) 3–115.

32. Boerger and Fischer, 'Problema Agrícola', 39.

33. Gabriel Terra, Minister of the Interior, *DSHCR*, 1920, Vol. CCLXXXVII.

34. *DSHCR*, 1923, vol. CCCV.

35. *La Mañana*, (Montevideo), 14 March 1939.

36. Wheat and beef cattle are selected as representative of crop and livestock production in view of the size and rate of growth of the former, and the fact that sheep tend to be grazed on thin soils less suitable for cultivation. The trade-off is likely therefore to be greater between these two products than between any other representative pair.

37. DGEC, *Anuario Estadístico*.

38. Raúl Ochoa, 'La Mecanización Agrícola en Nuestro País', *Revista de Economía*, v, no. 27 (1952).

39. MGA–CIDE, *Estudio Económico y Social de Agricultura*, vol. ı, p. 271.

40. Barrán and Nahum, *Historia Rural*, vol. ı, pp. 559–60.

41. Marta Díaz Rebajoli, *El Valor de Producción en el Sector Agropecuario*, (Instituto de Economía 1966), p. 165. Similar figures are reported in CLEH–CINAM, *Uruguay Rural*, p. 109.

42. Quoted in Solari, *Sociología Rural*, p. 336.

43. MGA–CIDE, *Estudio Económico y Social de Agricultura*, vol. ı, p. 8.

44. Ibid., vol. ı, pp. 308–40.

45. Ibid., vol. ı, p. 333.

46. As a proportion of total imports and of imported capital goods, imports of capital goods for agriculture were at their greatest before the First World War, declining in the 1920s (Table 6.3).

47. Criadores del Uruguay, *Cincuentenario de la Fundación de los Registros Genealógicos de la Asociación Rural del Uruguay*, (Montevideo, 1937), pp. 443–4.

48. MGA, *Recopilación*, pp. 127–8. Guillermo Vázquez Franco, 'El Uruguay Entre la Convención de Paz y los Convenios de Ottawa', in *Uruguay: Las Raíces de la Independencia*, Cuadernos de Marcha, no.4 (Montevideo, 1967), estimates that by 1930 93 per cent of cattle contained Hereford or Shorthorn blood (p. 31).

49. UN ECLA /FAO, *Livestock in Latin America; Status, Problems and Prospects. I. Colombia, Mexico, Uruguay and Venezuela* (New York, 1962, E/CN. 12/620) p. 53; CIDE, *Estudio Económico*, vol. ı, p. ıı 24; MGA–CIDE, *Estudio Económico y Social de Agricultura*, vol. ıı, p. 309. The observation of Martínez Lamas, that 'according to experts, only 30 per cent of the cattle of the country have been satisfactorily improved in terms of yield', appears to have been unduly pessimistic (*Riqueza y Pobreza*, p. 231).

50. *DSHCR*, 1928, vol. CCCXLVI, 573.

51. A full account of the problem is in MGA, *Plan Agropecuario Nacional*, pp. 167–71.

52. For an early attack on the landowners as 'an obstructionist and avaricious class', see Luis E. Azarola Gil, *La Sociedad Uruguaya y Sus Problemas* (Paris: Libería Paul Ollendorff, 1911), p. 95.

53. *El Libro del Centenario*, p. 131.

54. BROU, *Producción Agropecuaria*, p. 17; BCU, *Indicadores de la Actividad Económica-Financiera*.

55. BROU, *Producción Agropecuaria*, pp. 67–70; BCU, *Indicadores*.

56. The justification for doing so is the difficulty of explaining the apparent net loss of 14.8 million sheep in the following eight years. Ruano Fournier explains it by higher rates of slaughter by *frigoríficos* and for consumption, by exports of live animals, and by disease: Agustín Ruano Fournier, *Estudio Económico de la Producción de las Carnes del Río de la Plata* (Montevideo: Peña y Cia., 1936) p. 46. However, even doubling the recorded slaughter leaves 6.9 million to die by disease.

57. Instituto de Economía, *El Proceso Económico del Uruguay* (Montevideo: Universidad de la República, 1969), p. 99.

58. BROU, *Producción Agropecuaria*, pp. 19–22.

59. See Boerger and Fischer, 'El Problema Agrícola'; Montañes, *Desarrollo de la Agricultura*, pp. 46–50.

60. Russell H. Brannon, *The Agricultural Development of Uruguay* (New York: Praeger, 1967), p. 109.

61. Ibid., pp. 94–107.

62. MGA–CIDE, *Estudio Económico y Social de Agricultura*, vol. ii, p. 336.

63. MGA–CIDE, *Estudio Económico y Social de Agricultura*, vol. ii, pp. 321–2.

64. ECLA/FAO, *Livestock in Latin America*, p. 58.

65. Ibid., p. 59.

66. See Brannon, *Agricultural Development*, ch.5.

Chapter 4 *Taxation and Agricultural Stagnation*

1. See, for example, Eric N. Baklanoff, 'Notes on the Pathology of Uruguay's Welfare State', *Mississippi Valley Journal of Business and Economics*, ii, (1967); Herman E. Daly, 'The Uruguayan Economy: Its Basic Nature and Current Problems', *Journal of Inter-American Studies*, vii, (1965), and 'Historical Question'; Arturo C. Porzecanski, 'Uruguay's Continuing Dilemma', *Current History*, lxvi, no. 389 (1974).

2. Julio Martínez Lamas, *Riqueza y Pobreza del Uruguay: Estudio de las Causas que Retardan el Progreso Nacional*, (Montevideo: Palacio del Libro, 1930).

3. Speech to the Convention of the Colorado party, June 1925, reprinted in Antonio M. Grompone, *La Ideología de Batlle*, 3rd ed. (Montevideo: Editorial Arca, 1967) pp. 122–33.

4. Batlle, in ibid., p. 127.

5. Batlle, in ibid., p. 129. The basis of this scheme in the writings of Henry George is discussed in Luis Carlos Benvenuto, *La Quiebra del Modelo*, Enciclopedia Uruguaya no. 48 (Montevideo, 1969), pp. 152–3.

6. Grompone, *Ideología*, p. 131.

7. A further reason for leaving the *aforos* unaltered, in spite of the recommendations of a study commission at the turn of the century, was that the decline in the import price level at that time compared with the *aforos* would have required an increase in the tariff rate to produce an equal revenue. (Acevedo, *Anales*, vol. v, p. 210.)

8. Submission of the Cámara Nacional de Comercio to the tariff study commission of 1898, quoted in Eduardo Acevedo, *Notas y Apuntes; Con-*

tribución al Estudio de la Historia Económica y Financiera de la República *Oriental del Uruguay*, vol. II (Montevideo: El Siglo Ilustrado, 1903) p. 464.

9. Martínez Lamas, *Riqueza y Pobreza* p. 333.

10. Debate on the cost of living, *DSHCR*, 1913, vol. CCXXVII, 285.

11. See table 4.2, note 2.

12. Departments outside Montevideo were each divided into between two and six regions (79 in all), in each of which a single valuation per hectare applied. (Acevedo, *Notas y Apuntes*, vol. II, p. 474.)

13. Martín C. Martínez, *DSHCR*, 1903–4, vol. CLXXIV, 146, 150.

14. *DSHCR*, 1915, vol. CCXLV, 535–7. The debate was reprinted as *El Problema de Caminos y el Plan Financiero del Gobierno* (Montevideo: Dornaleche, 1916).

15. Vanger, *Batlle y Ordóñez*, p. 73.

16. Alberto Methol Ferré, *Adonde Va el Uruguay?* (Montevideo, 1958) p. 11.

17. CLEH–CINAM, *Uruguay Rural*, pp. 436–8.

18. As subsequent estimates have shown, Martínez Lamas was correct in discounting official population figures which gave a total population in 1926 of 1,720,000, of whom 439,000 were resident in Montevideo (*Anuario Estadístico* 1926). His own calculations indicated a total of 1,600,000 with 600,000 resident in Montevideo, and an additional 120,000 Uruguayans resident in Brazil and Argentina (*Riqueza y Pobreza*, part 1, ch. 5).

19. Martínez Lamas, *Riqueza y Pobreza*, p. 73.

20. Ibid., p. 56.

21. MGA–CIDE, *Estudio Económico y Social de Agricultura*, vol. I, p. 219.

22. This is presented most succinctly in *Riqueza y Pobreza*, part 2, ch. 5.

23. In 1932, the Federación Rural published his paper *La Situación Económica del Uruguay* and submitted it to President Gabriel Terra.

24. Martínez Lamas, *Riqueza y Pobreza* pp. 213–14.

25. Chapter 3, note 34.

26. Martínez Lamas, *Riqueza y Pobreza*, p. 213, footnote 162.

27. Ibid., p. 341.

28. Hanson, *Utopia*, p. 142; in the early 1960s, nearly 40 per cent of monthly paid labourers in the livestock sector were paid less than the legal minimum wage. (CLEH–CINAM, *Uruguay Rural*, pp. 450–2.)

29. Martínez Lamas, *Riqueza y Pobreza*, p. 326.

30. Pereira and Trajtenberg, *Población*, table II. 69.

31. 'The average wage of a *péon* is $15 monthly, and it may be supposed that $10 of this is spent on personal consumption; add to that $5 for the cost of food (excluding that of rural origin) which the employer buys for the consumption of the worker . . .' (*Riqueza y Pobreza*, p. 319). Note the extraordinary implication that employers bought in food to the value of one-third of wages for distribution to the work force.

32. MGA–CIDE, *Estudio Económico y Social de Agricultura*, vol. I, p. 802.

33. Martínez Lamas, *Riqueza y Pobreza*, p. 318.

34. Quoted in Acevedo, *Anales*, vol. V, p. 340.

35. David Ricardo, *The Principles of Political Economy and Taxation* (London: Dent, Everyman's Library, 1973), p. 132; Martínez Lamas, *Riqueza y Pobreza*, pp. 325–30.

36. Hanson, *Utopia*, p. 138.

37. Martínez Lamas, *Riqueza y Pobreza*, p. 237.

38. 'The nation's savings, instead of finding useful employment, flee from productive investment and stubbornly seek a comfortable, peaceful and lazy placement in public debt bonds.' (Report of Comisión de Hacienda, Cámara de Representantes, in *Boletín del Ministerio de Hacienda*, XIII, no. 3 [1926].)

39. Speech to the Congreso de las Sociedades Rurales del Pais, October 1939, reprinted in Pedro Cosio, *Doctrinas y Hechos Económicos* (Montevideo, 1940), p. 30.

40. This account of the evolution of exchange rate policies in the 1930s is based on Raúl Ochoa, 'Contralor de Cambios en el Uruguay', *Revista de la Facultad de Ciencias Económicas y de Administración*, year 4, no. 5 (1943) 215–529; Carlos Quijano, *Evolución del Contralor de Cambios en el Uruguay* (Montevideo, 1944); Santos Ferreira, 'Antecedentes y Naturaleza Financiera del Ingreso Cambiario en el Uruguay', *Revista de la Facultad de Ciencias Económicas y de Administración*, no. 7 (1954).

41. Eduardo Acevedo Alvarez, *La Gran Obra de los Poderes Constitucionales Frente a la Crisis* (Montevideo, 1934) pp. 105–27; Millot, Silva and Silva, *Desarrollo Industrial*, pp. 63–5.

42. See IMF, *Balance of Payments Yearbook*.

43. F. H. Schott, *The Evolution of Latin American Exchange Rate Policies Since World War II* (Princeton Essays in International Finance no. 32, 1959).

44. R. Mexigos, *Los Subsidios en Finanzas Públicas*, (Montevideo: Instituto de la Hacienda Pública, 1958).

45. Bank of London and South America, *Fortnightly Review*, 9 May 1959.

46. A more complete consideration of the Reform is made in Chapter 8.

47. H. E. Daly, 'A Brief Analysis of Recent Uruguayan Trade Control Systems', *Economic Development and Cultural Change*, XV (1967). The exchange rate equivalents were calculated as the dollar value of the export (import) category multiplied by the official exchange rate, minus export taxes (plus import taxes), divided by the dollar value of the category.

48. CIDE, *Estudio Económico*, vol. II, table II 77; CECEA, *Plan, Compendio*, p. 366; Instituto de Economia, *Estudios y Coyuntura 2* (1971) p. 44.

49. CECEA, *Plan, Compendio*, p. 361. The inverse relationship also holds. When the government of Pacheco Areco held exchange rates constant as part of the stabilisation programme of the late 1960s, the yield of retentions fell (in constant 1966 pesos) from $2.1 million in 1968 to $0.8 million in 1970 (Instituto de Economía, *Estudios y Coyuntura 2*, p. 44).

50. Carlos F. Diaz Alejandro, *Essays on the Economic History of the Argentine Republic* (New Haven and London: Yale University Press, 1970).

51. Redding, 'Economic Decline', 58.

52. MGA–CIDE, *Estudio Económico y Social de Agricultura*, vol. I p. 631.

53. CECEA, *Plan, Compendio*, vol. I, p. 272.

54. MGA–CIDE, *Estudio Económico y Social de Agricultura*, vol. I, pp. 563–651.

55. Ibid., vol. I, p. 632.

56. Ibid., vol. I, pp. 515–21.

57. Solari, *Sociología Rural*, pp. 404–6.

58. Brannon, *Agricultural Development*, p. 203.

59. Ibid., pp. 206–8.
60. CLEH–CINAM, *Uruguay Rural*, p. 112.
61. Brannon, *Agricultural Development*, p. 209.
62. MGA–CIDE, *Estudio Económico y Social de Agricultura*, vol. I, pp. 684–5.
63. CLEH–CINAM, *Uruguay Rural*, pp. 130–1.
64. Instituto de Economía, *Proceso Económico*, p. 90.
65. CLEH–CINAM, *Uruguay Rural*, pp. 106–7.
66. 'There are *estancias* better equipped, with better livestock, better fences, better buildings, etc., but they do not seem to produce substantially more. If this has been the general rule it is useless to expect investment in intensification.' (CLEH–CINAM,*Uruguay Rural*, p. 479.)
67. Following a World Bank/FAO mission to Uruguay and the visit of a study group to Australia and New Zealand in 1950–1, preparation began in 1952 of a livestock development programme which would attract foreign aid. The Plan Agropecuario came into existence in 1957 but not until 1960—following the IMF-inspired financial reforms of the Blanco administration—was the first World Bank loan made. See 'El Plan Agropecuario', in Asociación Rural del Uruguay, *Cien Años de la Asociación Rural del Uruguay* (Montevideo: 1971) vol. I, pp. 96–119.
68. The low yield on capital invested in artificial pasture is analysed in Instituto de Economía, *Proceso Económico*, pp. 101–13.
69. Raúl Vigorito, 'En Torno a las Praderas Artificiales', Instituto de Economía, *Estudios y Coyuntura 1* (Montevideo, 1970) esp. p. 130.
70. MGA–CIDE, *Estudio Económico y Social de Agricultura*, vol. I, p. 515.
71. Brannon, *Agricultural Development*, pp. 240, 251.
72. Ibid., pp. 327–8.
73. The reaction has been positive only in the sense that producers have switched from one form of rural production to another as relative prices within the sector have changed. This explains the apparent elasticity of total output to price changes, lagged two years in certain periods. (MGA–CIDE, *Estudio Económico y Social de Agricultura*, vol. I, pp. 481–3.)
74. CLEH–CINAM, *Uruguay Rural*, pp. 478–80.
75. Ibid., p. 478.
76. CIDE, *Estudio Económico*, vol. I, pp. II 156–7.

Chapter 5 Exports and the Meat Industry

1. BROU, *Producción Agropecuaria*, p. 111. The importance of exports in transit, especially from Argentina, during 1879–1903 is discussed in DGEC, *Anuario Estadístico*, 1902–3, pp. 633–5.
2. 'Wholesale Prices of Commodities in 1916', *Journal of the Royal Statistical Society*, LXXX, part II (1917) 296.
3. See Vázquez Franco, 'El Uruguay Entre la Convención de Paz y los Convenios de Ottawa'.
4. Boerger and Fischer, 'El Problema Agrícola'.
5. Calculated from DGEC, *Anuario Estadístico*, 1902–3, pp. 634–5.
6. Pedro Seoane, *La Industria de las Carnes en el Uruguay* (Montevideo, 1928).

7. Barrán and Nahum, *Historia Rural*, vol. I, p. 106. However, the proportion was evidently increasing in the nineteenth century, estimated at 34.1 per cent in 1883 (Ruano Fournier, *Producción de Carnes*, p. 33) and 51.0 per cent in 1896 (Barrán and Nahum, vol. III, p: 314).

8. Barrán and Nahum, *Historia Rural*, vol. III, p. 308. This compares with 21 in 1872 (Barrán and Nahum, vol. 1, p. 98), and 22 in 1885–6 (Seoane).

9. Adolfo Vaillant, *La República Oriental del Uruguay en la Exposición de Viena*, (Montevideo, 1873) p. 151.

10. On the unsuccessful attempts by *saladeristas* to win acceptance for *tasajo* in the main European markets, see Barrán and Nahum, *Historia Rural*, vol. II, pp. 111–16. The *Memoria del Ministerio de Industrias*, 1911, reported a government proposal to open new markets, including Japan, but the scheme fell through.

11. Slaughter by Liebig's represented 40 per cent of total slaughter in the Littoral region during 1886–1904 (Barrán and Nahum, *Historia Rural*, vol. III, p. 333). However, a proportion of Liebig's cattle purchases for slaughter in Uruguay were made across the river in Argentina.

12. Hanson, *Utopia*, p. 200. By the end of the century, of course, Liebig's were also producing outside Uruguay.

13. S. G. Hanson, *Argentine Meat and the British Market*, (Stanford, Stanford University Press, 1938), p. 31.

14. Barrán and Nahum, *Historia Rural*, vol. II, pp. 101–5.

15. Acevedo, *Anales*, vol. v, pp. 596, 464.

16. Hanson, *Utopia*, p. 218.

17. Acevedo, *Anales*, vol. v, p. 584.

18. Ministerio de Industrias, *Anuario de Estadística Agrícola*, 1918–19, table 131.

19. Ibid., table 92.

20. J. A. Brewster, 'The South American Trade', in F. Gerrard (ed.), *The Book of the Meat Trade* (London: Caxton Publishing Co., 1949) vol. I, p. 216.

21. Peter H. Smith, *Politics and Beef in Argentina* (New York and London: Columbia University Press, 1969) p. 58.

22. *DSHCR*, 1916, vol. CCLI.

23. Ministerio de Industrias, *Anuario de Estadística Agrícola*, 1926–7, tables 123 and 139.

24. The pool is analysed in Hanson, *Argentine Meat*, pp. 165–9.

25. J. T. Critchell and J. Raymond, *A History of the Frozen Meat Trade* (London: Constable, 1912), p. 144.

26. Ministry of Agriculture and Fisheries (MAF), *Report on the Trade in Refrigerated Beef, Mutton and Lamb* (London: HMSO, 1925) p. 27. 'Vestey packed beef in its own plants, shipped cargo in its own boats, insured voyages through its own company, deposited meat in its own cold-storage rooms, and sold it to the public through its own butchers' (Smith, *Politics and Beef*, p. 113).

27. MAF, *Report on Trade in Refrigerated Beef*, p. 52.

28. Ibid., pp. 52–3.

29. Smith, *Politics and Beef*, p. 114.

30. Hanson, *Argentine Meat*, pp. 242–51.

31. Frigorífico Artigas declared a loss of 7.5 per cent in 1926, while Swift had losses of 0.6 per cent and 4.8 per cent in 1925–6 (G. Bernhard, *Comercio de*

294   A POLITICAL ECONOMY OF URUGUAY SINCE 1870

Carnes en el Uruguay [Montevideo, Aguilar e Irazabal, 1958] pp. 157–9).
32. *La Federación Rural: Su Origen y Desarrollo*, p. 39.
33. Submission to Cámara de Representantes dated October 1924, quoted in *DSHCR*, 1925, vol. cccxxiv.
34. Paraphrasing the view expressed in the Report of the Special Commission of Representatives, June 1928: *DSHCR*, 1928, vol. cccxliv, 319.
35. An assessment of its early years is in Hanson, *Utopia*, pp. 86–93.
36. Department of Overseas Trade, *Economic Conditions in Uruguay, August 1930* (London: HMSO, 1930) p. 15.
37. Hanson, *Utopia*, p. 92.
38. Data on market shares is from P. Cosio, 'El Problema Internacional de las Carnes', *Boletín del Ministerio de Hacienda*, xx, no. 2 (1933) 81. Cosio noted: 'The quantity of meat exported depends completely on European demand, since shipments from Uruguay are the first to suffer when the trade is restricted.' A further aspect of weakness relative to Argentina was the lower price paid for cattle in Montevideo compared with Buenos Aires—16 per cent to 29 per cent less per head for cattle yielding 3 or 4 per cent less meat, according to a 1927 study commission (Acevedo, *Anales*, vol. vi, p. 486). While higher export taxes in Uruguay had an obvious bearing on the latter, an important factor explaining both was the seasonal character of cattle slaughter in Uruguay because of dependence on natural pasture. This both increased *frigorífico* costs because of idle capacity during the winter and spring, and prevented a continuous and regular supply to Smithfield.
39. I. M. Drummond, *Imperial Economic Policy 1917–1939* (London: Allen and Unwin, 1974), p. 31.
40. Exports of Australasian beef and veal to Britain, which in 1930 were only one-tenth the size of South American exports, had increased by 1934 to one-third (J. H. Richardson, *British Economic Foreign Policy*, [London, Allen and Unwin, 1936] p. 179).
41. Drummond, *Imperial Economic Policy*, p. 264.
42. Bernhard, *Comercio de Carnes*, pp. 32–3.
43. Much important documentary material relating to the contracts and the meat trade in the post-war decade is collected in ibid., ch. 2.
44. *La Mañana* (Montevideo), 12 April 1945.
45. The seventh British contract (October 1946) stipulated an absolute volume of meat, rather than a proportion of the exportable surplus as in previous contracts. (Bernhard, *Comercio de Carnes*, p. 43.)
46. Final report of the Comisión Administradora del Fondo de Compensaciones Ganaderas, 27 June 1950, reproduced in ibid., pp. 47–51.
47. Ibid., p. 62.
48. John Miles and Ricardo Gazzano, *Costos Internos y Precios Internacionales de la Carne Vacuna Congelada y Conservada (1942–1957)* (Montevideo: Universidad de la República, Instituto de Teoría y Política Económicas, 1961) pp. 17–18.
49. *Marcha*, 15 August 1952.
50. Memorandum to Consejo Nacional de Gobierno (CNG), 17 April 1953.
51. Memorandum to CNG, 15 October 1953.
52. During 1956 press reports estimated contraband sales to Brazil at 300,000 per annum. BOLSA (*Fortnightly Review*, 27 October 1956) reporting this,

believed it to be an overestimate but did not doubt that substantial losses were occurring. A decade later, the general manager of the Anglo is reported to have estimated, to the Comisión de Ganadería of the CNG, the annual contraband of cattle to Brazil at over 150,000. (G. Bernhard, *Los Monopolios y la Industria Frigorífica* [Montevideo: Ediciones de la Banda Oriental, 1970] p. 71.) In 1972 Benito Medero, Minister of Agriculture, estimated the contraband of cattle to Brazil in the period of July 1971 to June 1972 at 150,000 (*Marcha*, 27 October 1972).

53. In January 1953 the subsidy was limited to a fixed sum per kilo of meat delivered to retailers. Previously it was unrestricted, to meet the difference between cost and wholesale price. The slaughterhouses were more attractive to cattle producers because they paid cash promptly; payments for sales to the Nacional were subject to delay.

54. Calculated from Miles and Gazzano, *Costos y Precios de Carne Vacuna*, p. 35.

55. At the beginning of the 1960s the Nacional was estimated to have a ratio of administrative to manual workers of 1 : 2, compared with 1 : 7 or 1 : 8 in the other traditional *frigoríficos*. (Organización de las Naciones Unidas para la Agricultura y la Alimentación [FAO], *Informe para el Gobierno del Uruguay Sobre Aspectos Técnicos y Económicos de la Reorganización de la Industria de la Carne en el Uruguay* [Rome, 1963].)

56. A. Melgar, E. Peguero and C. Lavagnino, *El Comercio Exportador del Uruguay 1962–1968*, vol. I (Montevideo: Universidad de la República, Instituto de Economía, 1972) pp. 120–1.

57. CIDE, *Plan Nacional, Sector Industrial*, p. In 129.

58. Bernhard, *Los Monopolios*, p. 59. The decision to end the period of *abasto libre* in 1964 was taken by the municipal government of Montevideo, although the regime had been introduced by the national government. The reason was that the licensed suppliers, who had dominated the trade in competition with the Nacional, now refused to supply Montevideo unless the price of meat was raised. The *municipio* reacted by cancelling their licenses. (*Marcha*, 14 August 1964.) The effect of the Blanco government's policies on the price of meat in Montevideo was severe: in real terms it was 116 per cent of the 1953 level in 1955–8, rising to 179 per cent in 1959–60.

59. CIDE, *Plan Nacional, Sector Industrial*, p. In 127.

60. Melgar, Peguero and Lavagnino, *Comercio Exportador*, table 40.

61. Ibid., p.125.

62. FAO, *Informe Sobre Reorganización de Industria de Carne*, p. 275.

63. CIDE, *Plan Nacional, Sector Industrial*, pp. In 133–4; Commonwealth Secretariat, *Meat: A Review* (London: 1969) pp. 33, 40, 98 and (1973) pp. 28, 34, 92; Ministerio de Hacienda, *Carnes: Producción, Industrialización y Comercialización* (Montevideo, 1955) p. 13.

64. Bernhard, *Los Monopolios*, p. 25.

65. *Boletín del Ministerio de Hacienda*, xxiv, nos. 1–4 (1937).

66. Omar R. Freire, 'Estudio Sintético de la Gestión Cumplida Por el Frigorífico Nacional', *Revista de la Facultad de Ciencias Económicas y de Administración*, year 4, no. 4 (1943) 674–5; *Carnes: Producción, Industrialización y Comercialización*, p. 9.

67. Bernhard, *Monopolios*, pp. 72–3.

Chapter 6 Imports and Industrialisation

1. Faced with a 400 per cent increase in the price of coal during the First World War, the Central Uruguay Railway in 1917 began the conversion to oil of its coal-burning locomotives. By the mid-1920s conversion was largely complete. (Central Uruguay Railway Company of Montevideo Limited, *Report of the Directors to the Proprietors*, 1917 and 1924.)

2. Jorge Grunwaldt Ramasso, *Historia de la Quimica en el Uruguay 1830–1930* (Montevideo: Instituto Histórico y Geográfico del Uruguay, 1966) pp. 155–6.

3. The classification of sugar (up to 7 per cent of total imports) poses some problems. Before 1924 most sugar was imported as 'unrefined', apparently to take advantage of a lower rate of duty. After 1924, when the degree of refinement was laid down, almost all imports were of 'refined' sugar, i.e. a foodstuff rather than a raw material. Before 1910, both refined and unrefined sugar have been classified here as a consumption good. (See Pedro Cosio, *Economía y Hacienda*, [Montevideo: Maximino García, 1926] pp. 182–91.)

4. Luis A. Faroppa, *El Desarrollo Económico del Uruguay* (Montevideo: CECEA, 1965); Instituto de Economía, *Proceso Económico*; and Millot, Silva and Silva, *Desarrollo Industrial*, are all centrally concerned with the process of industrialisation, but only in the post-1929 period.

5. There is no data for manufacturing production for this period, apart from a few individual commodities, though it had been proposed in 1913 to establish an office of industrial statistics. There was also a decree in that year to hold an industrial census, but the first full census was not taken until 1930.

6. For the history of tariff protection, see especially Acevedo, *Notas y Apuntes*, vol. II, pp. 165–94; Juan Carlos Quinteros Delgado, *La Industria y el Estado*, 2nd ed. (Montevideo: Maximino García, 1926), ch. 7; Juan Carlos Guarnieri, 'Noticia Histórica sobre Nuestras Industrias y los Origenes del Proteccionismo Industrial en el Uruguay', in Cámara de Industrias, *Panorama de la Industria Nacional* (Montevideo: 1956). Imports of 'Raw Materials' were not classified separately in DGEC, *Anuario Estadístico* until 1927, although the classification was employed in some publications of the Oficina de Estadística Comercial a decade earlier.

7. A source of major importance for the early history of Uruguayan industrial development is *El Libro del Centenario*, pp. 761–853.

8. Secretary, London and River Plate Bank, Montevideo, quoted by Peter E. Winn, 'Uruguay and British Economic Expansion, 1880–93', unpublished PhD thesis, Cambridge University, 1972.

9. A similar conclusion is reached by Silvia Rodríguez Villamil, 'Un Antecedente del Espíritu de Empresa: El Industrialismo', in Oscar Mourat *et al.*, *Cinco Perspectivas Históricas del Uruguay Moderno* (Montevideo: Fundación de Cultura Universitaria, 1969), p. 186.

10. *Revista del Ministerio de Industrias*, VI, no. 37 (1918) 255.

11. *El Libro del Centenario*, p. 797.

12. *El Libro del Centenario*, p. 804.

13. The industrial and commercial census of Montevideo in 1908 found that of 7037 establishments reported (of which 2345 were wholly or partly engaged in 'manufacturing'), 61 per cent were owned by non-Uruguayans, whereas only 36

per cent of the labour force employed were not Uruguayan-born. (DGEC, *Anuario Estadístico*, 1909–10.)

14. Grunwaldt Ramasso, *Historia de la Química*, ch. 10; *Revista del Ministerio de Industrias*, III, no. 18 (1915), and IV, no. 20 (1916).

15. *Revista del Ministerio de Industrias*, IV, no. 21 (1916) 88.

16. Survey of the Oficina Nacional de Trabajo, reported in Acevedo, *Anales*, vol. VI, pp. 521–2.

17. Such production may be designated 'primary manufacturing', its characteristics being a low proportion of value added in manufacturing, raw materials mostly domestic in origin, production competitive in world markets and destined for export. Secondary manufacturing industry has a higher proportion of value added, and is generally confined to domestic markets, being frequently high-cost. The analysis in this chapter is mainly concerned with the latter group.

18. *Boletín del Ministerio de Hacienda*, XIII, no. 6 (1926); Acevedo, *Anales*, vol. VI, pp. 342–4.

19. Acevedo, *Notas y Apuntes*, vol. II, pp. 187–92; Oficina de Estadística Comercial, *Comercio Exterior de la República Oriental del Uruguay 1917* (Montevideo: Imprenta Nacional, 1919).

20. The selection of these periods is arbitrary and dictated by the availability of data in Oficina de Estadística Comercial, *Comercio Exterior 1917* and DGEC, *Anuario Estadístico*.

21. Universidad de la República, Facultad de Humanidades y Ciencias, *Proteccionismo y Librecambio: El Programa de la 'Liga Industrial' de 1880* (Montevideo, 1967).

22. 'Unión Industrial Uruguaya', in *Panorama de la Industria Nacional*, p. 67.

23. Acevedo, *Notas y Apuntes*, vol. II, pp. 172–5. Acevedo was Minister of Industries during the first half of the second administration of José Batlle y Ordóñez (1911–13). The Ministry itself was created in 1907–8.

24. For example, Octavio Morató, *La Industria Manufacturera en el Uruguay* (Montevideo, 1927).

25. José Serrato, 'Carta-Prólogo', in Quinteros Delgado, *Industria y Estado*, 2nd ed., p. 11.

26. Primary manufacturing industry producing for export markets might however employ arguments similar to those of protectionists. Thus an application by the washed wool industry for export tax exemptions was justified by the need to create industry, thus freeing the country from foreign bondage and from a bureaucracy overburdened by employees who could not find work elsewhere. (*DSHCR*, 1921, vol. CCXCVI, 325.)

27. Martínez Lamas, *Riqueza y Pobreza*, p. 25.

28. '. . . progressive historical judgment tends to take a very positive view of the industrialisation process which *Batllismo* propelled . . .' (Carlos Real de Azúa, *El Impulso y su Freno*, [Montevideo: Ediciones de la Banda Oriental, 1964], p. 52.)

29. Examples are to be found in González Conzi and Giúdice, *Batlle*, pp. 398–9.

30. UN ECLA, *The Process of Industrial Development in Latin America*, (E/CN.12/716/Rev.1, New York, 1966) p. 13.

31. Ministerio de Industrias y Trabajo, *Censo Industrial de 1936*, (Montevideo, 1939).

32. Reproduced in Instituto de Economía, *Proceso Económico*, p. 158.
33. Pedro C. M. Teichert, *Revolución Económica e Industrialización en América Latina*, 2nd ed. (Mexico D.F.—Buenos Aires: Fondo de Cultura Económica, 1963) p. 271.
34. BROU, *Cuentas Nacionales* (Montevideo, 1965) p. B 165; BCU, *Boletín Estadístico Mensual*. The data in *Cuentas Nacionales* is a revision of estimates published in CIDE, *Estudio Económico*, vol. II, table 10.
35. See, for example, K. B. Griffin, *Underdevelopment in Spanish America* (London: Allen and Unwin, 1969) p. 270.
36. Ramón Oxman, *Energía* (Montevideo: Universidad de la República, Instituto de Teoría y Política Económicas, 1961) p. 36.
37. *Boletín del Ministerio de Hacienda*, XXVIII, nos. 7–11 (1941).
38. Millot, Silva and Silva, *Desarrollo Industrial*, tables 1 and 23.
39. DGEC, *Anuario Estadístico*.
40. *Boletín del Ministerio de Hacienda*, XXVIII, nos. 7–11 (1941).
41. 'The stagnation in quality and quantity of our exportable production and the sharp fall in its value, especially in the last two years, has resulted in a large economic deficit and left the country without the financial means to continue buying from abroad the mass of articles whose consumption and use became customary after the European War, as a result of the large profits secured at that time and of the resources obtained by loans afterwards. This disproportionate growth in the flow of foreign commodities attracted enterprise and private capital by its profits, harming the operation and productive investment of industry; the internal crisis which had been developing for ten years broke violently in 1930 . . .' (Minister of Industry [Edmundo Castillo], *Mensaje del Consejo Nacional de Administración a la Asamblea General 1932* [Montevideo: Imprenta Nacional, 1932], p. 44. Quoted in Faroppa, *Desarrollo Económico*, p. 39.)
42. Millot, Silva and Silva, *Desarrollo Industrial*, p. 72.
43. Ibid., table 14.
44. Ibid., p. 58.
45. Ibid., p. 151.
46. CIDE, *Estudio Económico*, vol. I, p. II 42.
47. See BROU, *Cuentas Nacionales*, part II, input-output table. Exceptions to this are tobacco and wood products, both of which import a large proportion of their raw material.
48. BROU, *Cuentas Nacionales*, p. B 179.
49. See Universidad de la República, *Estadísticas Básicas*, table 25; BCU, *Indicadores*; Instituto de Economía, *Estudios y Coyuntura 2*, p. 16.
50. ECLA, *Economic Survey of Latin America*, 1970, table 25.
51. ECLA, *Latin America and the International Development Strategy*, vol. I, p. 73.
52. See R. Weisskopf and A. Figueroa, 'Traversing the Social Pyramid: A Comparative Review of Income Distribution in Latin America', *Latin American Research Review*, XI (1976) table 1.
53. On some social aspects of consumption propensities in Uruguay, see Solari, *Desarrollo Social*, pp. 175–8.
54. CIDE, *Plan Nacional, Sector Industrial*, p. In 4.
55. ECLA, 'Foreign Investments in Uruguay' (E/CN.12/166/Add.6, 2 May 1950) p. 7.

56. US, Department of Commerce, *Survey of Current Business*.
57. Bernhard, *Comercio de Carnes*, pp. 157–9.
58. Millot, Silva and Silva, *Desarrollo Industrial*, pp. 49–51.
59. Solari, *Sociología Rural*, p. 402.
60. Vivián Trías, 'Reforma Agraria, Industrialización y Revolución Nacional en el Uruguay', *Tribuna Universitaria*, no. 8 (1959), 47.
61. This and the following data on US investment are from US, Department of Commerce, *Survey of Current Business*.
62. Juan Arturo Grompone has argued the significance of the growth of technical education at the beginning of this century, reflecting the rise of the national bourgeoisie in opposition to the landowning oligarchy and to British imperialism (*Marcha*, 7 May 1971).
63. Comisión Especial para Fomento de Laboratorios Tecnológicos e Investigaciones Industriales, *Antecedentes Relacionadas con la Creación en el Uruguay de un Centro de Asistencia Técnica para la Industria* (Montevideo, 1956).
64. Ibid., p. 47.
65. DGEC, *Censo Económico Nacional 1968: Industrias*.
66. Instituto de Economía, *Estructura Industrial del Uruguay*, vol. I (Montevideo: Universidad de la República, 1972) table 3.5.
67. ECLA, *The Process of Industrial Development*, p. 63.
68. Instituto de Economía, *Estructura Industrial del Uruguay*, vol. I.

Chapter 7 Public Utilities and Public Corporations

1. On attempts by Uruguay to secure British protection during 1838–48, see Peter Winn, 'British Informal Empire in Uruguay in the Nineteenth Century', *Past and Present*, no. 73 (1976) 107.
2. FO 371 7794, Kennedy (Montevideo) to Foreign Office, 2 March 1911.
3. DGEC, *Anuario Estadístico*. South American shipping excluded.
4. 'It is likely that their investments in Uruguay yielded as high returns over the years as their capital in almost any other Latin American country.' (J. Fred Rippy, *British Investments in Latin America, 1822–1949* [Hamden, Conn.: Archon Books, 1966] p. 143.)
5. As the British Minister in Montevideo pointed out, 'the influence of foreign public companies and the influence of foreign diplomacy does undoubtedly affect the internal policy of the country'. (FO 371 10074, Innes [Montevideo] to Foreign Office, Annual Report 1913.)
6. Pereira and Trajtenberg, *Población*, table 60.
7. Letter, chairman of Central Uruguay Railway to Foreign Office, 15 March 1945 (FO 371 AS 1593/1593/46). The practice was likely to have been even more prevalent before 1914. See Leland H. Jenks, 'Britain and American Railway Development', *Journal of Economic History*, XI (1951) 384–5.
8. FO 371 36367 Kennedy (Montevideo) to Foreign Office, 1 October 1906.
9. Claims by British landowners and the railways for compensation for losses incurred in the insurrection of 1904 were also met 'more or less satisfactorily'. (FO 371 2936, Kennedy [Montevideo] to Foreign Office, Annual Report 1907.)
10. 'Since the outbreak of war what was before friendliness has developed into what can only be termed open enthusiasm. There is nothing in reason that

every department of the Government will not do for us.' (FO 371 77828, Innes [Montevideo] to Foreign Office, 6 November 1914.) The Foreign Office was probably sceptical, having endorsed an earlier Innes telegram: 'Mr. Innes is not an ordinary diplomatist' (FO 371 25430, 6 June 1914). Certainly Innes's reports were quite exceptional for their ironic criticisms of the British community's hostility to Batlle. 'Providence has gifted us with the singular power of being able to live all our lives among foreigners without learning to see their side or to understand their characters . . . We English must possess admirable qualities to carry us over the obstacles that our stupidity erects in our path.' (FO 371 37969, 17 July 1914.)

11. *Memoria del Ministerio de Obras Públicas*, 1908 (Montevideo: Barreiro y Ramos, 1909) pp. 827, 904.

12. The construction costs of the Northern and Eastern Extensions (both guaranteed) were reported to be £5596 and £5700 respectively per kilometre; and of the main line and Western Extension (both without guarantees) £9140 and £3788. (CUR, *Report of Directors*, 1902, p. 12.)

13. And by spreading as much as possible of the fixed costs of the unguaranteed sections of the system onto the guaranteed sections. On attempts to control this and other accounting devices of the railways, see Barrán and Nahum, *Historia Rural*, vol. ii, pp. 581–6.

14. The Oficina de Control de Ferrocarriles estimated the excessive length of the MUR, NWUR and UNR, at 5 per cent, 8 per cent and 5 per cent respectively. (*Memoria del Ministerio de Fomento*, 1892–3, pp. 313–29, quoted in Barrán and Nahum, *Historia Rural*, vol. ii, pp. 562–3.)

15. At the beginning of the 1890s the train from Montevideo to Rivera reached a maximum point-to-point speed of 31 km per hour. (Carlos García Acevedo, *Estudio Sobre Ferrocarriles*, [Montevideo: Imprenta Artística, 1892] p. 34.) In 1915, Luis Alberto de Herrera denounced the average speed of passenger trains to Paysandú (25 km per hour), Rivera (28 km per hour), Minas (25 km per hour). Artigas, 543 km from Montevideo, was reached in 46 hours. (*DSHCR*, 1915, vol. ccxliv, 114.)

16. Barrán and Nahum, *Historia Rural*, vol. iii, p. 436.

17. Ibid., pp. 438–9.

18. Quoted by Herrera, *DSHCR*, 1916, vol. ccxlvii, 415.

19. FO 371 5009, O'Reilly (Montevideo) to Foreign Office, Annual Report 1911.

20. In 1888 this was reduced for new concessions to 8 per cent.

21. See Cámara de Senadores, *La Intervención del Estado en las Tarifas Ferroviarias* (Montevideo: Imprenta Artística, 1922).

22. FO 371 A 1463/1463/46, Mallet (Montevideo) to Foreign Office, 3 February 1921.

23. Martínez Lamas, *Riqueza y Pobreza*, p. 227.

24. FO 371 AS 2684/1593/46, letter, Phillimore (Treasury, writing from Montevideo) to Powell (Bank of England). The text of Grindley's letter to the Minister of Public Works suggesting purchase, dated 18 December 1945, is reproduced in F. C. Central del Uruguay, *La Cuestión Sobre Homologación de las Tarifas Ferroviarias* (Montevideo, 1946).

25. Message accompanying the proposed railway law of 1888: quoted in Barrán and Nahum, *Historia Rural*, vol. ii, p. 569.

26. FO 371 A 4302/4302/46, Mallet (Montevideo) to Foreign Office, 22 June 1923.

27. F. C. Central, *Homologación*.

28. Barrán and Nahum, *Historia Rural*, vol. III, pp. 458–64.

29. CUR, *Report of Directors*, 1906.

30. FO 371 3898, Kennedy (Montevideo) to Foreign Office, Annual Report 1906.

31. Asociación de Ingenieros del Uruguay, *Síntesis Histórica de la Ingeniería en el Uruguay* (Montevideo, 1949) p. 8.

32. *The Economist*, 17 October 1925, 617.

33. Department of Overseas Trade, *Report on the Financial and Economic Conditions in Uruguay, September 1927* (London: HMSO, 1927) p. 22.

34. Department of Overseas Trade, *Economic Conditions in Uruguay, August 1930* (London: HMSO, 1930) p. 28.

35. Hanson, *Utopia*, p. 60.

36. Acevedo, *Anales*, vol. VI, pp. 185, 321.

37. Asociación de Ingenieros, *Síntesis Histórica*, p. 10.

38. F. C. Central del Uruguay, *Memoria Anual*, 1949.

39. CIDE, *Estudio Económico*, vol. I, p. II 77.

40. Barrán and Nahum, *Historia Rural*, vol. III, pp. 454–5.

41. Acevedo, *Anales*, vol. V, p. 239. Acevedo was himself a member of the commission.

42. FO 371 33059, Kennedy (Montevideo) to Foreign Office, 7 September 1906.

43. *DSHCR*, 1907, vol. CXCII, 16.

44. FO 371 40733, Kennedy (Montevideo) to Foreign Office, 11 November 1906.

45. *El Libro del Centenario*, p. 738.

46. Ibid., p. 737.

47. In 1927 Baltasar Brum had argued, in relation to the CUR, that 'bad management by the State would always be preferable, from the point of view of the national economy, to highly efficient management by foreign capitalists' (González Conzi and Giúdice, *Batlle*, p. 276.) The report declared: '. . . a bad or expensive service by the State will always be worse than a good and cheap one by a private company, provided the latter is under the permanent control of the former.' (*DSHCR*, 1928, vol. CCCXLVII, 187.)

48. *The Economist*, 1 January 1949; *El Día* (Montevideo), 15 January 1948.

49. *Register of Defunct and Other Companies 1957* (London: Skinner, 1957).

50. *El Libro del Centenario*, p. 744.

51. DGEC, *Anuario Estadístico*.

52. The Telephone Company distributed an average dividend in excess of 6 per cent in the twenty years before its sale to North American interests in 1927. But, 'the communicating service the company offers to the public is execrable, and in addition to the persecution of the muncipality it is anathematised by everybody who is compelled, of necessity, to use it.' (FO 371 A 2521/2521/46 Mallet [Montevideo] to Foreign Office, Annual Report 1923.)

53. FO 371 4196, Kennedy (Montevideo) to Foreign Office, Annual Report 1908.

54. CUR, *Report of Directors*, 1908.

55. FO 371 22746, Kennedy (Montevideo) to Foreign Office, 17 May 1911.
56. FO 371 A 5562/2370/46, Mallet (Montevideo) to Foreign Office, 20 August 1923.
57. Department of Overseas Trade, *Economic Conditions in the Republic of Uruguay 1933* (London: HMSO, 1934) p. 25; Hanson, *Utopia*, p. 194.
58. *Agreement between His Majesty's Government in the United Kingdom and the Uruguayan Government regarding Trade and Payments*, London, 26 June 1935, Cmd. 4940.
59. 'Informe del Asesor Letrado Muncipal, Dr. Juan J. Carbajal Victorica, Montevideo, abril 20 de 1939', in CUTCSA, *La Concesión de la Cooperativa Uruguaya de Transportes Colectivos S. A.* (Montevideo, 1944) p. 85. See also Julio Castro, 'Amdet Quiere Arrendar a Cutcsa', *Marcha*, 9 April 1954.
60. Examples of the first, generally adulatory, approach are González Conzi and Giúdice, *Batlle*, and Domingo Arena, *Batlle y los Problemas Sociales en el Uruguay* (Montevideo: Claudio García, 1939). Vanger also places the emphasis on Batlle's personal leadership. The second approach is exemplified by Julio A. Louis, *Batlle y Ordóñez*, 2nd ed. (Montevideo: Nativa Libros, 1972), and Vivián Trías, *El Imperialismo en el Río de la Plata* (Buenos Aires: Ediciones Coyoacán, 1960).
61. The proposal to establish an insurance monopoly, 26 April 1911. (*DSHCR*, 1911, vol. ccxii, 79.)
62. For the reaction of a number of domestic industries to the proposed eight-hour day, including that of paper, match, vegetable oil, metal-working, and textile manufacturers, see *DSHCR*, 1913, vol. ccxxiii.
63. *El Día*, 3 April 1908, quoted in Hanson, *Utopia*, pp. 22–3.
64. Battle is quoted extensively on this theme in González Conzi and Giúdice, *Batlle*, pp. 390–2.
65. G. W. Rama, 'Las Clases Medias', p. 66.
66. Acevedo, *Anales*, vol. v, p. 566.
67. Grunwaldt Ramasso, *Historia de la Química*, pp. 158–9.
68. Cámara de Representantes, *Monopolio del Alcohol* (Montevideo, 'El Siglo Ilustrado', 1923) p. 219.
69. FO 371 37969, Innes (Montevideo) to Foreign Office, 17 July 1914.
70. FO 371 53593, O'Reilly (Montevideo) to Foreign Office, 16 December 1912.
71. FO 371 4196, Kennedy (Montevideo) to Foreign Office, Annual Report 1908.
72. *The Statist*, 1 July 1911.
73. Uruguay, Ministerio de Relaciones Exteriores, Carpeta No. 803, letter from Kennedy to Romeu, 17 August 1911.
74. Reported in FO 371 8728, Robertson (Montevideo) to Foreign Office, Annual Report 1912.
75. Hanson, *Utopia*, p. 31.
76. See, for example, FO 371 A 885/885/46, Reid Brown (Montevideo) to Foreign Office, Annual Report 1926.
77. Juan Ferrando, *Reseña del Crédito Público del Uruguay*, vol. i (Montevideo, Ministerio de Hacienda, 1969) pp. 155 and 172; Agustín Cisa, 'Forma de Financiación de los Entes Autónomos en el Período Batllista', *Enfoques Sobre el Período Batllista*, Cuadernos de Ciencias Sociales No. 2 (1972) 67–95.

78. DGEC, *Anuario Estadístico*, 1940, vol. I, 351.
79. DGEC, *Anuario Estadístico*, 1920, 102–3.
80. Ley Orgánica, Administración de las Usinas Eléctricas del Estado, caps. II–IV.
81. Hanson, *Utopia*, p. 116, gives a brief summary.
82. Ibid., p. 117.
83. Ibid., pp. 49–50.
84. DGEC, *Anuario Estadístico*.
85. Weinstein, *Uruguay*, p. 64.
86. Luis C. Caviglia, *La Defensa* (Montevideo), 4 February 1926. Caviglia, who had earlier held ministerial office, became president of the Consejo Nacional de Administración in 1927.
87. Of the members of the council of the Montevideo Port Administration (ANP), the British view was that most had been appointed as a reward for political services. 'Not one of its members possesses any administrative ability. . . None of them have even experience of administrative work'. (FO 371 A 1394/1394/46, Ricardo [Montevideo], to Foreign Office, Annual Report 1919.)
88. Industries in the public sector were almost all organised as *entes autónomos*, the designation used in para. 100 of the 1919 constitution, translated here as 'public corporations'.
89. Prólogo, p. v., to R. Ramela de Castro, *Entes Autónomos: Organización Administrativa del Dominio Industrial del Estado* (Montevideo, 1923).
90. Domingo Arena, *DSHCR*, 1926, vol. CCCXXVII, 430. His figure of 60 was inexact, but the actual disposition of the 103 employees is an illuminating commentary on the use made of the pensions system and the state of the labour market at this time. Fifty-three of the 103, with their required 30 years' service 'more or less complete', decided to accept a pension; 27 were found work elsewhere within AFTE; 12 were eligible for a pension which they did not wish to accept; 7 or 8 emigrated; 1 died; and 2 or 3 found work with private employers (p. 437).
91. *Boletín del Ministerio de Hacienda*, XI, no. 1 (1924). Thirty thousand forms were to be printed, but the results of the census are unknown.
92. *Presupuesto General de Gastos para el Ejercicio Económico de 1924/25* (Montevideo, Imprenta Nacional, 1925–6); *Presupuesto General del Estado, Ejercicio Económico 1931/32* (Montevideo: Imprenta Nacional, 1932); Pereira and Trajtenberg, *Población*, p. 181. Thirty thousand has sometimes been taken as *total* public employment in 1930, and contrasted with the total for 1932 to yield what would be (if it were true) the remarkable conclusion that 'The period from 1930–32 showed an increase in public employment from 30,000 to 52,000' (Weinstein, *Uruguay*, p. 69). This error is shared by Néstor Campiglia, *Estatización y Burocracia*, Enciclopedia Uruguaya no. 40 (Montevideo, 1969) p. 185. In both cases it seems to derive from a misreading of apparently comparable figures reproduced in Blanca París de Oddone, Roque Faraone and Juan Antonio Oddone, *Cronología Comparada de la Historia del Uruguay 1830–1945* (Montevideo: Universidad de la República, n. d.) pp. 113, 117.
93. Hanson, *Utopia*, p. 94. Imports reached a maximum of 51,000 metric tons in 1928.
94. The pact is dealt with in Göran G. Lindahl, *Uruguay's New Path: A Study in Politics During the First Colegiado 1919–33*, (Stockholm: Library and

Institute of Ibero-American Studies, 1962) pp. 166–72.
    95. *Presupuesto General del Estado, Ejercicio 1937* (Montevideo: Contaduría de la Nación, 1937). The figure of 43,000 for 1937 quoted by Acevedo Alvarez, *Economía y Finanzas Públicas* (Montevideo, 1937), is inflated by the inclusion of certain public corporations whose legal status had been changed by Terra.
    96. Hanson pointed out that although the public corporation in Uruguay had proved to be 'an effective organization in its control of expenditure, in its regulation of the rate of expansion, in its capacity for producing revenue', and in spite of interest in other countries in autonomous public enterprise, Uruguay was increasing centralised control (*Utopia*, p. 121).
    97. Gustavo Gallinal, *El Uruguay Hacia la Dictadura* (Montevideo, Editorial Nueva América, 1938) pp. 256–68. His estimate of a 50 per cent increase in total public employment nonetheless seems substantially exaggerated.
    98. For the history of the project, see Asociación de Ingenieros, *Síntesis Histórica*, pp. 103–70.
    99. *Boletín del Ministerio de Hacienda*, xxviii, nos. 7–11 (1941).
    100. Hanson, *Utopia*, p. 258.
    101. The Uruguayan delegation was led by Gustavo Gallinal, who gave an account of the negotiations in 'El Reciente Convenio de Pagos Anglo-Uruguayo', speech to Bolsa de Comercio, 30 October 1947 (Montevideo: Cámara Nacional de Comercio, 1947). See also 'Convenios Financieras con Gran Bretaña', *Revista de Economía*, i, no. 1 (1947); *The Economist*, 26 July 1947, 6 March 1948.
    102. The company had been continuously profitable, its ordinary dividend free of tax averaging over 4 per cent between 1914 and 1946 (*The Statist*, 18 January 1947), and this doubtless explains why the company did not seek to dispose of its assets. Its dividend record thereafter was more variable, and the last dividend to be paid from earnings was in 1954 (Interview, general manager, 16 June 1969). Dividends of 4 per cent and 3.5 per cent were paid out of reserves in 1961 and 1962. The company was reluctantly acquired by the government in 1971.
    103. BROU, *Cuentas Nacionales*, pp. B160, B212.
    104. Ferrando, *Crédito Público*, vol. ii, p. 103.

Chapter 8 The Economic Crisis 1955–1970

    1. 'The Measurement of Latin American Real Income in US Dollars', *Economic Bulletin for Latin America*, xii, no. 2 (1968) table 11.
    2. BROU, *Cuentas Nacionales*, p. B165.
    3. Ibid., p. B167.
    4. For an account of such legislation in this period, see Roque Faraone, *El Uruguay en Que Vivimos (1900–1968)*, 2nd ed. (Montevideo: Editorial Arca, 1968), pp. 100–5.
    5. Universidad de la República, *Estadísticas Básicas*, tables 2, 7 and 11; *BCU, Indicadores*.
    6. 1969–70 figure from ECLA, *Latin America and the International Development Strategy*, vol. i, p. 99; other years, Universidad de la República, *Estadísticas Básicas*, table 7.

7. ECLA, *Latin America and the International Development Strategy*, vol. I, p. 99.

8. *Censo 1963, Fascículo I, Demografía*, p. 1, and *Fascículo III, Población Económicamente Activa*, p. 81.

9. CIDE, *Estudio Económico*, vol. II, table 19. The estimate of 39.6 per cent for 1957 made by Pereira and Trajtenberg, *Población*, p. 181, was on the basis of the much less complete information then available.

10. CIDE, *Estudio Económico*, vol. I, pp. I 10–14.

11. *Censo 1963, Población Económicamente Activa*, pp. 81–2.

12. Estimates based on survey data for 1965–8, summarised in Universidad de la República, *Estadísticas Básicas*, table 105; and for 1972, DGEC, *Encuesta de Hogares, Ocupación y Desocupación*.

13. CIDE, *Estudio Económico*, vol. I, p. I 15.

14. Universidad de la República, *Estadísticas Básicas*, table 11.

15. *Censo 1963, Población Económicamente Activa*, table 2, pp. 52–60. The proportion is of the economically active population for whom information was available, excluding those seeking work for the first time.

16. CIDE, *Estudio Económico*, vol. I, p. I 15.

17. BCU, *Producto e Ingreso Nacionales* (1977) p. 2

18. ECLA/FAO, *Livestock in Latin America*, p. 61.

19. Universidad de la República, *Estadísticas Básicas*, table 64.

20. Data on industrial production and imports at constant prices from CIDE, *Estudio Económico*, vol. I, p. II 46 and table II.52.

21. In 1962, less than 5 per cent of new machinery and equipment installed was of national origin (BROU *Cuentas Nacionales*, p. B82).

22. Instituto de Economía, *Estructura Industrial del Uruguay*, vol. I, table 6.1.8.

23. CIDE, *Plan Nacional, Sector Industrial*, p. In 5.

24. Universidad de la República *Estadísticas Básicas*, table 80.

25. It was, however, clearly perceived by Luis Batlle, the dominant figure in the governing Colorado party in the 1950s: 'It is an immense error to think that the development of national industry is valuable for itself, and that as a problem it is defined by what national industry might be. No; the development, strengthening and wealth of the nation's industry go side by side with our social, economic and political stability. If it should fail, we might face insoluble problems.' (Speech, 11 October 1957, quoted in Luis Batlle Berres, *Pensamiento y Acción*, vol. I [Montevideo: Editorial Alfa, 1965] p. 560.)

26. Speech of Luis Batlle Berres, president of the Consejo Nacional de Gobierno to the Asamblea General, 1 March 1955, in Batlle Berres, *Pensamiento y Acción*, vol. I, p. 443.

27. BOLSA, *Fornightly Review*, 21 April 1956.

28. Ministerio de Hacienda, *Uruguay y la Alianza Para el Progreso* (Montevideo, 1962) p. 5.

29. The analysis of the Reform and subsequent anti-inflation policy is based on M. H. J. Finch, 'Stabilisation Policy in Uruguay since the 1950s', in T. R. Thorp and L. Whitehead (eds.), *Inflation and Stabilisation Policy in Latin America*, (London: Macmillan, 1979).

30. Rosemary Thorp, 'Inflation and the Financing of Economic Development', in Keith Griffin (ed.), *Financing Development in Latin America* (London: Macmillan, 1971), pp. 204–5.

31. CIDE, *Plan Nacional de Desarrollo Económico y Social 1965–74* (Montevideo, 1965). The Plan is most accessible in an abbreviated two-volume version (*Plan, Compendio*) published in 1966 by the Centro de Estudiantes de Ciencias Económicas y de Administración (CECEA).

32. CIDE, *Estudio Económico del Uruguay: Evolución y Perspectivas*, 2 vols. (1963). Editions of the report were also published by CECEA, and in BROU, *Boletín Mensual*, nos. 247–8 and 249–50 (1963).

33. BROU, *Cuentas Nacionales*, p. A5. For Earlier estimates, see Raúl Ochoa, 'Mediciones de la Renta Nacional en el Uruguay', *Revista de Economía*, vol. II, no. 8 (1948), and Julio Giuria, 'Una Estimación de la Renta Nacional del Uruguay', *Revista de Economía*, II, no. 12 (1949).

34. CIDE, *Estudio Económico*, vol. I, p. I 28.

35. Ibid., vol. I, p. I 5b.

36. CIDE, *Plan, Compendio*, vol. I, p. 132.

37. 'This Development Plan is a technical instrument for the objectives of the national society. Its preparation obeys certain technical norms, but its substantive content depends on the objectives to which society aspires'. (CIDE, *Plan, Compendio*, vol. I, p. 5)

38. Ibid., vol. I, pp. 5–20, esp. p. 11.

39. Instituto de Economía, *Proceso Económico*, p. 289.

40. 'In 1967, then, the growing interest of the internal defenders of the present system will coincide with the greater leverage of the IMF to establish a formula for stabilisation: a coincidence, if not patriotic, at least anti-inflationary' (Pedro Seré, '1967: Año de la Estabilización', *Marcha*, 11 November 1966).

41. Seré, *Marcha*, 11 November 1966.

42. On the political background to the change in economic policy, see Carlos María Gutiérrez, 'El General Ha Elegido', *Marcha*, 27 October 1967.

43. Instituto de Economía, *Estudios y Coyuntura 2*, table 34.

44. See Felipe Pazos, *Chronic Inflation in Latin America* (New York: Praeger, 1972) ch. 11.

45. BCU, *Indicadores*.

46. BCU, *Boletín Estadístico Mensual*.

Chapter 9 The Military Regime since 1973

1. Although the IMF reportedly did not press its demands for a devaluation of the peso in order not to undermine Pacheco's position (Economist Intelligence Unit, *Quarterly Economic Review*, Uruguay, 1970, no. 3, p. 6), his obduracy in refusing to negotiate with the Tupamaros for the release of kidnapped diplomats exacerbated relations with the governments of Brazil, USA and UK.

2. On the evolving relationship of the military and the political system, see especially Carlos Real de Azúa, 'Ejército y Política en el Uruguay', *El Militarismo*, Cuadernos de Marcha No. 23 (March 1969), and Liliana de Riz, 'Ejército y Política en Uruguay', *Uruguay: Poder, Ideología y Clases Sociales*, Cuadernos de Ciencias Sociales 1 (Montevideo, 1970).

3. *Latin America*, IV, no. 24 (12 June 1970).

4. Organization of American States, Inter-American Commission on Human

Rights, *Report on the Situation of Human Rights in Uruguay* (OEA/Ser. L/V/II.43, 31 January 1978).

5. The communiqués were reprinted in *7 Días que Conmovieron a Uruguay*, Cuadernos de Marcha No. 68 (March 1973).

6. This is not confined to left-wing criticisms of the regime, as the suspension of the liberal, monetarist-inspired review *Búsqueda* in 1977, and the arrest of the head of military intelligence in 1978, for his part in the publication of a clandestine military journal critical of General Alvarez, both show.

7. Alejandro Végh Villegas, *Economía Política: Teoría y Acción*, (Montevideo: Ediciones Polo, 1977) pp. 44, 70.

8. 'Memorándum de Végh Villegas sobre las Perspectivas Políticas del País, principios de 1976', typescript.

9. *Comercio Exterior* (Mexico), xxv, no. 3 (1979) 110.

10. This section is based on M. H. J. Finch, 'Stabilisation Policy in Uruguay since the 1950s', in T. R, Thorp and L. Whitehead, *Inflation and Stabilisation Policy in Latin America* (Macmillan: London, 1979).

11. Presidencia de la República, Oficina de Planeamiento y Presupuesto, *Plan Nacional de Desarrollo 1973–1977*, 2nd ed. (Montevideo, 1977).

12. Ibid., vol. i, p. 24.

13. Ibid., vol. i, p. 30.

14. Ibid., vol. i, p. 36.

15. Ibid., vol. i, p. 37.

16. Presidencia de la República, Oficina de Planeamiento y Presupuesto, *Definición de Políticas y Estrategias del Gobierno Uruguayo y Análisis de la Instrumentación del Plan Nacional de Desarrollo* (Montevideo, October 1973) p. 4.

17. Report to Comisión de Economía y Finanzas of the Consejo de Estado, 22 July 1974, reproduced in Végh Villegas, *Economía Política*, p. 33.

18. Interview with Végh Villegas, *Búsqueda*, (Montevideo), no. 34 (1975).

19. Speech to Cámara Nacional de Comercio, 26 April 1976, reproduced in Végh Villegas, *Economía Política*, p. 92.

20. Nonetheless, the rate of inflation in the twelve months to March 1976 was 49.9 per cent, greatly in excess of the undertaking given to the IMF that the rate would be reduced to 30 per cent. BOLSA, *Review*, ix, no. 7/75 (1975) 420.

21. BCU, *Boletín Estadístico Mensual*.

22. BCU, *Indicadores*.

23. World Bank, Latin America and the Caribbean Regional Office, *Economic Memorandum on Uruguay* (Washington D.C., December 1977) pp. 5–7.

24. Interview with José Gil Díaz, president of the Central Bank, *Búsqueda*, no. 57 (1977).

25. César Aguiar Beltrán estimates the loss of active population during 1963–75 at about 11 per cent of the 1975 labour force. *Uruguay, Población y Desarrollo: El Flujo Emigratorio*, [Montevideo: Centro Latinoamericano de Economía Humana, 1978] p. 80.)

26. Presidencia de la República, *Plan 1973–7*, vol. i, p. 495.

27. BCU, *Indicadores*.

28. *El Día* (Montevideo), 27 February 1978.

29. 'On various occasions I have declared that industry needs the continu-

ation of the regime of *reintegros* to give it the incentive to go on with the process of winning markets abroad.' (Helios Maderni, President of the Chamber of Industry, quoted in *El País* [Montevideo], 8 April 1978.)

30. Eduardo Lanza, vice-president of the Chamber of the Tanning Industry, *El Día*, 26 December 1977.

31. An alternative view is that the liberalisation of the rural sector in 1978 'appears to be due to improved relations between the government and the livestock sector, which is presumably related to a transitory change in the composition of forces in the military command'. ('Uruguay: en el Círculo Vicioso del Estancamiento y la Inflación', *Economia de América Latina* [Mexico], no. 1 [September 1978] p. 125.)

32. Végh Villegas, *Economía Política*, p. 83.

33. *Comercio Exterior de Mexico*, xxv, no. 3 (1979) 108.

34. The Plan projected a doubling of exports between 1970 and 1977 (Presidencia de la República, *Plan 1973–7*, vol. I, p. 152), against an actual increase by a factor of 2.6.

35. *El Día*, (Mexico), 17 December 1976, quoted in Grupo de Información y Solidaridad Uruguay (GRISUR), Informaciones, no. 61, 11 January 1977.

36. Speech of 5 August 1975, quoted in Végh Villegas, *Economía Política*, pp. 72–3.

37. GRISUR, *Informaciones*, no. 61, 11 January 1977; and Economist Intelligence Unit, *Quarterly Economic Review, Uruguay*, 1976, no. 1, p. 2.

38. Indeed, criticism by the military provoked Végh to resign in 1975, but he was promptly reinstated.

39. President of the Central Bank, *Búsqueda*, no. 57 (1977). The Chicago influence among Uruguayan *técnicos* was emphasised by the publication of Juan José Anichini, Jorge Caumont and Larry Sjaastad, *La Política Comercial y la Protección en el Uruguay* (Montevideo: Banco Central del Uruguay, 1977). The work, an attack on Uruguay's traditionally protectionist policies, was prepared under the auspices of AID and the Banco Central.

40. Reported in GRISUR, *Informaciones*, no. 86, 29 August 1978.

41. BOLSA, *Review*, xiii, no. 5/79 (1979) 319; Economist Intelligence Unit, *Quarterly Economic Review, Uruguay*, 1979, no. 2 pp. 6–7.

42. According to a report of the Ministry of Labour and Social Security, unemployment in the industry was 18 per cent at the beginning of 1979. (GRISUR, *Informaciones*, no. 96, 29 June 1979.)

Appendix

1. Acevedo, *Notas y Apuntes*, vol. II, pp. 443–6.

2. Acevedo, *Anales*, vol. VI, pp. 368–9.

3. According to Oficina de Estadística Comercial, *Comercio Exterior de la República Oriental del Uruguay 1917* (Montevideo, 1919), the estimates of real import values for 1917 were made from a sample of 124 commodities (p. iii).

4. D. C. M. Platt, 'Problems in the Interpretation of Foreign Trade Statistics before 1914', *Journal of Latin–American Studies*, III (1971); Yehuda Don,

'Comparability of International Trade Statistics: Great Britain and Austria-Hungary before World War I', *Economic History Review*, xxxi (1968).

5. Acevedo, *Notas y Apuntes*, vol. ii, pp. 459–62.

6. Acevedo, *Anales*, vol.v , pp. 301–2.

7. Pedro Cosio, *Aduanas de Fronteras* (Montevideo: Ministerio de Hacienda, 1905) p. 68.

8. Platt, 'Interpretation of Foreign Trade Statistics', p. 126.

Select Bibliography

Unless indicated, all works in Spanish were published in Montevideo.

Government Publications

Administración de Ferrocarriles y Tranvías del Estado, *Memoria*
——*Situación Económica de la Institución* (1927)
Anichini, J. J., J. Caumont and L. Sjaastad, *La Política Comercial y la Protección en el Uruguay* (Banco Central del Uruguay, 1977)
Asamblea General, *Diario de Sesiones de la Honorable Cámara de Representantes*
Banco Central del Uruguay (BCU), Asesoría Económica y Estudios, *Aspectos Básicos de la Industria de Carnes del Uruguay* (1974)
——*Boletín Estadístico Mensual*
——*Endeudamiento Externo del Uruguay* (1978)
——*Formación Bruta de Capital* (1977)
——*Indicadores de la Actividad Económico-Financiera*
——*Producto e Ingreso Nacionales* (1977).
——*Reseña de la Actividad Económico-Financiera*
——*Selección de Temas Económicos*
——Departamento de Investigaciones Económicas, *La Lana en el Uruguay y en Los Principales Mercados Mundiales 1967–72* (1973)
Banco de la República Oriental del Uruguay (BROU), *Banco de la República Oriental del Uruguay 1896–24 de Agosto-1917* (Barreiro y Ramos, 1918)
——*El Banco de la República en su Cincuentenario, Memoria Histórica 1896–1946* (n.d.)
——*Labor del Directorio 1928–1931* (Barreiro y Ramos, 1931)
——*La Política del Oro y del Cambio* (1930)
——*Memoria y Balance General*
——*Producción Agropecuaria* (1966)
——*Sinopsis Económica y Financiera del Uruguay* (1930)
——*Suplemento Estadístico de la Revista Económica*
——Departamento de Investigaciones Económicas, *Cuentas Nacionales* (1965)
Banco Hipotecario del Uruguay, *Leyes Sobre Fomento Rural y Colonización* (1923)

310

——25 *Años, Banco Hipotecario del Uruguay 1912–1937* (Oficina de Publicaciones y Propaganda, n.d.)

Cámara de Representantes, *Monopolio del Alcohol* (El Siglo Ilustrado, 1923)

Cámara de Senadores, *Cooperativas Agropecuarias* (1940)

——*Instituto Nacional de Colonización* (1948)

——*La Intervención del Estado en las Tarifas Ferroviarias* (Imprenta Artística, 1922)

Castro, J. J., *Estudio Sobre los Ferrocarriles Sud-Americanos y las Grandes Líneas Internacionales* (Ministerio de Fomento, 1893)

Cataldi, A., *Población y Fuerza de Trabajo* (CIDE, n.d.)

Censo Municipal del Departamento y de la Ciudad de Montevideo 1889–90 (1892)

Comisión de Inversiones y Desarrollo Económico (CIDE), *Estudio Económico del Uruguay: Evolución y Perspectivas* 2 vols. (1963)

——*Plan Nacional de Desarrollo Económico y Social 1965–1974* (1965)

Contaduría General de la Nación, *Presupuesto General del Estado*

Cosio, P., *Aduanas de Fronteras* (Ministerio de Hacienda, 1905)

Dirección General de Comercio Exterior, *Estadísticas de Comercio Exterior*

Dirección General de Estadística y Censos (DGEC), *Anuario Estadístico*

——*Censo Económico Nacional 1968*

——*V Censo de Población y III de Vivienda, 1975, Muestra de Anticipación*, (1977)

——*IV Censo de Población y II de Vivienda, 1963*

——*Encuesta Anual de Producción, Sector Industrial*

——*Encuesta de Hogares, Ocupación y Desocupación*

——*Indice de los Precios del Consumo*

——*Indice Toponímico de los Lugares Poblados, 1963*, (1972)

Ferrando, J., *Reseña del Crédito Público del Uruguay*, 2 vols. (Ministerio de Hacienda, 1969)

Intendencia Municipal de Montevideo, *Boletín: Censo y Estadística*

Junta de Comandantes en Jefe, *La Subversión*, vol. i of *Las Fuerzas Armadas al Pueblo Oriental* (1977)

Ministerio de Ganadería y Agricultura (MGA), *Censo General Agropecuario*

——*El Uruguay Como País Agropecuario, 1932–1936* (Imprenta Nacional, 1937)

——*La Industria Lechera en el Uruguay* (1949)

——*Plan Agropecuario Nacional* (1947)

——*Planes de Fomento Agropecuario*, (1951)

——*Recomendaciones Para el Desarrollo Agrícola del Uruguay* (1951)

——*Recopilación de la Estadística Agropecuaria del Uruguay* (1950)

——CIDE, *Estudio Económico y Social de la Agricultura en el Uruguay*, 2 vols. (1967)

Ministerio de Hacienda, *Boletín*
——*Carnes: Producción, Industralización y Comercialización* (Imprenta Nacional, 1955)
——*El Reajuste Económico-Financiero* (1935)
——*La Revaluación del Encaje Metálico* (1935)
——*Programa Anti-Inflacionario* (1965)
——*Proyecto de Contribución Inmobiliaria* (Barreiro y Ramos, 1910)
——*Uruguay y la Alianza Para el Progreso* (1962)
Ministerio de Industrias, Dirección de Agronomía, *Anuario de Estadística Agrícola*
——*El Salario Real, 1914–1926* (Imprenta Nacional, 1927)
——Dirección de Agronomía, *La Industria Harinera en el Uruguay* (Imprenta Nacional, 1927)
——*Memoria*
——*Revista*
Ministerio de Industrias y Trabajo, *Censo Industrial de 1936* (1939)
——*Clasificación Industrial de Ramas de Actividad Económica del Uruguay; Digesto de la Actuación de los Consejos de Salarios entre los Años 1943–1952; Costo de la Vida 1943–1952* (1953)
Ministerio de Instrucción Pública y Previsión Social, Comisión de Inversiones y Desarrollo Económico, Comisión Coordinada de los Entes de Enseñanza, *Informe Sobre el Estado de Educación en el Uruguay*, 2 vols. (1966)
Ministerio de Obras Públicas, *Memoria*
Ministerio de Relaciones Exteriores, *Colección de Tratados, Convenciones y Acuerdos Económico-Comerciales*, 2 vols. (1947)
——*El Tratado de Amistad, Comercio y Desarrollo Económico de 23 de Noviembre de 1949* (Imprenta Nacional, 1950)
Ministerio del Interior, *Los Mensajes de la Presidencia de la República a la Asamblea General, 1931–1936* (1939)
Oficina de Estadística Comercial, *Comercio Exterior de la República Oriental del Uruguay 1917*, (Imprenta Nacional, 1919)
Opinión de la Presidencia de la República Sobre la Forma de Resolver el Problema Agrícola y el de la Carestía de la Vida: Subdivisión de la Tierra, Cooperativismo, (Imprenta Artística, 1920)
Presidencia de la República, Oficina de Planeamiento y Presupuesto, *Definición de Políticas y Estrategias del Gobierno Uruguayo y Análisis de la Instrumentación del Plan Nacional de Desarrollo*, (1973)
—— ——*Plan Nacional de Desarrollo 1973–1977*, 2nd ed., 2 vols. (1977)
Reglamento Para la Contabilidad y Control de Ferrocarriles, (El Siglo Ilustrado, 1908)

Books and Journals

Acevedo, E., *Anales Históricos del Uruguay*, 6 vols. (Barreiro y Ramos, 1936)

——*Economía Política y Finanzas*, (Barreiro y Ramos, 1936)

——*Historia Nacional Desde el Coloniaje Hasta 1915*, (Imprenta Nacional, 1933)

——*Notas y Apuntes; Contribución al Estudio de la Historia Económica y Financiera de la República Oriental del Uruguay*, 2 vols. (El Siglo Ilustrado 1903)

Acevedo Alvarez, E., *La Economía y las Finanzas Públicas Después del 31 de Marzo* (1937)

——*La Gran Obra de Los Poderes Constitucionales Frente a la Crisis*, (1934)

Agee, P., *Inside the Company: CIA Diary*, (Harmondsworth: Penguin Books, 1975)

Aguiar Beltrán, C., *Uruguay: Población y Desarrollo—El Flujo Emigratorio*, (Centro Latinoamericano de Economía Humana, 1978)

Andreasen, C., *Panorama Actual de la Industria de la Construcción en el Uruguay*, (Universidad de la República, Facultad de Arquitectura, 1961)

Antuña, J. P., *Reglas Tendientes a la Extensión, Unificación y Consolidación del Sistema de Seguros Sociales* (1939)

Arena, D., *Batlle y los Problemas Sociales en el Uruguay*, (Claudio García, 1939)

——*'Don Pepe' Batlle*, (Editorial Arca, 1967).

Ares Pons, R., *La Inteligentsia Uruguaya*, (Ediciones de la Banda Oriental, 1968)

——*Uruguay en el Siglo XIX*, (Ediciones del Río de la Plata, 1964)

——*Uruguay: Provincia o Nación?*, 2nd ed. (Ediciones del Nuevo Mundo, 1967)

Arias, J. F., *Banco Agrario-Industrial del Estado* (Tipografía Augusta, 1924)

Asociación de Bancos del Uruguay, *Resumen de los Principales Aspectos de la Actividad Económica del Uruguay*

Asociación de Ingenieros del Uruguay, *Síntesis Histórica de la Ingeniería en el Uruguay* (1949)

Asociación Rural del Uruguay, *Cien Años de la Asociación Rural del Uruguay 1871–1971*, 2 vols. (1971)

Astori, D., *Latifundio y Crisis Agraria en el Uruguay*, (Ediciones de la Banda Oriental, 1971)

——R. Zerbino, J. Rodríguez López and A. Tisnés *Inversión Extranjera y Desarrollo Económico*, (Fundación de Cultura Universitaria, 1975)

Azarola Gil, L. E., *La Sociedad Uruguaya y Sus Problemas*, (Paris, Librería Paul Ollendorff, 1911)

314   A POLITICAL ECONOMY OF URUGUAY SINCE 1870

Azzini, J. E., *La Reforma Cambiaria* (Amalio M. Fernández, 1970)
——and H. A. de Marco, 'The Tax System of Uruguay', *Public Finance*, XI (1956)
Bagú, S. *et al.*, *El Uruguay en la Conciencia de la Crisis* (Universidad de la República, 1971)
Baklanoff, E. N., 'Notes on the Pathology of Uruguay's Welfare State', *Mississippi Valley Journal of Business and Economics*, II (1967)
Bañales, C. and E. Jara, *La Rebelión Estudiantil*, (Editorial Arca, 1968)
Bank of London and South America, *Fortnightly Review*, and *Review*
Barbagelata, A. L. *et al.*, *Alcances y Aplicaciones de la Nueva Constitución Uruguaya* (Instituto de Estudios Políticos para América Latina, 1967)
Barbato de Silva, C., *Comercialización y Faena de Ganado Vacuno en Uruguay: Información Cuantativa*, (Centro de Investigaciones Económicas, 1977)
Barrán, J. P., *Apogeo y Crisis del Uruguay Pastoril y Caudillesco*, (Ediciones de la Banda Oriental, 1977)
——*Latorre y el Estado Uruguayo*, Enciclopedia Uruguaya No. 22 (Editores Reunidos, 1968)
——and B. Nahum, *Bases Económicas de la Revolución Artiguista*, 2nd ed. (Ediciones de la Banda Oriental, 1964)
—— *Historia Rural del Uruguay Moderno, 1851–1914*, 7 vols. (Ediciones de la Banda Oriental, 1967–78)
Barrios Pintos, A., *Montevideo: Los Barrios*, 2 vols., Series Montevideo Nos. 4 and 8 (Editorial Nuestra Tierra, 1971)
Batlle, Cuadernos de Marcha Nos. 31 and 32 (1969)
Batlle, Su Vida, Su Obra, (Editorial 'Accion', 1956)
Batlle Berres, L., *Pensamiento y Acción*, 2 vols. (Editorial Alfa, 1965–6)
Bauza, E. A., *Abasto de Carnes*, (1952)
Bellán, O. P. and O. Nuñez Orens, *La Política de los Contingentes y la Orientación del Uruguay en su Intercambio Internacional* (1938)
Benvenuto, L.C., *Breve Historia del Uruguay* (Editorial Arca, 1967)
——*La Evolución Económica*, Enciclopedia Uruguaya, III (Editores Reunidos, 1968)
——*La Quiebra del Modelo*, Enciclopedia Uruguaya No. 48 (Editores Reunidos, 1969)
——*et al.*, *Uruguay Hoy* (Buenos Aires, Siglo XXI, 1971)
Bernhard, G., *Comercio de Carnes en el Uruguay* (Aguilar e Irazabal, 1958)
——*La Reforma Agraria en los Paises Latinoamericanos*, (1962)
——*Los Monopolios y la Industria Frigorífica* (Ediciones de la Banda Oriental, 1970)
——*Nuestra Industria Frigorífica, Tiene Futuro?* (Nativa Libros, 1968)
——*Realidad Agropecuaria del Uruguay a través de los censos, 1956–1966*, (Nativa Libros, 1969)

——*Uruguay en el Mundo de la Carne* (Aguilar e Irazabal, 1967)

Berreta, T. and J. L. Buzzetti, *Esquema de un Planeamiento Económico y Social* (1946)

Boerger, A. and G. Fischer, 'El Problema Agrícola de la República Oriental del Uruguay', *Revista del Ministerio de Industrias*, x, no. 63 (1922)

Bolsa de Valores de Montevideo, *Análisis Estadístico de 50 años de Bolsa 1925–1975*, 2 vols. (n.d.)

Brannon, R. H., *The Agricultural Development of Uruguay* (New York: Praeger, 1967)

Brause, L. A., *La Industria Lechera en el Uruguay* (1951)

Brena, A. C., *El Problema Pesquero en Uruguay* (Editorial Florensa y Lafon, 1946)

British Mission to South America, *Report* (Montevideo: Asociación de Fomento del Intercambio Comercial Anglo-Uruguayo and the British Chamber of Commerce in Uruguay, 1940)

Brotos, C., *La Granja en el Uruguay* (1927)

Bruschera, O., *Los Partidos Tradicionales en el Uruguay* (Ediciones del Río de la Plata, 1966)

Bucheli, M., *El Sistema Dinerario del Uruguay* (Montevideo: Facultad de Ciencias Económicas y de Administración, 1957)

Buzzetti, J. L., *Historia Económica y Financiera del Uruguay* (1969)

——*La Magnífica Gestión de Batlle en Obras Públicas* (Editorial Ceibo, 1946)

——*Planificación y Desarrollo de las Obras Públicas 1944–1949* (1945)

Cámara de Industrias, *Panorama de la Industria Nacional* (1956)

Campal, E. F., *Hombres, Tierras y Ganados* (1967)

——*La Pradera*, Nuestra Tierra No. 28 (1969)

Campiglia, N., *El Uruguay Movilizado* (Giron Editorial, 1971)

——*Estatización y Burocracia*, Enciclopedia Uruguaya No. 40 (Editores Reunidos, 1969)

——*Los Grupos de Presión y el Proceso Político* (Editorial Arca, 1969)

——*Migración Interna en el Uruguay* (Universidad de la República, 1968)

——*Montevideo: Población y · Trabajo*, Series Montevideo No. 7 (Editorial Nuestra Tierra, 1971)

Caprario Bonavia, A., *Apuntes Para La Historia de los Ferrocarriles Uruguayos* (1966)

Castellanos, A. R., *Montevideo en el Siglo XIX*, Series Montevideo No. 3 (Editorial Nuestra Tierra, 1971)

Caviglia, Luis C., *Estudios Sobre la Realidad Nacional*, 3 vols. (Urta y Curbelo, 1952)

Central Uruguay Railway Company of Montevideo Ltd, *Report of the Directors to the Proprietors*

Centro de Comercio Internacional del Uruguay, *Lana Uruguaya:*

Producción, Industrialización, Comercialización (1958)
Centro de Estudiantes de Ciencias Económicas y de Administración (CECEA), *Plan Nacional de Desarrollo Económico y Social 1965–1974, Compendio,* 2 vols. (1966)
Centro Latinoamericano de Economía Humana (CLEH)–CINAM, *Situación Económica y Social del Uruguay Rural* (Ministerio de Ganadería y Agricultura, 1964)
Centro Uruguayo de Estudios Económicos y Sociales, *Búsqueda*
Charlone, C., 'The Economic and Social Situation of Uruguay', *International Labour Review,* XXXIII (1936)
Cluzeau-Mortet, J., *Aspectos del Estatismo en el Uruguay* (A. Monteverde, 1934)
Collado, E. G. and S. G. Hanson, 'Old-Age Pensions in Uruguay', *Hispanic American Historical Review,* XVI, no. 2 (1936)
Collin Delavaud, A., *Uruguay: Moyennes et Petites Villes* (Paris, Institut des Hautes Etudes de L'Amérique Latine, 1972)
Comisión Especial Para Fomento de Laboratorios Tecnológicos e Investigaciones Industriales, *Antecedentes Relacionados con la Creación en el Uruguay de un Centro de Asistencia Técnica Para la Industria* (1956)
Convención Nacional de Trabajadores, *C.N.T.: Declaración de Principios, Programa y Estatutos* (Centro Estudiantes de Derecho, 1967)
Cooperativa Uruguaya de Transportes Colectivos Sociedad Anónima, *La Concesión de la Cooperativa Uruguaya de Transportes Colectivos S. A.* (1944)
Cosio, P., *Aspectos Económicos del Año 1926* (Maximino García, 1927)
——*Las Defensas Económicas Contra la Gran Depresión* (Maximino García, 1936)
——*Doctrinas y Hechos Económicos* (1940)
——*Económia y Hacienda* (Maximino García, 1926)
——*Estudios Económicos* (Imprenta Artística, 1922)
——*Problemas de Nuestro Banco* (1930)
Couriel, A. and S. Lichtensztejn, *El F.M.I. y la Crisis Económica Nacional* (Centro Estudiantes de Derecho, 1966)
Critchell, J. T. and J. Raymond, *A History of the Frozen Meat Trade* (London, Constable, 1912)
Daly, H. E., 'A Brief Analysis of Recent Uruguayan Trade Control Systems', *Economic Development and Cultural Change,* XV (1967)
——'A Note on the Pathological Growth of the Uruguayan Banking Sector', *Economic Development and Cultural Change,* XVI (1967)
——'An Historical Question and Three Hypotheses Concerning the Uruguayan Economy', *Inter-American Economic Affairs,* XX (1966)
——'The Uruguayan Economy: Its Basic Nature and Current Problems', *Journal of Inter-American Studies,* VII (1965)

D'Elía, G., *El Movimiento Sindical*, Nuestra Tierra No. 4 (1969)

Demicheli, A., *Los Entes Autónomos* (El Siglo Ilustrado, 1924)

Díaz Rebajoli, M., *El Valor de Producción en el Sector Agropecuario* (Instituto de Economía, 1966)

Dickstein, N. and M. N. Val Santalla, *Nuevo Régimen Cambiario Para el Comercio Exterior* (Asociación de Idóneos de Comercio y Administración Pública, 1958)

Directorio del Partido Nacional, *El Partido Nacional y la Política Exterior del Uruguay* (1947)

Dondo, P., *Los Ciclos en la Economía Nacional* (1942)

Dotta, M., D. Freire and N. Rodríguez, *El Uruguay Ganadero* (Ediciones de la Banda Oriental, 1972)

Durán, J. L., *Por un Uruguay Mejor*, 2 vols. (1966)

Echegaray, A., I. Hodara, W. Sarli and C. Steneri, *Plusvalía Agropecuaria del Uruguay 1930–54*, 2 vols. (Fundación de Cultura Universitaria, 1971)

Economist Intelligence Unit, *Quarterly Economic Review, Uruguay*

El Libro del Centenario del Uruguay 1825–1925 (Capurro & Cia., 1925)

El Militarismo, Cuadernos de Marcha No. 23 (1969)

El Problema de Caminos y el Plan Financiero del Gobierno (Juan J. Dornaleche, 1916)

Errandonea, A., 'Apuntes Sobre la Conformación de las Clases Sociales en el Medio Rural Uruguayo', *Uruguay: Poder, Ideología y Clases Sociales*, Cuadernos de Ciencias Sociales, 1 (1970)

——and D. Costabile, *Sindicato y Sociedad en el Uruguay*, Biblioteca de Cultura Universitaria (1969)

Faraone, R., *El Uruguay en que Vivimos (1900–1968)*, 2nd ed. (Editorial Arca, 1968)

——*La Prensa de Montevideo* (Biblioteca de Publicaciones Oficiales de la Facultad de Derecho y Ciencias Sociales de la Universidad de la República, 1960)

——*Medios Masivos de Comunicación*, Nuestra Tierra No. 25 (1969)

——*Origenes de Algunos Grandes Problemas Económicos del Uruguay de Hoy* (Mercedes, Uruguay, Equipo Editor de la Ciudad de Mercedes, 1968)

Faroppa, L. A., *El Desarrollo Económico del Uruguay* (CECEA, 1965)

——*La Crisis Económica Actual*, Enciclopedia Uruguaya No. 55 (Editores Reunidos, 1969)

——*Perspectivas Para un País en Crisis*, Nuestra Tierra No. 47 (1970)

——and I. Wonsewer, *La Política Económica del Uruguay* (Universidad de la República, Facultad de Ciencias Económicas y de Administración, 1956)

—— ——, R. Oxmán and A. Tisnés, *Posibilidades y Perspectivas de una Programación Para el Desarrollo Económico de la Economía del Uruguay* (Universidad de la República, Facultad de Ciencias Económicas y de Administración, 1960)

F. C. Central del Uruguay, *La Cuestión Sobre Homologación de las Tarifas Ferroviarias* (1946)

Federación de Estudiantes Universitarios del Uruguay, *Tribuna Universitaria*

Fernández y Medina, B. and J. L. Bengoa, *El Uruguay en su Primer Centenario, 1830–1930* (Madrid, Imprenta Católica, 1930)

Ferrari, F. de, *Los Principios de la Seguridad Social* (Facultad de Derecho, 1955)

Fierro Vignoli, P., *Comercio Exterior del Uruguay* (El Siglo Ilustrado, 1967)

Finch, E. A., *The Politics of Regional Integration: A Study of Uruguay's Decision to Join LAFTA* (Centre for Latin-American Studies, University of Liverpool, Monograph 4, 1973)

Finch, M. H. J. 'Stabilisation Policy in Uruguay since the 1950s', in R. Thorp and L. Whitehead (eds.), *Inflation and Stabilisation Policy in Latin America* (London: Macmillan, 1979)

——'Three Perspectives on the Crisis in Uruguay', *Journal of Latin American Studies*, III (1971)

Fitzgibbon, R. H., 'Adoption of a Collegiate Executive in Uruguay', *Journal of Politics* (1962)

——*Uruguay: Portrait of a Democracy* (New Brunswick, New Jersey: Rutgers University Press, 1954)

Freire, O. R., 'Estudio Sintético de la Gestión Económica Cumplida por el Frigorífico Nacional', *Revista de la Facultad de Ciencias Económicas y de Administración*, IV (1943)

Frente Amplio, Cuadernos de Marcha Nos. 46, 47 and 53 (1971)

Frick Davie, C., *Cuál Reforma Agraria?* (Barreiro y Ramos, 1964)

Frigorífico Nacional. Con Motivo de su Discusión en la Cámara de Diputados (Barreiro y Ramos, 1925)

Frigorífico Nacional, *Frigorífico Nacional 1928–1951* (n.d.)

Frugoni, E., *La Revolución del Machete* (Buenos Aires, Editorial Claridad, n.d.)

——*Los Nuevos Fundamentos* (Maximino García, 1919)

——A. Rubio, A. Gonzáles Vidart and A. Martínez Trueba, *Sobre la Reforma Agraria en el Uruguay* (Publicaciones del Club Banco Hipotecario, 1944)

Gallinal, G., *El Reciente Convenio de Pagos Anglo-Uruguayo* (Cámara Nacional de Comercio, 1947)

——*El Uruguay Hacia la Dictadura* (Editorial Nueva América, 1938)

Gallinal, J. P. et al., *Estudios Sobre Praderas Naturales del Uruguay*, (Imprenta Germano Uruguaya, 1938)

Ganón, I., *Estructura Social Del Uruguay* (Editorial As, 1966)

——*Introducción a la Sociología Nacional* (Centro Estudiantes de Derecho, 1966)

García Acevedo, C., *Estudio Sobre Ferrocarriles* (Imprenta Artística, 1892)

Gerassi, M., 'Uruguay's Urban Guerrillas', *New Left Review*, No. 62 (1970)

Gnazzo, E., *Ingresos Públicos del Uruguay* (Universidad de la República, Facultad de Ciencias Económicas y de Administración, 1965)

Gómez, E., *Historia del Partido Comunista del Uruguay* (Editorial Elite, 1961)

González Conzi, E. and R. B. Giúdice, *Batlle y el Batllismo*, 2nd ed. (Editorial Medina, 1959)

Graceras, U., *Los Intelectuales y la Política en el Uruguay*, (Cuadernos de El País, 1970)

Grompone, A. M., *Las Clases Medias en el Uruguay*, 2nd ed. (Ediciones del Río de la Plata, 1963)

——*La Ideología de Batlle*, 3rd ed. (Editorial Arca, 1967)

Grunwaldt Ramasso, J., *Historia de la Química en el Uruguay 1830–1930* (Instituto Histórico y Geográfico del Uruguay, 1966)

Grupo de Información y Solidaridad Uruguay, *Informaciones* (Geneva)

Haedo, F. G., and E. Soares Netto, *Cómo Estabilizar la Agricultura Nacional*, 2 vols. (El Siglo Ilustrado, 1932)

Hall, J. O., *La Administración Pública en el Uruguay* (Instituto de Asuntos Interamericanos de los Estados Unidos de América, 1954)

Hanson, S. G., *Argentine Meat and the British Market* (Stanford: Stanford University Press, 1938)

——*Utopia in Uruguay* (New York: Oxford University Press, 1938)

Harberger, A. C. and D. L. Wisecarver, 'Private and Social Rates of Return to Capital in Uruguay', *Economic Development and Cultural Change*, xxv (1976–7)

Herrera, L. A. de, *La Formación Histórica Rioplatense* (Buenos Aires, Ediciones Coyoacán, 1961)

Herrera Vargas, J. and J. Sartrillo, *La Penetración Extranjera en la Economía Uruguaya* (Editorial Diaco, 1969)

Historia de la Rambla Sud (Tipografia Inglesa, 1912)

Hugarte, R. P. and D. Vidart, *El Legado de los Inmigrantes*, 2 vols., Nuestra Tierra Nos. 29 and 39 (1969)

Iglesias, E. V., *El Balance Monetario del Uruguay* (Universidad de la República, Facultad de Ciencias Económicas y de Administración, 1959)

——*El Redescuento Bancario en la Política Monetaria Nacional* (Universidad de la República, Facultad de Ciencias Económicas y de Administración, 1955)

——*Uruguay: Una Propuesta de Cambio* (Editorial Alfa, 1966)

'Immigration and Settlement in Brazil, Argentina and Uruguay: II', *International Labour Review*, xxxv (1937)

Instituto de Estudios Políticos para América Latina (IEPAL), *Uruguay: Un País Sin Problemas en Crisis*, (1967)

Instituto Nacional de Agronomía, *Aplicación de un Gran Empréstito*

Nacional Para Obras de Carácter Productivo (Imprenta Nacional, 1924)

Iribarren, S., *Economía Agraria y Colonización* (1942)

——*La Empresa Rural y la Reforma Agraria* (Universidad de la República, Facultad de Ciencias Económicas y Administración, 1961)

Kirby, J., 'On the Viability of Small Countries: Uruguay and New Zealand Compared', *Journal of Interamerican Studies and World Affairs*, xvii (1975)

Kneit, J. E., *La Previsión Social en el Uruguay*, 2 vols. (Universidad de la República, Facultad de Ciencias Económicas y de Administración, 1964)

Labrousse, A., *The Tupamaros* (Harmondsworth, Penguin Books, 1973)

La Era Militar, Cuadernos de Marcha No. 69 (1973)

La Federación Rural: Su Origen y Desarrollo (Talleres Gráficos, 1916)

La Gamma M., *et al.*, 'Desarrollo de los Ingresos Públicos Nacionales', *Revista de la Facultad de Ciencias Económicas y de Administración*, Year I (1940)

Latin American Newsletters, *Latin America*

Lindahl, G. G., 'Uruguay: Government by Institutions', in M. C. Needler (ed.), *Political Systems of Latin America* (Princeton, Van Nostrand, 1964)

——*Uruguay's New Path: A Study in Politics During the First Colegiado 1919–33* (Stockholm: Library and Institute of Ibero-American Studies, 1962)

Llovet, E., *Comentarios Sobre Colonización* (Instituto Nacional de Colonización, 1949)

——*La Colonización en el Uruguay* (Urta y Curbelo, 1931)

Louis, J. A., *Batlle y Ordóñez: Apogeo y Muerte de la Democracia Burguesa*, 2nd ed. (Nativa Libros, 1972)

McDonald, R. H., 'Electoral Politics and Uruguayan Political Decay', *Inter-American Economic Affairs*, xxvi (1972)

——'The Rise of Military Politics in Uruguay', *Inter-American Economic Affairs*, xxviii (1975)

Maggi, A., *Los Ferrocarriles en la Economía Nacional* (1951)

Marcha

Marchesi, E. and A. Durán, *Suelos del Uruguay*, Nuestra Tierra No. 18 (1969)

Marmouget, L. M., *Los Transportes*, Nuestra Tierra No. 41 (1970)

Martin, P. A., 'The Career of José Batlle y Ordóñez', *Hispanic American Historical Review*, x (1930)

Martínez, J. J., *La Telaraña Bancaria en el Uruguay* (Ediciones Pueblos Unidos, 1969)

Martínez, M. C., *La Renta Territorial* (Imprenta El Siglo Ilustrado, 1918)

Martínez Ces, R., *El Uruguay Batllista* (Ediciones de la Banda Oriental, 1962)

Martínez Díaz, N., *Capitales Británicos y Ferrocarriles en el Uruguay del Siglo XIX* (1966)

Martínez Lamas, J., *A Dónde Vamos?* (Impresora Uruguaya, n.d.)

——*Riqueza y Pobreza del Uruguay* (Palacio del Libro, 1930)

——*La Situación Económica del Uruguay* (Federación Rural, 1932)

Martínez López, N., *Las Organizaciones de Los Trabajadores y el Conflicto Industrial* (1966)

Medina Vidal, M., *Orígenes de los Servicios Eléctricos en el Uruguay*, (Organización Taquigráfica Edina, 1946)

——*Reseña Histórica de la UTE* (Organización Taquigráfica Edina, n.d.)

Melgar, A., E. Peguero and C. Lavagnino, *El Comercio Exportador del Uruguay 1962*–1968, 2 vols. (Universidad de la República, Instituto de Economía, 1972)

Mercader, A., and J. de Vera, *Tupamaros: Estrategía y Acción*, (Editorial Alfa, 1969)

Methol Ferré, A., *Adónde va el Uruguay?* (1958)

——*El Uruguay Como Problema*, 2nd ed. (Ediciones de la Banda Oriental, 1971)

——*La Crisis del Uruguay y el Imperio Británico*, (Buenos Aires: Editorial A. Peña Lillo, 1959)

Mexigos, R., *Los Subsidios en Finanzas Públicas* (Instituto de la Hacienda Pública, 1958)

Mezzera, B., *Coyuntura Europea y Economía Uruguaya* (Imprenta Gutenberg, 1957)

Miles, J. and R. Gazzano, *Costos Internos y Precios Internacionales de la Carne Vacuna Congelada y Conservada (1942–57)* (Universidad de la República, Instituto de Teoría y Política Económicas, 1961)

Millot, J., C. Silva and L. Silva, *El Desarrollo Industrial del Uruguay de la Crisis de 1929 a la Postguerra* (Universidad de la República, Instituto de Economía, 1973)

Montañés, M. T., *Desarrollo de la Agricultura en el Uruguay* (1948)

Montero Bustamante, R., *El Banco Comercial y la Epoca de Reus* (Universidad de la República, Instituto de Investigaciones Históricas, 1966)

Monteverde, M., *Agricultura-Ganadería e Industrias Derivadas*, 3rd ed. (Monteverde y Cía., 1930)

——*El Problema de Las Jubilaciones* (Monteverde y Cía., 1939)

——*Sobre Algunos Problemas del Momento* (Monteverde y Cia., 1947)

——*Sobre un Gran Problema de Actualidad* (1951)

Monteverde, P. M., *Hacienda y Finanzas del Estado* (Impresora Uruguaya, 1931)

Montevideo Entre dos Siglos (1890–1914), Cuadernos de Marcha no. 22 (1969)

Morató, O., *La Industria Manufacturera en el Uruguay* (1927)

——*Problemas Sociales* (O. M. Bertani, 1911)

——*Surgimientos y Depresiones Económicos en el Uruguay a Través de la Historia* (Universidad de la República, Facultad de Ciencias Económicas y de Administración, 1938)

Morón, I., *Problemas de la Colonización en el Uruguay* (1945)

Mourat, O., *La Crisis Comercial en la Cuenca del Plata (1880–1920)*, 2nd ed. (Ediciones de la Banda Oriental, 1973)

——*et al.*, *Cinco Perspectivas Históricas del Uruguay Moderno*, (Fundación de Cultura Universitaria, 1969)

Nahum, B., *La Epoca Batllista 1905–30* (Ediciones de la Banda Oriental, 1975)

——*La Estancia Alambrada*, Enciclopedia Uruguaya No.24 (Editores Reunidos, 1968)

Narancio, E. M. and F. Capurro Calamet, *Historia y Análisis Estadístico de la Población del Uruguay* (Peña y Cia., 1939)

Oddone, J. A., *Economía y Sociedad en el Uruguay Liberal* (Ediciones de la Banda Oriental, 1967)

——*La Emigración Europea al Río de la Plata* (Ediciones de la Banda Oriental, 1966)

——*La Formación del Uruguay Moderno* (Buenos Aires, Editorial Universitaria de Buenos Aires, 1966)

——*Una Perspectiva Europea del Uruguay* (Universidad de la República, Instituto de Investigaciones Históricas, 1965)

Oficina Internacional del Trabajo, *Informe al Gobierno de la República Oriental del Uruguay Sobre Seguridad Social* (Geneva, 1964)

Organización de las Naciones Unidas Para la Agricultura y la Alimentación, *Informe Para el Gobierno del Uruguay Sobre Aspectos Técnicos y Económicos de la Reorganización de la Industria de la Carne en el Uruguay* (Rome, 1963)

Organization of American States, Inter-American Commission on Human Rights, *Report on the Situation of Human Rights in Uruguay* (OEA/Ser. L/V/II. 43, 31 January 1978)

Oxmán, R., *Energía* (Universidad de la República, Instituto de Teoría y Política Económicas, 1961)

——*Transportes en el Uruguay* (Universidad de la República, Facultad de Ciencias Económicas y de Administración, 1961)

Paris de Oddone, B., R. Faraone and J. A. Oddone, *Cronología Comparada de la Historia del Uruguay (1830–1945)*, 2nd ed. (Universidad de la República, n.d.)

Pazos, F., *Chronic Inflation in Latin America* (New York: Praeger, 1972)

Pereira, J. J. and R. Trajtenberg, *Evolución de la Población Total y Activa en el Uruguay 1908–1957* (Universidad de la República, Instituto de Economía, 1966)

Petrucelli, J. L., *Migración y Perspectivas de la Población en el Uruguay* (Centro de Informaciones y Estudios del Uruguay, 1975)
——*Notas Sobre el Proceso de Poblamiento Uruguayo* (Centro de Informaciones y Estudios del Uruguay, 1976)
Pintos, F. R., *Uruguay: de la Liberación al Afianzamiento de la Burguesía* (Ediciones Pueblos Unidos, 1966)
Pivel Devoto, J. E. and A. Ranieri de Pivel Devoto, *Historia de la República Oriental del Uruguay (1830–1930)* (Editorial Medina, 1966)
Platt, D. C. M. (ed.), *Business Imperialism 1840–1930* (London: Oxford University Press, 1977)
Porta, E. S., *Uruguay: Realidad y Reforma Agraria* (Ediciones de la Banda Oriental, 1969)
Porzecanski, A. C., 'Uruguay's Continuing Dilemma', *Current History*, LXVI, no. 389 (1974)
——*Uruguay's Tupamaros* (New York: Praeger, 1973)
Quijano, C., *Evolución del Contralor de Cambios en el Uruguay* (1944)
——*La Reforma Agraria en el Uruguay* (Ediciones del Río de la Plata, 1963)
Quijano, J. M., 'Uruguay: Balance de un Modelo Friedmaniano', *Comercio Exterior* (Mexico), XXVIII (1978)
Quinteros Delgado, J.C., *La Industria y el Estado*, 2nd ed. (Maximino García, 1926)
——*La Política Económica y la Reforma de Nuestros Aranceles* (Sociedad Uruguaya de Economía Política, 1931)
——*Vida y Obra de Pedro Cosio* (1937)
Rama, C. M., *Batlle: la Conciencia Social*, Enciclopedia Uruguaya no. 34 (Editores Reunidos, 1969)
——*Historia Social del Pueblo Uruguayo* (Editorial Comunidad del Sur, 1972)
——*Las Clases Sociales en el Uruguay* (Ediciones Nuestro Tiempo, 1960)
——'Movimientos Campesinos y Problemas Agrarios en el Uruguay de Fines del Siglo XVIII a Nuestros Días', *Revista de Ciencias Sociales*, (Universidad de Puerto Rico), XV (1971)
——*Obreros y Anarquistas*, Enciclopedia Uruguaya no. 32 (Editores Reunidos, 1969)
——*Sociología del Uruguay* (Buenos Aires: Editorial Universitaria de Buenos Aires, 1965)
——*Uruguay en Crisis* (El Siglo Ilustrado, 1969)
Rama, G. W., *El Ascenso de las Clases Medias*, Enciclopedia Uruguaya No. 36 (Editores Reunidos, 1969)
——*El Club Político* (Editorial Arca, 1971)
——*Grupos Sociales y Enseñanza Secundaria* (Editorial Arca, 1963)
——*La Democracia Política*, Enciclopedia Uruguaya no. 44 (Editores Reunidos, 1969)

324   A POLITICAL ECONOMY OF URUGUAY SINCE 1870

——'Las Clases Medias en la Epoca de Batlle', *Tribuna Universitaria*, No. 11 (1963)

Ramela de Castro, R., *Entes Autónomos: Organización Administrativa del Dominio Industrial del Estado* (1923)

Real de Azúa, C. (ed.), *Antología del Ensayo Uruguayo Contemporáneo* (Universidad de la República, 1964)

——*El Impulso y su Freno* (Ediciones de la Banda Oriental, 1964)

——*La Clase Dirigente*, Nuestra Tierra no. 34 (1969)

——*La Historia Política*, Enciclopedia Uruguaya I (Editores Reunidos, 1968)

Redding, D. C., 'The Economic Decline of Uruguay', *Inter-American Economic Affairs*, xx (1967)

Revista de Economía

Revista de la Facultad de Ciencias Económicas y de Administración

Revista de la Federación Rural

Revista Uruguaya de Ciencias Sociales

Reyes Abadie, W., *Aparicio Saravia* (Ediciones del Río de la Plata, 1963)

——and J. C. Williman, *La Economía del Uruguay en el Siglo XIX*, Nuestra Tierra no. 32 (1969)

Ricaldoni, A. P., J. E. Santías and L. Silva, *El Regimen de Promoción Industrial* (Fundación de Cultura Universitaria, 1975)

Rippy, J. F., *British Investments in Latin America, 1822–1949*, (Hamden, Conn.: Archon Books, 1966)

Rodríguez, H., *Nuestra Industria Textil, Tiene Futuro?* (Nativa Libros, 1967)

——*Nuestros Sindicatos*, 2nd ed. (Centro Estudiantes de Derecho, 1966)

Rodríguez López, J., *La Política Monetaria y Los Cambios* (Editorial La Facultad, 1931)

Rodríguez Villamil, S., *Las Mentalidades Dominantes en Montevideo (1850–1900)*, I (Ediciones de la Banda Oriental, 1968)

Ros, F. J., *Modesta Colaboración en Algunos de Nuestros Problemas Nacionales* (El Siglo Ilustrado, 1926)

Rothman, A. M., 'Evolution of Fertility in Argentina and Uruguay', *International Population Conference, London, 1969*, vol. I (Liége, International Union for the Scientific Study of the Population, 1971)

Rovetta, V., *La Crisis Agraria en el Uruguay* (Ediciones Ciudadela, 1961)

——*Peón Rural y Rancherío* (Ediciones Ciudadela, 1962)

Ruano Fournier, A., *Estudio Económico de la Producción de las Carnes del Río de la Plata* (Peña y Cía., 1936)

Ruiz Díaz, M., *Los Barómetros Económicos del Uruguay* (1936)

Sampognaro, V., *L'Uruguay au commencement du XXᵉ siècle* (Brussells, published for the Brussels Exhibition, 1910)

San Román, R. C., *Cuadros Estadísticos y Comentarios Sobre las Cajas de Jubilaciones y Pensiones del Uruguay* (1948)

Sanguinetti, J. M. and A. Pacheco Seré, *La Nueva Constitución* (Editorial Alfa, 1967)

Seoane, P., *La Industria de las Carnes en el Uruguay* (1928)

Seregni, L., *Discursos* (Editorial Arca, 1971)

——*Solamente el Pueblo* (Comisión del Frente Amplio, 1972)

Serrano, G., and C. M. Leis, *Problemas de las Exportaciones del Uruguay a la Zona Latinoamericana de Libre Comercio* (Universidad de la República, Facultad de Ciencias Económicas y de Administración, 1966)

7 Días Que Conmovieron a Uruguay, Cuadernos de Marcha no. 68 (1973)

Simoens Arce, F., *El Problema Cambiario en el Uruguay* (Barreiro y Ramos, 1943)

Solari, A. E., *El Desarrollo Social del Uruguay en la Postguerra* (Editorial Alfa, 1967)

——*El Tercerismo en el Uruguay* (Editorial Alfa, 1965)

——*Estudios Sobre la Sociedad Uruguaya*, 2 vols. (Editorial Arca, 1964–5)

——*Sociología Rural Nacional*, 2nd ed. (Biblioteca de Publicaciones Oficiales de la Facultad de Derecho y Ciencias Sociales de la Universidad de Montevideo, 1958)

——N. Campiglia and G. Wettstein, *Uruguay en Cifras* (Universidad de la República, 1966)

Street, J., *Artigas and the Emancipation of Uruguay* (London: Oxford University Press, 1959)

Taylor, P. B., *Government and Politics of Uruguay* (New Orleans, Tulane University, 1960)

——'Interests and Institutional Dysfunction in Uruguay', *American Political Science Review*, LVIII (1963)

——'The Uruguayan Coup d'Etat of 1933', *Hispanic American Historical Review*, XXXII (1952)

Terra, G., *Política Internacional* (Barreiro y Ramos, 1918)

Terra, J. P., *La Vivienda*, Nuestra Tierra no. 38 (1969)

Touron, L. S. de, J. C. Rodríguez and N. de la Torre, *Evolución Económica de la Banda Oriental*, 2nd ed. (Ediciones Pueblos Unidos, 1968)

——————*Estructura Económico-Social de la Colonia* (Ediciones Pueblos Unidos, 1967)

Trías, V., *El Imperialismo en el Río de la Plata* (Buenos Aires, Ediciones Coyoacán, 1960)

——*Las Montoneras y el Imperio Británico* (Ediciones Uruguay, 1961)

——*Imperialismo Geopolítica y Petroleo* (Ediciones de la Banda Oriental, 1971)

——*Imperialismo y Rosca Bancaria en el Uruguay* (Ediciones de la Banda Oriental, 1971)

Turiansky, V., *La UTE y la Crisis Nacional* (Centro Estudiantes de Derecho, 1967)

United Kingdom, *Agreement between His Majesty's Government in the United Kingdom and the Uruguayan Government regarding Trade and Payments* (London, HMSO, Cmd. 4940, 26 June 1935)

——*Annual Statement of the Trade of the United Kingdom with Commonwealth and Foreign Countries*

——Department of Overseas Trade, *Report on the Financial and Economic Conditions in Uruguay, September 1927* (London, HMSO, 1927)

——*Economic Conditions in Uruguay, August 1930* (London, HMSO, 1930)

——*Economic Conditions in the Republic of Uruguay 1933* (London, HMSO, 1934)

——*Economic Conditions in the Republic of Uruguay 1935* (London, HMSO, 1936)

——Ministry of Agriculture and Fisheries, *Report on the Trade in Refrigerated Beef, Mutton and Lamb* (London, HMSO, 1925)

United Nations, Economic Commission for Latin America, *Foreign Investments in Uruguay* (E/CN.12/166/Add.6, 2 May 1950)

——Economic Commission for Latin America/Food and Agriculture Organisation, *Livestock in Latin America: Status, Problems and Prospects, I. Colombia, Mexico, Uruguay and Venezuela* (New York 1962, E/CN.12/620)

United States, Department of Commerce, *Foreign Commerce and Navigation of the United States*

—— ——Trade Promotion Series no. 39: W. R. Long, *Railways of South America Part II* (Washington, Government Printing Office, 1927)

—— *Survey of Current Business*

——Federal Trade Commission, *Report on Trade and Tariffs in Brazil, Uruguay, Argentina, Chile, Bolivia, and Peru* (Washington, Government Printing Office, 1916)

——Tariff Commission, *Mining and Manufacturing Industries in Uruguay* (Washington, 1945)

Universidad de la República, Facultad de Agronomía, *La Cuenca Lechera de Montevideo* (1968)

——Facultad de Derecho y Ciencias Sociales, *Enfoques Sobre el Período Batllista*, Cuadernos de Ciencias Sociales, no. 2 (1972)

—— ——*Uruguay: Poder, Ideología y Clases Sociales*, Cuadernos de Ciencias Sociales no. 1 (1970)

——Facultad de Humanidades y Ciencias, *Proteccionismo y Librecambio: el Programa de la 'Liga Industrial' de 1880* (1967)

——Instituto de Economía, *El Proceso Económico del Uruguay* (1969)

—— ——*Estructura Industrial del Uruguay*, vol. I (1972)

—— ——*Estudios y Coyuntura* nos. 1–3 (1970–3)

—— ——*Uruguay: Estadísticas Básicas* (1969)

——Instituto de Investigaciones Históricas, *La Crisis del Noventa*, (1967)

'Uruguay: en el Círculo Vicioso del Estancamiento y la Inflación', *Economía de América Latina* (Mexico), no. 1 (1978)

Uruguay, las Raices de la Independencia, Cuadernos de Marcha no. 4 (1967)

'Uruguay: Ten Years of Crisis', *Comercio Exterior de Mexico*, xxv (1979)

Vallarino, J. C., *Economía Dirigida 1934–35* (Editorial Moderna, n.d.)

Vanger, M. I., *José Batlle y Ordóñez of Uruguay: The Creator of His Times, 1902–1907* (Cambridge: Harvard University Press, 1963)

——'Uruguay Introduces Government by Committee', *American Political Science Review*, vol xlviii (1954)

Vasconcellos, A., *Febrero Amargo*, 2nd ed. (1973)

Vázquez, F. P., *Carreteras y Ferrocarriles del Estado* (1931)

Vázquez Franco, G., *El País Que Batlle Heredó* (Fundación de Cultura Universitaria, n.d.)

——*Ingleses, Ferrocarriles y Frigoríficos*, Enciclopedia Uruguaya no. 25 (Editores Reunidos, 1968)

Végh Villegas, A., *Economía Política: Teoría y Acción* (Ediciones Polo, 1977)

Veiga, D., *Regional Development and Population Distribution in Uruguay* (Centro de Informaciones y Estudios del Uruguay, 1979)

Vicario, L., *El Crecimiento Urbano de Montevideo* (Ediciones de la Banda Oriental, 1970)

Visca, C., *Emilio Reus y Su Epoca* (Ediciones de la Banda Oriental, 1967)

Weinstein, M., *Uruguay: The Politics of Failure* (Westport, Conn. and London: Greenwood Press, 1975)

Winn, P. E., 'British Informal Empire in Uruguay in the Nineteenth Century', *Past and Present*, no. 76 (1976)

——'Uruguay and British Economic Expansion, 1880–1893', unpublished PhD thesis, Cambridge University, 1972

Wonsewer, I., L. A. Faroppa and E. V. Iglesias, 'Política de Subvenciones en el Uruguay', *Revista de la Facultad de Ciencias Económicas y de Administración*, no. 5 (1953)

——E. V. Iglesias, M. Buchelli and L. A. Faroppa, *Aspectos de la Industrialización en el Uruguay* (Universidad de la República, Facultad de Ciencias Económicas y de Administración, 1958)

—— ——and L. A. Faroppa, *El Desarrollo Económico Nacional* (Universidad de la República, Instituto de Teoría y Política Económicas, 1960)

World Bank, Latin America and the Caribbean Regional Office, *Economic Memorandum on Uruguay* (Washington, D.C., 1977)

Zabaleta, R., E. G. de Olaondo, J. M. Gimeno Sanz and N. W. Ruocco, *El Contralor de las Importaciones y Exportaciones en el Uruguay* (1954)

Zum Felde, A., *Proceso Histórico del Uruguay*, 5th ed. (Editorial Arca, 1967)

——*Proceso Intelectual del Uruguay*, 3rd ed., 3 vols. (Ediciones del Nuevo Mundo, 1967)

Index

Authors of works cited are omitted unless referred to by name in the text.

329

external debt, 229–31, 268–9
London, 191–2, 194
New York, 12, 192

Fábrica Nacional de Papel, 162
Fábrica Uruguaya de Neumáticos SA
(FUNSA), 175
Farquhar Syndicate; see Uruguay
Railway Company
Federación Obrera Marítima, 58
Federación Obrera Regional
Uruguaya (FORU), 54–7, 59
Federación Regional de la República
Oriental del Uruguay, 54
Federación Rural, 98, 105,
as pressure group, 15, 101, 118, 141,
169, 199, 251
formation, 11, 96, 140, 279n10
Ferrocarril y Tranvía del Norte, 45,
210, 215
First World War, 199
and left wing, 58
and rural sector, 73, 75
effect on production, 44, 164, 210
trade during, 84, 93, 128–9, 275
fiscal policy
and rural sector, 96, 99–103, 106–
114
in 1960s, 227–8, 238
of Batlle y Ordóñez, 92–6, 194
of military regime, 254, 259–260,
268–70
fishing, 223, 253
Florida
(department), 64
(town), 201
Fondo de Compensaciones
Ganaderas, 144–5
Fondo de Diferencias de Cambio; see
Exchange Profits Fund
foreign currency reserves, 221, 229–
31, 268
France, 88, 132, 143, 192, 211
Fray Bentos (town), 134, 138, 149
Frente Amplio, 62, 247, 249, 263
Frigorífica Uruguaya, La; see
Sansinena
Frigorífico Anglo, see Vestey
Frigorífico Artigas, see Armour

Frigorífico Castro, 147–8
frigorífico industry, 11, 77, 79, 82, 84,
86, 133, 135–52, 210, 283n58; see
also Armour and Co., Frigorífico
Nacional, Sansinena, Swift and
Co., Vestey Brothers
Frigorífico Montevideo; see Swift and
Co.
Frigorífico Nacional, 15, 137, 140–1,
143–9, 151, 212, 215, 219, 266,
295n53, 295n55
Frugoni, Emilio
and Batlle y Ordóñez, 56–7, 59,
286n104
and Socialist party, 56–9, 62
on immigration, 46
on protection, 12, 95
fuel
alcohol as, 210
consumption of, 161, 260, 296n1
import of, 157–9, 216
oil price rise (1970s), 254, 256, 270
oil refining, 217; see also Administración Nacional de Combustibles Alcohol y Portland
Fynn, Enrique, 202

Galicia, 163
Gallinal, Gustavo, 217
George, Henry, 289n5
Germany (pre-1945)
in Second World War, 60, 217
investment by, 192, 194, 204
social legislation in, 43
trade with, 18, 132, 143, 192, 194, 217
East Germany, 132
Gestido, President Oscar, 242
Giraud, Félix, 162
gold mining, 192
Greece, 132
Grindley, H. H., 200
Grompone, Antonio M., 35

Hanson, Simon G., 41, 48, 213–14,
217–18
Herrera, Luis Alberto de, 14, 16, 18,
137, 216, 300n15
Herrera y Obes, President Julio, 7,
279n7

INDEX

337

prices; *see also* inflation
  of cattle, 136–7, 141, 146, 151
  of exports, 126–7, 275–6
  of imports, 154–5, 275–7
  of land, 103–5, 119–20
  of rural production, 112–13, 118–19
principistas, 5
protection, 153, 161–2, 186, 190
  and Terra regime, 16, 173
  attack on (1970s), 260–1, 266, 271–2
  debate on (1920s), 161, 169–70
  effect on imports, 158, 166
  in 19th century, 8, 94
  tariff levels, 162, 166–8, 266, 271
Proudhon, Pierre-Joseph, 54
public employment, 213–19, 227, 268, 270
  and coparticipation, 13, 20, 214–15
  and middle class, 11, 39, 209
  as bureaucracy, 51–2, 147, 152, 214, 218–19
  during Terra regime, 16, 216–17
public sector, 207–19, 235, 240, 270; *see also* public employment
public utilities, 12, 18, 39, 193–210, 212–13, 215, 217–19
  British-owned companies; dividends of, 203–5; employment policies of, 39, 193, 209; government acquisition of, 200, 204, 207, 208, 218; tariffs of, 197–206; *see also* railways, tramways
Puerto Rico, 179
Punta del Este (town), 273

Quintela, Manuel, 140
Quinteros Delgado, Juan Carlos, 169

railways, 6, 7, 97, 140, 192–202, 217, 219,
  deficiencies of, 197–9
Rama, Germán W., 37–8
Refinería Nacional de Azucar, 162
reintegros (export tax rebates), 254, 264–6, 271, 307–8n29
Representatives, House of, 41, 59, 204

repression
  in 1930s, 18
  in 1960s, 20–1, 28, 61, 243–5
  in 1970s, 248–9, 252
Ricardo, David, 101, 104
Rimlinger, Gaston V., 43–4
Rincón de Baygorría, 217
Rincón del Bonete, 174, 217
Rio Grande do Sul (state), 25, 134, 197
Río Negro
  (department), 64
  (river), 174, 195, 201, 207, 217
Río Santa Lucía, 202
Rivera (town), 195, 198, 300n15
River Plate, 191, 198
River Plate Fresh Meat Co., 135
road transport, 158–9, 161, 194, 201–2, 205–7, 219
Roca-Runciman Agreement (1933), 142
Rodríguez, Héctor, 61
Rostow, Walt W., 43
Russia
  revolution (1917), 55, 58–9
  Soviet Union, 43, 60, 88, 161
  Tsarist, 43

saladero industry, 8, 35, 82, 128, 133–6, 293n10
Salto
  (city), 7, 29, 66, 195–7
  (department), 64
Salvo, Campomar y Cia., 162
San José
  (department), 64
  (town), 201
San Luis (town), 200
San Miguel (conclave, 1973), 254, 267
Sansinena, 135–41, 151
Santos, President Máximo, 7
Saravia, Aparicio, 10, 32, 54, 56, 194
Sayago (suburb), 166
Second World War, 18, 200, 204
  economic growth during, 172, 175–6, 184, 190, 217
  foreign currency reserves, 221, 230
  trade during, 127, 130, 143, 155, 201
Senate, 249
Serrato, José, 100